PRAIS⸺ 999

'A fascinating read crammed with gossip, jokes, insights and anecdotes ... Loathing for artifice and pretence, along with fundamental decency, make Mullin a captivating tour guide.' *Spectator*

'Perceptive, witty, humane, indignant and self-lacerating by turn, Mullin has the qualities of all enduring diarists' *Guardian*

'Mullin's insights are still unrivalled' *Sunday Times*

'His acerbic wit, independence of mind and self-deprecating honesty have proved a refreshing antidote to the spin that marked life under Tony Blair and Gordon Brown' *Financial Times*

PRAISE FOR *A VIEW FROM THE FOOTHILLS 1999–2005*

'His quiet humour and intense personal integrity make this book compulsively readable ... an important service for democracy' Peter Oborne, *Daily Mail*

'By far the most revealing and entertaining [diary] to have emerged from the now-dying era of New Labour ... a diary that tells us as much about British politics as that great television series *Yes Minister*' *Economist*

'Every once in a while, political diaries emerge that are so irreverent and insightful that they are destined to be handed out as leaving presents in offices in Whitehall for years to come. *A View from the Foothills* is one such book.' David Cameron, *Observer Books of the Year*

PRAISE FOR *DECLINE & FALL 2005–2010*

'The most enjoyable and insightful of all the political diaries I have read' Jonathan Dimbleby

'Mullin's supreme virtues are an eye for the absurd and an incorruptible independence of outlook ... an indispensible hangover cure for anyone who has ever been drunk on the idea of power' *Guardian*

'Mullin's name will live in these diaries when the great host of New Labour careerists has been cast into oblivion' Andrew Gimson, *Daily Telegraph*

ALSO BY CHRIS MULLIN

Diaries
A View from the Foothills
Decline & Fall

Novels
A Very British Coup
The Last Man Out of Saigon
The Year of the Fire Monkey

Non-fiction
Error of Judgement: the truth about the Birmingham bombings

CHRIS MULLIN was the Member of Parliament for Sunderland South from 1987 until 2010. He is a former chairman of the Home Affairs Select Committee and was a minister in three departments. He is the author of three novels, the best known of which, *A Very British Coup*, was made into an award winning television series. His two previous volumes of diaries, *A View from the Foothills* and *Decline & Fall* have been widely praised. He was a judge of the 2011 Man Booker Prize and is currently chairman of the Heritage Lottery Fund for the North East of England.

RUTH WINSTONE was a senior library clerk in the House of Commons and edited Tony Benn's diaries. She is now a freelance researcher and editor.

A WALK-ON PART

Diaries 1994–1999

edited by Ruth Winstone

PROFILE BOOKS

This paperback edition published in 2012

First published in Great Britain in 2011 by
PROFILE BOOKS LTD
3a Exmouth House
Pine Street
London EC1R 0JH
www.profilebooks.com

1 3 5 7 9 10 8 6 4 2

Text design by Sue Lamble
Typeset in Stone Serif by MacGuru Ltd
info@macguru.org.uk

Printed and bound in Great Britain by
CPI Group (UK) Ltd, Croydon, CR0 4YY

A CIP catalogue record for this book is available from the British Library.

ISBN 978 1 84668 524 8
eISBN 978 1 84765 753 4

With love to Ngoc, Sarah and Emma;
in memory of Leslie and Teresa Mullin
and with gratitude to the people of Sunderland

CONTENTS

Preface

This is my third and final volume of diaries. It covers the period from the day of John Smith's death in May 1994 to the moment of my assumption into government in July 1999. Although published out of sequence, the complete work embraces the rise and fall of New Labour from the moment of its inception to the moment that Gordon Brown walked out of Downing Street.

Looking back to those early years, long before the shadow of Iraq fell across the New Labour project, several thoughts occur to me. First, how much Tony Blair got right. He was surely right about the need to seize the middle ground and stay there. His decision to rewrite Clause IV of the Labour Party constitution – implying as it did nationalisation of the means of production, distribution and exchange – was in retrospect a master stroke, though it didn't feel that way at the time. His strategy of promising little and delivering more, in contrast to the over-promising and under-delivering of previous governments, was also surely vindicated. Likewise his determination to tackle the huge benefit culture (ironically, the new government's most enduring legacy from the Thatcher decade) and to reform public services, education in particular. And as we contemplate a Tory government, propped up by Liberal Democrats, laying waste to the public sector, who can say that Blair was mistaken in his desire to realign politics by bringing the Lib Dems into New Labour's big tent? Had he succeeded we might not be where we are today. The extent to which Blair had changed the political landscape was first brought home to me in January 2001 when I was invited to address the sixth form at Harrow, one of our most distinguished public schools. Afterwards I dined with several teachers and was amazed to discover that not one had voted Tory at the previous election. 'We think you will win by an even bigger margin next time,' said one.

'What on earth makes you think that?'

'Because we talk to the parents and they are no longer afraid of you.'

Most of the fault lines which would come to haunt New Labour in the years ahead – control freakery, a soft spot for rich men, the obsession with spin – were also apparent from the outset. One thing not apparent (at least to those of us outside the magic circle), however, was the dysfunctional relationship between the two most powerful figures in the government. Nor was it yet apparent that New Labour's love affair with the markets would end as disastrously as it did. Not that much could have been done, even had it been apparent. No amount of regulation could have protected us from the financial tsunami that came from America in the autumn of 2008.

Looking back at those early years I am struck, too, by the extent to which certain issues assumed an importance that many readers will find mystifying. The pressure to ban hunting with hounds is the obvious example. Even in terms of animal welfare, it was not a large issue. The difficulty was that expectations had been aroused, undertakings given. It became an issue of confidence. A test of whether a Labour government with a clear mandate and a large majority was capable of facing down the mighty vested interests and unlimited resources represented by the hunting fraternity. Such was the strength of feeling that this was one of the rare issues on which Blair was forced to back down, a decision he now says he regrets, though the polls continue to suggest that most of us don't.

The fate of Peter Mandelson is the other matter that crops up incessantly. Among colleagues in Parliament and in government, some of whom had been on the receiving end of his black arts, he was cordially loathed. I lost count of the number of people who warned Blair of the damage his evident dependence on Mandelson was doing. It is also apparent from the diaries of Alastair Campbell that managing Mandelson occupied a good deal of time at the highest level. Yet Blair stuck with him through thick and thin. Even successive resignations do not seem, save for the briefest of interludes, to have diminished his access. How do we explain this extraordinary resilience? In part because Mandelson was a man of excellent judgement in every respect, except in relation to his own affairs. 'Peter goes gaga in the presence of rich men,' someone who once worked for him remarked. As a minister and as a strategist he was widely respected for his ability to make calm, clear, considered decisions. His third and final visit to government, in the autumn of 2008, arguably made the difference between mere defeat and annihilation. None of this, however, was apparent in the early days.

As in previous volumes, I have tried to inject a flavour of life as a representative of a northern working-class city which took quite a battering during the Thatcher decade. Entire industries disappeared – shipbuilding, mining, textiles, glass, the local brewery and a fair swathe of our engineering. The 1980s saw the growth of a huge, alienated underclass, trapped in a world of benefit, amid soaring levels of crime and anti-social behaviour, from which escape was difficult if not impossible. By the late eighties there were parts of my constituency where civilised life had broken down to such an extent that entire streets had to be demolished because they were no longer habitable. For ten years or more, at almost every surgery I was faced with people begging to be evacuated from the most blighted parts of the city. Although in opposition we had the luxury of being able to blame all bad news on the Tories, it will be apparent from these pages that the collapse of much of Sunderland's manufacturing sector continued into the early years of the Labour government when almost the only bright spot was the survival of Nissan, although there was a moment when even that looked wobbly. Hand on heart, however, I can say that, whatever the disappointments, thirteen years of Labour government made a significant difference to the lives of my least prosperous constituents. Unemployment, especially among the young, fell to levels not seen since the early seventies and, as unemployment fell, so did the epidemic of crime and anti-social behaviour that blighted the lives of my poorest constituents. Gradually, Sunderland reinvented itself. New businesses replaced old ones – Doxford International, a business park in my former constituency, was a green field in the mid-nineties. By the time I retired 7,500 people worked there.

Also as before, I have tried to inject a flavour of family life. I came late to fatherhood and watching my two daughters grow up has been one of the great joys of my life. As this volume opens my older daughter, Sarah, is just five years old and Emma, my younger daughter, is as yet unborn. They are now bright, attractive young women. Every day I count my blessings.

I am aware that I do not always come out well from these pages. That is the nature of an honest diary. First, because I have a tendency towards pessimism. Second, because I am a bit of an agoniser. On the advice of my esteemed editor, Ruth Winstone, much pessimism and agonising has ended up on the cutting-room floor, but enough has been retained to leave the reader with a flavour of my weakness in this regard.

The success of the two earlier volumes has come as a pleasant surprise. Readers of the previous volume, *Decline & Fall*, will recall that I approached retirement with trepidation. I am pleased to report, however, that it has worked out well. A small industry has developed around the diaries and, as a result, I am flooded with invitations. The political meeting is not dead, it has merely transferred to the literary festival. The Live Theatre in Newcastle has launched a stage version of the diaries which, who knows, may eventually find its way further south. Also, from time to time, my opinion is still sought on matters political – and even literary. Currently I am helping to judge entries for this year's Man Booker Prize. In the long term, of course, the test will be whether these diaries, like those of Alan Clark, Chips Channon or Jock Colville, are still read in twenty or thirty years by those wanting a flavour of our life and times at the end of the twentieth and the beginning of the twenty-first century. On that, however, the jury is still out.

Chris Mullin
Sunderland, August 2011

Acknowledgements

As ever, I owe thanks to many people. My constituents in Sunderland South for having allowed me the honour of representing them for twenty-three years. Members of the Sunderland South Labour Party for having allowed me to be their candidate through five general elections. My friends and erstwhile colleagues in Parliament for the pleasure of their company.

My thanks also to Andrew Franklin and his cheerful and industrious team at Profile, to Trevor Horwood for his meticulous copy-editing and to my agent, Caroline Dawnay. Above all, to Ruth Winstone for her help in cutting the manuscript down to size and for offering much useful advice.

I take this opportunity, too, to remember my late good friends Jacky Breach and Joan Maynard, whose passing is recorded in these pages and whom I shall never forget.

Cast

Listed mainly according to responsibilities held for the period covered by this volume of the diary, May 1994–July 1999

John Smith, Leader of the Labour Party 1992–4

Tony Blair (aka The Man), Leader of the Labour Party 1994–2007; Prime Minister 1997–2007

Significant Others

Margaret Beckett MP, Deputy Leader of the Labour Party 1992–4; Cabinet minister 1997–2007

Tony Benn MP, former Cabinet minister, fellow diarist and friend of CM

Gordon Brown MP, Shadow Chancellor 1992–7, Chancellor of the Exchequer 1997–2007, Prime Minister 2007–10

Nick Brown MP, Chief Whip 1997–8 and 2008–10; Minister of Agriculture 1998–2001

Steve Byers MP, Minister of State, Education 1997–8; Chief Secretary to the Treasury 1998; Secretary of State for Trade and Industry 1998–2001

Denis Carter, Chief Whip, House of Lords 1997–2002

David Clark MP, Shadow Secretary of Defence 1992–7; Chancellor of the Duchy of Lancaster 1997–8

Robin Cook MP, Shadow Foreign Secretary 1994–7; Foreign Secretary 1997–2001

Donald Dewar MP, Opposition Chief Whip, 1995–7; Secretary of
    State for Scotland 1997–9; First Minister, Scotland 1999–2000

Bill Etherington, MP for Sunderland North 1992–2010

Charlie Falconer QC, Lords 1997– ; Solicitor General 1997–8;
    Cabinet Office minister 1998–2001; long-term friend of Tony
    Blair

Derek Foster MP, Opposition Chief Whip 1983–95

George Galloway, MP for Glasgow Hillhead, 1987–2005

John Gilbert MP, Minister of State, Defence 1997–9; Lords 1999–

Tommy Graham, MP for Renfrewshire West, 1987–2001

Bruce Grocott MP, Parliamentary Private Secretary to Tony Blair
    1994–2001

Roy Hattersley MP, Deputy Leader of the Labour Party 1983–92;
    Lords 1997–

Commander Michael Higham, Secretary, Grand Lodge

Derry Irvine, Lord Chancellor 1997–2003

Neil Kinnock MP, Leader of the Labour Party 1983–92; EU
    Commissioner 1995–2004

Tom King MP, chairman, Intelligence and Security Committee 1994–
    2001 and a former Secretary of State for Defence

Stephen Lander, director general, MI5 1996–2002

Ken Livingstone, MP 1987–2001; Mayor of London 2000–8

John Major MP, Prime Minister 1990–7

Peter Mandelson MP, close friend and adviser to Tony Blair, Cabinet
    Office minister 1997–8; Secretary of State for Trade and Industry
    1998 (July–Dec.); Secretary of State for Northern Ireland
    1999–2001

Joan Maynard, MP for Sheffield Brightside 1974–87, close friend of
    CM

Alan Milburn MP, Chief Secretary to the Treasury 1998–9; Secretary
    of State for Health 1999–2003

Mo Mowlam MP, Secretary of State for Northern Ireland 1997–9

Sally Morgan, political officer, 10 Downing Street

Sir Patrick Neill, chairman, Committee on Standards in Public Life
    1997–2001

Frank Nicholson, managing director 1984–99

Paul Nicholson, chairman, Vaux Group 1976–99

Lord Nolan, chairman, Committee on Standards in Public Life
     1994–7
John Prescott MP, Deputy Prime Minister 1997–2007
Stella Rimington, director general, MI5 1992–6
Jack Straw MP, Shadow Home Secretary 1994–7; Home Secretary
     1997–2001
Ann Taylor MP, Leader of the House 1997–8; Chief Whip 1998–2001
Sir Humphry Wakefield, owner of Chillingham Castle,
     Northumberland, friend of CM
John and Sheila Williams, friends of CM
Audrey Wise, MP for Preston 1987–2000
Martin and Mori Woollacott, former *Guardian* foreign editor and GP
     respectively, friends of CM

Media Moguls

John Birt, director general, BBC 1992–2000
David Elstein, head of programming, Sky TV 1993–6; chief
     executive, Channel Five Television 1996–2000
Ray Fitzwalter, editor/executive producer *World in Action* 1976–93;
     head of current affairs, Granada Television 1987–93
Liz Forgan, managing director, BBC Radio 1993–6; director,
     Guardian Media Group 1998–
Michael Grade, chief executive, Channel Four Television 1987–97
Michael Green, chairman, Carlton Television 1983–2003
David Montgomery, chief executive, Mirror Group 1992–9
Rupert Murdoch, chairman and chief executive, News Corporation,
     whose empire includes the *Sun*, *The Times*, the *News of the
     World*, the *Sunday Times*, and a controlling interest in Sky TV
     and Fox News
Bob Phillis, deputy director general, BBC 1993–7
Stewart Purvis, chief executive, ITN 1995–2003
Gerry Robinson, chairman, Granada Group 1992–2001

Members of the Home Affairs Select Committee*
1994–7

Janet Anderson, David Ashby, Gerry Bermingham, Peter Butler, Steve Byers, Jean Corston, Jim Cunningham, John Greenway, John Hutton, Jill Knight, Sir Ivan Lawrence (chairman), Chris Mullin, Walter Sweeney, David Winnick

1997–9

Richard Allan, Robin Corbett, Ross Cranston, Janet Dean, Nick Hawkins, Warren Hawksley, Douglas Hogg, Gerald Howarth, Beverley Hughes, Melanie Johnson, Martin Linton, Humfrey Malins, Chris Mullin (chairman), Bob Russell, Marsha Singh, Paul Stinchcombe, David Winnick

Parliamentary Committee July 1997–July 1999
Backbench Members of Parliament

Charlotte Atkins, Ann Clwyd, Jean Corston, Llin Golding, Helen Jackson, Andrew Mackinlay, Chris Mullin, Clive Soley (chairman), Charles Williams (representing the Lords)

Sunderland Office Staff

Pat Aston, Jacky Breach, Sharon Spurling

Family

Nguyen Thi Ngoc, wife of CM
Nguyen Thi Hanh, sister-in-law of CM
Sarah (b. 1989) and Emma (b. 1995), children of CM
Leslie and Teresa Mullin, parents of CM

---

*Not everyone served a full term; there were only eleven members at any one time.

CHAPTER ONE

1994

Thursday, 12 May 1994

John Smith is dead. Carol Roberton at the *Echo* broke the news. A massive heart attack, she said. He had been rushed to Bart's Hospital. No announcement yet, but obituary material coming through on the wire. After I put the phone down I turned on the television just as the surgeon at Bart's was announcing his death.

The House met at 3.30 for tributes. The Prime Minister and Margaret Beckett spoke movingly. Margaret was with John until late last night. I don't know how she managed to keep control. I couldn't have done. The best line came from a Liberal, Menzies Campbell, who had known John since university – 'He had all the virtues of a Scottish Presbyterian and none of the vices.'

After the tributes, business was cancelled and the House adjourned for the day. People hung around in little groups discussing the succession in low tones.

I stayed upstairs working on a lecture I have to give at Hull in two weeks and at about nine o'clock I went down to watch the BBC news in the Family Room. By now the House was deserted and most of the lights were turned down. When I went back upstairs I found my office had been locked, containing the keys to my flat. Eventually I unearthed a security man and rescued my keys. On the way out I met Robin Cook in the gloomy corridor leading from the Members' Lobby to the Library. We chatted briefly about the succession. He says he hasn't made up his mind whether to stand, but I think he will. And why not? His problem will be getting support elsewhere since his talents are not as widely appreciated as they should be. Early days, but I could see myself voting for him.

We talked about Gordon Brown. I said that I used to be impressed with him, but he had been chanting the same old slogans for years and they were wearing thin. Robin said 'Gordon is intellectually lazy. With someone like Tommy Graham you know he is doing his best and you respect that, but Gordon is capable of much more than he is offering.'

Friday, 13 May

The report stage of Kevin Barron's Bill to ban tobacco advertising which the government is in the process of wrecking. Loads of amendments have been tabled in order to kill it off. I stayed for the first two votes and then headed north. Travelled up with Steve Byers, one of the brightest and most agreeable of the new intake. We agreed that winning the next election was paramount. We can't afford to take even a little gamble. That being so, he sees no alternative but to vote for Blair. He may well be right.

We're all under a vow of silence as regards the leadership to allow a decent interval to elapse until John is buried. The *Independent on Sunday* rang to ask how I would vote and I refused to say.

Saturday, 14 May
Sunderland

To a party at Bryn Sidaway's in the evening to celebrate his election as council leader. I asked everyone who they would support for the leadership. Prescott was mentioned surprisingly often. He seems particularly popular with the northern working-class males. When you ask who is most likely to lead us to an election victory the answer was almost always the same: Blair.

Tuesday, 17 May

To the Home Office for a much-delayed meeting with the Home Secretary Michael Howard to hand over my dossier of alleged miscarriages. His room is massive. One enters from the far end and walks across acres of carpet towards a distant figure in shirtsleeves enthroned behind a long table. On the wall two large oils of battlefield scenes, one the Battle of Blenheim. Behind, laid out neatly, the day's newspapers. I sat alone on one side, facing him. On his side, a woman from C3 (the Division for the Perpetuation of Miscarriages of Justice) and a man from the press office.

Besides the dossier I raised with him the long delay in reconsidering the Carl Bridgewater case and his plans for an independent review tribunal. He was amiable but unhelpful. He didn't even glance at the dossier and repeated the usual bland assurances that all new evidence would be carefully considered. On Carl Bridgewater the woman from C3 said how difficult it was since the convicted men's representative kept making new submissions. I replied that the last one of which I was aware was dated 1 February and she confirmed that this was so. Three and a half months ought to be ample. What can they be playing at? As for the review tribunal, he could offer no estimate of a timetable for its creation, even though yet another Criminal Justice Bill is expected in the new year. The fact is, of course, there are no votes in it, so it isn't a high priority. I pressed him as hard as I could on the need for the tribunal to have at least a reserve power to conduct its own investigations, and not to be dependent on the police. He said he would think about this, although clearly he is minded to leave investigations to the police, which, I said, would be a fatal flaw.

Although all candidates for the leadership are staying impressively silent, everyone else is talking. Alice Mahon said to me, 'I'm in the Stop Blair camp.' To which I replied, 'I am in the Win the Next Election Camp.'

Later, coming out of the division lobby, John Gilbert invited me to his room. The proposition on which he was seeking my opinion was this: with the exception of Margaret Beckett, who held a junior post in the Callaghan government, none of the likely candidates for the leadership had Cabinet experience. Indeed none had ever set foot in a government department, except to protest at some aspect of government policy. This was going to be a serious handicap both in winning the election and, in the event of victory, of governing. There was, however, one person (not yet a candidate) who had the requisite experience. His name? Roy Hattersley. Apparently (and I am inclined to believe) this is not Roy's idea, although he has been consulted. He is understandably reluctant to run and would need to be convinced that there was serious support. Soundings are therefore being taken to see if the idea is a runner. If it is, a delegation led by Cledwyn Hughes would go to Jim Callaghan and suggest that he persuade Blair and the others to stand down in favour of Roy and in the interests of the party. The calculation being that Roy would only be likely to serve one term (I wouldn't bet on that, if we won) and that by the time he went the others would be better equipped to shoulder the burden of office.

The idea has a superficial attraction. No one could ever allege that Roy wasn't up to the job. Indeed there were many occasions during the Kinnock years when one would have given a great deal to see Roy in charge. On the other hand, he is over sixty. His retirement has been announced. He represents the past rather than the future. On top of which he has never been all that popular either with the public or with the party, despite his undoubted ability. I agreed to sound out friends and report back.

Wednesday, 18 May

A depressing meeting of the Campaign Group, always at its worst when discussing election slates. The gist of most contributions seemed to be that Blair must be stopped at any cost. Scarcely anyone mentioned issues or the desirability of winning the election. For a while it looked as though they were going to throw their lot in with John Prescott although Dennis Skinner, who knows him well, is very much against. I can't bear the thought of another phoney-left leader. Give me an honest right-winger any day. The division bell intervened before I could contribute and the meeting ended inconclusively.

Friday, 20 May

To Edinburgh for John Smith's funeral. I caught the seven o'clock from Sunderland and ran into Derek Foster, Ronnie Campbell, David Clark, Steve Byers and John McWilliam on the platform at Newcastle. John Prescott and a crowd of members from Yorkshire were further down the carriage and, to judge by the laughter emanating from that direction, in surprisingly high spirits.

We were in Edinburgh by 9.20 a.m. and walked together down the Royal Mile to the car park beside Holyrood Palace where coaches were waiting to take us to Cluny Parish Church, round the corner from John's home in the south of the city. Everywhere photographers with long lenses. The surrounding streets sealed to traffic. A rumour that the Israeli Prime Minster was coming, which was why security was especially tight. In the event, there was no sign of him.

We were in our seats an hour and a half before the service. I sandwiched between the Ulster Unionist John Taylor and Barbara Roche. The Prime Minister and his wife, who arrived about thirty minutes in advance, were five rows in front. John's coffin surmounted by a wreath of white lilies, rested before the altar.

For all practical purposes, a state funeral. The Queen was represented by Jim Callaghan. A frail, solitary figure in morning dress, he arrived in a Daimler flying the Royal Pennant, escorted by police outriders. The last to take his seat before the immediate family.

A lean, spare service, no kneeling, a few good hymns. Tributes from Donald Dewar and Derry Irvine, who had both known John since university, and acting Labour leader Margaret Beckett on the verge of tears. A psalm in Gaelic beautifully sung by Kenna Campbell. Finally, the coffin was carried out to begin its journey to Iona where he will be buried privately tomorrow.

So much grief for one man who never made more than the most minor impact in government. What we were mourning, of course, was promise unfulfilled. After years in the wilderness, a thoroughly decent man appeared from almost nowhere and offered us the hope of rebuilding our shattered social fabric, and then, suddenly he is gone.

Briefly I attended the reception at Parliament House. As I left, a pane of glass, half an inch thick, fell from a skylight about sixty feet up. My briefcase was smothered with fragments. A few feet more and the next funeral might have been mine.

Tuesday, 24 May

Tony Blair came to a poorly attended meeting of the Civil Liberties Group to tell us about civil liberties under Labour, although none of us now expects that he will be Home Secretary in a Labour government. I asked if he would support a requirement that Freemasons in public office should be obliged to disclose. 'Yes, why not,' he replied, 'but don't expect me to make a major issue out of it.'

Wednesday, 25 May

Not many takers for a Hattersley ticket. Bruce Grocott, Dawn Primarolo and Tony Banks all said 'no'. I espied John Gilbert consulting Dennis Skinner, an unlikely duo if ever there was, and he told me afterwards that Dennis sounded interested.

Tuesday, 31 May

To Windsor Castle with Ngoc's friends, Mr and Mrs Thanh, whom we collected from Heathrow earlier this morning.

'What's this room?' asked Sarah as we entered an apartment stuffed with pictures by Rubens and Van Dyck.

'It's the Queen's Drawing Room,' I read from the sign above the door.

'Does that mean the Queen did those drawings?'

Sunday, 5 June
Brixton Road

After lunch, we loaded up the car and set out for Sunderland. As we passed Sherwood Forest, Ngoc explained to Sarah about Robin Hood. This prompted many questions. 'When did Robin Hood live? Before you and Dad were born? Before Granny and Grandpa? Did he ever visit Vietnam?' Finally, she remarked that Robin Hood wouldn't give us any money because we had a lot. In fact, he would probably take our money and give it to the poor.

Wednesday, 8 June

This evening I chaired a rally at Farringdon School for our European Parliament candidate, Alan Donnelly. Roy Hattersley was the main speaker. 'You will be fair,' he said. 'Why of course, Roy. What do you take me for?'

Like all Donnelly events, the rally was organised like an American convention – balloons, a band, a starlet or two, plus a couple of hundred ultra-loyal pensioners. The only hiccup came at the end when a net full of balloons was unleashed onto the band, who were struggling to play a tune suitable for our triumphal exit.

When I returned home, I found a message to ring John Gilbert. You'll never guess, I said, I've just spent the evening with Roy Hattersley. John was ringing to say that his little plan to install Roy in the leadership had come to nought. The great man had declared that he wanted none of it.

Friday, 10 June

A call from Giles Radice. Might I be persuaded to vote for Tony Blair? I could be, I said, but I hadn't yet made up my mind. 'You'd be a big catch,' he said. What he means is they'd like a left-winger to show the breadth of their support and I'm the most likely sucker.

Saturday, 11 June

A call from Tony Blair. Could he count on my support? Possibly, I said, but I didn't want to commit myself at this stage. Also, I would like to hear his views on coping with the power structure. We left it that I would call his assistant for an appointment next week.

Sunday, 12 June

Stella Rimington, the head of MI5, gave the Dimbleby lecture before an invited audience at the Banqueting House. She was full of assurances that MI5 didn't spy on politicians or on legitimate dissenters (no mention of CND, the National Council for Civil Liberties or the miners' strike). I'm inclined to believe her, if she is talking about the present, but she rather damaged her case by pretending that nothing of the sort had happened in the past.

Monday, 13 June

Ann Taylor rang to see if I would vote for Blair. I seem to be a prime target, but I can't think why they bother. Tony's going to walk it.

Wednesday, 15 June

An hour at the Campaign Group. Unsurprisingly, Ken Livingstone has failed to find the necessary thirty-four nominations and has withdrawn from the leadership election.

Later, I gatecrashed a meeting of the Tribune Group and listened to the leadership candidates. All very fluent, but a little thin on detail.

Thursday, 16 June

Northern Ireland questions. I asked why the RUC were still resisting the use of tape recorders at Castlereagh and refusing to admit solicitors to interrogations. Who better, I asked, to introduce these elementary reforms than a Secretary of State who, as Attorney General, had presided over a series of disasters in the English legal system? A pathetic reply from the Minister of State, John Wheeler. I flashed a smile at the Secretary of State, Patrick Mayhew, who was sitting beside him, but he was not amused.

Nominations for the leadership closed at 4 p.m. Blair has over 150 and Margaret Beckett and John Prescott about forty each. Given that there is no serious ideological difference between the three of them, it seems only logical to vote for the one most likely to help us win the election and that's obviously Blair. I decided not to nominate him, however, in order to distinguish myself from the jobseekers who are flocking to his banner.

Monday, 20 June

Ngoc delivered me to Durham for the 10.46. On the way down, I read a shocking article in the *Guardian* about a new famine in Ethiopia. This one threatens to be worse even than the last. It said that parents were having to choose which of their children to feed, in the hope that at least one or two would survive. Not for the first time, I find myself wondering whether I wouldn't be more use to the world if I worked for an aid agency instead of being a minor politician ministering to the generally sullen and relatively prosperous. The trouble is I have no skill to offer, except as a propagandist. I speak no foreign language, couldn't drill a water hole or administer medicine. I am entirely useless. Perhaps one day I shall be the Overseas Development Minister. Nothing would give me greater pleasure.

Thursday, 23 June

Tea with Tony Blair. We sat on the little terrace outside his office on the first floor of One Parliament Street. A lovely little enclave, but for the dust and noise from the building site next door. Tony confirmed that he was committed to a national minimum wage, which is, for me, the bottom line. I wanted to hear the words from his own lips, because it has been suggested that he is not sound on this issue. However, it is referred to in his statement of values published today (which, that apart, is a rather thin document).

I pressed him to think about how he was going to deal with the power structure. He confirmed that he will go for disclosure of political donations and also that he will disqualify hereditary peers from voting in the Lords. He also confirmed that he would make the intelligence services accountable to Parliament rather than to the executive. On the media, he was non-committal. I told him that we won't survive unless we tackle ownership. Tony listened, but said nothing except that they could do an awful lot of damage. I suspect he will err on the side of caution. I shall keep badgering.

I also tackled him about the kind of regime he envisaged. He confirmed that it will be broad-based. 'I am not bothered about left or right as much as competence.' He said one other interesting thing. 'There is a tradition in the Labour Party of talking big and acting small. It should be the other way round.' We should learn from the Tories, who always did much more than they said they would. Amen to that.

Monday, 27 June

To London on the 10.46. Alan Milburn, a strong Blair supporter, joined me at Darlington. I expressed concern that Tony was too close to Peter Mandelson. Alan said he had put this to Tony and that Tony had said he recognised that his association with Mandelson was damaging. Alan takes the view that Peter is hooked on manipulation. 'He just can't stop himself.' By way of evidence, he pointed to evidence of Peter's hand in some of the press speculation the weekend after John Smith's death. Alan agreed that Peter was bound to be a minister in a Blair regime, but doubts that he'll ever make the Cabinet. 'He's only got two supporters in the Shadow Cabinet – Blair and Brown.' Quite so.

Later, a drink on the terrace with Charles Clarke, who used to work for Neil Kinnock. He came to discuss the minority report on party funding, which I drafted for the select committee. He was very complimentary, said it would form the basis for legislation and advised me to get something drafted. He had one or two reservations: it would be unwise to exclude recent donors from receiving political appointments because that would include trade unionists and we were short of talent to take over some of the Tory quangos. State funding, he said, could only be introduced with all-party support. The only way that could be obtained would be to introduce disclosure and then wait two or three years for the Tory funding to suffer, as it would be bound to. Then they might be more sympathetic. Good thinking, but I'd prefer not to have to introduce it at all.

It was apparent that, unlike many in the Labour Party, Charles had given serious thought to coping with the power structure. So, he claimed, had Kinnock. The problem, he said, had been Hattersley, with whom there had been considerable tension. Cledwyn Hughes had apparently drafted a two-clause Bill for Neil, which would have disenfranchised hereditary peers. He also said that Neil had been determined to do something about Murdoch.

This evening, to the Foreign Office for a drinks party given by Douglas Hogg for veterans of the Intelligence Services Bill. The spooks were out in force – the head of all three services, MI5, MI6 and GCHQ. I chatted to a man from SIS who has the responsibility of preparing the service for the dawning of what passes for democracy. I asked if he could cope with an oversight committee that was responsible to Parliament rather than to the Prime Minister. He went a bit red in the face and said it would be a matter for the politicians. (Maybe, but I bet they would fight it like hell.)

I asked the head of GCHQ if it was true that they bugged domestic as well as international telephone calls. Far from denying it, he said there was nothing to stop them, 'providing it was properly warranted'. I asked what there was to stop an employee on the nightshift indulging in a little freelance tapping. He said that the system of cross-checking was such that it would show up on the computer and could not easily be erased.

Tuesday, 28 June

A drink with the *Sunderland Echo*'s new lobby correspondent, a young journalist called Tom Baldwin, who is hungry for stories. I explained to him that I was anxious to keep many of my more interesting activities out of the *Echo* since they only lead to a wave of anonymous letters demanding to know why their MP was taking an interest in matters beyond the roundabout at the end of the Durham Road. I must try to keep him supplied with local stories if he is to be kept out of mischief.

Thursday, 30 June

One of those rare days – there are about two or three a year – on which I am permitted to address the nation, albeit in sound bites. Sir John May's inquiry into the Guildford and Woolwich cases reported, four years and eight months after it was set up. All very hush-hush, considering it was supposed to be a public inquiry. Most of his interviews have been conducted in private. The contrast with the judicial inquiry being conducted by Lord Justice Scott into the Iraqi arms affair is stark. Even finding out where and when the press conference was taking place proved difficult. My secretary, Jacky, rang the Inquiry number, but obtained no answer. I rang the Private Secretary to the Attorney General and he said the Home Office were dealing with it. I rang the Home Secretary's Private Secretary and he referred me to a civil servant who had worked for the Inquiry, but had now returned to another department. He turned out not to have come in because of the train strike. I rang the Press Association legal correspondent and she said she had been sworn to secrecy. Very odd. Anyway, I eventually tracked the press conference down to the Royal Institute of Mechanical Engineers, just over the road from Parliament.

I persuaded the Home Office to send me over an advance copy, which I received at 12.45. Having read the introduction and the conclusions, I drafted a short statement, made about twenty copies and wandered over to the press conference in good time to distribute my statement to the waiting hacks.

Just as well I did. The report was more or less a snow job, absolving just about everyone except the Guildford Four. There is mild criticism of the police and the DPP, but no names are named. No criticism of the forensic scientist who rewrote his evidence at the suggestion of the police and the prosecution. No view as to how the confessions were obtained – and you would have to have fallen off a Christmas tree to believe they were voluntary. No criticism of his fellow judges, no evidence indeed that Sir John has even interviewed them. And at the end he absolves the legal system as a whole.

At the press conference he was repeatedly asked to express a view about the guilt or innocence of the four and declined to do so, offering instead weasel words about their being entitled to be regarded as innocent. He added that his judicial training constrained him from expressing a view. Well it certainly hasn't constrained some of his judicial colleagues and they didn't have the benefit of an inquiry lasting four years and eight months.

While the press conference was still going on, I nipped downstairs and recorded interviews with ITN, BBC Television, BBC Radio, RTE, Sky and one or two others. I then returned to the House to finish a piece for the *Guardian* which I faxed over just after five. Finally, a quick telephone interview with the *PM* programme and then to King's Cross for the train to Sunderland. All in all, a good day's work.

Monday, 4 July

Sarah said to me at breakfast this morning, 'I know what you wish, Dad.'

'What's that, Sarah?'

'You wish you didn't have to go to your Parliament so you could stay here with me.'

As she was leaving for school, she said, 'Bye, Dad; I hope you won't be bored in your Parliament.'

A brief chat with Livingstone in the division lobby at ten. I put it to him that, if he had made more effort, he would have been a contender for the leadership by now. 'No I wouldn't,' he said. 'There has been an irreversible shift to the right. It always happens when we are in opposition for a long time. It happened in the fifties. Look at Tony Banks. He has worked hard in Parliament and where has that got him? Forty or fifty votes in Shadow Cabinet elections. Maybe I would have got a few more, but not many.'

Ken thinks everything will change when we get into government. He is very gloomy about the economy which, he believes, is in a worse state than anyone anticipates and, if so, that will be his chance. All I can say is he'd better start doing some ground work. Funnily enough he was optimistic about a Blair regime facing up to the power structure. 'They might be quite good on things like that, because they won't be able to afford to do anything else. We might even get some decent gay rights legislation.'

A few minutes later I was sitting scribbling in the Members' Lobby when Nicholas Soames and Tristan Garel-Jones bore down upon me. 'Tell me, Mullin,' boomed Soames, 'supposing Labour wins the next election, what job are you going to get?' He added quietly, 'They'll put you in the Home Office, won't they?'

'I don't think I'll be allowed anywhere near the Home Office.'

To which Garel-Jones added, 'Of course he won't. When Labour becomes the government people like Jim Callaghan and Walter Harrison take over. People like Mullin will have to move from one safe house to another under cover of darkness.'

Wednesday, 6 July

This evening I chaired a meeting organised by Amnesty International at the Friends Meeting House for an American nun, Sister Helen Prejean, who is campaigning against the death penalty. About 200 people attended. Sister Helen is over here to launch her book *Dead Man Walking*, a moving account of her work with death row prisoners in Louisiana. She held everyone spellbound for ninety minutes. 'Only politicians benefit from the death penalty,' she said. 'It enables them to pretend they are tough on crime without actually addressing the causes of crime.' She was in favour of public executions on the grounds that once the public knew the full horror, they'd react against it. An interesting thought, but I have my doubts. The best hope, she said, was that the Supreme Court would eventually put a stop to it, as they had done once before. Already President Clinton had appointed two Supreme Court justices who were more or less opposed and others were coming up for retirement. She also said that Hillary Clinton is against. Perhaps we should be lobbying her, rather than her husband.

Friday, 8 July
Sunderland

At this evening's surgery, a young woman who said she had been summoned by a DSS fraud officer who had accused her of cohabiting. She denied this, but said he wasn't interested in hearing her side of the story. Instead he propositioned her. He gave her the weekend to think about it and asked her to call back next week. I took a signed statement from the woman and rang the head of the DSS fraud section. He told us to tell her to go ahead with the appointment and he would arrange for the interview to be monitored.

Saturday, 9 July

This week's *Tribune* carries my article on why I am voting for Tony Blair, accompanied by a simply awful photograph. I fear it is going to get me into trouble with some people.

To Durham for the Miners' Gala. I walked in with the Wearmouth banner. Just before we reached the County Hotel we were joined by John Prescott and his wife Pauline and the cameras homed in on us. Pauline, I suspect, is not entirely at home in the world of politics. John introduced us but my name clearly didn't ring a bell. Seeing the camera round my neck she inquired, 'Are you a freelance photographer?'

Whereupon John hissed, 'I told you, you should have stayed on the balcony'.

Wednesday, 13 July

To the Queen Elizabeth Conference Centre for Mo Mowlam's media conference. There was a lot of crap about information superhighways and the wonders of optical-fibre networks all designed to intimidate us into doing away with regulation and allowing the market to let rip. A dreary man from BT told us that it was already possible to transmit the entire contents of the Encyclopedia Britannica around the world in less than half a second and that optical fibre made possible a simultaneous two-way conversation between every man, woman and child on the planet. A fat lot of use if you are starving. A man from Sky told us that nothing needed doing about anything. A man from cable TV said that they must be let in on the act as soon as possible. There was even a man from the *Guardian/Observer* who wanted to sweep away such limits as there are on cross-media ownership so he could get into television. He promised that the *Guardian*'s high standards would be maintained, but as someone pointed out, the *Guardian* was already a big shareholder in GMTV which is junk television incarnate.

There was a session on ownership. David Glencross of the ITC said that the market share of advertising should be the determining factor. He suggested a maximum of 25 per cent. Greg Dyke made a good speech. Multichannel TV was coming whether the Labour Party liked it or. The key issue was not delivery systems, it was programmes. Sky is buying 93 per cent of its programmes from the US. Off-the-peg American drama can be bought in at $50,000 an hour, whereas British-made drama cost $600,000 an hour. We had to find a way of encouraging programmes. The EC rule about 51 per cent local content should be applied to Sky, together with the same quotas on news, current affairs and regional television that applied to terrestrial TV. He said the rules on cross-media ownership had been fixed by Thatcher for the benefit of Murdoch. News International must be prevented from controlling both the delivery system and the encryption, otherwise no one else would get in on the market.

I put my tuppence ha'penny worth in from the floor. We shouldn't be intimidated by all this technobabble, I said. We should be concerned about the social, political and cultural consequences. We already had junk newspapers, now we were faced with junk television and soon we would have a junk culture. We had to find a way of preventing a handful of megalomaniacs from taking control of everything we see and read. It went down like a lead balloon, although one or two people (including Bob Phillis, deputy director general of the BBC) came up to me later and said they agreed.

Afterwards I put it to both Greg Dyke and Bob Phillis that, in crude political terms, a Labour government had about six months after taking office to do something about Murdoch or else he would do something about us. They both agreed. Greg said go for the encryption system. Phillis said he would invite Murdoch to choose between his newspapers and his television interests. I asked if either of them were talking to Mo or Robin Cook. Neither of them are. I just hope someone manages to smuggle a message through to the top, otherwise we are doomed.

Thursday, 14 July

To John Smith's memorial service at Westminster Abbey and then home on the six o'clock train. For most of the journey I was alone in the carriage except for a party at the far end who seemed to be receiving an unusual level of service. Staff from the dining car were whizzing back and forth with food and gin and tonics. At first I assumed it was some British Rail bigwigs, but after a while curiosity overcame me and I went to take a look. It was the Duke of Edinburgh. There were three people with him, one of whom appeared to be a detective. He got off at Darlington carrying a battered briefcase.

Saturday, 16 July

My old friend Hugh MacPherson has used his *Tribune* column to denounce me for supporting Blair. He even suggests that I have done it in pursuit of a job, which is a bit low. Never mind, my back is broad.

Monday, 18 July

A day in the office dictating letters to Sharon and then Jacky drove me to Durham for the 17.02. Sarah came too. 'Don't be boring in your Parliament, Dad,' she said.

Wednesday, 20 July

At the suggestion of Dale Campbell-Savours I put down an amendment to delete Sir Marcus Fox from the committee being set up to look at the cash-for-questions scandal and, to my amazement, it was called. As a result, we spent an amusing hour and a half challenging the composition of the committee on the grounds that it is choc-a-bloc with vested interests. The Tory members have eighteen directorships and nine consultancies between them. The whole thing is a fiasco. What a shameless bunch they are.

At 11.30 p.m. I went to the Chamber for a debate on the newspaper price war triggered off by Murdoch's attempt to sink the *Independent* and the *Telegraph*. I had intended just to listen to the debate, but in the end felt inspired to make a little speech along the lines that Murdoch was polluting our culture and something must be done about him. It was 2 a.m. by the time I got home.

Thursday, 21 July

To Shenfield to see Uncle Terence, aged eighty-six, who is dying of cancer but in remarkably good spirits. We sat in the garden. He told some lovely stories about his early years working in the City on a starting salary of £52 a year. He stood at the gate waving as I walked away. 'I have no bitterness,' he said. 'That's one of the things you learn when you get older – not to be bitter or to hate anyone.'

I took the train back to Liverpool Street and caught the Circle Line back to the House. It wasn't until I saw someone reading an *Evening Standard* that I remembered that today is the day that we elect our new leader. It only goes to show how much has changed. Fifteen years ago, I'd have been on tenterhooks, following every detail. Today, it is all predictable. Tony Blair won 57 per cent on the first ballot. John Prescott is to be deputy.

Friday, 22 July

A coffee with the local head of Barclays Bank who is called, appropriately, Mr Sunderland. Barclays is based in one of the new pavilions overlooking the river at North Hylton. The purpose of the meeting was for Mr Sunderland to assure me what a customer friendly, socially minded institution Barclays is. I left him with details of a constituent who borrowed from Barclays to purchase a business which was grossly overvalued and which predictably went bust. Having extracted everything possible from the sale of the business, Barclays is now after his home as well.

From Barclays, I went across to Grove Cranes on the opposite side of the river for a meeting with management and unions. Groves, which is American owned, is about to lay off another 300 workers.

The company's cranes are state of the art, but demand is low and the prospects gloomy. The management are hoping for a big order from the Ministry of Defence, but they didn't think that there was anything we could do to hurry it along. This is the sort of situation where I feel entirely useless. What my constituents need most is work, but in the eight years I have represented them we have lost the shipyards, the pit and a large slice of our engineering capacity, and I cannot think of a single job that has been created or saved as a result of my efforts. Even Bob Clay's heroic efforts to save the Pallion shipyard ended in failure. To paraphrase John Garrett, 'Britain has been in decline for the last hundred years. The role of Parliament has been to provide a running commentary.'

Wednesday, 27 July

Jan Gordon, a mature student from Hull University, has been helping to sort through my Birmingham Six papers. One box is filled entirely with abuse, much of it of a crude and disgusting nature and mostly anonymous, but every now and then a gem. My favourite, which I used to read out at public meetings during the Birmingham Six campaign, is from Mr R. C. Sindle of Mid-Glamorgan. Dated 26 February 1992, it was prompted by an exchange I had with a retired judge on *Newsnight*. It reads:

> ... you certainly came across as a smug sanctimonious git, if ever I saw one. Lord Lane has done more for his country than all the muck-raking scum of the Labour Party put together. And, if the name of Mullins implies what I think it does, then why are you not peddling your crusade for human rights in Ireland? God almighty! What country needs it more?
>
> Mind you Mullins, they are probably silly questions, aren't they? Crusaders among the bigots of Ireland are just as likely to get the shit shot out of them, and we couldn't have that happen to you, could we? But then again, why not?

Tuesday, 9 August

Awoke to hear that Rupert Murdoch has said he could 'imagine' backing Blair. I can imagine him backing Blair too, but solely as a means of protecting his assets if he thinks there is going to be a Labour victory. There is bound to be a lot of free-lunching going on between now and the next election. I pray that we don't fall for it, although I can't say I'm entirely confident.

Wednesday, 31 August

To Shenfield to record an interview with Uncle Terence. Increasingly emaciated, but still in good spirits. What a wonderful old gent he is. Morphine three times a day. A liquid diet. Never once have I heard him complain. His voice was strong. His mind crystal clear. His first memory was of the little white coffin in which his infant sister, a cot death, was carried away and of his mother's distress. That was in 1911.

We recorded for about an hour and a half and it didn't seem to tire him at all. Afterwards he took a walk in the garden with Sarah and we filmed that, too. Finally, Sarah sang him some of her Vietnamese songs and we said goodbye.

Saturday, 3 September

We were invited to a party at Sedgefield to celebrate Tony Blair's accession. I would like to have gone, but gallantly turned it down because we had already agreed to attend a neighbour's silver-wedding party. He had a good job on the oil rigs until he was made redundant, since when he has made heroic efforts to find employment. He tried running a mobile hot-dog stand at Seaburn, then he tried his hand at carpet cleaning, then he took a job as a security man – seventy hours a week, two quid an hour. Now he has grown a ponytail and runs a little New Age shop near the Park Lane bus station and seems to be getting by.

Sunday, 11 September

John Major has made a speech about yob culture. Incredible that the party that gave us mass unemployment, the Broadcasting Act (which introduced an era of junk television) and which enjoys the unqualified support of newspapers like the *Sun* and the *Daily Star*, now has the nerve to lecture us about yobbery.

Friday, 16 September

The novelist Joanna Trollope was on *Desert Island Discs* this morning. Among the records she chose was Mozart's Great Mass in C, which, she said, was the theme tune from 'Alan Plater's *A Very British Coup*.' A bit much.

Monday, 19 September

The chimney sweep came. 'Still on holiday?' he asked slyly. I despair. I have worked every weekday this month. I have engagements on fifteen out of thirty evenings and still most of my constituents believe I am sunning myself.

Wednesday, 21 September
Sunderland

I spent the morning visiting community service projects run by the Probation Service. Like many people I was sceptical about their value, but having seen them in operation I am persuaded. Attendance is enforced rigorously. Three failures to turn up, or even late arrivals, result in a report to the court with a possibility that a custodial sentence can be substituted. I was taken around by a senior probation officer who explained that there were about 320 people on projects in the city. They work mainly in supervised groups of up to six. The projects I visited included a carpentry workshop, a flat in the Garths which had been converted into a crèche and the conversion of a piece of wasteland in Plains Farm into a garden for disabled children from Portland Special School. I also dropped in on a group who were maintaining a cemetery in Silksworth, and a project where bollards were being installed to prevent joyriding on the riverside at North Hylton. The kids on the schemes have been convicted of offences ranging from burglary, car theft, misuse of drugs and violence. Some were career criminals. Several were young women. For most, this was the only real work they had ever done in their lives. Some were actually proud of what they were doing. A young woman at Plains Farm in her twenties told me how moved they had all been at the sight of the disabled children using the youth centre where they were working. Even the hard men on the project had been moved. One or two were even coming back out of hours as volunteers.

Monday, 26 September
Strasbourg

A little Euro junket organised by Jack Cunningham. We arrived about two and went immediately to the European Parliament – a monstrous carbuncle of steel, concrete and glass grafted onto a magnificent medieval city. Our party consists of about twenty MPs, including several good friends. Object of exercise: to familiarise ourselves with the EC and meet our Euro colleagues. About time I learned about the EC since, like it or not, it is destined to play an ever greater role in our lives. I am astoundingly ignorant about Europe. This is the first time I have set foot in France for twenty years.

We began with a briefing from Wayne David and Christine Crawley, leader and deputy leader of the large Labour contingent. Everything about the European Parliament seems ludicrous. The committees meet three weeks a month in Brussels and in the fourth week the entire circus moves to Strasbourg for the plenary session. Every month tons of papers are transported back and forth in a long convoy of pantechnicons, trailed by hundreds of officials. Outside every MEP's room is a steel trunk into which the members pack their papers for transport back to Brussels or vice versa. The Parliament has virtually no power over the executive. Commissioners make statements, but cannot usually be cross-examined. Obtaining an answer to a written question can take weeks.

I spent an hour in the hemicycle listening to an antiseptic debate on air-traffic control. Speakers are chosen by party so there are no dissenters. They are allocated between one and five minutes, according to the size of their group. Debate consists of statements read into the record. No interventions are permitted and passion is entirely absent.

In the evening, dinner with a group of MEPs. They all think the Parliament should be in Brussels, alongside the executive. Apparently a suitable chamber already exists, but the French will have none of it, even though the Strasbourg Parliament is hardly used for the forty-one weeks a year that it is not sitting. It gets worse. When the EC takes in the Scandinavians and Austria, the existing building will not be large enough to accommodate everyone so the French are building a new Parliament alongside the existing one. They got their way by blackmailing the Edinburgh summit. The new monster is costing billions and no one, except the French, want to use it.

The more I learn about the EC, the more opposed to proportional representation I become, especially anything involving the list system. The great strength of the British system is that our elected representatives are accountable to constituencies which, to some extent at least, keeps their feet on the ground. Most continental Europeans are appointed from lists drawn up by their party apparatus. Once elected they are accountable only to the apparatus. All kinds of corruption surrounds the drawing up of the list. Some countries use it as a way of rewarding or exiling distinguished or errant national politicians – like a sort of House of Lords – and the unscrupulous can make a great deal of money by manipulating the lavish allowances that MEPs enjoy as a substitute for power. Christine Crawley said that in the last session her seat was next to the former Italian Prime Minister Bettino Craxi, but she had seen him only once in five years.

Tuesday, 27 September
Strasbourg

A huge catastrophe in the Baltic. A ferry travelling between Sweden and Estonia has gone down. At least 800 dead.

After breakfast I rang home. Sarah said, 'Are you in France, Dad?'
'Yes.'
'Did you go there by aeroplane?'
'Yes.'
'Is France near Vietnam?'

I walked to the Parliament, about a mile and a half along the canal which later becomes a river. On the way in I met an Englishman who interprets in three languages, including Dutch. He said that some of the Greek members were just turning up, signing in and going home again.

An hour in the hemicycle listening to the debate on Ireland. John Hume spoke well and received a standing ovation. The only real dissent came from Ian Paisley, who was cut off after two minutes. It seems that Paisley is no more popular in the Euro Parliament than he is in ours.

Later, a briefing with Dave Feickart, one of the Trade Union Congress's growing team of lobbyists in Brussels. He made the very fair point that the TUC gets nowhere at Westminster, but achieves a lot of what it wants in Brussels. Maybe it is where the future lies, after all. It certainly will be, if we can't win an election soon.

A brief meeting with Klaus Hänsch, President of the Parliament, who was at pains to assure us that the future lay in redistributing power between the Euro Parliament and the Commission and not in extracting more power from national parliaments.

I have been haunted all day by the ferry disaster. I find myself thinking, as I often do at times of disaster, supposing it happened to us. What must it be like to be confronted by your children screaming 'Daddy, Daddy, help me' and being able to do nothing? The only thing more terrible than dying in such circumstances, would be to survive alone.

Wednesday, 28 September
Strasbourg

Meetings with Bruce Millan, who is on the point of retiring after five years as an EC commissioner, and Pauline Green, leader of the socialist group in the European Parliament. Bruce was fairly downbeat. The Treaty, he said, was basically a free-market treaty. There were few socialist commissioners (although this situation will improve after the Scandinavians and Austria come aboard). At present there are sixteen commissioners, some of whom slavishly follow the line of their government, despite taking an oath of impartiality. After the new entrants had signed up, there would be twenty-one, each with his own cabinet of six officials. It was going to be very hard to find work for them all. At the moment, since the Commission was coming to the end of its term, there was not much political will. It is hard to get agreement on difficult issues.

Several important matters were being dodged. No one was giving much thought to the budgetary and structural consequences of bringing in Hungary and Poland. Likewise the growing concentration of media ownership. There is an Italian in charge of looking at that, which might explain why. As for legislation, the situation was chaotic. 'There are seven different procedures,' Bruce said, 'and even after five and a half years I don't understand them.'

Tony Blair and his family have been staying with Alan Haworth* at his house in southern France. Alan told me that Tony had recently dined with Murdoch, but he didn't know what had been discussed. I am not shocked by this. In his place I would do the same: accept his invitations, listen carefully to what he had to say, nod in all the right places – and strike with deadly force during my first week in office. I said that, although we stood a good chance of forming a government after the election, it was not a foregone conclusion and we were unlikely to have a majority of more than minus five to plus five. Alan said, 'That's Tony's assessment, too.'

---

*Secretary of the Parliamentary Labour Party; now in the Lords.

Monday, 3 October
Labour Party Conference, Blackpool

A debate on the minimum wage. A lot of posturing about the rate at which it should be set. I would rather start low and phase it in. If it starts at a rate which is unsustainable I shall have sacked workers from Dewhirst's* banging on my door demanding to know why we have priced them out of their jobs.

Tuesday, 4 October
Blackpool

Awoke to see Tony Benn on television saying with approval that the Labour Party hasn't changed. If that's true, we are doomed. Happily, the tabloids are preoccupied with a book about an ex-army officer who claims to have had an affair with Diana.† That should keep them off our backs for a day or two.

Blair's first speech as leader. He entered to some rather naff music and a synthetic standing ovation. The speech was generally excellent. The best I can recall from a leader in twenty-four years of conferences, but it was ruined by a bombshell at the end. He wants to rewrite Clause IV. How can he be so foolish? It means we are destined to spend the next twelve months navel-gazing instead of addressing the nation. It will dominate next year's conference as well as this. The hacks loved it. They see another year of fratricide ahead.

Anne Clwyd told me that a Sunday newspaper in Wales carried a report last week suggesting that Peter Mandelson was drawing up a list of her defects with a view to keeping her out of the Shadow Cabinet. She has confronted him, but needless to say he denies all.

Predictably, Blair's plan to ditch Clause IV dominates the television news. Mandelson is everywhere. At the crucial point both the early TV news bulletins cut to him applauding vigorously. In the evening I went along to the Tribune Rally in the Spanish Room, which

---

*A Sunderland-based clothing manufacturer.
†*Princess in Love* by Anna Pasternak, which documented the affair between Diana and Major James Hewitt.

was overflowing. As I entered I was pounced upon by *News at Ten*. What did I think of Tony's plan to do away with Clause IV? I refused to play. I guess we're in for a lot of this nonsense over the next year or so. It will require great restraint.

Later, at the Northern Region do in the Blackpool Trades Club, Mo Mowlam recounted how Mandelson, who was sitting next to her during Tony's speech, in the seats reserved for members of the Shadow Cabinet, had just walked up, peeled off the label and sat down. The man's arrogance is astounding. Mo also told me that she didn't know Mandelson had been advising Tony during the leadership campaign until she read about it in the papers. Incredible, considering that she was one of his campaign team. She also said that she had warned Blair that his association with Mandelson was doing him no good in the parliamentary party. Derek Foster said he gave Tony a similar warning, but he's obviously taking no notice. Derek agrees that this Clause IV business is a mistake and suspects Jack Straw had something to do with it. Well, it's too late now. All we can do is try to limit the damage.

Tony and Cherie put in a brief appearance at the Northern do, in a whirl of television cameras and groupies. Poor Cherie looks very tense and awkward, trailing around after her man. I asked how she was coping. She replied, 'What I dislike most is having to keep my mouth shut.'

Wednesday, 5 October
Blackpool

A wonderful piece of anti-Mandelson invective from Ken Livingstone in today's *Independent*. Apparently Peter had described Ken as 'the enemy' on a radio programme yesterday. Asked to comment, Ken replied: 'There must be something really tragic that happened to him in his childhood, but I am so used to his views that I am prepared to forgive him his bitter little asides and I hope he will get better soon. The alternative is that he is a Martian sent to the planet to extermi-nate all forms of life on Earth. But I take a charitable view.'

The media are already formulating new demands now that Clause

IV is to be disposed of. Blair was asked on TV this morning if he intended to change the name of the Labour Party. Naturally he denied all, but who knows?

At lunchtime I went to hear the *Guardian* financial journalist Will Hutton speak at a fringe meeting on the media. He said there must be no compromise with Murdoch, but we shouldn't demonise him. Murdoch is paying virtually no corporation tax. He recommends: (1) A thorough review of the tax status of the Murdoch empire in collaboration with the Australians and American revenue authorities who are also interested. (2) Tighter criteria for the Monopolies and Mergers Commission before making any new referrals. (3) Sticking to the existing rules on cross-ownership (which is interesting, considering that the board of the *Guardian* are among those pressing for the rules to be relaxed). (4) Enforcing existing quotas for TV imports. (5) Limits on the amount of advertising broadcast per hour. (6) A review of auditing procedures for big corporations with a view to tightening them.

Afterwards I dropped in on the BBC lunch at the Imperial and had a pleasant chat with John Humphrys. The Corporation, he says, is not iconoclastic enough – 'It's not okay until someone with a title says it.' He said there had been a big increase in 'guidance' from above during recent years. Especially on royal stories. 'Ten years ago, when the fairy tale was still intact, we were expected to include a royal story in every bulletin. Now the guidance is that we don't use royal stories unless everyone else is going with it.' He said, 'I went in the other day at 4 a.m. and asked, "Has the word come down on the Hewitt book?" Sure enough, it had. We were not to discuss it. There is now guidance on 100 issues on which there didn't use to be.' Humphrys said that in his view broadcasters shouldn't accept gongs. Robin Day had been wrong to do so. He confirmed that Mandelson had been acting for Blair throughout the leadership campaign. We also talked about sound bites. He said the average sound bite on American television news was down to six seconds or eighteen words. On the BBC, 'We start getting jittery at twenty seconds.'

Thursday, 6 October
Blackpool

A resolution endorsing Clause IV was narrowly carried against the advice of the platform. A shot across the bows for our new masters. The spin doctors are already saying that it won't make the blindest bit of difference and I am sure it won't. Blair will get his way, but only at the price of squeezing a little more spirit out of the party. If we lose the election, this will be seen as the turning point.

I ran into an elderly woman who had been brought up in Sunderland in the 1920s, one of eleven children living in two rooms. They lived mainly on porridge and were always hungry. At fifteen she had gone to London with sixpence in her pocket to work as a servant in the house of the Governor of the Bank of England on Queensgate, Kensington. Her masters, she said, ate seven-course meals which they stretched out for hours – 'because they were so bored'. She now lives in Richmond, North Yorkshire, and her children have done well. A useful reminder of how things used to be.

Monday, 10 October
Sunderland

To St Anthony's to address sixth formers. One girl asked if it was ever right to break the law. I said yes, if it was an unjust law and you were prepared to take the consequences. I mentioned the Tolpuddle martyrs, but I should have referred to the suffragettes. Another asked whether tax would increase under a Labour government. I said yes, for the best off. She asked me who the best off were and I gave a long and not very clear answer. I am beginning to sound like Gordon Brown.

Thursday, 13 October

This afternoon a meeting with shop stewards from clothing factories in and around Sunderland. Women from a factory at Seaham said a climate of fear prevails among employees with less than two years' service. Up to that time they can be dismissed at whim without any recourse to a tribunal (the deadline used to be six months until the Tories changed it, first to one year and now to two years). As the two-year deadline approached, some women became nervous wrecks, wondering whether they would have a job the next day. They dare not take a day off through sickness for fear of providing management with an excuse for dismissal. The union official responsible for the textile industry said that reducing the deadline for access to employment tribunals was the single most useful reform a Labour government could make. I came away refreshed. It is always good to meet the people at the sharp end rather than the theorists and spin doctors.

Tuesday, 18 October

Frantic lobbying for the Shadow Cabinet election. Every post brings a new batch of begging letters from hopefuls. It is impossible to get from the door of the Tea Room to the counter without being nobbled. I have adopted a lofty posture – asking no one to vote for me and making no promises. My vote is likely to go down this year, the price of voting for Tony Blair.

Robin Cook joined me at lunch. I told him that he was my – and many other people's – candidate for Shadow Chancellor, but he said there was no chance of Gordon being shifted. If he can't be Shadow Chancellor, he would prefer to hang on to the Trade and Industry portfolio. I said it was rumoured that he might be shifted to Foreign Affairs. He replied, 'I am absolutely uninterested in being Shadow Foreign Secretary.'

I chaired a meeting of the Civil Liberties Group at lunchtime. Mike O'Brien said that Michael Howard had recently told a private meeting of Police Federation officials that a tribunal to deal with miscarriages of justice will only be introduced this session if he comes under sufficient pressure.

Wednesday, 19 October

Tony Blair addressed the parliamentary party. He began with an absolutely clear statement of what we stand for, and then delivered a little homily on how hard we all need to work to win. 'Losing is the greatest betrayal.' He promised to run an 'inclusive' regime without cliques or cabals. The quid pro quo, he said, was mutual support and discipline. All good stuff. A stark contrast to Kinnock's mixture of threats, waffle and rant, but I am just a little sceptical as to how inclusive the new regime will be. Time will tell.

The Shadow Cabinet results were announced at 8.30. Robin Cook topped the poll, followed by Margaret Beckett and Gordon Brown. I received fifty-nine votes, ten down on last year, but respectable for a balding, middle-aged, middle-class left-wing male. Harry Barnes pointed out I was highest of the non-office holders.

Thursday, 20 October

The *Guardian* is running a big story alleging that two ministers – Tim Smith and Neil Hamilton – took money from the Al Fayeds which they neglected to declare. Smith has resigned; Hamilton is staying put and suing. The sleaze factor dominated PM's Questions and Blair was on top form. The new Shadow Cabinet was announced in the evening. Gordon, needless to say, remains as Chancellor and Robin becomes Shadow Foreign Secretary (so much for his protestations that he was entirely uninterested).

To the Reform Club for a party to celebrate Alastair Campbell's departure from *Today* newspaper. Everyone who was anyone was there, even old Jim Callaghan. Clare Short agrees that it is a mistake to move Robin away from economic policy. 'Gordon's fingerprints are all over it,' she said. 'Tony thinks he's in Gordon's debt. He's not, but he doesn't know it.' She also said that she had warned Tony about Mandelson. She must be the tenth person who claims to have done that. She added that, despite his many obvious qualities, Tony is indecisive and that's why he heeds Peter.

Caught the 22.00 train north, getting home around 1.30 a.m.

Friday, 21 October

At lunchtime, Bill Etherington and I addressed a demonstration of NHS workers at the gate of the General Hospital. A couple of domestic workers from Ryhope Hospital told me that their jobs had been put out to tender. They'd won them back by agreeing to lower pay and fewer hours. They'd been assured that their jobs were safe, at least until Ryhope closes in four years' time. Now they have been told that they will have to go out to tender again. What a mess our masters are making of people's lives. And how typical that they always pick on the lowliest to try out their half-baked economic theories.

Tuesday, 25 October

At lunch I shared a table with Charles Kennedy who told a hilarious tale about Roy Hattersley. Apparently Roy was visiting New York where Ned Sherrin had fixed him up an appointment with Stephen Sondheim, of whom Hattersley is an admirer. At the appointed hour Roy turned up at a lavish mansion in New York. The door was answered by a maid who showed him into a huge living room, gave him a drink and said that Mr Sondheim would be down shortly. The best part of an hour went by, but there was no sign of either the maid or Sondheim. Roy, becoming annoyed, scribbled a note saying that he had to leave and headed for the hall. As he did so, a door opened upstairs and the man himself leaned over the banister. 'If Hattersley doesn't show up soon, we'll have to go ahead with the audition.'

Blair is now appointing the junior spokesmen and all around there are urgent little groups of hopefuls awaiting the call. Ann Clwyd, who has been runner-up in the Shadow Cabinet elections for the last two years, was first offered a lowly post which she sensibly rejected. Then he came back and offered her a junior post in the Foreign Office team and she rejected that, too.

The big news is that Major has set up an inquiry under Lord Justice Nolan into the business interests of MPs. Neil Hamilton (who is, with supreme irony, the minister in charge of business ethics at the DTI) has resigned as a result of the allegations made by Al Fayed. He has gone with particular ill grace. The argument seems to be about whether or not he should have registered a free stay at the Ritz Hotel in Paris (owned by the Al Fayeds) at which he ran up a hefty bill. The more interesting question is, what was he doing there in the first place?

I walked to the bus stop with Derek Fatchett, who was very scathing about the Shadow Cabinet appointments. He says that anyone who has any different ideas from Gordon has been moved out of economic policy. Dealing with Gordon was the first big test of Tony's leadership and he's failed miserably. He added that Margaret Beckett should have been treated with more respect and given one of the big jobs. 'The trouble with Tony,' he said, 'is that, faced with pressure, he backs down.'

Wednesday, 26 October

With Bruce Grocott to lunch at the ITV network centre. Bruce has just been appointed Blair's Parliamentary Private Secretary – just about the most sensible of the new appointments. He and I have a common interest in the media – and in particular persuading our masters to do something about Murdoch. We dined with Andrew Quinn and Stuart Prebble who were at pains to assure us that, far from having declined, the quality of commercial television was as high as ever. Stuart, who is in charge of factual programmes, insisted that there were more than ever – although a little probing revealed that the definition of 'factual' includes such in-depth analysis as *Hollywood Women*. Domestic content was 65 per cent (although Murdoch's Sky TV is exempt). They are still anxious to get the *News at Ten* out of the way to make way for more junk movies at prime time. Channel Four was plunging downmarket, only 40 per cent of its programmes were original. Bruce remarked that so far as he could see the Broadcasting Act had led to a lot of people being made redundant and a handful of people becoming very rich. No one contradicted him.

To the Home Affairs Committee where we discussed our future programme. The clerk has prepared a draft report on organised crime which confirms that we have absolutely no original thoughts on the subject. Once again I suggested that we should draw a line under it, but the Tories seem keen to press on. The reason, it soon became apparent, is because it provides a convenient alibi for a freebie. Ivan Lawrence told us he has wangled £319,000 from the Liaison Committee to fund a fact-finding mission to The Hague, Bonn and Rome. A complete waste of public money. Ironic, considering that the Tories are always accusing Labour of profligacy. They're in for a bad surprise. Steve Byers said he wasn't going. Gerry Bermingham won't be interested. My inclination is not to go either. In which case they'll have no one to pair with, unless they go in the recess, which they most certainly won't want to do. Ivan mentioned that the newly formed select committee on Northern Ireland had received approval for a trip to Korea at a cost of £40,000. If nothing else, they deserve a prize for ingenuity.

Monday, 31 October

Peter Mandelson has been appointed a whip. As Brian Sedgemore remarked, 'It shows that Blair's got bottle. He's taken on the whole parliamentary party.'

Tuesday, 1 November

Jack Straw, Shadow Home Secretary, came to the Civil Liberties Group at lunchtime. I pressed him on disclosure for Freemasons and he was in favour. I shall hold him to that.

A bizarre row with Ray Powell (the whip responsible for the allocation of offices) about Bob Cryer's old room. A room with a window is my only remaining political ambition and Bob's has been vacant for months. I first dropped Ray a note on the subject before the summer recess and he told me that Mildred Gordon needed it for health reasons. I was surprised to find, when Parliament returned in October, that Mildred was still in her old office and, when I inquired, her secretary told me that she had turned it down. Back to Ray, who says there are others, more senior than I, who qualify. Name one, I said, and he named someone who was elected four years after me. Then he mentioned Terry Lewis, who already has an office with a window, larger than Bob's. Finally, he blurted the truth. It is going to James Kilfedder, a pleasant old Independent Unionist. I pointed out that Kilfedder already has the office next to Bob's. Ray replied that he needs a second one.

'Why?'

'Because he is the leader of his party.'

'But Ray, he is the only member of his party.'

I suggested that, if Kilfedder needs a second office (and I can't for the life of me see why he should), then he can have mine – the one without a window. In any case, Kilfedder is for all practical purposes a Tory; I naively thought that Ray was supposed to be representing the Labour interest. Ray then started babbling about it all being part of some complex deal which will lead to a suite of offices at One Parliament Street being put at Ray's disposal. I can't make head or tail of it. I only know that it stinks.

Wednesday, 2 November

At the House we were discussing whether to refer to the Privileges Committee *Guardian* editor Peter Preston's foolish forgery on House of Commons notepaper, used to obtain a copy of Jonathan Aitken's bill for his stay at the Ritz in Paris. The Tories see it as a lifeline and have seized eagerly upon it. They were virulent in their denunciations. Julian Brazier shouted out that it was 'wickedness'. I said to him afterwards that he wouldn't recognise wickedness if it hit him in the face. What a load of Pharisees. It could still all blow up in their faces. Preston is asking the Privileges Committee to hear his case in public, which they won't be keen on. An amusing exchange with Roger Gale, who was huffing and puffing about the wickedness of the *Guardian*. 'The honourable gentleman, like me, is a journalist by profession,' I said. 'Isn't he even mildly curious to know what the Minister of Defence Procurement was doing in an hotel in Paris at the same time as three Saudi arms dealers?' Needless to say he wasn't.

When I referred to our both being journalists someone on our side called out, 'He's from a different school.' Whereupon Lady Olga

Maitland, who is not terribly bright, was heard to say, 'What's his school got to do with it?'

No one believes Aitken and a number of Tories are saying so privately.

On the train this evening, my wallet was stolen.

Thursday, 3 November

A message on the office answerphone from British Rail at Newcastle to say that my wallet, minus the cash, but with everything else intact had been found when the train was cleaned and was in Lost Property. I went there at lunchtime and they charged me £3 to retrieve it, which I thought was a bit rich. Later a British Rail policeman rang. After he had noted the details he said, 'How's the campaign against freemasonry going? You've got a lot of support among the police, but they wouldn't dare put pen to paper.' He said that freemasonry wasn't too bad in Newcastle, but it was a problem in many police forces. He added that his neighbour was a Northumbria Ambulance Service officer. 'He's not a Mason, but he keeps getting notes through the door.'

Wednesday, 9 November

The mid-term elections in the USA have gone badly for Clinton. Perhaps we shall hear a little less from the New Labour modernisers about learning from the Democratic Party. Elections in the US are a dismal affair with each candidate stooping lower and lower in pursuit of votes from a public which, collectively, is all but fascist. In Texas and Florida they are vying with each other over the number of death warrants they will sign. I heard the other day that someone from the Labour Party has been over there learning about negative campaigning. Unhappily, it seems to work. Fortunately we've got two things going for us – strict limits on spending (at least at local level) and a ban on politicians buying airtime on TV.

Thursday, 10 November

I have written to Lord Justice Nolan enclosing the minority report which I drafted for the select committee on party funding and suggesting some areas into which he might like to inquire. I also wrote to the director general of the Inland Revenue suggesting he investigate a little scam reported in the *Independent* on Tuesday where a Tory front organisation called the Blaby Industrial Council is holding a £150-a-head dinner to raise funds for the Tories. Participants have been told it will be billed as a budget seminar so they can claim it against tax. Finally, I faxed a note to Paul Nicholson seeking his assurance that the Northern Industrialists Association, another Tory front which is holding a similar dinner this evening in Newcastle, will not be advising members to claim tax relief à la Blaby. I obviously touched a raw nerve. A reply containing his 'absolute assurance' came back within ten minutes.

Monday, 14 November

A call from Frank Dobson. He has persuaded Tony Blair to make a serious push on reform of party funding and is setting up a small team for that purpose. Would I like to join? You bet.

Wednesday, 16 November

To London on the 10.46. On the way down I read that the Queen's Speech would contain proposals for the long-promised Criminal Cases Review Authority, but in the event there was no mention of it. Only a reference to 'further measures of law reform'. It wasn't until John Major spelled it out towards the end of his speech that it became clear that there will be a review body. Major said it would be 'independent of the government and the courts', but will it be independent of the police? That's what I want to know.

The select committee commenced an inquiry into the private security industry which is full of cowboys and criminals. Anyone can buy a dog and an old van and call himself a security guard. We began by interviewing the employers. Interestingly, they want government regulation, which is not what the government wants to hear. I managed to squeeze out of the witnesses what they paid their employees. It's as low as £2.25 an hour – and these are the good guys. They were apologetic, but excused themselves on the ground that they were being undercut by cowboys. 'In that case,' I said, 'a national minimum wage would be beneficial to good employers like you.' Needless to say they didn't think so, but the logic is inescapable.

Thursday, 17 November

To a meeting with Tony Blair at his request. The first time I had been in the Leader's office since I interviewed Michael Foot for *Tribune* twelve years ago and he abruptly terminated the interview when the questions got too sticky. Would I accept a front-bench job? I had thought the recent appointments were with us for the duration, but apparently not. He talked of 'pepping up' the front bench and 'giving it a radical edge'. An odd conversation to be having only two weeks after he had appointed his team. He said he wanted to add some 'sensible radicals'. So many of the left, he said, are ...

'Impossibilists,' I suggested.

'I was going to say, conservative. Their idea of being radical is to defend the status quo.' A fair point when you think about it. So many of my Campaign Group colleagues merely want to revert to the status quo ante. Repeal all Tory trade union laws, throw out all the changes in the NHS without pausing to consider whether any of them have merit.

It's clear that Tony was railroaded into reappointing a lot of people he didn't want. (Anji Hunter, his assistant, told me a while ago that the reshuffle process had been an horrendous ordeal.)

He asked what jobs I was interested in and I listed half a dozen – Heritage (if we are intending to do anything about media ownership), Home Office, Foreign Office, Agriculture (with responsibility for farm animal welfare – that surprised him). Above all, I said, I was interested in addressing the power structure.

We talked about his dinner with Murdoch who, apparently, hadn't tried to sound him out on our plans. Tony said he had the impression that these days Murdoch's principal interests were in Asia.

'If he thinks we are going to win, he will go easy on us, but if he thought we could lose, he would turn on us.' He added, 'If the press misbehave badly during the election campaign, I will stop everything for two days and we will have a debate about what they are up to, who owns them, the lot.'

'Did you say that to Murdoch?'

'Not in so many words.'

I said that, while I accepted that we should do nothing to alienate the media in advance, if we wanted to survive, we would have to strike with deadly force soon after we took power. He was non-committal but had clearly thought about it, which is more than can be said for any other Labour leader in my lifetime.

We talked about doing away with hereditary peers – something he has clearly set his sights on – he was apologetic about the recent nominations to the Intelligence Services Committee. 'Unfortunate' was the word he used. He hinted that there were factors beyond his control, a reference no doubt to the Whips Office. I said that, if the war in Ireland was over, there was scope for saving some public money. Perhaps by amalgamating MI5 and MI6 (now there's a job I would enjoy). He said, 'You try telling them that' (nothing would give me greater pleasure).

I was with him for about twenty-five minutes. For the last ten, a young woman was making him up for a television interview. At the end he said to me, 'So you've no objection in principle to going on the front bench.'

'Not at all,' said I. 'If something's about to change for the better, I would like to play a part.'

'It may all end in tears and disillusion.'

'There's no reason it should.'

'My absolute priority is to win. I know that sounds unprincipled, but I just see it as my role in life.'

Later, a talk with Alan Milburn who had been hoping to get on the front bench this time. He said that Tony had taken him aside and told him that there would be another opportunity before the election. He said that Tony had completely lost control of the reshuffle – and just given up on most of the junior appointments.

Friday, 18 November

The debate on the Home Affairs section of the Queen's Speech was thinly attended, which meant that I was called reasonably early (i.e. after only two and a half hours). I got stuck in on the proposed review body for alleged miscarriages of justice. It's clear that Howard, despite all the advice to the contrary, is intending to leave investigations in the hands of the police, which will make it as useless as the Police Complaints Authority.

Afterwards a Tory member said that he agreed with everything I had said about the police. Seven years practising at the criminal Bar had taught him they were not to be trusted. He must be at least the thirtieth Tory to say something similar in private during the last five years. A pity they can't bring themselves to say it out loud.

Saturday, 19 November

The first National Lottery is drawn today. The tabloids have been full of lottery fever all week. I can't say I share their enthusiasm, but all the same I went to the post office and purchased three tickets. There was a long queue. The jackpot is said to be £7 million. If we win, the first person to benefit will be poor Mr Le Qua* and his family. After that I will buy a walled garden and give most of the rest to charity. This is not, however, a dilemma with which I am likely to have to wrestle. The odds against winning are about fifty million to one.

Monday, 21 November

A message from Mum to say that Terence died at about eleven o'clock last night.

---

*A Vietnamese building worker who lost both arms in an accident and whose family I supported.

Tuesday, 22 November

One of the whips told me that there are forty or fifty Labour members who can't be relied upon to turn up regularly and they have to be kept sweet by being given foreign trips, good offices and so on. The worst offenders, he says, are those who are not standing again.

Thursday, 24 November

I showed a group of kids from a secondary school in one of the poorer parts of Sunderland around the House. Afterwards we had a short question-and-answer session. The examination league tables were published this week and their school is once again the lowest in Sunderland and, perhaps, in the country. They asked what Labour would do to help them find jobs and I waffled on about increasing investment and releasing capital receipts to boost public housing development. The sad truth is that, for many of them, it is too late.

In the evening I spent an hour at a reception in the Locarno Room at the Foreign Office given by Alastair Goodlad. Alan Howarth, a very decent Tory, lamented Foreign Office cynicism about the arms trade. He said, 'At home Foreign Office civil servants are perfectly civilised people who tend their gardens, play in string quartets and so on, but when they come to work they abandon any sense of morality and set about protecting the balance of payments by any means possible.' He added that the arms trade was not only wrong, but had no future. He wondered if a Labour government would be any different. I wonder, too.

    An interesting talk with a senior colleague in the Tea Room. She said that before the last election John Major had sent the Cabinet Secretary, Sir Robin Butler, to address the Shadow Cabinet. She was surprised and embarrassed by the deferential tone of many of her colleagues' questions. She added, 'They'll have circles run around them in government.' We talked about Gordon. She agreed he is a problem. So hyped up that he will burn out. His fingernails are bitten to the quick. She added that it was a mistake to move Robin (just about everyone thinks that).

Saturday, 26 November

Ngoc has told Sarah that Uncle Terence is dead. 'He has gone to heaven because he was very old and ill.' What a useful concept heaven is for explaining death to children.

'Did they put him in a box?'

'Yes'.

'And did they put the lid on?'

'Yes.'

'Why?'

'Because that's what happens when people die.'

Tuesday, 29 November

Budget Day. I didn't go in since my presence or absence won't make the blindest bit of difference. Instead I went to University College at Euston to talk to the Law Society on miscarriages of justice. About fifty people attended including some members of staff and afterwards there was a good discussion. I sold five copies of *Error of Judgement*, which, apart from two or three on my shelves, are the last I possess. About 64,000 copies were printed and they are all gone.

Wednesday, 30 November

I caught the 20.00 from Kings Cross and was home by midnight. The Director of Public Prosecutions, Barbara Mills, and several senior officials were on the train and we talked for about half an hour. I said the review authority would be useless if it didn't have power to conduct its own investigations, but I am not sure she took the point even though I laid it on with a shovel. She asked whether I thought it should have the power to examine evidence that would otherwise be inadmissible and I said it should. I asked about Masons and she said she had never come across them and that they certainly weren't a problem in her organisation which, in any case, was 60 per cent female. A pleasant, bright woman, but naive.

Thursday, 1 December
Sunderland

A day in the office wading through piles of casework. Also, a desperate plea from an Englishwoman in Missouri who has married a man on death row who is due to be executed next Wednesday. I faxed a letter to the governor, but I don't hold out much hope. In five years of writing appeals on the death penalty to American politicians, I have never even had an acknowledgement. We rang the poor woman and she said she had been to the prison this morning and they were already rehearsing the execution.

It is reported today that Tony Blair is sending his son to an opted-out school. The Tories are cock-a-hoop. A big row brewing.

Friday, 2 December

At the management committee this evening, a huge row about Blair's son. Council leader Bryn Sidaway said it is going to put the council in a very difficult position. So far, he had managed to persuade the Catholic schools to stay with the local authority, but that would obviously be more difficult in the future. No one came to Tony's defence. It was agreed to write expressing concern.

Sunday 4 December

This evening on television, a shocking report by Julian Pettifer from Vladivostok, home of the Russian Pacific Fleet. The harbour is full of rusting nuclear submarines, leaking radiation. The old reactors and much else besides are being dumped into the Sea of Japan. Meanwhile, Japanese logging companies, having worked their way through the forests of Thailand and Indonesia, have begun demolishing the Siberian forests. What a mess we are in. It can only be a matter of time before the chickens come home to roost.

Tuesday, 6 December

Great excitement this evening. The government was defeated by eight votes over increasing VAT on fuel. Six Tories voted with us. About the same number abstained and, for once, all the Ulster Unionists deserted the government. Much talk about this being the beginning of the end, but I am not so sure. There are two years to go yet until the election and they will certainly hang on until then. By that time, VAT on fuel will be forgotten – just like poll tax.

Wednesday, 7 December

At the select committee we took evidence from the police on the private security industry. Like everyone else we have interviewed so far, they were in favour of statutory regulation. John Stevens, the Chief Constable of Northumberland, was the chief police witness. Afterwards, I bent his ear about a remarkable case brought to me recently by a constituent who apparently got word that he was going to be fitted up by the local police, so he took the precaution of filing a letter with his solicitor and carrying a copy with him. Sure enough, he found himself being trailed, stopped, breathalysed and harassed. When he showed the officers who had stopped him the letter he had filed, they became agitated. A murky business. Everyone involved, including the victim, seems to be a Mason. I had written to John Stevens, but he had not seen my letter. I asked him to take a personal interest, and he promised to do so.

A silly row at the Campaign Group in the evening. Lynne Jones was in the chair and Dennis Skinner was giving his report on the National Executive Committee. As usual, he was making a meal of it, and Lynne attempted to hurry him (the meeting had been going nearly two hours), and Dennis threw a tantrum. Lynne, who is fearless, remained calm, but Dennis kept on about it. As ever, when Dennis throws a wobbly, everyone else kept quiet. One or two even intervened on his side. I was the only one who spoke up for Lynne. Later, in the Tea Room, I told him he had behaved badly and he started shouting at me. Tony Benn said afterwards that you can't have a relationship with Dennis until you have had a row with him.

Thursday, 8 December

Bruce Grocott and I had a quiet talk with Shadow Heritage Secretary, Chris Smith, about the media. He is still feeling his way and doesn't seem to have come to any firm conclusions yet, but we pressed upon him the need to have a plan for dealing with Murdoch, Michael Green et al. I floated my one daily, one Sunday per proprietor scheme and stressed the need to limit cross-media ownership – including satellite. We pointed out that Carlton and Granada already had 36 per cent apiece of ITN. Chris was non-committal, although he did say that he was at least as worried about Michael Green as Murdoch. He also said he proposed to talk in generalities until after the election. After which, I suggested, he could then amaze everyone by doing more rather than less than we implied we would. Chris will be a much better Heritage Secretary than Mo. At least he doesn't appear to be dazzled by all that information superhighway nonsense.

At lunch in the Strangers' Cafeteria, I sat at the same table as Tom King, who is the Tory rep on the Nolan Committee. He said that my letter about Masons had prompted a furious reply from Commander Higham, Secretary of Grand Lodge. To my surprise, he was hostile to the Masons. He mentioned Calvi, the Italian banker found hanging under Blackfriars Bridge, and seemed amenable to the idea of doing away with the secrecy around the Masons. A most unlikely ally.

I stayed long enough to hear Ken Clarke's emergency mini budget to make up for the other night's defeat on VAT on fuel. He has decided to clobber drinkers, drivers and smokers, which is fine by me. Considering the hole he had to dig himself out of, Clarke was on excellent form. Gordon was as gloomy and doom-laden as ever. Give me Clarke any day. He actually looked as though he was enjoying himself, rarely glancing at his notes, casually leaning on the Dispatch Box, brazenly denouncing Gordon for our complete absence of an economic policy. He is undoubtedly the Tories' greatest asset in Parliament. How stupid of us not to oppose him with our best performer, Robin Cook.

I wonder whether we would have been better off losing the vote on VAT? Had it been implemented, it would have hung around Tory necks for years to come, but without it, we shall have to look for something else to pin on them and that may not be easy. 'You've shot your fox,' Tom King said to me at lunch. John Fraser used the same expression two hours' later. They may well be right. We can no longer rely on VAT to camouflage the fact that we don't have any economic policy.

Home on the 17.00. In the newspaper on the way back, there was a one-line report saying that a man and a woman had been stoned to death in Iran yesterday.

Saturday, 10 December
Sunderland
Passed the day in the garden, spreading compost and horse manure. A pleasant stink pervades.

Thursday, 15 December
I was at the House by 8 a.m. to wait in the Public Bill Office for a chance to table a ten-minute-rule Bill – aimed at breaking up media monopolies. While waiting, I chatted to Tessa Jowell, one of the brightest of the new London MPs and a keen Blairista. She said that most of Tony's supporters had voted for him because they believed he was a winner and, if he turned out not to be, his support would swiftly melt away. We talked about education. She said Tony's decision to send his son to an opted-out school eight miles from home was not controversial among most of her electorate. Education in parts of Southwark was in a state of collapse. Dulwich, her constituency, is full of private schools and most of the middle classes have long since evacuated their children. She wants to see inner-city schools providing breakfast for the poorest children and homework clubs for those whose home environment doesn't enable them to do homework. She also wants to see independent schools encouraged to open their facilities to local state schools – which she says already happens in Dulwich. If they don't, she says, we should take away their charitable status.

John Major seemed rattled at Question Time. Several people rubbed his nose in the announcement by British Gas that they are cutting the salaries of their salesroom staff – three weeks after awarding their chairman a whopping 75 per cent increase. The timing is impeccable, on the day of the by-election at Dudley.

Friday, 16 December

A swing of 29 per cent to Labour at Dudley. A catastrophic result for the Tories. Beware of triumphalism, however. Two years into a Labour government, it will happen to us. The electorate is in a mean and greedy frame of mind. The relentless pursuit of self-interest, unleashed by the Thatcher decade, has uncorked all sorts of ugly forces which no one can satisfy.

Monday, 19 December

A chat with Tony Benn, Joan Lestor and Derek Foster in the Tea Room. Derek said he had just spent half an hour telling Tony Blair that his decision to send his son to an opted-out school was a mistake. They took the same view of the plan to rewrite Clause IV. Tony Benn said that Gaitskell had tried it in 1960 and backed off. Instead, he had accepted a compromise where Clause IV was retained and a statement 'clarifying' it was issued. Within a few weeks, the statement had been forgotten. Apparently, a similar solution had been suggested to Tony Blair, but he is having none of it. Joan said she was going to see if she could persuade him.

Saturday, 24 December

Sarah wrote a note to Santa Claus to say that she would be staying with her aunty Liz and I went out to post it. On the way to the post box I was waylaid by a woman who owns a number of properties in the area, several of which have recently been burgled. What, she demanded, was I going to do about it? I pointed out that, having been burgled on many occasions, I was as keen as she that something should be done. What did she have in mind? 'It's up to you, you're the government.' I pointed out as gently as I could that, on the contrary, I was the Opposition. Government for the last fifteen years had been in the hands of the Conservative Party – for which, I just restrained myself from saying, she had no doubt voted throughout. What we were now faced with was, to a large extent, the social consequences of fifteen years of Conservative rule to which there were no magic solutions. She continued to rage so I pressed her again about what she wanted done. 'Capital punishment,' she said.

'For thieves?'

'Well, chop off their hands.'

Debate continued at this level for ten minutes or so. I curtailed it by saying that, if she felt strongly enough to write me a letter, I would be glad to represent her views to the Home Secretary, although I doubt even Michael Howard could be persuaded to start chopping off hands.

Saturday, 31 December

The last day of 1994. The human race is in a worse state now than at any time I can remember. Catastrophe in Africa. A war in Europe for the first time in fifty years. The Soviet Union disintegrating. The Pacific Rim, where, we are assured, the future lies, is in the grip of market forces more virulent and more destructive than any we have so far seen. The planet is being remorselessly looted and polluted. Everywhere rampant market forces have triumphed. Resistance, we are forever being told, is futile. Politicians are losing control over events and, as a result, becoming increasingly discredited.

For the first time we have a Leader of the Labour Party who is younger than I am. Attractive, capable, well motivated, but it remains to be seen where he is taking us. No day seems to pass without news that some old policy or principle has been discarded. I only hope we have something to replace them with and so far that is not at all clear.

No use complaining. I voted for the new order (and there wasn't anything better on offer). I have signed up for the journey. I shall not jump ship halfway.

CHAPTER TWO

1995

Sunday, 1 January 1995
Brixton Road

I was loading the cases into the car outside the flat in preparation for our journey north when a skeletal old boy sidled up and bummed a lift. He had come from Croydon on a 109 bus, got off at Brixton and was looking for a cafe in which to have a cup of tea and a sausage roll. I drove him to the bottom of the Brixton Road where there are a couple of cafes, but they were both closed. So was the one by the Oval. He was familiar with them all so I guess he often did this, using his bus pass to while away the lonely days. I don't suppose he could cook for himself either. Christmas and New Year must be the worst time of year for people like this. I dropped him at Stockwell tube station, suggesting that he go to Victoria where there are bound to be cafes open. As he got out he tapped me for a couple of quid.

David Blunkett was on the news this morning saying that Labour is considering removing charitable status from private schools and imposing VAT on fees. By lunchtime he was on *The World this Weekend* assuring the nation that there would be no VAT on school fees after all. So much for the well-oiled machine.

Frederick West, the alleged mass murderer, has been found dead in his cell.

Wednesday, 4 January

With Ngoc to hospital for another scan. The baby is alive and well. Ngoc said she could see its arms and legs moving.

Thursday, 5 January

Three lifers have escaped from Parkhurst. The latest in a series of mishaps in the Prison Service. Everyone is calling for Howard's head. I had a call from *The World at One*, but I declined to join in. It's a silly game which will rebound on us one day. Prisoners are just as likely to escape under a Labour government as under a Conservative one. Unless someone can demonstrate that Michael Howard actually left the doors open, I can see no good reason why he should go.

Sunday, 8 January

Hanh, Sarah and I took a picnic and went for a walk, starting at the Penshaw monument. Would you believe, half the floodlights have been stolen? The padlocks have been cut with bolt-cutters, the cages prised open and the lights expertly disconnected. No doubt they are now illuminating someone's allotment. From Penshaw we walked down the river, through Cox Green to Fatfield and back to Penshaw – about four and a half miles. A lovely walk, if it wasn't for the plastic bags and the fact that all the 'Wear Heritage' signs and maps put up by the council have been vandalised. There was even a stolen car in the river.

Wednesday, 11 January

An hour and a half being interviewed for BBC documentary on the Labour Party up to the death of John Smith, resisting the suggestion that Labour's downfall in the late seventies and early eighties was the result of a left-wing conspiracy. Although I am perceived (wrongly) as an Establishment figure these days, I remain one of that small band who believes that had Tony Benn become leader in 1981 Labour would be in a far stronger position today than it is. We would never have wasted years hunting for Trotskyites in the back streets of Liverpool. Nor would we have gone around apologising for our past. Instead Thatcher would have been countered head on. To be sure we would have been beaten by Thatcher, given the Falklands and all the other things she had going for her such as North Sea oil, but we would certainly have given her a run for her money.

In the afternoon I moved my Media (Diversity) Bill. I was lucky with the timing. There were no statements and so I had a good audience and the BBC televised my speech live. It was aimed as much at our front bench as at the government.

Ann Clwyd told me that she finds Robin Cook very difficult to work with. She says he is insufferably arrogant and won't share with his colleagues. Apparently, he kept his team meeting waiting twenty minutes this morning and then left the room to take a long telephone call. Depressing, really; Robin is undoubtedly our finest mind. If this is how he carries on in opposition, goodness knows what he'll be like in government.

The news bulletins this evening are full of Blair's trip to Brussels which has been entirely sidetracked by a row with the Euro MPs over Clause IV. More than half of them signed an advert in the *Guardian* calling for Clause IV to be retained. Blair accused them of being infantile, but frankly he has only himself to blame.

Thursday, 12 January

It's clear we are in trouble over Clause IV. If Blair wins, it will only be by the skin of his teeth and only at the cost of further demoralisation and by making it an issue of confidence – which it obviously is. 'Blair tells his party it's time to grow up', says a headline in one paper. Exactly the sort of mess that Kinnock got us into. Ken Coates* has an article in today's *Telegraph* slagging off the new management – and the paper leads its front page with it. Foolish of Ken. He is allowing himself to be used, but I guess we are in for a lot more of this. The

*Euro MP 1989–99.

polls say we are a record forty-one points ahead, but I don't believe a word of it.

Friday, 13 January

A call from Alan Bannister, on death row in Missouri. I wrote a strong letter to the governor on his behalf, but as usual received no acknowledgement. He was due to die last month, but received a last-minute stay of execution. I had thought he was dead. An eerie feeling speaking to the living dead. He sounded calm and confident and even optimistic. I don't know what grounds he has for optimism. Since the Republican victory in November the tide in America is moving heavily towards barbarism. Texas has scheduled six executions for a single week later this month.*

Tuesday, 17 January

I attended my first meeting of What's Left, the latest grouplet set up to talk policy behind the backs of our leaders. Those present include Jean Corston, Mike Connarty, Derek Fatchett, Richard Burden, Dick Caborn, Roger Berry and Peter Hain. We spent the first forty-five minutes discussing Clause IV, which dominates everything these days. The consensus was that the planned rewrite was wholly unnecessary, but the existing wording could not be defended and we should concentrate on lobbying for a new version which included the redistribution of power and wealth as well as a strong reference to public ownership. We decided to send a delegation to see Tony.

Roger Berry then addressed the meeting on the economy. He said that until recently our economic policy had consisted mainly of calling for interest rates to be 1 per cent lower than whatever the Tories said they should be at any given time, but lately we had gone quiet about interest rates. The other main plank was to call for more training, but training was no good if there were no jobs to go to. Government policy, he said, consisted of targeting inflation and nothing

---

*Bannister was eventually executed by lethal injection on 22 October 1997.

else. There was nothing wrong with what he called 'a decent rate of inflation', which was the quickest way to wipe out the insecurity caused by negative equity. There was also no reason we shouldn't have a target for reducing unemployment. A reduction of 1.5 million was perfectly realistic. Investment in manufacturing would not necessarily produce more jobs. The main scope for expansion was in services and infrastructure. In the short term this could only be achieved by increased public spending. The only way to raise the money was by either borrowing or increasing taxes for the better off. It was straightforward Keynesian stuff, but in the current climate even that sounds dangerously radical.

Wednesday, 18 January

A riveting meeting of the parliamentary party. At Roy Hattersley's suggestion there was a debate on education, prompted by Tony Blair's decision to send his son to an opted-out school. Roy kicked off from the floor. It was Hattersley at his best: passionate, principled and robust. He attacked the 'myth' of parental choice. Ninety per cent of parents, he said, had no choice. League tables have no purpose unless we are trying to justify competition by social class. He dealt unambiguously with the need to bring the grant-maintained schools back into the public sector and not to allow the middle classes to opt out. Tony Blair looked uncomfortable. Criticism came from the most unlikely people. Gerry Steinberg, a former head teacher, said that because of what Tony had done we now found ourselves criticised wherever we went. Paul Flynn began by describing himself as 'an incurable, serial leadership loyalist', but said that Tony's action had been a body blow. He used words like 'inexplicable' and 'indefensible'. There was real anger. Tony looked miserable. I have never seen a leader told off to his face like that before. The Blair bubble seems to have burst. I only hope he doesn't take us all with him.

Thursday, 19 January

To see Lord Nolan in the hope of persuading him to examine the role of freemasonry in public life. He has a suite of offices on the fourth floor at the back of the Treasury – previously used by Lord Denning for the Profumo inquiry. Nolan had replied to my letter saying I was the only person to mention freemasonry. I solved that problem by getting Jack Straw to write me a note confirming that the Labour Party was interested and would address the subject in its next submission. Nolan said he had discussed freemasonry with his committee, but only one member (he hinted that it was Tom King) had expressed interest. He had also asked if any were Masons and none were. He said he had never come across freemasonry in the judiciary although there was a lodge in his Inn. I told him Lord Templeman was the most senior judicial Mason. That seemed to surprise him. I showed him the photo of the inaugural meeting of the Scotland Yard lodge, the Manor of St James, and we chatted pleasantly for about an hour. He is a mild-mannered, soft-spoken man, entirely lacking in pomposity and he appears to have an open mind. I am not sure the same can be said for everyone on his committee, however. I shall have to up the ante.

A chat with David Heathcoat-Amory during this evening's division. He has held six ministerial jobs in as many years and said Labour was going to find it difficult when it gets into government, having so few people with ministerial experience. 'You will either give a lot of power to civil servants or you will make a lot of mistakes. As for becoming Prime Minister without previous experience, that's scary.' He added, 'It's easier for us because we just want to run the system as it is, but you chaps want to change things. It takes about four months to get on top of a new ministerial job, but the learning curve is steep. Government is about a lot of small decisions that you never normally hear about, unless one goes wrong.'

We agreed that the outcome of the next election was far from being a foregone conclusion. 'We're ruthless,' he told me, 'and we have big reserves.' He said the Tory Party had big institutions behind it. 'The Liberals have no institutions on their side, that's why they're small.'

Home on the 20.00 train with Derek Foster's wife, Anne, who is nostalgic for the days of John Smith. The party had been at ease with itself, she said. Now everyone was sitting around the Tea Room plotting and looking over their shoulders.

Friday, 20 January

Today's *Tribune* lists the MPs who are said to be supporting the Save Clause IV campaign. Basically, it's the Campaign Group plus four or five others, of whom the most surprising is Gwyneth Dunwoody. My name is among them, although no one has bothered to ask me. The time has come to grasp the nettle. I write *Tribune* a letter saying that, while it was a mistake ever to have raised the issue, I couldn't defend the existing wording. Having seen at first hand – in Vietnam, Laos and elsewhere – the catastrophic effect of common ownership of 'the means of production, distribution and exchange' I couldn't possibly advocate such a system here. I then faxed this through to *Tribune* and copied it to about twenty colleagues. It will do me some damage, but what else can I do and remain honest?

Increasingly I find myself at odds with most of my Campaign Group colleagues on key issues. They are so deeply conservative and so obsessed with dogma at the expense of the big picture. The Clause IV campaign has really brought them to life, but most of them don't seem to understand that, if they win, we are doomed to at least another five years of opposition. It's not their fault, of course; they didn't start all this nonsense. I wonder if I ought to allow my membership of the Group to lapse. The trouble is there is a long history of people who started on the left abandoning their friends when the prospect of office looms. I am determined not to go down that road. If they don't want me, they can kick me out.

Saturday, 21 January

Today's *Independent* has splashed its front page with a story prompted by my meeting with Lord Nolan, saying that the committee may look at Masonry. It also says that the Home Affairs Select Committee may

look at the subject (which I am sure it won't in the foreseeable future).
An unhelpful story, I'm afraid.

Tuesday, 24 January

With Bill Etherington to see Tom Sackville at the Department of
Health about the proposed bed cuts in Sunderland. We left him with
a copy of Saturday's *Journal* which leads with a story that Newcastle
hospitals are having to bus up to 200 patients a month all over the
region because they are short of beds. The pressure on space is so great
that one patient went to the toilet and when she came back she found
someone else in her bed. We told Sackville that we didn't want that
happening in Sunderland. I doubt whether anything we say will make
the blindest bit of difference, but at least we went through the
motions. Afterwards both Bill and I did interviews with BBC *Look
North* and for once it was my clip that was used. A pleasant change to
be quoted on an issue that my constituents care about – instead of
terrorists and Freemasons.

In the evening, with five others, to see Tony Blair about Clause IV.
Derek Fatchett was the prime mover. We said that we all thought it
was a mistake ever to have embarked on the campaign. We were
worried about the bad atmosphere it had created in the party; there
were little groups plotting all around the Tea Room. We accepted
there was no going back and expressed the hope that his new version
would include a firm commitment to redistribute wealth and power
and a friendly reference to public ownership. Tony was relaxed and
amiable, but unrepentant. As to whether rewriting Clause IV was a
good idea or not, we would have to agree to differ, he said. Thatcher
won by establishing her values in the public mind and we should try
to do likewise. As regards a formula he said, 'I probably agree with you
more than you realise.' He promised to call off the ultra-loyalists who
are demanding that everyone sign a loyalty oath.

After seeing Tony we retired to the Smoking Room, which I
cannot recall having visited before, where Jean Corston recounted a
conversation she recently had with a Tory dissident, Christopher Gill.

He had remarked, 'You don't have the Stasi in your party.' Was that a reference to the Tory whips, she asked, and he confirmed that it was. Then he added, 'If I was to write my memoirs now, there would be an election immediately and Labour would win and go on winning.' What on earth can he know that we don't? Let's hope he gets round to writing his memoirs sooner rather than later.

A call from the *Kilroy* programme. They want me to go on tomorrow morning to discuss Private Clegg, a soldier in the Parachute Regiment who was jailed for his part in killing two young joyriders in Belfast. The Shire Tories are working themselves up into a frenzy over the case. Hilarious really. All the hangers and floggers suddenly interested in a miscarriage of justice. I declined the invitation. The *Kilroy* programme is not a forum for rational argument and besides, I can't bear the thought of all that hate mail again.

Wednesday, 25 January

Gwyneth Dunwoody, usually a loyalist, has been sounding off about Blair. 'The man doesn't understand the Labour Party. He didn't realise the degree to which his family would be in the spotlight. He is isolated, depressed and receiving bad advice from someone who is malevolent' – presumably a reference to Mandelson. 'He won't last beyond the end of the year.'

At the select committee in the afternoon it emerged that no Labour member has volunteered for the trip to Italy and Holland to investigate serious crime. All the Tories want to go, however, but they are snookered because there is no one on our side to pair with. The chairman, Ivan Lawrence, gave us a little lecture about 'playing the game'. The plain fact is that the serious crime inquiry has only been kept alive as an alibi for a freebie. The trip is just a pointless waste of public money and the only people keen on it are those who are forever accusing Labour of squandering public money.

Thursday, 26 January

The headline in today's *Times* is, 'Clause IV knocks ten points off Labour lead'. Meanwhile hysteria about Private Clegg is sweeping the country. Petitions are being presented at Downing Street. Sackfuls of mail are being delivered to his prison cell. A hundred Tory MPs, hangers and floggers to a man, have signed a motion calling for the case to be reopened. The tabloids are busy whipping up a frenzy in a blatant attempt to spring the man from jail. So much for the rule of law that they are always lecturing the rest of us about.

I have been trying to stay off the subject since it will only get me into trouble, but it is hard not to be indignant in the face of such a massive display of hypocrisy. A reading of the House of Lords judgment makes clear that Clegg and his mates are far from the heroes they are made out to be. A great deal of perjury was committed at the trial.

I was listed number eight for PM's Questions and didn't expect to be reached. However, Dale Campbell-Savours misbehaved and the Speaker allowed injury time so I was called at 3.31 p.m. A hilarious episode followed. The Prime Minister thought that questions were over. I shouted out my number, but he remained seated so I stretched out my arms and indicated that he should get up and eventually he did. When he had said his piece, I gave him the thumbs up to general hilarity. I couldn't resist asking about Clegg. 'Did the Prime Minister welcome the sudden interest among Conservative MPs in miscarriages of justice? Would he join me in hoping that their interest would extend to victims of miscarriages of justice who did not happen to be members of the Parachute Regiment – such as the three innocent people convicted of murdering Carl Bridgewater who were now beginning their eighteenth year in prison?' Within an hour I had a message of thanks from Ann Whelan (the mother of one of the convicted men) so it obviously went out on telly, even though it was out of time.

Monday, 30 January

This evening a sad little row with Tony Benn. I had copied to him my letter to *Tribune* saying that I could not defend 'common ownership of the means of production, distribution and exchange' having seen it applied in Vietnam and Laos with catastrophic effects. Tony said it was the saddest letter he had ever received. 'I wept when I read it.' He said that I had repudiated everything that had happened in Vietnam – the struggle against colonialism, imperialism, repression. In vain did I protest that the only thing I had repudiated was the Stalinisation of the means of production, distribution and exchange and in the end he stalked off. I was depressed all evening. I may be wrong, but I fear this marks a turning point in our relationship. I do so deeply resent the fact that this Clause IV debate has set us all against one another.

Tuesday, 31 January

Ray Fitzwalter, who now runs an independent production company, came in for a drink in the evening. We spent an hour lamenting the declining standards in commercial television. His company is struggling. He says that Granada is being squeezed for every penny of profit by the new masters. They have been paying bills up to nine months in arrears and there is continuous downward pressure on costs. Not only at Granada, but the BBC as well. There is little interest in foreign stories or documentaries that require any element of risk. Eighty per cent of the drama scripts at the ITV network centre are for police or detective series. Ratings *über alles*. To survive he is having to grovel to people he used to employ. He talked of getting out of TV. A sign of the times when there is no place in television for a journalist of Ray's calibre.

Wednesday, 1 February

A presentation from the party's pollsters. The message was that, despite our massive lead, we have nothing to be complacent about. Blair's election is said to have led to a huge increase in our core support, much greater than under John Smith, which I find surprising. All this was pre-Clause IV and the row over Blair junior's schooling, of course. It would be interesting to see what effect they have had on his poll rating. However we are still not credible on the economy.

Despite the fact that the penny has finally dropped about the Tory tax-cut fraud, most people believe we will put up tax. As ever, people are still claiming that they are willing to pay more to protect health and education, but experience suggests that in the privacy of the ballot box they will renege. Can any party suspected of wanting to spend on anything – except war and the police – ever again hope to be elected in this country?

Thursday, 2 February

A visit from a couple of American academics, one of whom is attached to the School of Law at Warwick University for a year. We last met ten years ago when he was preparing a paper on the Labour Party. This time he is studying miscarriages of justice. They both said how much the country had changed for the worse since they were here in 1985. A huge increase in road congestion, private health insurance and fear of crime. Also, dirtier streets. They think we are heading down the American road. I replied we still had some advantages over the urban US – no gun lobby, no religious right and the fact that politicians can't buy advertising space on TV. True, they said, but at least the American economy was booming. Unemployment down to 5 per cent and falling. Here we are cursed by the cost of maintaining three million people permanently unemployed. That's why, despite all their rhetoric, the Tories have not succeeded in cutting public spending – which was 44 per cent of GDP in 1979 and is still 44 per cent today. The only difference is that we used to invest in public enterprise, health and education and now these are being slashed to pay for unemployment and for more police to beat the underclass back into the ghetto at regular intervals. Today it was announced that 12,000 jobs are to go at the Inland Revenue. All in the name of efficiency, but in fact the problem is just being transferred from one public sector budget to another.

Home on the 20.00 train, arriving just after midnight.

Friday, 3 February
Sunderland

A visit to Sunelm, a sheltered workshop for disabled which the council is proposing to close. Actually, it's a factory making high-quality pine-wood furniture. The place was humming with activity. Some of the machinists were virtually blind. I met the union reps, all of whom seemed to be able-bodied. They were very bitter. Much talk of betrayal. How could a socialist council could do such a thing, etc.? Why couldn't they make a stand like Liverpool? Why not raid the balances? To be fair, most of the bullshit came from one man. They all expressed the view that, if closure was inevitable, priority should be given to finding work for the seriously disabled, who would just be sitting at home festering if it were not for Sunelm. I promised to do what I could, but told them plainly that I was not optimistic. Later, I telephoned Bryn Sidaway, the council leader, and Colin Sinclair, the chief executive. They both said the same: the subsidy required to keep Sunelm going was just too high. Bryn said he's been having sleepless nights over what he is being asked to do.

Monday, 6 February

I am making inquiries about my pension. I'm happy to stay on as long as there is something useful for me to do, but I'm damned if I am going to spend the next fifteen years ya-booing on the back benches. If we win the election and I am given something worthwhile to do, I will stay on until I am sixty. If we lose, I would like out as soon as possible. There are still plenty of things I want to do.

Tuesday, 7 February

I had the first question to the Employment Secretary, Michael Portillo, and asked about the cost of maintaining three million people out of work. He conceded nothing in reply, but the more I think about it the Tories have been well and truly shafted by the cost of unemployment – and so will we, if we can't get it down.

Wednesday, 8 February

There is a tree in Victoria Tower Garden with an absolutely stunning display of deep pink blossom, the first I have seen this year. I hope it is not ambushed by frost.

At the select committee we commenced our inquiry into the mandatory life sentence. The former Chief Justice, Lord Lane, was among the witnesses and was strongly in favour of giving discretion to the judges. The arguments in favour were overwhelming, but needless to say the Tories on the committee would have none of it. They love the idea of Tory Home Secretaries showing how macho they are by keeping people inside for ever (except Private Clegg, of course). My first encounter with Lord Lane since he turned down the Birmingham Six appeal six years ago. My last dealing with him, in the wake of the Birmingham Six release, was a motion calling for his resignation which attracted a considerable number of signatures. At the Old Bailey, I used to gaze for hours upon his gloomy countenance. Today, however, he came across as a genial, grandfatherly figure, positively liberal in fact. I warmed to him as he shredded Ivan Lawrence, himself a part-time judge, making no attempt to hide his irritation at some of the fatuous points put to him. One of the Tories demanded to know what the editor of the *Sun* would have to say if the Home Secretary were to surrender his power to decide the length of a life sentence, at which point I intervened, 'We must never hand justice to the mob, must we, Lord Lane?'

'I take that as axiomatic,' he growled.

Had he noticed, I inquired, that most of those who were demanding the release of Private Clegg were also in favour of retaining the mandatory life sentence?

'Doesn't surprise me in the least,' he said wearily.

Thursday, 9 February

Rodney Bickerstaffe, leader of the public employees union Unison, was on the radio this morning making a number of 1979-type noises about the need for higher pay in the public sector.

To Ruskin College Oxford to address the Labour Club on

miscarriages of justice. About forty-five people turned out. A number of depressing conversations about Clause IV. Several people who had been active in the party said they were giving up. No amount of reasoning would persuade them that we were worth fighting for. The sooner this Clause IV nonsense is over the better. I took a stroll around the gardens of Worcester College and was back at the House in time for the debate on the future of the BBC.

I am getting letters and calls about the cuts the council is proposing in the health and education budgets. Besides Sunelm, the plug is being pulled on several advice centres (including the Citizens Advice Bureau in the town centre), nursing homes, music teaching and swimming lessons. Derwent Hill (the outdoor centre in the Lake District, which for many of our kids is the first they see of the countryside) is also threatened. The English as a Second Language course, which caters for 240 mainly Bengali children who come from homes where not a word of English is spoken, is to be wiped out. Maternity and sickness cover is to be withdrawn and structural maintenance cut by 12 per cent. Already some head teachers are talking about opting out of local authority control – which is, of course, exactly what the Tories want. Frankly, the council has not handled this well. It may well be that they have no other choice, but little effort has been made to convince people of that. Being a one-party state, everyone knows that the real decisions are taken in private at the Labour Group. By the time the proposals reach committee, the decisions are cut and dried and no real debate takes place, except a bit of posturing for the gallery. It is treason to say so aloud, but Sunderland could do with some serious opposition.

Monday, 13 February
Sunderland

To a conference of community workers organised by Save the Children at the Swallow Hotel in Seaburn to publicise the results of an evaluation of work carried out with young people in Pennywell, one of the poorer parts of my constituency, last summer. Unsurprisingly it concluded that giving youngsters something to do had done wonders for the crime rate. Total cost of running trips to the seaside and country for 630 kids, £28,000. About half the cost of keeping one delinquent locked up for a year. Despite the obvious benefits for so small an outlay, they are having trouble raising the money to repeat the scheme this summer. With four months to go they are still £18,000 short.

Tuesday, 14 February

To a meeting of the regional government group addressed by Jack Straw. He said that the Tory strategy was to accuse us of wanting to Balkanise Britain and to add another huge and expensive tier of bureaucracy. This tactic was working – at least in England. Local government reform was extremely difficult. The Tories had recently attempted to introduce unitary government in the Shire counties and had only succeeded in eight out of thirty-nine. We had to ask ourselves, do we have the stomach for a further bout of local government reorganisation? 'If we don't get this right, we could be out of power for a further generation.' All the polls indicated that people gave much higher priority to jobs, health, education than to regional government. This was true even in Scotland. He foresaw two stages: First, repair the democratic deficit with measures that did not require legislation – re-establish regional health authorities; restore democratic control over economic development, planning and transport. Second, create a framework for elected regional councils which could be set up, or not, according to local demand.

Dale Campbell-Savours said a four-tier system of government was not credible. Neither was our position on Scotland. It simply wasn't credible to say that the Scots should vote on English legislation, but that we couldn't vote on theirs. Nor in his view would the problem be resolved by granting regional government to the rest of the UK.

I said I favoured starting with a few simple measures such as a national minimum wage that would improve the quality of life of our least prosperous constituents, adding that I dread the possibility of becoming bogged down in endless wrangles about structures. Just the sort of dispute that Labour Party members love and the public can't stand.

Several people, most notably Dick Caborn, then made speeches about the absolute necessity to introduce regional government as rapidly as possible. It is clear, however, that for many people regional government is just a slogan to which we have become committed without any serious thought as to the practicalities.

Although a devolver by instinct, I can't help noticing that not a single constituent has ever written to me on the subject.

Saturday, 18 February
Sunderland

Arose in a deep depression. I am supposed to spend the weekend, until Sunday lunchtime, at the National Policy Forum in Gateshead Civic Centre. Just to fill in the gap this evening the district Labour Party has organised a fund-raising event which I am also obliged to attend. That should take me up to midnight. There are people all over Sunderland thinking of ways of filling my every waking hour.

Sunday, 19 February

A glorious sunny day with a cold wind. I decided to forego the pleasure of a morning in Gateshead Civic Centre and instead join a workshop with my family. We drove to the churchyard at Castle Eden Dene which is carpeted with snowdrops and aconites. After lunch, Sarah and I went to Foxholes Dene, just south of Easington, which has recently been purchased by the National Trust, and walked about a mile along the cliff top and then back along the beach.

Tuesday, 21 February

Jack Straw and Mo Mowlam came to the Civil Liberties Group to discuss the Prevention of Terrorism Act which comes up for renewal shortly. It is rumoured that the government may be offering concessions and they took the view that we might have to abstain. I said I hoped we would continue to vote against for as long as people could be held for seven days and nights without charge. We'd taken an honourable stand up to now and there was nothing to be gained by backing down.

Wednesday, 22 February

The Bill to set up the long-awaited Criminal Cases Review Commission was presented today. When I asked for a copy at the Vote Office I was told that it was embargoed until after Howard's press conference tomorrow at 9.30 a.m. Typical of the contempt with which Parliament is treated. I rang Howard's Private Secretary and asked if I could attend the press conference, since that appeared to be a better way to find out what was going on than being a Member of Parliament. He rang back three hours later and said he had no objections.

Thursday, 23 February

At 9.30 a.m. I presented myself at the Home Office only to be told that my name wasn't on the list. I held up my pass. 'What's that?' said the young woman on reception.

'That,' I said, 'is a pass to the Houses of Parliament, to which the Home Office is supposed to be accountable.' At which point she gave a good-natured shrug and let me in.

Just as well I went along. The Bill is fatally flawed. Despite all the advice to the contrary, Howard has left investigations in the hands of the police. I distributed a little statement to everyone present and then stood outside on the pavement conducting interviews which ran on all bulletins for most of the day. Afterwards I rewarded myself with a stroll around St James's Park. The crocuses and daffodils magnificent in the bright sunshine.

Later, a chat with Audrey Wise in the Tea Room. She told me about last night's meeting of the Campaign Group at which Tony Benn moved that the group amend its standing orders to incorporate Clause IV. He also proposed that the group should be rechristened the

'Socialist Group of MPs', the implication being that we are the only socialists in Parliament. Talk about a bunker mentality. Audrey was furious and said she would have left the group if it had gone ahead. Of the thirteen present, only the two Dennises – Skinner and Canavan – were in favour. Alan Simpson pointed out that, here they were complaining about being bounced into changing Clause IV by Tony Blair, while proposing to change the Group's constitution without any reference to the supporters. That killed it stone dead.

Monday, 27 February
At Heritage questions a Tory helpfully raised the issue of cross-media ownership only to be diverted by Chris Smith onto some irrelevant point about Bernard Ingham. The sad truth is we are scared to even talk about media ownership for fear of exposing the fact that we have nothing to say.

At the Tibet Group in the evening a talk by a monk who had escaped from Tibet after thirty-three years in prison, six years longer than Nelson Mandela. He was a little wizened old man whose parchment skin was stretched in a triangle from his cheekbones to his pointed jaw. My goodness, he had suffered, but his spirit was unbroken. Remarkably, before leaving Tibet he had managed to bribe a prison guard into parting with instruments of torture which are, apparently, standard issue in Chinese jails. He had walked out of Tibet carrying them with him. Most gruesome of all was an electric baton, designed to administer 7,000 volts. He had had one put in his mouth, knocking out most of his teeth. He passed the evil thing around the table for us to study. Its place of manufacture – Jiangsu Rado Factory Number 4 – was marked clearly in Chinese and English.

Tuesday, 28 February
In the Tea Room I had a chat with Tam Dalyell about John Smith. He knew Smithy well and paints a less rosy picture than most people. Tam said John could be ruthless with colleagues – a reference to the

way he dealt with Tam during the devolution debate of the mid-seventies. Tam described him as Callaghan's attorney. 'He never cared passionately about anything outside the mainstream and never took a risk.'

'What about Europe? He was one of the sixty-nine Labour members who voted for it. Surely that was a risk.'

'Ah,' said Tam, 'a calculated risk.'

I am not sure this is entirely fair. After all, Smithy also turned down his first offer of a job in the government, but perhaps there is something in his alleged ruthlessness. Michael Meacher said much the same to me a while ago.

Wednesday, 1 March

Sensational news. Barings Bank has been bankrupted by a twenty-eight-year-old trader in its Singapore office. He allegedly ran up debts of more than £700 million gambling in something called derivatives and none of his superiors noticed. He has promptly disappeared and the world is being scoured for him. Meanwhile TV news bulletins have been full of frantic scenes of demented young spivs, on seven-figure salaries, screaming at each other across the dealing floors. God help all of us if we are at the mercy of these people. What a fragile flower capitalism is.

Half a dozen of us went to see John Prescott about Clause IV. It wasn't my idea, but I tagged along anyway. He has what must surely be the best rooms in the place, on the Labour side at any rate. A suite which was once the Serjeant-at-Arms' apartment and later John Smith's office. From what was once a living room, there is a magnificent view along the river to Hungerford bridge. Above the fireplace a charcoal portrait of Attlee (not a good likeness, too long in the face). JP was amiable, but slobbish. In shirtsleeves, tie hanging loose, slumped in an armchair with one leg over the side. Not a good listener. Each comment or question triggering a long stream of consciousness. Tony, he said, first told him last summer that he was planning to rewrite Clause IV. 'I said, "don't". Tony said, "John, I can't do it without you."

I said, "Fine, we're not doing it then," but it became clear he was going ahead anyway, so I had to decide whether or not to back him. He is the leader. The party didn't vote for division, so I backed him.'

John added that he had been proved wrong. The debate over Clause IV had been generally good-natured, not divisive.

JP is different from Blair in just about every respect, but clearly admires him. Tony, he said, is confident, courageous, a long-term thinker. He listens and when he is wrong, backs off. 'Unlike Kinnock, he doesn't bully, but he's a luvvie. He's used to everyone kissing him, but since becoming leader he's had a few nasty shocks – the rows over Shadow Cabinet appointments and his son's education – but he's learning fast.'

This afternoon, a debate on Europe. An attempt to exploit Tory divisions on a single currency. The trouble is that we are at least as divided. Most of us don't understand it and those who do are strongly opposed. The only reason it doesn't show is that we are not the government. Tony was brilliant. Relaxed, witty, clear. As good as I have ever seen him. There were, he conceded, divisions on our side, but he was clear where he stood. He put five questions to Major, and after each one gave his own answer – thereby avoiding the usual Tory charge that we have no policy of our own. I am not sure the problem is as simple as he made out, but there is no doubt the lad is a star.

This evening, an hour in the Library dipping into the memoirs of Lawson, Thatcher and Ridley in the hope of finding clues as to how they prepared for power in the late seventies. An interesting passage in the Ridley book. Thatcher, he said, always concentrated on attacking the government and rarely gave hostages to fortune in the shape of policy positions of her own. 'I know what a godsend to government Opposition policy statements are ... It is never wise for an Opposition leader to expose his or her detailed policies to the possibility of ruthless dismemberment by the government ... Her basic beliefs were clear enough.' There is a lesson for us there. The trouble is most Tories knew they could count on Thatcher to deliver and didn't need to see every dot and comma spelled out. Our people aren't confident that our leaders will deliver and so they seek reassurance in long and tedious policy statements. Perhaps Tony is right to stick to generalities, as long as he has a plan. Does he, I wonder. Gordon Brown doesn't, that's for sure.

Newsnight featured a documentary on child labour in India. Little mites as young as eight working for 30 pence a day for up to seventeen hours a day in textile factories making clothes for sale in the developed world. The whole thing is fuelled by the demands of Western consumers and GATT has made it worse. Olenka Frankel, the reporter, remarked, 'There is no room for sentimentality about childhood in this brave new world we are building.'

Thursday, 2 March

To Canary Wharf for lunch with David Montgomery at the *Mirror*. The first time I have been on the Docklands Light Railway. The public transport of the future. No drivers. The only visible human intervention, an occasional ticket inspector. It runs on an overhead railway past monstrosities of black glass and concrete, the brutal effect of which is mitigated only by the water.

We last met on the Mirror Group training scheme twenty-five years ago. In those days he was just a harmless little Ulsterman; now he is top dog. His office is on the twentieth floor with stunning views to the south and to the west along the Thames as far as Big Ben. I had expected to find him difficult to talk to, but he wasn't. What he had to say was fascinating. He had worked for Murdoch – or Rupert, as he called him – all through the siege of Wapping and it hadn't dawned on me how much he despised Murdoch or shared my fear of his growing power. 'Rupert has contempt for the rules, contempt even for governments. He can't enjoy success unless he is causing someone else pain.'

Rupert had been allowed to get away with using profits generated elsewhere to slash prices in a deliberate attempt to sink his rivals. David added that when Murdoch wasn't much of a threat the Labour Party was always going on about him, but now he was a serious threat, Labour had little or nothing to say on the subject.

The price war is doing enormous damage. The *Mirror* has only survived because of much tighter management and the *Independent* is on the brink. David explained in detail how Murdoch was carving up television. Not only did he control the encryption system, but he was buying rights on flagship sporting events and films until well into the next century so that no one else could get a look in. As things stood there was nothing to stop him buying into Channel 5 and sewing that up too.

I said that at least Murdoch was getting old, but David replied that he is only sixty-four and pursuing world domination with increasing urgency. Also, there are three little Murdochs, two sons and a daughter, coming up behind.

He was equally scathing about Michael Green and Gerry Robinson who, he said, already had most of Channel 3 advertising between them. He called them 'Murdoch imitators'.

He was careful to distinguish between proprietors – who want to interfere in newspaper content – and shareholders, who simply wanted sound management. He regards himself as a manager and says he has no ambition to be a proprietor.

He had made changes at the *Mirror*, however. 'There was a lot of anti-Tory abuse. I stopped most of that. The *Mirror* had lost respect for its readers. *Mirror* readers are not failures. Seventy per cent of them own their own homes; 50 per cent go on foreign holidays. They deserve to be taken seriously.' He said the first thing he did on arrival at the *Mirror* was clear out his cocktail cabinet. 'The others didn't follow suit immediately, but they did when I stopped signing the bills.'

In a blinding flash it occurred to me that Murdoch's rivals fear him as much as we do. Instead of trying to take them all on at once, we must team up with them and go for Murdoch. Step by step, like Thatcher with the unions.

Friday, 3 March
Sunderland

Sarah thinks all men go to Parliament. She said to Ngoc the other day about her little friend Martha, whose father works in an advice centre in South Shields, 'Her dad comes home from his parliament every night, why does my dad have to stay at his?'

Monday, 6 March

The second reading of the Criminal Appeal Bill. I was called first on our side and spoke for about thirty minutes, mainly on the need for the new commission to have power to conduct investigations independently of the police. Now I know how it feels to be treated like Edward Heath. I was permitted a leisurely speech without the pressure of time limits, away in time for dinner before sauntering back for the wind-up. Most speakers, including the Home Secretary, made friendly references to my role in the events that led up to the Bill. David Ashby, who made one of the best contributions, said that when I first started going on about Birmingham and Guildford everyone on his side thought I was just a loony lefty, but he now realised what a sensible chap I was and that I had been right all along. Mustn't let all this praise go to my head. The fact is it is a thoroughly unsatisfactory Bill.

Tuesday, 7 March

To the annual meeting between North East MPs and the Northern Engineering Employers' Federation. The employers are worried about the Social Chapter.* They said that social costs were already causing problems for the Germans and that, although the French had signed up to the Social Chapter, it was largely ignored in France. Their chief worry was the ability to compete outside Europe. There was, one said, a fierce, brutal market throughout the world. I put it to them that the ultimate logic of competing with the Asians on their own terms was to reduce our wages and social provision to the levels in Bangladesh or Vietnam. Needless to say they all denied any such intention. Actually the Asian countries with whom we are really competing in engineering are South Korea, Japan and Taiwan and they all have rapidly

---

*The EU Social Chapter required EU states to adopt common policies on issues such as maximum working hours, trade union rights and equality for working women. Mrs Thatcher refused to sign. Tony Blair signed in 1997.

rising wages and social costs. Japanese skilled wages are far higher than our own. As usual, they were critical of the refusal of the banks to invest in productive activity. One employer said to me afterwards, 'If I could change one thing, it would be the short-termism of the banks.' Several spoke warmly of the service they were getting from the Department of Trade and Industry under Heseltine. The head of an engineering company in Darlington said he had recently had a call from the DTI drawing his attention to a contract in Trinidad. 'That's the first positive experience I have had of the DTI in thirty years.' Someone whose company built power stations said that their home market had been virtually wiped out by the dash for gas that followed electricity privatisation – another little chicken coming home to roost.

Wednesday, 8 March

To lunch with Michael Green at the headquarters of Carlton Television, a Georgian mansion just off Hanover Square – the third encounter with a media mogul to arise from my Media (Diversity) Bill. Bruce Grocott also came to provide covering fire. Green is an engaging fellow. My age, almost to the day. Slim, but not tall, with a shock of mousey hair, brown-rimmed specs and a ready smile. He talks with passion and gesticulates like an Italian. No visible airs, although according to Bruce he can be ruthless. He has come from nowhere in five years. His company is worth £2 billion. He was accompanied by a rosy-cheeked, soft-skinned young man who radiated upper-class self-confidence and didn't hesitate to interrupt his master. I heard later that he used to work for Michael Howard.*

As ever, much of the talk was of Murdoch. Green began by saying that he did not detect the slightest sign that anyone was going to take anything off Murdoch. Green wants to be allowed into newspapers, cable and satellite TV and he wants the encryption system taken off Murdoch. It was crazy, he said, that the Americans, Bertelsmann or Berlusconi can buy into British newspapers or satellite television and British companies couldn't. 'Regulate content by all means, but not

---

*My first encounter with David Cameron.

size.' He denied that there had been a decline in the quality of ITN, and justified his 36 per cent share of ITN by saying that he had invested over £70 million and a great deal of time in rescuing it.

The government, he said, was afraid of Murdoch although, 'at the highest level', they were not at all keen on him. I asked about his donations to the Conservative Party. He said they were personal, not from Carlton (an academic distinction as far as I am concerned). He believes that satellite will survive cable because once people had bought their dishes, they would become attached to them.

He had read up on both Bruce and me. He had a copy of my speech introducing my Media Bill with passages highlighted in green. After lunch he smoked a fat cigar, which was just about the only thing he appears to have in common with the stereotypical tycoon. He took us upstairs to his office and showed us his cable system. Reuters were offering live feed from just about anywhere in the world – a statement by the Spanish finance minister on the peso and another from the Danish government, the state of the Japanese markets, you name it.

I came away thinking that we could do business with Green – and for that matter Montgomery. The bottom line is that they want to make a profit and we want a plural democracy and the protection of our culture. The key is to regulate the mix of programmes, to insist on diversity and above all to break Murdoch. Bruce suggests we draft a memo for Tony and Chris Smith.

Tuesday, 14 March

The new Clause IV has been published. Worthy but wordy. As Paddy Ashdown remarked, 'Words by Blair, punctuation by Prescott.' The second sentence is nearly eighty words long and that is the one that's going on our membership cards. Surely they could have made it read-able after all that agonising.

Thursday, 16 March

I was called in Prime Minister's Questions for the second time this year. The former Tory, Lord McAlpine, was on the radio this morning saying that a spell in opposition would be good for the Tory Party, so I asked Major if this was a rare example of the interests of the Tories and those of the nation coinciding. It went down well, but he was ready with a good answer: 'I understand Lord McAlpine was promoting his book. It is a work of fiction.'

A Philippine maid is due to be hanged in Singapore tonight and I kept thinking of her as the last hours of her life ticked away.

Sunday, 19 March

To Roseberry Topping with Sarah. We walked across the edge of the moor to Captain Cook's monument and back around the other side – about seven miles in all. The weather stayed clear apart from two small showers of hail. Sarah pretended we had horses with us. Sometimes we rode them and sometimes we had to lead them by the reins. Now and then we had to get off and feed them, or else her imaginary friend Sally had to be given a ride. She kept this up for two hours. Whenever I forgot that I was supposed to be leading a horse by the reins she would remind me. Then she suddenly announced that the horses had gone. 'I'm bored with playing horses.' And that was that. They were never mentioned again.

Tuesday, 21 March

Bruce Grocott says that he has discussed what to do about Murdoch et al. with Tony Blair, but that Tony was 'paranoid' about upsetting Murdoch before the election. That I readily understand, but I still think we need to talk about it, however discreetly.

In the evening I went across to Millbank for a chat with Gordon Brown. One of a number of little meetings he is having with backbenchers. There were five of us – Mike O'Brien, Alan Milburn, Andrew Miller, John Gunnell and myself. Gordon talked for about half the time and sat uneasily through the second half while we chipped in. I had gone in search of some long-term thinking, but there was no sign of any. He was full of sound bites about a 'fairness agenda' and the need to 'invest in skills' and handed out a thick wodge of press releases, but it was all very shallow. In an attempt to provoke a debate I asked whether we should be looking at early retirement and job-sharing as the only hope of making a real impact on unemployment, but all he said was that it didn't suit us to have that sort of debate in opposition. Gordon is a very bright man, a workaholic who is burning himself up for no apparent purpose. His fingernails are bitten right down. When most of us go home to our families at the weekend, he goes home to work out how to get on the weekend news bulletins. And the chilling thing is that one weekend in two he succeeds but, having got there, he has nothing to say beyond calling for 'a package of measures'.

Wednesday, 22 March

Bruce and I had lunch with Stewart Purvis, the editor of ITN. He denied that ITN was deliberately headed downmarket and said they now had seven overseas bureaux as opposed to only two a few years ago. He said that Green and Robinson did not interfere in content but were interested only in ratings. When I put it to him that this was the whole point he did not disagree and said it was useful to have pressure from the opposite direction. I asked what had to be done in order to jack up the ratings and he said 'less foreign news and shorter items', which is, of course, exactly what is happening. I asked what contact ITN had with the intelligence services and he said there was no formal link. 'In that case what was Patrick Walker doing at David Nicholas's retirement party?'* Stewart replied smoothly that he had just been taking advantage of the opportunity to meet journalists as part of MI5's coming-out process. Hmmmm.

Friday, 24 March

A call from Jonathan Powell, the new head of Tony Blair's office (and younger brother of Charles who used to work for Margaret Thatcher

---

*Patrick Walker, director general, MI5 1988–92; David Nicholas, editor and chief executive, ITN 1977–89.

– my goodness what a small world). Had I seen the article in today's *FT* suggesting that Labour has no plans to do anything about Murdoch? I hadn't. 'Well, Tony just wanted to let you know there is no truth in it.' I said I was quite content for Murdoch to believe that we weren't going to do anything about him, just so long as he was wrong. Powell said that Tony would want to talk to me on Monday. Obviously a sensitive subject.

Sunday, 26 March

A forty-mile section of the Antarctic ice cap has detached itself and is floating free. Evidence of global warming? Scientists are estimating that, if the entire ice cap were to melt, the seas would rise by between 120 and 300 feet. Of course it will take several generations, but that is not a long time in the history of the world. By the end of Sarah's life the process could be well under way, unless we wake up in time, but I don't think we will. One half of the human race is entertaining itself to death and the other half is clinging to life by its fingertips. Only a catastrophe which hits western Europe or North America will make any difference – and by then it will be too late.

Monday, 27 March

To London on the 8.43. Peter Mandelson was on the train. We chatted amiably about the Kinnock regime. He said that David Hare's play *An Absence of War* was cruelly accurate. He also confirmed that John Smith and Kinnock did not get on.

Tea with Lord Runciman in the Pugin Room. I want him to write to *The Times* saying he would have no objection to the Criminal Cases Review Commission having a reserve power to commission investigations from sources other than the police. I also want him to support an amendment to this effect when the issue comes before the Lords. To my surprise he was fairly positive, but wanted to be convinced that his intervention would be decisive (a luxury not given to many of us). He confessed to being very out of touch on the issue and hadn't even seen a copy of the Bill until I sent it to him last week. In passing, he remarked that he had had several discussions with the Lord Chief Justice and that he was no radical. Although he had remarked, apropos of many of Michael Howard's plans, 'You have no idea how much rubbish I have had to see off.'

Later, a call from Anji Hunter in Tony Blair's office asking if I would be available to take a call just after four o'clock. He would ring from his car on the way to Heathrow for a flight to Glasgow. I went to my room and waited, but the call never came.

Tuesday, 28 March

A morning on the Criminal Appeal Bill. The minister, Nicholas Baker, reads woodenly from his brief while his sidekick, David Maclean, just looks bored most of the time. The truth is the Tories aren't at all interested. There are no votes in miscarriages of justice. The Bill has been forced upon them by events and they want to get it over with as soon as possible. With the exception of Lady Olga Maitland and Peter Butler, who provide occasional light relief, the rest of the Tories keep their heads down. John Hutton remarked that it is the first time he has come across a government Bill about which the Opposition are more enthusiastic than the government.

I mentioned to Bruce Grocott that I had been told to expect a call from Tony Blair and he said he would find out what it was about. Later he came back to me and said Tony couldn't remember. I have now seen the *FT* article which prompted Jonathan Powell's call on Friday. It quotes 'senior Labour officials' and there was a similar piece in the *Independent*. There must have been something in it. I asked Chris Smith and he claimed to know nothing. Never believe anything until it has been officially denied, as Claud Cockburn used to say.

Wednesday, 29 March

I am wearing a suit this week and everyone keeps remarking on it. It happens whenever I wear a suit. Portillo once remarked that you could tell the men of principle on the Opposition benches because their jackets didn't match their trousers. I am happy to be included in that small group.

In the afternoon the Home Secretary came to the select committee to explain why he should keep his power to determine the length of life sentences. He is just about the only witness who wants the power to stay with the Home Office. Most others, including the victims' organisations, want to do away with mandatory life sentences and give discretion to the judges. Even our chairman, Ivan Lawrence, appears to be coming round to that view.

Monday, 3 April

This evening a little party for Tony Benn's seventieth birthday. A select group of his closest political associates, friends, family and young people who had worked in his office, plus several Tories came – Richard Shepherd, John Biffen and Ivan Lawrence (Tony's pair). Also Peter Shore, Evelyn and Jack Jones. Jack, aged eighty-two, looks as fit as ever. He had just been to Plymouth and back for one of his pensioners' meetings. A transparently decent man. He lives modestly in south London having rejected offers of a place in the Lords and spends his life campaigning for pensioners. A group of female singers – Velvet Fist – sang songs about the Levellers and South Africa, even managing to keep singing through the division bell. Then we all trekked across Westminster Hall and down into the Crypt where Tony Banks presented Tony with a brass plaque to go alongside the one which he had put up in the broom cupboard where a suffragette hid herself on the night of the 1911 census. The inscription read, 'This historic broom cupboard is dedicated to Tony Benn MP on the occasion of his seventieth birthday in recognition of his lifelong work for Parliament and the People. Monday, 3 April, 1995'. Tony made a little speech in which he said that he had learned three things in life: 'First, that experience is the only teacher. Second, that all progress comes through struggle. Third, that all real achievement is collective and that nothing is ever achieved by one person acting alone.' He said that he had been a dissident since the age of five when he had fallen foul of his Sunday school teacher, Miss Babcock, who had complained to his parents, 'When I start, he starts.' She once began a lesson by saying, 'When God is angry ...' and Tony had interrupted to say, 'But Miss, God is love. God is never angry.'

Finally, we all trooped back upstairs where Tony cut a huge cake in the shape of Parliament with a Victoria Tower which leaned like the Tower of Pisa. He started by cutting up the House of Lords and we offered the first piece to Jack Jones since he had once moved the abolition of the Lords at annual conference.

Postscript: Richard Shepherd reported that he had been talking to Margaret Thatcher some months ago and had said to her, 'When you next see John Major ...'

'I hardly ever see him,' she had replied, adding, 'I never really knew him.'

Tuesday, 4 April

This evening I tabled an early-day motion on Nicky Ingram, a British citizen who has been on death row in Georgia and is due to go to the electric chair on Thursday at midnight our time.

Friday, 7 April

I heard on the ten o'clock news that Nicky Ingram has been given another seventy-two hours. What an evil business it is. Last night he came within less than an hour of death. His head and legs have been shaved to make him a better conductor for electricity. Needless to say they are all staunch Christians in Georgia. How many times do you have to die to satisfy the bloodlust of a Georgia Christian?

Saturday, 8 April

Nicky Ingram was electrocuted after all. He went to the chair at about two o'clock this morning after a higher court had overruled the seventy-two hour stay. Just as well. They would have got him anyway.

Although it's been a big story over here, there has been hardly a ripple in America, where executions take place every week. What, I think, has shocked most people has been the sheer torture involved in stretching the process out over twelve years, stopping and starting the clock at intervals while a corrupt, incompetent legal system plays with your life. If a Third World country did this there would be uproar. The next Olympics are due to be held in Atlanta. I shall write to Amnesty International and suggest either a campaign for a boycott or some organised protests. That may be the only way to get a message to the American public.

Monday, 24 April

To the School of Oriental and African Studies for a reception in honour of Bui Tin, the North Vietnamese officer who took the surrender of the South Vietnamese government after smashing through the gates of the presidential palace on the back of a tank. It was organised by Judy Stowe, who has just translated his memoirs into English. Sadly, Bui Tin is now a refugee. He came to Paris five years ago on study-leave and broadcast a series of interviews on the BBC World Service which were strongly critical of the regime. His interviews had an enormous audience back home and caused a big debate inside the Vietnamese Communist Party. The poor man desperately wants to go home. His family are still in Hanoi, he has no relatives in France and he is struggling to make ends meet. He said that if he were to go back now there is a fifty–fifty chance he would be imprisoned. In two years he reckoned it would be safe. Bui Tin cannot easily be written off since he is a lifelong Party member, has an impeccable war record and was friendly with all the top people. He said he had sent the Vietnamese version of his book to Prime Minister Vo Van Kiet and had received a handwritten acknowledgement which suggests he still has friends in high places.

Tuesday, 25 April

Attended a reception organised by the Andrew Lee Jones Fund, an American-run organisation which campaigns against the death penalty in the USA. Nick Scott, a very civilised Tory, presided and Ann Ingram, whose son, Nicky, was recently executed, was also there. I spent some time bending the ear of David Rose of the *Observer* about organising a boycott – or at least a protest – at the Georgia Olympics. He promised to try and persuade his masters to take up the idea. If we could talk some of the athletes into wearing black armbands or, better still, T-shirts with an appropriate logo, we might cause a real upset. We must get Amnesty onside, if we are to make a go of it. There was a man from Amnesty there and I pressed him too.

Wednesday, 26 April

To Archbishop's House, Westminster, for a meeting with Cardinal Hume's delegation to discuss the Criminal Appeal Bill. In the event there was only Merlyn Rees, Lord Scarman and the cardinal's adviser, Paddy Victory. Scarman is a lovely old gent. Thin as a rake, but with a sharp mind and a gentle sense of humour. I briefed them on the Bill's passage through the Commons and we discussed what to do when it goes to the Lords.

I had the number one question to the Scottish Secretary which caused one or two raised eyebrows among Scots colleagues. The Scots have exempted themselves from the Criminal Appeal Bill and I wanted to know why. Needless to say, I got no very satisfactory answer. A smug lot, the Scottish legal establishment.

At the report stage of the Criminal Appeal Bill, I moved new Clause I, which gives the commission power to conduct investigations independently of the police. Roy Hattersley and Gerald Kaufman had added their names, together with four Tories (David Ashby, Richard Body, Alan Howarth and Richard Shepherd) and Alan Beith, the Lib Dem home affairs spokesman. I spoke for about twenty minutes, reading from a prepared text, and so it probably came over as a bit flat. Only two Tory backbenchers spoke and they were both on my side. David Ashby made a generous little speech saying this was for all practical purposes my Bill. I had been right before and the government should listen to what I had to say. The government, of course, weren't listening. The Home Secretary wasn't there and his place was taken by David Maclean who hardly bothers to conceal his lack of interest.

Saturday, 29 April

Tony Blair's new Clause IV has been approved overwhelmingly. The news bulletins are full of it. Without doubt a triumph for Blair. He took a big risk and it's paid off. My only worry is that it's knocked the stuffing out of many activists upon whom we depend to keep our rusty old machine working. Despite all the talk of new members flooding in, there's no sign that the new recruits are prepared to do any work.

Monday, 1 May
Sunderland

Unison organised a May Day rally to protest against the cuts. Most of those taking part were local authority workers. We assembled behind the library in Mowbray Park, marched once round the town and back to the park for speeches. I had been worrying all weekend about what to say. In the end I just said that, despite what you may have read in the papers over the weekend, socialism is alive and well – the health services, universal education, the welfare state were entirely socialist concepts to which most people (including many Tories) remained committed. I added, apropos of all those letters from Tories in the *Echo* demanding that the school music service be preserved, that you can't vote for tax cuts and simultaneously expect to be immunised from the consequences. You had to choose. That went down reasonably well. Bill Etherington spoke for longer than me and was much better. He speaks straight from the heart and is untroubled by doubt. How I envy his certainty.

Tuesday, 2 May

Today's *Guardian* has run a series of pictures of a public beheading in Saudi Arabia, together with an eyewitness account. I cut it out and sent it to the Saudi Ambassador with a note saying, 'Please do not send me any more of your glossy brochures extolling life in Saudi Arabia ...'

Wednesday, 3 May

Richard Wilson, the new Permanent Secretary at the Home Office, came to the select committee. He agreed that diverting potential offenders from criminal activity was more cost effective than locking them up. In that case, said I, could you please draw my attention to the part of the Home Office annual report that deals with spending on diversion? Of course, he couldn't. He didn't really seem to understand the concept, waffling about the virtues of volunteering. The truth is that the entire Home Office strategy is geared entirely towards locking people up. Spending on projects designed to provide fulfilling and constructive activity simply isn't a priority.

Home on the 20.00 train. Ngoc met me at Durham.

Thursday, 4 May
Sunderland

Local elections day. Apathy the prevailing sentiment. Only in Hendon, where the council leader Bryn Sidaway is up for re-election, has any effort been made to canvass. Elsewhere there has been difficulty even finding enough people to distribute leaflets. The same diminishing band of old faithfuls. No sign of any of these New Labourites who are alleged to be flocking to our standard.

Monday, 8 May

Dreamed last night that I was at a party in John and Norma Major's house in Huntingdon. That's the third night running I have dreamed I was in the company of a Tory Cabinet minister. It was Douglas Hurd on Saturday night and before that Michael Howard. Goodness knows what it all means, but I dream continuously as if there's a newsreel in my head. It starts rolling even if I nod off for a few moments.

This evening, to Seaburn to watch the mayor light a beacon commemorating the fiftieth anniversary of VE Day. It was still raining lightly and the beacon had to be liberally laced with paraffin to make sure it ignited. When the flare was fired to mark the start of the two-minute silence it triggered off a car alarm and so most of Sunderland's silence was accompanied by a high-pitched whine.

Tuesday, 9 May

A reply from the Saudi Ambassador to the note I sent him last week. It is courteously worded, but he says that I should not seek to impose my Western values on his country and warns me against cultural imperialism. I have written back saying I am against barbarism wherever it occurs. This country included. 'And as for cultural imperialism, I note that the part of their colonial culture to which former colonies like Singapore, Malaysia and Jamaica cling most tenaciously is the gallows.'

Thursday, 11 May

The House was almost deserted in the evening. The only people around were Tories bemoaning the Nolan Committee's first report* which was published today. I overheard two in the Library. One said it had all gone badly wrong. When the original cash-for-questions scandal had arisen it had only been natural to set up a committee to kick the issue into the long grass. To which the other replied, 'Yes, but the grass wasn't long enough.' Another, immensely rich, remarked that it wouldn't be possible to persuade Tories to stand for Parliament if they had to live only on their official salaries. 'What you don't understand, Chris,' he said with passion, 'is that no Tory can *survive* on £33,000 a year.' He said it within the hearing of one of the ladies

---

*On standards in public life.

behind the counter in the Members' Cafeteria which made me curl with embarrassment since their salaries are less than a third of ours.

Although I find it hard to sympathise, I understand the point he was making. Labour members by and large represent people who earn much less than we do. Indeed, many of our voters think we are grossly overpaid. Tories, on the other hand, represent people with serious money. They move in circles where great store is attached to keeping up appearances. The cost of a house in Surrey or Sussex is three or four times that in Sunderland. I have never been so well off in my life, but for many Tories £33,000 a year represents genuine hardship. Which is why so many of them have their noses in the trough. Never mind, I'm sure they'll soon find ways of subverting Nolan.

Friday, 12 May

Awoke to hear Tony Blair on the radio berating Ken Clarke for not following the advice of the Governor of the Bank of England on inter-est rates. My heart sinks. Surely Tony must be aware that every Labour government comes into conflict with the Bank, usually within days of taking office. It's all in Harold Wilson's memoirs. Are we really saying that we will do everything the Bank tells us? If so, we might as well come out with our hands up now.

Monday, 15 May

The Lords debated the Criminal Appeal Bill. No sign of Runciman, Scarman or Roy Jenkins, but all the right points were made. Merlyn Rees described me as 'a classic nuisance figure'. He added, 'He does much better on the back benches than he would ever do as a minis-ter.' I am sure Merlyn meant well, but I would like to be remembered as more than a nuisance.

Tuesday, 16 May

Ran into Merlyn and thanked him for putting the black spot on me. He said he had meant it as a compliment. I had far more influence as a backbencher than any junior minister – or even a Minister of State. In that case I'd better get into the Cabinet.

Ted Heath told me that he is reading *The Private Life of Chairman Mao*, written by his former doctor, which I am just finishing. Both riveting – and shocking. So many heroes have feet of clay and none more so than Chairman Mao. What is so amazing is that his colleagues let him get away with his monstrous excesses. The real disappointment is Chou En-lai, who comes over as a weak man, utterly in awe of Mao. I am not sure that's an entirely fair picture. A pity he never wrote his memoirs.

Wednesday, 17 May

At the select committee we started our inquiry into judicial appointments. With characteristic complacency Sir Thomas Legg, Permanent Secretary in the Lord Chancellor's Department, outlined the present system of informal soundings. I gave him a hard time, but unfortunately the hearing wasn't broadcast. As Tony Benn, says, it's like smuggling a message out of prison.

Thursday, 18 May

We debated Nolan. I've never seen the Tories so upset. It is clear that they are going to fight tooth and nail to preserve the secrecy of their financial arrangements. They are angry with Major, too, for going along with it. For the first time, I begin to think that he may not survive. Ted Heath led the rebellion with a disgraceful speech. It's a long time since he has been a hero on the Tory back benches, but they were cheering him on. I looked him up in the register of interests. They include several companies trading in China, which no doubt explains not only his attitude towards Nolan, but also his performance in the debate on China two weeks ago when he went so far as to say that most Tibetans didn't support the Dalai Lama.

Monday, 22 May

Gordon has been making one of his Iron Chancellor speeches over the weekend. He's going to be a perfectly disastrous Chancellor. Tony's been in the City saying that keeping down inflation is the 'prerequisite' of a Labour government economic policy. Silly me, I thought it was reducing unemployment.

Tuesday, 23 May

In the afternoon Stephen Dorrell announced his long-awaited plans to relax restrictions on cross-media ownership. Better than I thought. Everyone can expand except Murdoch and the Mirror Group. Would we have been so bold?

Re Nolan. The most likely outcome is a massive salary increase for MPs in return for an agreement (no doubt riddled with loopholes) to restrict outside interests. In other words, it is perfectly possible that the only concrete outcome of Nolan would be that MPs pay themselves more. I bounced this off Dennis Skinner, but he thought the government would never dare before an election. However, they would if they could take our front bench with them. I mentioned this to several other people in the Tea Room and they all jumped at the idea. One said he thought we were worth £50,000 a year. My goodness, how we overrate ourselves. There are 650 of us. We each manage a budget of no more than £40,000 and employ at most two people. Individually our influence over government policy is negligible. There is no shortage of candidates for our jobs. I don't see any case at all for a salary hike. Quite apart from which we would have to be barmy to risk it in the current climate. I may be wrong, but I feel that one is in the air. We shall see.

Wednesday, 24 May

Harold Wilson died today.

To Channel Four to see Michael Grade. They have moved from Charlotte Street to a ghastly new Richard Rogers building in Horseferry

Road. Grade was in short sleeves and multicoloured braces. Accompanied by a man who had spent three years on the board of Carlton. He seemed pleasantly surprised by Dorrell's announcement yesterday, but says that newspaper owners will shamelessly plug their own products and rubbish those of their rivals – just as Murdoch is already doing with Sky in the *Sun*. He believes the decline in the quality of commercial television is inevitable and believes nothing can be done to reverse it. 'There are no programme-makers, like my uncle Lew or Sidney Bernstein, in commercial TV any more. It's all profit driven.'

Grade reckons that the only hope is to concentrate on building up the BBC and Channel Four. The Beeb, he says, should stop trying to be a world player and concentrate on making quality programmes.

I put it to him that we should go for Murdoch with the aim of seeing him off the premises within two to three years. He believes it's feasible, but that Tony Blair and Chris Smith lack the political courage. He described the *Sun* as 'the house magazine of yob culture' and agreed that it's fatal to try to reach an accommodation with Murdoch. The most likely scenario, he says, is that the *Sun* will give us lukewarm backing next time; the Tories will go for someone like Portillo and the *Sun* will then fall in behind him with enthusiasm.

Dorrell told Grade yesterday that he had spoken to Rupert Murdoch before making his announcement and Murdoch ranted at him, 'I thought you were the party that believed in competition.'

The tributes to Harold Wilson in the afternoon were muted. There was no sense that we were mourning a statesman. Only a great manipulator. The truth is that he was mainly admired not for what he achieved in office, but because he won four out of five elections. A Tory remarked to me afterwards that John Major's tribute sounded 'as if he was reading his own obituary'.

Thursday, 25 May

This evening, to the open day at Springwell Special School, which deals with drop-outs and exclusions from mainstream schools – about fifty boys and only three girls. The school was very well equipped. A pupil–teacher ratio of one to nine, but gradually creeping up under budget pressure. It has worked wonders with some very difficult customers. Just about all of them will be found some sort of employment, which is a miracle. A teacher told me that twenty years ago there were no such schools in Sunderland. Now there was a huge demand for places. I asked to what he attributed the growth. 'Margaret Thatcher,' he replied.

Sunday, 28 May
Chillingham Castle, Northumberland

After breakfast Sarah and I kicked a football about on the lawn for a while and then we set off for a gentle stroll in the woods. In the trees at the end of the lawn we came upon two young deer. We walked up a muddy track which leads to the wild cattle. After a few hundred yards the track divides and a grassy path fringed with bluebells leads to a picnic table at a spot overlooking a lush valley and beyond that the Cheviots. The forecast was sunshine and showers. We could see the rain clouds coming at us from the hills long before they arrived. Fortunately we were equipped with a large umbrella underneath which we huddled while the rain poured and then suddenly disappeared, leaving us in bright sunshine.

Monday, 29 May
Chillingham

Slept like a log. We awake in paradise. Why spend hours in airports, jetting off to crowded resorts, when this perfect place lies just an hour and a half away?

The Bosnian Serbs have taken UN soldiers, including some of ours, hostage. It's all a big mess and we're being drawn in ever deeper. Some people are calling for complete withdrawal. I am opposed. Whatever happens, we can't allow the ethnic cleansers a free hand. If the Serbs had been dealt with firmly in the first place, as some of us argued at the time, we might not now be in this mess.

Tuesday, 30 May
Chillingham

Across the lane from the castle there is a walled garden which appears to have gone to sleep many years ago. It is difficult to see into but tantalising glimpses can be had from the woodland walk. In the evening, under cover of twilight, I cut across an overgrown field and stuck my nose through the gate. The garden appears to be divided into two sections with decaying glasshouses running the length of the south-facing wall in the centre.

Thursday, 1 June
Chillingham

After dinner, under cover of twilight, I sneaked into the walled garden and explored. It is overgrown with brambles and tall grass, but it has been wonderful in its day. Glasshouses, with many of the panes smashed, run along the entire south wall. One contains a lonely climbing geranium in flower. A mass of self-seeded lupins poke up among the long wet grass. In the second part, beyond the archway in the centre, there is an orchard, the fruit trees covered in mildew. What a labour of love it would be to restore this place, situated as it is in an air pocket of absolute tranquillity. The garden is apparently owned by the Countess of Tankerville, the last living inhabitant of the castle (until the present owner Sir Humphry Wakefield came along fifty years later). She now lives in the former estate manager's house with her son, the Honourable Ian.

Meanwhile, back at the castle, the clock just above our apartment has stopped. It was struck by lightning.

Tuesday, 6 June

Andrew Marr has a piece in today's *Independent* calling for an end to Shadow Cabinet elections to make way for more bright young things. A number of journalists have been making similar noises recently. Who is putting them up to it?

Supper with Gerald Kaufman, who had just come back from

Harold Wilson's funeral. He spoke warmly of Harold, saying that, unlike Neil Kinnock or Nye Bevan, Harold had never sought the 'metropolitan embrace'. Roy Hattersley, he said, had the same attitude. After the ten o'clock division I was approached by a Tory who asked how my Masons Bill was getting on. He said some business friends of his had recently had difficulty with Masons and he thought it was disgraceful. He asked who the Masons were in the House and I referred him to Sir Gerald Vaughan.

Thursday, 8 June

To the Home Office for a vigil for the Carl Bridgewater defendants. A good turnout. Paul Foot, Richard Ingram, Jean Corston, Robin Corbett, Lynne Jones and Billy Power, one of the Birmingham Six. The *Sun* has paid out around £1.5 million in damages to the Birmingham Six, one of the biggest libel payouts in history, and nobody knows about it because neither side wants publicity.

There is nothing doing in the House. Business ran out last night, but I can't go home because I have to go to the bloody Policy Forum in Reading on Saturday. I sat for an hour in the Tea Room chatting to Derek Foster, Tony Benn and Andrew Mackinlay. Later we were joined by Ann Taylor and George Howarth. We talked about the coming Labour government and the mood was sombre. Expectations are low. Andrew asked how we were going to finance an employment programme without putting up taxes. Derek said he feared the removal of controls over the markets had rendered politicians redundant.

I sat upstairs until about 11.30 p.m. dictating replies to the two thick files of letters that Jacky has left me with. At one point I heard the rumble of what sounded like an explosion. I sat in the silence waiting for the sirens, but there were none. Later it occurred to me that it must have been workmen dynamiting the extension to the Jubilee Line which runs under Westminster.

Saturday, 10 June

To Reading for the National Policy Forum. Documents on the economy, employment and training, crime and the legal system had already been circulated and on arrival we were given one on the health service. Every copy was numbered and we had to hand it back before we left the premises because Margaret Beckett is intending to publish it on the fiftieth anniversary of the NHS and didn't want leaks. The two economic documents appeared to contradict each other. One implied that holding down inflation was the overriding priority and the other implied spending. The only clear commitment was a promise to ban tobacco advertising. Private practice was referred to only in passing (Nick Brown told me that a passage on the subject had been removed at the last moment). We are obviously terrified of upsetting the consultants. Some of it was impenetrable. On GP fund-holding, 'We will support a diversity of practice which reflects a diversity of local need.' Whatever that means. The gist seems to be that the Tories might be right about many of their reforms, but we dare not admit it. It is, of course, true (as Margaret said) that there is change fatigue in the NHS, as there is in the schools, and no one is going to thank us for tearing the whole system up by the roots, quite apart from the expense.

The section on care in the community contains the memorable sentence, 'Labour will not shirk its responsibilities – we will set up a Royal commission' which was the cause of much hilarity. Indeed we seem to be proposing to set up all sorts of commissions and quangos. There is to be a Fair Wages Commission to determine the level of the minimum wage. Restrictive practices in the legal profession may be referred to the Monopolies Commission. On private practice in the NHS, we will set up a study to determine its influence, 'positive or negative ...'. Why the hell can't we just govern? Goodness knows we will have had eighteen years to think about what we are going to do.

Monday, 12 June

John Garrett told me that after I had left the Policy Forum on Saturday he had managed to persuade our study group, in the teeth of fierce opposition from Paul Boateng, to support an amendment which would have done away with barristers' wigs. When he got to the plenary session next day there was no mention of this in the minutes so he inquired and was told that his proposal had been omitted because the facilitators didn't agree with it. It also emerged that the front-bench spokespersons had been present at the facilitators' meeting where this decision had been taken. What a fraud the whole process is. Anyway, John forced the matter to a vote and lost heavily (I heard afterwards that he had lost his temper and been rude about Boateng, which no doubt influenced the outcome). What a pass we have come to when we daren't even express a view about lawyers' wigs.

Tuesday, 13 June

An extraordinary statement by Heseltine about BMARC, the arms company of which Jonathan Aitken was a director. It appears that BMARC was supplying weapons to Iran via Singapore. So we weren't just arming the Iraqis during the Iran–Iraq war. We were arming both sides. Aitken was sitting on the front bench looking miserable. All the signs are that he intends, in the manner of his hero Richard Nixon, to tough it out but I can't see him lasting much longer.

Robin Cook came to the What's Left group and made a fascinating little speech. There was no doubt, he said, that Blair was delivering the votes of the middle classes to an extent that not even John Smith had achieved. Also, he was keeping his promise to run an inclusive leadership. Unlike Neil, he listens to advice. There was also no doubt that the era of naked greed has had its day and that the penny has dropped with most people – that there was no Thatcher miracle. 'All of which,' he added, 'begs the question, why are we all looking so glum?'

Robin gave three reasons. First, New Labour was repudiating too much of its past. No detergent manufacturer marketing a new brand would do so on the basis that the old brand was rubbish.

Two, the extraordinary detachment of Tony Blair's office from the party. Jonathan Powell, who was very dedicated, had been recruited into the Labour Party by Tony on a visit to Washington. Much more worrying was the fact that Derek Scott, the former SDP candidate for Swindon, an economist with a City bank, appears to be drafting our economic policy. Also, in a crisis, there was still a tendency to send for Peter Mandelson.

Three, we are making too many concessions to Middle England. The fact is that Thatcher was wrong about most things and we don't have to repudiate our past.

Four, all our forward thinking seemed to run out after the last eve-of-poll rally.

Robin added that no one would thank us for rocking the boat. All we could do was unite around what he called 'the Will Hutton agenda', quietly build alliances – particularly with local government – and await events. 'Tony is capable of changing his mind once he sees that something doesn't work.'

Wednesday, 14 June

Tony Blair addressed the parliamentary party this morning. I've heard him give the same speech several times now and he does it brilliantly. No cause for complacency. Emphasise values and themes, not policy. We must be disciplined and stop Labour local authorities doing stupid things that could drag us all down – a reference to Mid Glamorgan county councillors who propose to award themselves a four-fold increase in allowances. All sound stuff, but I hope someone, somewhere is thinking long term.

Later, Bruce Grocott and I went to lunch with Stewart Purvis at ITN. We were joined by Sue Tinson, a Thatcherite who used to edit *News at Ten* and who is now ITN's lobbyist; she was made a dame in Thatcher's retirement honours. I only just managed to resist asking what services she had performed in return for the honour. I asked whether she thought Major would survive. She said it was touch and go. A few months ago she would have said 'yes', but now she was uncertain. Interestingly, she identifies Nolan as the principal cause of his difficulty. That's my opinion, too.

Thursday, 15 June

For the first time it is beginning to look as if Major is in serious trouble. Nolan has tipped the scales. Derek Foster was on the train. He reckons Major will be gone by Christmas, replaced by Heseltine with Portillo as Foreign Secretary.

Friday, 16 June

The surgery in the evening was full of people complaining of harassment by neighbours. Three young women whose families have been under siege for more than a year. Two women, one dosed with tranquillisers. Afraid to go out, can't sleep. She wanted the council to put up secure fencing along the rear of her street to deter raiding yobs. Even the washing isn't safe. Also a young professional couple said they had been harassed by the same youth for the last five years – he is now fourteen. They've complained to his mother, but received only a mouthful of abuse. The police say they are powerless. They allege that the boy is destabilising the whole neighbourhood. Half a dozen neighbouring houses are empty – which they attribute mainly to the activities of this youth and his friends. They, too, have decided to sell up and get out. I promised to write to the housing association which owns the flats where he lives, but it is not likely to make much difference. I guess he will just carry on until he is old enough to be locked up indefinitely.

Yob culture is engulfing us and everyone is powerless. The yobs know it and they are without fear. They are winning. Where will it end? Floggings, kneecappings, death squads …

Sunday, 18 June

Emma Kim Van (Golden Cloud) Mullin was born at Sunderland General Hospital at 4.47 p.m. Despite being three weeks early she weighs a healthy six pounds. Very decent of her to arrive on a Sunday in daylight. If she has an average lifespan, she will still be around fifty years after I am gone. Her children may see the twenty-second century.

Monday, 19 June

I phoned my regrets to the whips, took the car for its MOT, bought a large bunch of flowers and a 'welcome home' card for Ngoc and paid a visit to the office. At 2.30 p.m. Hanh and I went to collect Ngoc and baby Emma from the hospital. Ngoc is blooming despite yesterday's ordeal and a night in an overheated hospital ward.

Tuesday, 20 June

Arrived at Westminster to find everyone giggling over poor John Major's latest misfortune. At Question Time he pronounced himself 100 per cent behind the decision by Shell Oil to dump Brent Spar in the Atlantic. About an hour later the company announced it had changed its mind and wouldn't be dumping it at sea after all. Frank Dobson was retailing a cruel little joke which he apparently heard from someone in Shell:

Question: 'What have John Major and Brent Spar got in common?'

Answer: 'Neither have been in full production for some time; they are both heavily contaminated and they are both being towed into deep water with a view to being broken up.'

Wednesday, 21 June

Bruce and I had lunch with Gerry Robinson who in January I denounced as a ruthless profiteer. As is so often the case with one's ogres, he turned out to be much nicer than his reputation suggests. Soft-spoken, mild-mannered, liberal in outlook. He said Granada was under growing pressure to move *World in Action* to a later and more obscure slot because the other ITV companies want to see it out of the way to make space for wall-to-wall movies. The BBC, he says, has lost its way (the same phrase as Michael Grade used). He would put Grade in charge of it. There was no need to turn it upside down in the name of efficiency. Half a dozen top-flight managers could eliminate the worst excesses. 'So what if there is inefficiency? A saving of £50 million or £100 million is nothing compared with its value as producer of a quality product.' I bet there are a lot of people who used to work at Granada who wish that philosophy had been applied there.

Robinson does not share the general loathing of Murdoch. On the contrary, he is an admirer. He would not limit Murdoch's ownership of satellite TV. Murdoch, he says, took a big risk with Sky and should be allowed to benefit from its success. He did, however, think the domestic content rules should apply to Murdoch, or Rupert as he kept calling him.

Four complacent QCs, representing the Bar Council, came to the select committee this evening to assure us that very little change was needed to our system of appointing judges. One, a woman called Anne Rafferty, positively glowed with self-satisfaction. I asked what purpose was served by the creation of QCs, except as a device for jacking up fees, and she became very indignant.

During the select committee Peter Butler, a Tory, whispered to me that he had been at a recent press gallery lunch addressed by Gordon and that he had been unimpressive. Later in the evening I discussed the Gordon problem with Doug Hoyle. Doug said he had tackled Gordon on economic policy at the recent Shadow Cabinet away day and there was nothing there. Doug says it's a serious problem. Tragic that Robin is not Shadow Chancellor.

Thursday, 22 June

John Major announced that he is resigning as Leader of the Tory Party and will stand for re-election, challenging his opponents to put up or shut up. A bold move which just goes to show that he is not at all the grey, incompetent man that his critics allege. If he gets away with it – and it looks as though he will – he will not only have routed his opponents but he will have got the whole thing out of the way before the Scott and Nolan inquiries cause further embarrassment. As for me, I am going to derive special pleasure from watching Michael Heseltine declaring his undying loyalty to the regime every night for the next two weeks.

Friday, 23 June

The *Today* programme was a procession of Cabinet ministers declaring their love for John Major, but there are signs that he may not have an easy run. As this morning's *Telegraph* says, there is no point standing to attention on the deck, saluting while the ship goes down. Even more interesting, the early editions of the *Sun* reported Major's decision in fairly neutral terms, 'Put Up or Shut Up' was the headline. Later editions, however, were headed 'Major's Suicide Note', which suggests that the editor had received a late call from Rupert. From our point of view the best outcome would be for him to survive, wounded.

At tonight's surgery several more victims of yob culture. A father with his son, wanting to be evacuated from his council home after being attacked by violent, drunken neighbours. The son had a black eye and two broken fingers. Two women whose homes backed onto what remains of a derelict row of shops whose homes were constantly under attack from stone-throwing youths. One had had eight bedroom windows, a toilet window and the window of her caravan shattered. She couldn't use her garden at all for fear of attack. She was surprisingly cheerful in the circumstances.

Monday, 26 June

John Redwood has resigned from the Cabinet to run against Major. As dry as dust and relatively lightweight, but he could inflict damage. What looked like a smart move by Major begins to look less clever. Everywhere little groups of Tories are standing in corners talking sotto voce. We mock them at our peril. Robin Corbett said he remembered Harold Wilson practically turning cartwheels in the Tea Room on the day that Margaret Thatcher overthrew Heath. 'Hee hee, they've done it now. They'll never get elected.' And look what happened. Tories have an uncanny instinct for survival. In the end they will do whatever is in their best interests – and our worst.

Tuesday, 27 June

Michael Meacher led the discussion of the What's Left group this evening. He said the exclusive emphasis on price stability was politically catastrophic. Look what's happened to Clinton. Our priority had to be sustainable growth, reduced unemployment balanced by holding down inflation. There had to be a just redistribution of rewards and we had to deal seriously with the excesses of the rich. Europe, he said, will dog us when we are in power, just as its haunts the Tories. Closer union must be conditional on (a) a referendum and (b) convergence. Michael thinks we will win the election, even against Heseltine, but we won't survive if we allow the Tories to make the intellectual running.

Roger Berry said that anyone who seriously believed that economic recovery was not about spending, taxing and borrowing didn't know what they were talking about. Blair's recent speech on the subject could have been written by a Thatcherite. Joan Lestor said that no one believed us when we claimed to have an answer to unemployment – especially the kids. David Blunkett said, 'We've thrown our hand in with the City, as opposed to manufacturing.' Derek Scott, Blair's economic guru, was entirely bound up with the City. I said we needed to issue a fatwa on him. More people must be made aware of his existence and the malign influence he exercised. I am urging friendly lobby correspondents to do a nice big profile of him.

I passed Stephen Dorrell in the corridor outside the Smoking Room and asked if it was true that Heseltine had been pushing for Murdoch to be allowed to own 20 per cent or more of our media. He replied, 'Yes, but not very strongly.' It hasn't done Hezza much good. The *Sun* is still against him.

Wednesday, 28 June

To Soho Square for a preview of Ken Loach's new film *Land and Freedom*, about a Liverpool lad who went to Spain to fight in the civil war and ended up with the Anarchists. Very moving. Ken's best so far, although it comes to a characteristically gloomy conclusion. I sat next to John Pilger. As we were going out he said, 'Chris, when are you going to give up all this nonsense?' – meaning Parliament. I told him that, if I had my time over again, I'd have worked for an aid agency or Greenpeace. Too late now, of course. I've booked my ticket and I'm in for the duration. I have a growing feeling, however, that I'm wasting my life.

Thursday, 29 June

Major was on excellent form at Question Time. The received wisdom now seems to be that he will survive. All the same I keep a small space in the back of my mind for the possibility that, one way or another, Hezza will end up on top of the pile. No hour passes without him pledging undying loyalty.

Journalists have discovered a house near Smith Square which is apparently being made ready for Portillo's campaign headquarters. He, too, is on the air daily pledging loyalty to the regime. What tame pussycats we in the Labour Party are compared to these people.

Monday, 3 July

The *Telegraph* has come out firmly against Major. Is it possible to be Leader of the Tory Party without the support of the *Daily Telegraph*? He might not make it after all.

Tuesday, 4 July

A vicious anti-Major leader on the front page of the *Mail*. All the main Tory papers have lined up against him, except the *Express* and the *Evening Standard*. I almost feel sorry for him. It's not his fault that he has had the bad luck to be Prime Minister when the bills for the Thatcher decade have started to hit the doormat. He looked very calm at Question Time and not at all tired although I don't suppose he can have got much sleep last night.

At five I went up to the Committee Corridor and stood outside Room 14 where the result was to be announced. The corridor was packed with Labour MPs, journalists, secretaries, researchers and assorted hangers-on. No one had the slightest idea of what the outcome would be. Having swung back and forward on each of the last few days, I thought Major had had it, but no. When the voice of Sir Marcus Fox came over the loudspeaker it was clear that he would survive. John Major, therefore, becomes the first Tory leader to see off a challenge under their remarkable electoral system. I am happy with the result. First, because it's exactly what we need – just enough to enable him to hang on, not enough to heal the wounds. Second, because a general election is the appropriate place for John Major to account for his stewardship. It was beginning to look as if the only change of government to which the British people are entitled is when the Tory Party decides to change leader a year before an election. Third, because I have a sneaking regard for anyone who can see off the combined might of the Murdoch press, the *Mail* and the *Telegraph*. It's going to be fun watching them worming their way back behind the Tories in time for the election.

This evening I was having a drink on the terrace with Gareth Peirce when the Prime Minister appeared, fresh from his triumph. Tony Banks went up and shook his hand and made some sort of barbed comment to the effect that it was exactly the result we wanted. Major rested his arm on Tony's shoulder and said, 'You blame me for everything. You blame me if Chelsea loses ...'

As I was leaving I passed an unhappy looking Tony Marlow, one of the nastier Tories. 'A fucking shambles,' he said. 'The PM calls for a vote of confidence and a third of the MPs refuse to vote for him and he calls that the greatest victory that any leader has ever had.'

Also, one of our number, looking very depressed. 'Tony,' he said, 'is a Tory in all but name. I like the guy. At least he listens, but a Labour government under him will achieve little or nothing.'

Tuesday, 11 July

The *Sun* is running a 'Shop a Scrounger' campaign, complete with a phone number for snitches to ring in with dirt on their neighbours. No doubt the East German Stasi had a similar arrangement. We can expect more of this sort of thing as pressure on the social security budget grows.

Several people at this evening's What's Left meeting had just come from a meeting between Tony Blair and the trade union group. Richard Burden said, 'He genuinely believes that Labour should be equidistant between capital and labour.' Personally, I'd settle for equidistance. That would be a considerable improvement on the present situation. We have a merchant banker writing Tony's speeches; the party's membership campaign is being run through the *Daily Mirror*, where trade unions are forbidden in all but name; next week Chris Smith is organising a media conference to be addressed by, among others, that much-loved social democrat Sir David English – and the National Union of Journalists hasn't even been invited. And to cap it all the leader himself is about to scurry halfway round the world to answer a summons from Rupert Murdoch and his evil empire. Give me equidistance any day.

Wednesday, 12 July

I passed Nick Budgen, a right-wing but amiable Tory, in the corridor and asked what the future held. 'It's only a question of whether you have a small majority or a large one. I think you'll have a small one and we'll soon get you out. The markets will do it. They are not kind to your party. You can't reimpose exchange controls.' He wasn't saying he approved. On the contrary, he is an ardent defender of British sovereignty. He was just remarking on what he regards as a fact of life. Tony Benn made the same point in a debate on the economy this afternoon, 'Globalisation has destroyed the value of the ballot box.' If that's true, then we are all wasting our time.

A statement from Foreign Secretary Malcolm Rifkind about the catastrophic situation in Bosnia. Dreadful, mealy-mouthed stuff. He spoke as if both sides were equally to blame. Fifty years after the defeat of fascism, ethnic cleansers are on the brink of triumph in Europe and no one wants to lift a finger. My view is the same as it has always been: overwhelming force. If it had been used at the outset, we wouldn't be in this mess now. The most sickening sight is watching those Tories who were baying for blood in Iraq and the Falklands demanding immediate withdrawal.

The Lord Chancellor, Lord Mackay, came to the select committee to talk about judicial appointments. An impressive man. Thoughtful, softly spoken, courteous and radiating integrity. His great strength is that he was brought in from outside the English legal system – and the Tory Party – in an attempt to bust the mighty vested interests. He hasn't entirely succeeded, but not for want of trying. One of Thatcher's better appointments. We could do worse than reappoint him.

Tuesday, 18 July

Tony Blair arrived back from his weekend in Australia with Murdoch this morning. He landed just before seven and by nine was making the opening speech at Chris Smith's conference on information technology. Then a full morning of engagements before taking on Major at Prime Minister's Questions at 3.15 p.m., looking as though he had never been away. Incredible stamina, but if he carries on like that his youthful good looks will soon fade.

Wednesday, 19 July

A big row at the party meeting. Derek Foster has been persuaded to stand down as Chief Whip and it was proposed that his successor be appointed from among the Shadow Cabinet instead of being directly elected. Derek himself proposed the change, although he has clearly been eased out by Tony in return for a promise of a place in the Cabinet. Several people complained about being bounced. Ken Livingstone said that the last thing Tony needed in government was to be surrounded by 'yes' men. But the change went through easily. I agonised a bit and then went along with it. Once again I found myself out of line with many of my old friends. My credit on the left is diminishing.

Blair spoke with great passion, reminding us that the outcome of the election was far from certain. We needed the biggest swing of modern times to win. Described himself as 'the eternal warrior against complacency'. Our ambition, he said, must be to govern for a generation, 'So that people will look back on us in years to come, as we look back on the 1945 government, and say that this was a government that did something for the people of Britain.'

A little triumph at the select committee this afternoon. My proposal for an inquiry into freemasonry was carried with the help of David Ashby. I haven't seen the other Tories so upset since we agreed to look into the funding of political parties. John Greenway (who I suspect is or was a Mason) was apoplectic. Butler kept going on about how paranoid I was and then revealed that he was a Mason. Ivan Lawrence, who isn't a Mason, wasn't at all happy. It is clear they will do everything in their power to sabotage our inquiry, but providing we can keep Ashby on board we should have some fun.

A debate on Bosnia. Portillo, who led for the government, was not his usual cocky self. As Dawn Primarolo said afterwards, for the first time in his life he is in grown-up politics and he is finding it hard going. Major sat next to him looking glum. Portillo tried to paint both sides as being nearly as bad as one another. Malcolm Rifkind did the same the other day. They are preparing alibis in case the UN decides to make a run for it. Douglas Hurd spoke for the first time from the back benches and stopped just short of advocating withdrawal. Not that there is much stomach for a fight on our side either. Even the Campaign Group is split down the middle. Calum MacDonald has been looking up the debates in 1938–9 and says that the same arguments for doing little or nothing about Hitler were deployed then.

Saturday, 22 July
Sunderland

I was walking down the terrace towards Backhouse Park with Sarah on her bicycle when a man said, 'You've got a nice long holiday.'

'Do you have the slightest idea what hours I work?'

'Sorry, mate, I didn't mean to suggest ...' But, of course that's precisely what he meant. No doubt I shall have to get used to this crap all summer, even from people who should know better. I must try not to be so sensitive, but I wish I could find some way of conveying to my constituents that all that happens during the recess is that I turn back into an ordinary human being and go to work in the morning and come home to my family in the evening.

Friday, 28 July

The Liberals won the by-election at Littleborough and Saddleworth. Serves us right. We conducted a very dirty campaign, orchestrated mainly by Mandelson, based almost entirely on attacking the Liberal candidate for some sensible remarks he had made about legalising cannabis. Then Andrew Smith launched a big assault because he had said the Liberals would increase taxes to spend more on education. How low can we sink?

I spent a couple of hours at Pennywell Neighbourhood Centre in what used to be called Plawsworth Square. The centre is funded partly by Save the Children and run by a cheerful young woman called Denise. It provides facilities which wouldn't otherwise be available to the citizens of Pennywell. A crèche, a toy library, a midwife, a health worker who holds daily clinics, contraceptive advice and all sorts of other activity. Local people are involved in the management. A ray of light in an area of darkness. Although the centre has been visited by all sorts of bigwigs from the Princess Royal down, no senior official of the council's Social Services department, let alone the director, has yet found time to make the four-mile journey from the Civic Centre. In May the Social Services' contribution to the £200,000 annual budget was cut from £6,500 to £2,500. I hadn't realised, but there is no doctor's surgery anywhere on the Pennywell estate which is huge and where the residents are in dire need of better health care. The GPs have, however, objected to the health worker operating out of the centre on the grounds that she should be based at a doctor's surgery. A view they stoutly maintain, despite the fact that no GP is willing to set foot there. Nor does Pennywell see much of the police, except for occasional raiding parties.

Wednesday, 2 August

Two hours with the new Director of Education, John Williams. He has previously spent ten years in the Isle of Wight, which is riddled with Masons, but he assures me he is not one. 'There,' he said, 'councillors had difficulty making up their minds about anything. Here there is more of a Somme mentality. Once decisions have been made they cannot be changed. I have had difficulty persuading people that revisiting some of the proposed cuts doesn't necessarily mean political humiliation.' His predecessor had drawn up an unnecessarily drastic list of possible cuts in the belief that it would frighten councillors off the education budget. The same trick had worked in previous years, but this time round it didn't and they were all voted through mechanically. He has managed to save something from the wreckage. English as a Second Language has been saved; £100,000 has been found for the music service – some will be used to help poorer students and some to keep the youth orchestras going. A plan is being drawn up which should enable the outdoor centre at Derwent Hill to survive. To my surprise he said the schools weren't keen on free milk. They apparently find it a hassle to administer and much of it is wasted. He said he was looking at the possibility of providing breakfasts for poorer children as they do in Cleveland.

It was his aim, he said, to make education a higher priority within the culture of the city. Expectations were too low. Many local teachers had never worked anywhere but Sunderland and, as a result, were insular in their outlook. I asked which schools he was worried about. He mentioned two in my constituency. Judged by league tables, we have several schools on what he called the national 'at risk register'. 'But,' he added, 'when you go there they are self-evidently well managed.'

Thursday, 3 August

I was picked up at 10 p.m. by a man in a Mercedes and taken to the BBC studios in Newcastle to do a live piece for *Newsnight* on dogs. When he dropped me back at around a quarter to midnight, I came across two separate parties of villains at work on the cars in the terrace. Outside number 3, a group of youths were attempting to batter their way into a car. I walked past and they ignored me. Outside number 8, I came across a pasty-faced yob attempting to chisel his way into our neighbour's car. When challenged he claimed to be looking for coins which he had dropped. 'I think you were trying to steal that car,' I said. Whereupon he emerged, beer bottle in hand, screaming that he was going to 'snap my fucking jaw off'. I scuttled quickly indoors and he made off down the street.

Monday, 14 August

A couple of hours with John Marsden, Social Services director. He says the hospitals were now much more ruthless about chucking out old people the moment they were deemed not to need a hospital bed. Social Services is cut down to the bone. Next time around there would be no fat to cut. Funding for community care was okay so far, but there were ominous signs for the future. He has had various run-ins with Unison, whose members, he says, equate quality of service with the number of people employed. Those days were over and it was about time Unison recognised this.

Friday, 8 September

To the psychiatric hospital, Cherry Knowle, for a look round the new residential unit for in-patients. A big improvement on the original Victorian monstrosity. One of the psychiatrists said she was getting many more men referred to her from Seaham and Murton where the pits have closed and work has run out. She said, 'They suffer from depression because there is no hope.'

Sunday, 10 September
Hanoi

A convoy of cars meets us at the steps of the plane and whisks us to a VIP lounge. The embassy have sent a young man called Giles to meet us. Our Vietnamese guide is Mr Khai, a handsome man in his thirties with a luminous smile. Besides speaking passable English, he is fluent in Russian and Japanese. The drive into town was less hair-raising than usual, with only half a dozen or so near misses.

Dinner with the Ambassador, Peter Williams, and his family at the residence. He has been here nearly five years and loves it. The Foreign Office has long pretended that Hanoi is a hardship post, but both our last two ambassadors have pleaded to be allowed to stay longer which rather gives the game away. Peter's predecessor, Emrys Davies, used to say that he had been briefed to expect East Germany and had found Mexico.

Monday, 11 September
The Government Guest House, Hanoi

My room overlooks the clock tower on the post office. Instead of the old air-raid siren it now plays a pleasant little tune at 6 a.m., after which sleep is impossible.

Our first call was on the chairman of the Foreign Affairs Committee of the National Assembly. An elderly apparatchik with dyed hair who reeked of insincerity and had the annoying habit of drumming his fingers on the arm of his chair while he spoke. The meeting began with a lengthy exchange of claptrap. Our leader, Sir Wyn Roberts, an amiable Tory, rose magnificently to the occasion; his fifteen years as a minister in the Welsh Office proved invaluable training for events such as this. Our host made no attempt to answer our questions and offered only one memorable remark, 'When you open the door, you let in flies as well as light.'

This afternoon, to the Prime Minister's office for a meeting with the Chef de Cabinet, Mr Trinh, a plumpish, youngish man with heavy jowls. (When I first came here fifteen years ago there were no fat people in Hanoi.) The meeting commenced with another lengthy exchange of claptrap which, I fear, is going to be a feature of all our encounters with officialdom. To be fair, it is difficult for a delegation of six people, five of whom have never set foot in the country before, to have any meaningful dialogue. I am on my best behaviour, trying to avoid showing off or butting in, but it requires great restraint.

Mr Trinh listed the government's infrastructure priorities – ports, airports, highways. Railways were not mentioned. He asked for our comments, which were never likely to be very serious on the strength of twenty-four hours in the country. I made my usual point: 'The only advantage of being poor is that you are not obliged to copy the mistakes of others. You can look around you and choose.' I mentioned that Oxford had introduced cyclos at about the same time as the Saigon authorities announced a ban on cyclos on fifty main roads to make more room for the motor car. Liam Fox said, 'Beware of politicians who praise bikes but drive cars.' Touché. Keith Mans said, 'The USA has lifted its trade embargo but when are the Vietnamese going to lift their own?' which was perceptive.

After dinner we took a stroll around the Hoan Kiem lake, stopping for a beer in a bar on the far side. Two girls in red *ao dais*, wearing sashes, were offering free Marlboro cigarettes. I asked if they smoked and of course neither did. It was a cancer-promotion drive. That's market forces for you.

Liam Fox, a government whip, boasted that in opposition the Tory whips would run rings round us. He confirmed that the Tory whips kept notes on every speaker on their side, but wouldn't say what use was made of them. Nick Brown, he said, was one of the most effective frontbenchers on our side. He also spoke well of Tony Banks. George Galloway bet Liam £50 that Labour would have an overall majority of at least fifty next time round. Liam reckoned there would be no overall majority. He once wrote speeches for Thatcher. 'I kept the bits she cut out. You'd be surprised how cautious she was.'

Tuesday, 12 September
To Ba Dinh Square to pay our respects to Uncle Ho, asleep in his glass coffin. Afterwards we visited his little house in the garden of the former Governor General's mansion, a far more appropriate memorial than that dreadful Soviet-style mausoleum.

The rest of the day was spent rushing about in air-conditioned limos for meetings, mainly about investment. The difference between us and the Tories is noticeable. Most of their questions are about contracts and percentages. We tend to concentrate on the social consequences. To be fair, I suppose they would argue that unless you construct a sound economy there won't be anything to spend on welfare. All the same, it would be nice to visit a hospital or a school, but there are none on the agenda.

The day's most interesting meeting was with Le Dang Doanh, a little man with thick glasses who heads the Institute of Economic Management. He said, despite all the talk of privatisation, the private sector was still weak, accounting for only about 28 per cent of industrial output. The state was reluctant to part with many of its vast array of assets and still owned hotels, taxis and even a barber's shop. Bookkeeping in the state sector was very unsatisfactory. Dishonesty was high. At least $3 billion of badly needed capital was still outside the banking system because no one trusted the banks. State education and health had all but collapsed as a result of losing what he called 'the Soviet cradle' – the withdrawal of Russian aid following the end of the war.

He frankly acknowledged the growth of inequality, but said that the egalitarianism of the past had been a sharing of poverty. There was no motivation. Before the recent reforms everything was scarce. Now rice production had doubled, coffee had increased ten-fold, and there were no more food shortages. He talked of the need for 'a war on egalitarianism', which upset George Galloway, who harbours many illusions about the joys of life under the Stalinist system.

This evening a visit to the Hanoi water puppets. Hilarious, ingenious, wonderful. A girl in a red *ao dai* played a solo on a one-string instrument. She was so stunningly beautiful that a gasp went up from the audience, men and women alike, when she appeared. 'Imagine her sitting at the end of your bed playing that instrument,' commented George in a rare lapse from socialist correctness.

Wednesday, 13 September

To the Hoa Binh hydro-electric plant on the Da (Black) River, ninety miles south-west of Hanoi. Hoa Binh supplies more than half the electricity for the entire country. 'A successful Soviet-aid project,' says our interpreter Mr Khai, adding cheerfully, 'There were many disasters.' For some, however, this too was a disaster. According to the man from Oxfam, several thousand minority people were forced out of their homes to make way for the 230-km lake formed by the dam. Some had to move as many as four times as the water rose.

The visit to the dam cheered George up. He talked approvingly of 'proletarian internationalism'. Everything else he finds rather upsetting. 'They could have had all this without a war,' he remarked, surveying the fantastic outbreak of market forces we see around us. I remarked that he will not meet anyone who thinks that life was better five years ago than it is now, but he is not convinced.

Saturday, 16 September

George and I were collected before dawn by an Oxfam driver and headed south, stopping for lunch at Vinh and staying overnight at Ha Tinh, where we were entertained to dinner by representatives of the People's Committee. American bombers destroyed everything in Ha Tinh during the war. The people lived underground, emerging at night to tend their crops. Almost everyone at the table had lost a member of his family. One had lost four brothers. This didn't stop George regaling them with tales of 'my first injury in the struggle', which turned out to be a kick he had received from a police horse during the 1968 anti-war demonstration outside the American embassy in Grosvenor Square.

Sunday, 17 September

A day touring Oxfam projects in the poorest part of this poor country. At a tree-planting project we were met by a headmaster and three small girls in the red, white and blue uniforms of Young Pioneers who gave us flowers. They showed us their school. Just two rows of bare whitewashed classrooms, catering for 500 children. The headmaster was a decent, conscientious man struggling in the face of great odds to provide a basic education for the children in his care. George admired a picture of Uncle Ho reading a newspaper that was hanging on the otherwise bare wall of the headmaster's little office. To our immense embarrassment, the next thing we knew, it was being taken down, rolled up and put into the back of our Land Cruiser.

We visited several miles of dykes funded by Oxfam to keep the sea water out of rice paddies along the coast in a commune regularly devastated by typhoons and floods.

Once again we were entertained by the local bigwigs. A red banner had been hung across the entrance to the district HQ which read, WELCOME THE SENATORS OF THE NATIONAL ASSEMBLY OF ENGLAND MR CHRIS MULLINS AND MR GEORGE GALLOWAY VISIT TO KY AN DISTRICT. Over lunch George again regaled the assembly with tales of his long service to socialism. The district chairman, a canny old boy, listened politely when George again referred to his 'first injury in the struggle'. Then, without batting an eyelid he inquired, 'And what was your second?'

Monday, 18 September

To Dong Hoi, the capital of Quanh Binh, the last province before the 17th Parallel which used to be the divide between North and South. We visited a hospital and then had a long lunch with the provincial chairman, Mr Phuoc, who struck me as honest and capable. Once again George took the opportunity to express his disappointment at the apparent triumph of the market. 'I am a socialist. Throughout my life I have lived according to socialist principles. Have I been wasting my time?' George is much given to lavish declarations of this sort. ('I do not have a bourgeois bone in my body,' he told the provincial bigwigs in Ha Tinh.) Mr Phuoc might have replied by asking George what experience he had of life under socialism or at least the version of it that prevailed in Vietnam. And, by the way, was that experience confined to occasional tours of inspection in air-conditioned limos, interspersed with official banquets, or had he been, so to speak, at the coalface? In fact, however, Mr Phuoc gave a good-natured reply, the gist of which was that public ownership of the means of production, distribution and exchange was not all it was cracked up to be.

We parted from the Oxfam people at Dong Hoi and paid US$100 for a lift to Hué, a drive of about three hours. The hotel in Hué was several stars up from the state-owned ones we have stayed in so far, which particularly pleased George. 'Is it private?' he inquired sheepishly. 'Yes,' I replied – and I couldn't resist adding that the run-down hotels we had stayed at in Ha Tinh and Ky An were state-run. He didn't respond, but I think the penny – or should I say the dong – is beginning to drop.

We paid three dollars apiece to a couple of cyclo drivers who took us for a tour of the city. The Royal Gate of the old imperial palace has been restored by UNESCO and illuminated. As we were driven past the Citadel George said, 'Chris, when did we take Hué?'

'*We*?' I don't know where you were, George, but I was studying for a law degree in Hull throughout the Tet offensive.

Friday, 22 September
Ho Chi Minh City

I visited a British banker of my acquaintance who has lived here for years. Usually, he is full of optimism, but this time his mood had changed. Greed and corruption, he said, were rampant. 'I used to say it was only on a small scale compared with neighbouring countries, but it is as big and getting bigger.' He also complained about the huge gulf between rich and poor, which was interesting coming from a Tory and a banker.

Sunday, 24 September

My best ever journey home from the Far East. Only an hour and a half to wait at Bangkok. Once we were airborne, at 11 p.m., I declined all offers of food, took a sleeping pill and slept until breakfast, an hour before landing. A three-hour wait at Heathrow and then on to Newcastle. When I got home there was a sign on the front door in Sarah's writing, WELCOME HOME DAD, and a little picture of a balding, bespectacled figure carrying a suitcase. Not a bad likeness. Baby Mullin is fatter and sleeping well.

In the afternoon we drove to Finchale Abbey and walked to Moorhouse Woods. The weather alternated between sunshine and rain. Good to be home.

Saturday, 30 September

Sarah saw a picture of a very old lady in the newspaper. Ngoc said, 'She had a long life because she had good health.' To which Sarah replied, 'Does that mean she never ate chips?'

Tuesday, 3 October
Labour Party Conference, Brighton

Ann Taylor told me that she had been delegated to obtain from her Shadow Cabinet colleagues details of their legislative priorities in the happy event that we should form a government. Only two had responded to her first invitation. She had circulated them again and had now received a third reply. It does make one wonder whether we are ready for government. Perhaps a further period in opposition is called for.

I watched the leader's speech from the comfort of my hotel room. Actually, it was pretty good. He addressed the nation, rather than the party. Some positive commitments on unions and on the minimum wage. He cheekily announced a deal with British Telecom to cable up schools and hospitals for free in exchange for entry into the cable market – which will upset the Tories, who like to think they have a monopoly on relations with business. There was some technobabble on 'virtual reality tourism' and a bit about providing computers for every schoolchild which sounded a mite fanciful. A good line about the Tories wrapping themselves in the fabric of the Union Jack while destroying the social fabric. Plus a lot of claptrap about Britain being a young country and much chanting of 'New Labour, New Britain' at regular intervals. That's obviously going to be our campaign slogan. A touch of Harold Wilson, circa 1964. White heat of technology and all that. Indeed, Mary Wilson was on the platform. Only one fly in the ointment. All the technobabble and talk about New Britain cannot disguise the fact that we do not have a serious economic policy. And the reason we don't is that it is impossible to have an honest debate about taxation. Tax has been turned into a dirty word. In fact it is a precondition of a civilised society and we ought to campaign on that basis. The problem is that no one believes we can be elected if we tell the truth – namely, that the only way to fund decent health and education – and reduce unemployment – is to raise the basic rate of tax. Sooner or later it will have to be faced up to. Or else it will be the death of us.

Dinner with Will Wyatt, managing director of BBC Television, in a suite at the Grand. Part of a big lobbying effort the BBC is mounting for the next Broadcasting Bill. It wants to break Murdoch's monopoly over the encryption system for satellite telly. Like everyone, they are terrified that his grip is tightening.

Later, at the ITN reception, I came across Alastair Campbell. 'We have a little something lined up for the Tory Party conference next week,' he said gleefully.

'Will I notice when it happens?'

'Oh yes, Chris, you'll notice all right.'

Wednesday, 4 October

Roy Hattersley received a standing ovation today during the education debate in which he sharply criticised our official line of appeasing foundation and direct-grant schools. This was immediately cancelled out by a standing ovation awarded to David Blunkett, who gave a rather sharp reply. Last night Roy was on the Tribune platform. Another first. Suddenly he finds himself on the left of the party. He said to me later, 'I've just stood still and everyone else is rushing past me.' Not quite true. Roy has always been a mite more daring out of office, than in. All the same, I have a sneaking regard for him. He stayed and fought his ground while most of his mates were deserting to the SDP and he did so with dignity. He would have been good at either Education or the Home Office.

Ann Taylor said she noticed I had made a note of what she said to me yesterday, she hoped I wasn't going to embarrass her. Fortunately she didn't press the point. No one knows I am keeping a diary and I want to keep it that way.

Sunday, 8 October

Alan Howarth, that most civilised of Tories, has defected to Labour. The first time anyone can remember a Tory MP crossing directly to Labour. This must be the surprise that Alastair Campbell tipped me off about on Tuesday evening. The timing is impeccable. Just in time for the Tory conference.

Monday, 9 October

The Tories are reeling from Alan Howarth's defection. They have been calling for ruthless spending cuts in order to fund tax cuts and here is someone from their own side telling them it is immoral. This is a turning point. Until now I have thought we will win only by our fingertips, but I now foresee victory by a comfortable majority. The entire political landscape is changing.

Thursday, 12 October

To Sandhill View School which operates in a catchment area with 52 per cent unemployment, and is heavily fortified against local criminal elements. Computers are kept in special strongrooms with metal shutters and steel reinforced doors. I was shown several places where local gangsters had broken through solid brick walls to make off with valuable equipment. The head teacher, a decent man, didn't think vandalism had got any worse during his twelve years in charge, but complained that the national curriculum obliged him to teach *Romeo and Juliet* to children with a reading age of twelve.

Vocational training had also had to stop as a result of the national curriculum.

Tuesday, 17 October

A tremendous row after Michael Howard has sacked the head of the Prison Service, Derek Lewis, following publication of a report into the breakouts at Parkhurst. Lewis isn't going quietly and is accusing Howard of constant interference. A somewhat different story from what he told us when he came to the select committee in January. Tony Blair led on the subject at PM's Questions. Everyone on our side is very excited because they scent Howard's blood. I'm not so sure.

Wednesday, 18 October

Shadow Cabinet elections. For the last three days the Tea Room has been wall-to-wall with candidates pressing the flesh. Gordon Brown even put in an appearance. I made a point of not asking anyone to vote for me or committing myself to voting for anyone. When the results were announced at 8.30 p.m. Margaret Beckett and Robin Cook topped the poll. Jack Cunningham was voted off. I scored 69, which wasn't bad.

At the select committee I moved that Derek Lewis be recalled to explain the evidence he gave us in January when he said that he and he alone was responsible for removing the governor of Parkhurst. He is now suggesting that it was Howard's doing. The Tories are not at all keen to have him back and we split along party lines, Ivan Lawrence using his casting vote to put the matter on the back burner.

Thursday, 19 October

A note from Tony Benn apologising for forgetting to vote in the Shadow Cabinet elections. So I would have got seventy. Not that it matters. To the House to find urgent messages left everywhere for me to ring Jonathan Powell in Tony Blair's office. Three of the numbers led to answerphones and the fourth was engaged so for about an hour

I laboured under the illusion that I was about to be appointed shadow something or other. When I eventually got through, it turned out to be about this afternoon's debate on the Prison Service. Tony had read my questioning of Derek Lewis at the select committee in January and wanted me to intervene in Howard's speech to say that in my opinion Lewis was telling the truth. The difficulty is that, in my opinion, he was dissembling – and therein lies the weakness of our case.

The debate was a disaster. Howard performed brilliantly and wiped the floor with Jack Straw, whom I suspect had been put up to this against his better judgement. The civil servants in the box, who were there to support the Home Secretary but who secretly loathe him, looked even more miserable than we did. The moral of the story is that we should stick to the high ground and not get involved in mud-wrestling. We should have stayed with the real issue – was it sensible to appoint the head of a TV rental company to run the Prison Service? Watching Howard, I couldn't help thinking how good it would be if Labour ministers stood up to their civil servants with the same vigour as he obviously does.

The new Shadow Cabinet was announced tonight. Despite his defeat, Jack Cunningham has been given Heritage. Michael Meacher, who was handsomely re-elected, was moved to Employment, where he will be an understudy to Blunkett, since the Tories have abolished the Department of Employment. Once again Michael has been treated badly. He does every job he is given with enthusiasm and competence yet the clique around Blair is determined to get him out. In government, he is unlikely to last beyond the first reshuffle.*

Saturday, 21 October
Steve Byers, Alan Milburn and Mike O'Brien have been given jobs on the front bench. All good appointments.

---

*In fact he lasted six years.

Monday, 23 October

No word from the Leader's office and as the day wore on I began to realise that I had been overlooked. Although I keep telling myself I don't care and that I am enjoying life on the select committee, the truth is that I am a little offended. At the grand old age of forty-seven I have been overtaken by the younger generation and there is no going back. A decisive day for me. Twenty-five years since I contested my first parliamentary seat and after eight years in Parliament I now know that I shall never see the inside of government. Instead I must concentrate on the select committee. I shall also be the diarist of the regime. That is where my political future lies – if I have one.

Tuesday, 24 October

Heseltine answered Prime Minister's Questions for the first time today (Major is at the UN). He was very nervous and uptight and his hands were shaking uncontrollably. John Prescott easily got the better of him. I've never seen Heseltine like that before.

At the What's Left group in the evening Peter Hain presented a little plan for employing a part-time organiser setting up a nationwide network. Very naive of him. He's only been on the front bench forty-eight hours and he's already setting up an opposition. I did my best to squash it and I think I succeeded.

Wednesday, 25 October

Peter Lloyd, a former Tory minister, came up to me in the Library. He had presided at the report back from our Vietnam trip yesterday where we had talked about the problems thrown up by the virulent outbreak of market forces. He said, 'All politicians fail. If they succeed, they just create a whole lot of new problems. That's why in the old days people used to retire to a monastery and contemplate eternity.'

I asked Jack Straw whose idea it was to have a debate on the Derek Lewis affair. As I suspected, he said the pressure came from Tony. Jack said he was against it at first on the grounds that we didn't have the evidence to pin Howard down, but Tony had decided to run with it. He added that Tony had been very decent about the aftermath – as well he might be. It is becoming obvious that, for all his immense talents, his judgement is far from perfect. His decision to abstain on the Criminal Justice Bill, to send his boy to an opted-out school, to favour Gordon over Robin for the Chancellorship and now the fiasco over Howard, these are all mistakes.

Tuesday, 31 October

David Roddan, general secretary of the Prison Governors Association, came in. He says that Howard has completely lost the confidence of the Prison Service. The day after the report on the Parkhurst escapes was published Ann Widdecombe had a meeting with the governors at which she expressed complete confidence in the acting head of the service, Richard Tilt. According to Roddan, she was met with derisive laughter. One governor told her to her face, 'You can see for yourself the low esteem in which we hold Home Office ministers.'

On the way out in the evening I walked as far as Horseferry Road with Tam Dalyell. He has been keeping a diary for more than thirty years, but he says it will never be published. He said that he and Tony Benn once compared their accounts of a meeting they had both attended with Richard Crossman. They also looked up Crossman's account of the meeting. All three had emphasised completely different points.

Thursday, 2 November

The Tories are kicking up about Nolan, which we are due to debate on Monday. What upsets them most is the suggestion that they should disclose earnings from work related to Parliament. Major, who once said he would support Nolan in full, is backing down, presumably because he has virtually no support on his own side. In my view Nolan doesn't go far enough. There are bound to be endless disputes about what qualifies to be disclosed. We are due to vote on the issue on Monday. I am toying with the idea of putting down an amendment calling for full disclosure of MPs' earnings from all sources. That would save us having to pay some retired civil servant £72,000 a year to decide what should be disclosed and what shouldn't. I rang the Public Bill Office and asked someone to draft an amendment.

Friday, 3 November

Called Ann Taylor to ask if she had any objections to my proposed amendment. It's a free vote, so I don't have to consult anyone really, but at the end of the day I am a team player. She said her instinct was that such an amendment would frighten off some of the Tories who were planning to vote with us, but she would consult Donald Dewar. Later she rang back and said his opinion was the same, 'with knobs on'. I also rang Richard Shepherd to see if he would add his name to an amendment for full disclosure. He said he didn't think it was justified so I abandoned the idea.

Monday, 6 November

The Nolan debate. The Tories were sickening. In eight years I can't recall ever having seen them so upset. They are terrified that their constituents will find out what they get up to, although some of them tried to dress it up as though some high constitutional principle was involved. I had thought Nolan rather weak, but it is obviously going to hurt so it can't be all bad. The ban on paid advocacy will affect us, too. Still, it may not do any harm to get our front-bench health team out of the hands of Unison. In the end about twenty Tories voted with us and there was a comfortable majority for disclosure. A good night's work. We must now do the same with party funding.

Saturday, 11 November
Sunderland

It rained all day and night. A large damp patch has appeared in the ceiling in the corner of my study. I put a bowl on the floor to catch the dripping water. There are also leaks in the living-room wall and in the bedroom on the top floor.

Monday, 13 November

An hour and a half with our new police superintendent, who said how much he regretted the way in which the police had been used during the miners' strike. We talked at length about the disintegration of the social fabric. 'A political problem,' he said. I agreed, but could not resist gently pointing out that the police had voted rather enthusiastically, perhaps by a margin of three or four to one, in favour of the Thatcher regime. 'You don't know how I vote,' he said testily. I said I wasn't personalising. It was just a fact. Thatcher knew she'd need lots of police to enforce her vision of society. That's why she had been so generous to the police in the early eighties and most policemen had gone along with her enthusiastically. Now the bills were coming in and the police were on the receiving end. He didn't disagree. He added that the lower ranks had made a good deal of money out of the miners' strike, but that it had done lasting damage to relations with the public in the mining areas.

Tuesday, 21 November

Tea with Joan Lestor and Doug Hoyle, who complained that Gordon Brown never consults anyone before coming out with new policy commitments – his latest being to reduce the lowest rate of tax to 10p in the pound. There was apparently a blazing row about it at the Shadow Cabinet last week. Joan said that Gordon is the most unpopular member and that his sums don't add up. She also said that John Prescott is very isolated. The new masters take decisions and inform him afterwards. She told him that he had better keep in touch with his friends on the left because he is going to need them one day, but he doesn't appear to have taken any notice. She also said the new masters want rid of her, Michael Meacher, Ron Davies and Ann Taylor. She and Doug were lamenting the fact that the parliamentary left has disappeared. We needed a leader and neither Tony Benn or Dennis

Skinner would do. 'Dennis hasn't changed his mind on anything and Tony hasn't had a new idea since planning agreements in the early seventies.' Doug was also critical of Clare Short. 'She's abandoned the left and the right don't want her. She doesn't know where she is.' My guess is that about two years into a Blair government, Robin Cook will emerge as a focus for dissent – whether he wants that role or not.

Wednesday, 22 November

Mo Mowlam asked me to talk to her front-bench team, and others, on the situation in Ireland. I declined and dropped her a note saying that I don't know the slightest thing about Ireland. My interest in the Birmingham and Guildford cases arose from an interest in justice – British justice. One of the ways in which I preserve my limited credibility is by not talking about things I don't know about. She has taken it well. When I saw her in the lobby this evening she said, 'Such modesty is rare in New Labour. Everyone cheered when your note was read out.'

Tuesday, 28 November

At 12.30 I attended a little meeting of What's Left with Robin Cook. The others present were Peter Hain (who set it up), Ken Purchase, Jean Corston, Richard Caborn and Richard Burden. Robin said he had had an unpleasant few days. He had strongly criticised Gordon's failure to consult at the Shadow Cabinet ten days ago and now he's being falsely blamed for leaking details of the exchange. About half a dozen stories had appeared in the last few days. They appear to have been put about by Gordon's spin doctor, Charlie Whelan. Robin is consulting lawyers.

Pathetic, really, but a symptom of serious tensions within the regime. Goodness knows what it will be like if we get into government. The problem is that Gordon is too big for his boots. This latest wheeze about denying benefit to anyone who doesn't take work or training – for which there is a strong case, let it be said – came out of the blue. Robin said he heard it on the radio. Chris Smith, who is responsible for social security, was not consulted either. The backbench Treasury Committee no longer meets. Neither does the Economic Policy Forum. In short, there are no restraints on Gordon. I said that all we could hope to do was mitigate the damage, given that there was not likely to be a showdown until at least two years into a Labour government. I gently put it to Robin that he should not waste energy and money on libel lawyers. Other people are more vulnerable than him. Notably Michael Meacher and Joan Lestor. To which someone added Ron Davies and John Prescott. Prescott in particular is very isolated. We agreed that like-minded members of the Shadow Cabinet should do their best to stick together. That we should exert what pressure we can on Gordon through the parliamentary party and the backbench committee. And that we should put the word about that Robin is innocent. We will meet again in the New Year.

Richard Caborn told me an interesting story. Apparently he made some remarks about referring Murdoch's control of the satellite TV encryption system to the Monopolies Commission. Quick as a flash he received a call from Tony Blair asking what he was up to. Richard replied that he was only restating party policy, to which Blair said he was meeting Murdoch at 3.30 that afternoon. I'm all in favour of keeping the bastard sweet until the election, but Tony does seem to be seeing rather a lot of him. What do they find to talk about?

At lunch Joan Lestor said there was some nasty personal gossip going round about Robin. She knew the source – a female member of the Shadow Cabinet. What a snakepit this place can be. I must try to stay above it. Joan also said the Shadow Cabinet had been briefed about the Budget. They weren't to mention cuts for fear of implying that we were committed to restore them. Instead they were to talk about broken Tory promises. A wholly incredible posture that can only damage our election prospects.

As it turned out the Budget was not nearly as irresponsible as everyone had been predicting. Nor, to judge by the glum looks on the faces of the Tory backbenchers, was it as irresponsible as they had been hoping. A penny off the basic rate, some fairly sensible adjustments to allowances for the lower paid and a wholly unjustifiable hike in the limits for inheritance tax. To be paid for mainly by cutting housing benefit for the under-twenty-fives. It's quite clear now that they are intending to soldier on to the last possible moment. Also, they are saving up for a massive giveaway this time next year. It wouldn't surprise me if they were to declare another miracle and reduce the basic rate to 20 per cent in a single leap next time. Who knows, it might just work.

In the evening I went to address sixth formers at Harrow School.

Wednesday, 29 November

A whispered chat with Dawn Primarolo about tax. She confirmed that we will raise the top rate,* but we haven't yet made up our minds whether we dare say so before the election. In any case, it won't bring us much money. Big money, she said, can be found by obliging the corporations to pay their share – Murdoch, for example, is paying just 2 per cent on profits of over a billion. Gordon's much-trumpeted 10 per cent rate is apparently only an 'objective'. (If you ask me, it was just a silly wheeze to get him on the weekend news bulletins.) Dawn said it was important to do something about the rate at which benefit tapers off when people start earning. At the moment they were losing a pound in benefit for every pound of earnings. A major disincentive to work. Absolutely barmy. Amazing that the Tories haven't tackled it. She also fears that the Tories will slash 4p off the basic rate next time round and then challenge us to reinstate it.

This evening I signed 350 Christmas cards while watching *Inspector Morse*. Afterwards, while waiting for a 159 bus in Whitehall, I saw Bill Clinton and his convoy sweep out of Downing Street.

---

*We didn't.

Monday, 4 December

I spoke in the budget debate. My first in the Chamber since March. Almost a complete waste of time. I had to wait four hours, mostly listening to sterile claptrap from both sides. By the time my turn came the audience consisted entirely of people waiting to make their own speeches – less than the attendance at an average Labour Party ward branch meeting. My speech was addressed as much to our own front bench as to the government. I said we shouldn't get involved in a Dutch auction over taxes with the Tories because we could never hope to win. It was the duty of honest politicians to make clear to people that if they wanted decent public services they would have to pay for them and so on.

Tuesday, 5 December

Walked in with Chris Smith. He confirmed that he had not been consulted about Gordon's plans to withdraw benefit from young people who don't accept work. Where had he heard about it? 'I read it in the *Daily Telegraph* on a plane coming back from Barcelona.' How did he feel? 'Incandescent.' Chris said there had been some big rows and Gordon had been left in no doubt about his colleagues' views. Had Gordon learned from the experience? 'I doubt it. Ironically, the row has brought him closer to Tony Blair.'

My speech yesterday was noticed after all. Dennis Skinner said he had been watching the football in his room and turned over when my name came up. Gordon Brown also said he had watched me in his room. He seemed in good humour, but word must have reached him that I am not his greatest fan. One forgets that these days everyone has a live feed from the Chamber.

Will Hutton came to the What's Left group to talk about paying for the welfare state. So refreshing to have someone from outside injecting new ideas into our incestuous little world. 'We should think the unthinkable,' he said and we all held our breath. Then he added, 'The welfare state is affordable.' He said that spending on education, health and social security was low to middling by west European standards. Government receipts from taxation were only 36.5 per cent of gross domestic product against an EC average of 45 per cent, so there was scope for raising taxes. Only in Japan, the US and Greece were taxes lower than in the UK. Company taxation, capital gains and inheritance taxes were particularly low. The problem was how to bind together a society where the gap between top and bottom was growing and the top 10 per cent were less and less willing to contribute to services that they no longer used.

Wednesday, 6 December

At the parliamentary party this morning there was a PowerPoint presentation by the campaign team which contained the rather sobering thought that a 6 per cent swing was needed before we could form a government and that we had not achieved this at any general election since 1945.

Thursday, 7 December

To Brompton Square to call on Jim Lawrie, the ABC correspondent who is moving to Hong Kong, who told an incredible story. He had been filming in a village in China not long after the Tiananmen Square massacre when a really angry man came up and started slagging off the regime to camera. The uncut footage was then shipped to Hong Kong for transmission by satellite to New York. Unknown to him, the Chinese were monitoring satellite transmissions out of Hong Kong as well as from China itself. They ran all the way through the footage, extracted the interview with the angry man and broadcast his photo on national TV. The interview was unbroadcast. It was transmitted from outside China. But the Chinese security service still managed to find their man in a country of 1.3 billion people. The man was handed in by a relative. He got five years. How's that for an efficient police state?

Tuesday, 12 December

A chat with John Hutton in the Tea Room. He remarked that the reason Shadow Cabinet members leaked to newspapers was because there was no other outlet for their views. There was no serious debate at Shadow Cabinet. Or at Walworth Road. Or in the weekly meeting of the parliamentary party. Decisions on policy appeared to be taken mainly in the Leader's office. He said, 'People come here intending to change the world and end up admiring the architecture.'

Friday, 15 December
Sunderland

To Pennywell for the annual meeting of the Youth Project. Fortunately it has been awarded lottery money, which means it is secure for the next two or three years. The new chief housing officer for the area says the situation is desperate. People are handing in their keys and fleeing rather than waiting to be rehoused. There are eighty-one houses on the estate that no one will take. Gangs of feral youths are roaming out of control. One street of houses were so badly damaged that they had to be demolished. A security guard had his Portakabin torched and was sent away with a beating. Everyone knows who the core villains are, but evidence that will stand up in court is hard to come by since everyone is afraid of retribution. Afterwards we went for a drive round. So far the worst problems are confined to a couple of areas. The tide could still be turned, but it won't take much to tip the whole area over the edge.

Thursday, 21 December

I called on a young woman who has been turned down for a place at the School of Education at the university because she is in a wheelchair. A cheerful girl without a trace of self-pity. I am determined to fight for her.

The rest of the day was spent in the office ploughing through mail. Impossible to concentrate. The telephone rang every few minutes. I can see no end to it. I am getting more and more depressed by all this drudgery.

Saturday, 30 December

Emma Nicholson has joined the Lib Dems. The second Tory MP to defect in six months. She claims she is leaving because the Tories have gone too far to the right, which is surprising because she never struck me as a rebel. On balance, it looks like a career move (she is already talking about being the Lib Dem Euro candidate for Devon next time round). Who cares about her motives? The point is that, after seventeen years, the regime is crumbling.

CHAPTER THREE

1996

Tuesday, 2 January 1996

A big thaw, pipes bursting all over the place. The water companies can't cope and are threatening to cut off most of the North East, Sunderland included.

I dragged myself to the office and wrote a letter to Environment Secretary John Gummer asking for an inquiry and put out a statement saying that we were used to severe winters in the north, but none had ever resulted in water cut-offs on the scale now contemplated. I stopped short of alleging it was all the fault of privatisation, but wondered whether there was any connection. The result was a sound bite on *World at One* and a mention on BBC radio news bulletins for most of the day. I went home and filled the bath and a five-gallon plastic barrel borrowed from a neighbour.

Tuesday, 9 January

Lunch with Adam Raphael of the *Economist* at a restaurant in St James's. He thinks we will win by up to thirty seats. I am less optimistic – between plus and minus ten. Adam says we will stand or fall on what we do about unemployment. That we have to look for new ways of raising tax – road taxes, VAT on newspapers (they will squeal, but they can afford it). He added that Labour must overcome its hostility to VAT and agreed that a minimum wage must be set initially at a disappointingly low level and updated annually. We must do something about the powers of the Monopolies Commission, which, he says, are woefully inadequate. On media ownership he was surprisingly radical. Why not a residence qualification for proprietors? Why not indeed?

Like others, he fears we are in danger of becoming bogged down in constitutional reforms. He asked which left-wingers were likely to be in government. I said, 'None of my generation. We carry too much baggage.' I did tell him to watch out for Steve Byers, though.

Wednesday, 10 January

We debated the security services. The government is introducing a Bill to allow MI5 to become involved in fighting organised crime. A lot of talk about evil drugs barons, but the plain truth is that MI5 has run out of threats and so a new one has been invented in order to head off embarrassing questions about its bloated budget. This ought to be one area where we could safely call for public spending cuts. Jack Straw, however, wants to go along with the Bill. He confined himself to proposing a few amendments. The definition of organised crime is breathtakingly wide – any offence which is likely to attract a sentence of three years or more. The thin end of a very big wedge. We had a little pre-meeting before the debate at which Jack explained his strategy. I will say one thing for Jack. He is very good about consulting colleagues. As I feared, however, he is wobbly on accountability. I asked whether we were still intending to make the security services accountable to Parliament. 'I haven't talked to Tony about it.' I warned that I would intervene during the debate. When I did, he gave a non-committal reply. 'Does that mean "no"?' asked Michael Howard. 'It means "maybe",' said Jack. Afterwards he sent me a note saying he hoped his assurance was 'bankable'. I wrote my bank account number on the bottom and returned it to him.

I counted eight MI5 employees in the gallery and there were several more in the officials' box. Most of them looked quite ordinary, but there was one well-scrubbed young public-school boy, blond with a pink striped shirt and cuffs that stuck out a mile. A Son of Somebody, no doubt.

A brief chat with Mark Fisher in the Tea Room. He said we have thirty more frontbenchers than there are places in the government, so there are going to be a lot of disappointments ahead. He clearly thinks he may be a casualty, but seemed relaxed about it. 'I shall have been an old has-been before I've finished being a young hopeful,' he said. Mark is fifty-one.

Thursday, 11 January

Derek and Anne Foster were on the train. We chatted about Blair's 'stakeholder' speech. Needless to say there was no discussion of it at the Shadow Cabinet until after the event. Now they are all scuttling around trying to explain, with varying degrees of credibility, what it means. Derek said he was surprised that no one had yet suggested a stakeholder Labour Party, rather than one that was run by diktat from the Leader's office. He said he had advised Blair repeatedly to adopt a more inclusive leadership, but although he had used the word 'inclusive' several times, it was just a word. Derek added, 'I'd be happy if just one person was removed from the leadership team.' No prizes for guessing who.

Derek said he was worried that Tony may be all words and no substance. He remarked on Tony's growing isolation. 'I haven't seen him in the Tea Room since he was elected, in stark contrast to John Smith who went out of his way to mix with the troops.' He agreed that Michael Meacher's treatment was disgraceful and confirmed that Jack Cunningham is still attending Shadow Cabinet meetings despite having been voted out. This sort of arrogance can only get worse when we are in government.

I slept with Emma to give poor Ngoc a night off, managing only three hours' sleep, between just after midnight and 3.20 a.m. Ngoc relieved me at 5.30 and I went upstairs for another three hours.

Saturday, 13 January

Awoke to hear Donald Dewar on the *Today* programme trying to explain what is meant by a 'stakeholder society'. He did his best, but he was clearly struggling. The sad truth is that it is all meaningless claptrap.

Sunday, 14 January

A call from the *Today* programme to ask if I would take part in a discussion tomorrow about MPs' salaries. The Tories are starting to demand that salaries be increased drastically in exchange for their cooperation with Nolan. I agreed, but only after extracting a cast-iron guarantee that the Sunderland BBC studio would be open. Several times recently I have turned up for prearranged interviews only to find it hermetically sealed.

Monday, 15 January

Up at 6.30 for the *Today* interview only to find a series of messages on the answerphone – from an Isobel, a Tim and a Lucy – saying the time of the interview had been changed to 8.30 a.m. I rang to ask if the person charged with opening the Sunderland studio – a Neil – had been informed. Yes, he had. Arrived to find that the building was locked. I persuaded a man unloading a van at the rear to let me in, but the studio, too, was locked. In the end the caretaker let me use the phone in reception. The discussion was cut short, but not before I had said enough to ensure enduring unpopularity with most of my colleagues. I emerged from the caretaker's office to be greeted by the young man who was supposed to be opening up the studio. He had come from Newcastle and, predictably, had been caught in a traffic jam. Incredibly, the BBC has no one working for it based in Sunderland.

Ngoc, who had only a couple of hours' sleep last night, had gone to bed. I am in charge of the Tiny Tyrant, who sits in her bouncing chair making good-natured blowing noises interspersed with occasional bouts of hysteria, as she does for much of the day and night. For how much longer will this go on?

Tuesday, 16 January

All the little Blairites are rushing around talking about a stakeholder economy as though they have been familiar with the concept all their lives, whereas in truth none of them had ever heard of it before Tony made his speech in Singapore last week. Ken Purchase said to me, 'If stakeholding is such a good idea, why have we had nothing to say about the destruction of "mutuality" in the building societies? – surely the very essence of stakeholding.' Quite so. The reason is, of course, because the societies are handing out big dollops of money to their members in exchange for their acquiescence and we dare not offend the middle classes by uttering home truths about greed and short-termism.

Wednesday, 17 January

Tony Blair addressed the party meeting. Brilliant as usual. Without a doubt the Great Communicator. As to substance, the jury is still out but I am not entirely pessimistic. Three themes – stakeholding, his so-called 'big idea'; a welfare state to be matched by social responsibility; and the devolution of power. All good stuff in theory, but where is the beef? If someone were to say to me, 'Relax, Chris. Don't keep on about it. There is a plan. Our finest minds are working on it even as we sit here,' I would shut up. But I strongly suspect that most of our masters don't have a clue about what they want to achieve in government. Witness the difficulty Ann Taylor is having obtaining details of their bids for a place in the legislative timetable. We have been in opposition so long that we have lost the habit of thinking positively. Victory has come to be defined in terms of when we get the jobs. My definition of victory is when something changes for the better.

John Reid rather spoiled the effect of Tony's speech by getting up and demanding that this year's Shadow Cabinet elections be dispensed with in the interests of unity. He earned a sharp riposte from Andrew Mackinlay. It is the thin end of a wedge, of course. As John told me afterwards, he is in favour of doing away with Shadow Cabinet elections altogether. Not if I have anything to do with it. The Leader already has quite enough power as it is.

Afterwards I buttonholed Tony in the corridor and said that if he wanted to avoid a repeat of what happened in the late seventies and early eighties, he should bear in mind that it was caused by the huge gulf which opened up between the leaders and the led. I said there were several occasions – the fiasco at Newham North East for example – when the judgement of the led proved superior to that of the leaders. He listened carefully and seemed to take it in the spirit in which it was intended.

Later, Giles Radice, who must have overheard my exchange with Tony, said that there were lessons for all of us from that period. He added unwisely, 'I remember your pamphlet.'

'Oh yes,' I said, 'What was it called?'

'"How to Deselect Your MP",' he replied without hesitation.*

The mythology of the seventies is still deeply engrained.

A long chat with Peter Shore at the Welsh table in the Tea Room. When I was at *Tribune* we said some harsh things about Peter, but I have long realised that he is a decent and substantial figure. He thinks we will win the election by a big margin, but that we risk being blown off-course by trying to defend sterling at an unrealistic rate within a single currency. If there is one lesson from the experience of previous Labour governments, it is that we shouldn't chuck everything overboard trying to defend sterling. Peter is on the Nolan commission and so I bent his ear on the Masons. I said, 'If you are serious about cleaning up public life, you can't avoid looking at the Masons. You might investigate and decide there is nothing to worry about, but you can't avoid it.' I think I made some headway. He said, 'I am glad we had this conversation. The subject has been in the back of my mind for some time, but it is now in the front.'

Tony Blair was spotted in the Tea Room this afternoon. The first recorded sighting (of which I am aware) since he became leader.

---

*It was called 'How to Select or Reselect Your MP'.

Thursday, 18 January

A little triumph at PMQs. I offered John Major some light-hearted advice about how to deal with plotters in his ranks. It went down well with all sides. Home on the 16.30 train feeling pleased with myself.

Friday, 19 January

Three people at this evening's surgery remarked that they had seen my intervention at PM's Questions yesterday. Probably the most useful thing I have done in weeks. What a silly world.

Saturday, 20 January

A grey day. Kevin Marquis, my agent, called round. We talked about what a Labour government might bring. About challenging benefit culture, extending compulsory education or job training, a minimum wage, and realised that we have both, to a surprising degree, bought the New Labour package. Kevin, even more than I, sees the terrible damage to the social fabric wrought by the rampant free market and realises that, if we are ever to repair the damage, we must abandon a lot of old shibboleths.

Monday, 22 January

Everyone is talking about Harriet Harman's decision to send her son to a selective school in Bromley. We were supposed to be discussing the Tories' lunatic scheme for nursery vouchers, but the debate was eclipsed by the row over Harriet. This is going to do us a lot of damage.

At the division this evening John Major commented on our exchange last Thursday. He asked, as he always does, whether I am writing and I told him I wasn't. He said, 'I thought you'd write a kiss-and-tell story,' which was an odd thing to say. 'That's Edwina's department,' I replied. A Tory asked me later, 'Do you and the Prime Minister have a special relationship? He always seems to take questions from you in good part.'

As I was leaving I ran into a Labour veteran in the Upper Corridor who teased me, as he often does about my voting for Blair. 'Well, Chris, do you regret voting for him yet?'

'Ask me two years after the election,' I said.

'Two years? We'll be hanging on by our fingertips within twelve months, whatever the majority.' He went on, 'We've got no economic policy. None whatsoever. I remarked on this to Tony and he said, "I know. I'm working on it." At first I thought, "Great, he's realised," but after a while I realised he was just talking about presentation.'

He was in a very black mood. 'Mark my words, in twenty years' time, when I am in my grave, fascism will start coming back. The Single Market is what started it. A single currency follows as night follows day. What's going to happen when people find they can't legislate to solve their own problems? Fascism will come back if politicians fail.'

Somewhere in the course of our exchange he said, 'I like Tony, but he's got no substance.'

Tuesday, 23 January

Everyone is seething about Harriet. It isn't just the fact that she's chosen a selective school, but the effrontery with which she defends her decision. Why couldn't she have sent the boy to the Oratory, where her other one goes, along with Tony's son? At least we've already weathered that storm. Most people think she should go, and quickly, but I don't think she will. She's part of the charmed circle. The party has been taken over by a sort of Metropolitan elite who believe that the rules that govern everyone else don't apply to them. It started, of course, with Tony's decision to send his son to the Oratory, although this is worse since it involves selection. The trouble is, Tony can't very well drop Harriet, because the Tories would go for him next. Sure enough, the subject dominated PM's Questions. Tony put up a brave fight, but it was a walkover. John Major made sarky remarks about being tough on hypocrisy and tough on the causes of hypocrisy. Tony, unwisely, made clear that he would stick up for Harriet come what may. Prescott's face, neatly caught in the frame on the news bulletins, was a picture of misery. He is said to be spitting feathers. The Tories are cock-a-hoop. They are going to play this for all it's worth. It's going to haunt us all the way through the election. I overheard Brian Sedgemore say, 'If our electoral fortunes change, we can date our decline from today.'

I asked Chris Smith when he first heard of stakeholding (a question I put to every Shadow Cabinet member I come across). He replied, 'Sitting in the High Commissioner's residence in Singapore, in the company of a number of bemused Singaporean businessmen.'

Wednesday, 24 January

A riveting meeting of the parliamentary party. Harriet sat up front, trying to look suitably penitent, but she obviously isn't. She was on the radio this morning robustly defending her decision. The mood was overwhelmingly hostile, but several people spoke up for her. One of the London yuppies made a perfectly awful speech and succeeded in alienating just about everybody, but the most surprising contribution came from Bernie Grant. He said he had three sons and felt he had let them down badly by sending them to local schools. He has a point, of course. Many of the schools in inner London are dreadful, particularly since the Tories abolished the Inner London Education Authority (a point which, oddly, no one has made), but that doesn't explain why Harriet had to choose a selective school.

Paul Flynn made a brave speech directed straight at Tony. He talked of 'a golden circle of beautiful people bound together by mutual admiration and remote from ordinary people'. He went on, 'Tony, you don't seem to understand. You are pushing us off the moral high ground, stealing our most precious possession – our idealism.' Clive Solely made the best speech. He said, 'This story won't go away, however loyal we are. It's not about education any more. It's about trust. About saying one thing and doing another. Harriet, for your own sake and for the party's sake, please resign.' Roy Hattersley stopped short of calling on her to resign, but hinted strongly that she should. He did say that she should stop going on the media to defend her decision, 'otherwise some of us will be provoked beyond endurance'. After everyone had spoken Harriet got up and stumbled through a pathetic little statement, every word of which was written out, and which actually contained the word 'apologise'.

Finally, Tony Blair gave a brilliant performance. I have never seen him speak with such passion. He threw his full weight behind Harriet. He said he wasn't going to let the Tories crucify a member of his Shadow Cabinet. As he was speaking, it occurred to me that there must be several members of the Shadow Cabinet – Michael Meacher, for example – who must wish they enjoyed the confidence of the Leader to the same degree as Harriet. (Ann Clwyd got the chop from the front bench for missing a single, non-essential, vote.) Tony got the headline he wanted in the *Standard*: 'Blair Crushes Revolt'. True, but he has used up a lot of goodwill. And what's he going to do when the Shadow Cabinet elections come round? She hasn't a hope in hell of being re-elected.

Chatted to Derek Foster in the Tea Room. He said, 'I have worked for four leaders. What struck me most about Neil Kinnock's office was the contempt his staff had, not only for the parliamentary party, but for half the Shadow Cabinet. The attitude of Blair's staff is exactly the same.'

Later, The Man himself came in and sat down at my table. That's the third Tea Room sighting in the last ten days. Obviously, the penny's dropping. I told him I was an eleven-plus failure and he seemed surprised.

Thursday, 25 January

Just when we hoped it had gone away, back it came. Blair unwisely raised education at Prime Minister's Questions and received yet another hammering about Harriet. I heard someone say, 'The magic's gone.' Too early to say yet, of course, but for the first time since he was elected we have glimpsed the possibility of defeat. Mick Clapham said to me afterwards, 'We are on the slippery slope.' Ken Purchase said, 'We are in deep shit.' If only John Smith were still with us.

Sunday, 28 January

Emma awoke every two hours, demanding attention. She has got very devious. She knows that if she screams loud enough she will get her way. Every so often she pauses to see whether her crying is having the desired effect. We have taken to calling her Civilised Baby, so-called by Ngoc after she had a deceptively easy night a few days ago.

Monday, 29 January
Sunderland

A couple of hours with Jules Preston, chief executive of the local Training and Enterprise Council, the quango charged with providing job training for the young unemployed. As TECs go, it appears to be very successful, but, as Jules said, nothing he can do will make up for the thousands of skilled jobs that once existed in the shipyards. One interesting fact: I asked what the definition was of a successful transition from training to a real job. The answer: two pay packets in six months. No wonder the claimed rate of success is so high.

To London just in time for a meeting on the Security Services Bill, about which there is a strong, and not entirely healthy, whiff of consensus in the air.

Tuesday, 30 January

The Security Services Bill, the purpose of which is to extend the functions of MI5 into investigations of serious crime. In theory MI5 is supposed to be assisting the police, but in practice, I am sure it will do as it pleases. The government is putting it about that only twenty or thirty personnel will be involved, but it is clearly the thin end of a very big wedge. Alun Michael, who leads for our side, is a likeable Stakhanovite with absolutely no eye for the big picture. No serious opposition is planned. Just a lot of probing amendments which are then withdrawn without a vote. The minister, David Maclean, who is usually very combative, was uncharacteristically reasonable. There was none of the usual nonsense to the effect that opposition to whatever foolishness is being proposed equates with sympathy for the villains. Alun has been invited to the Home Office for background meetings with officials. We have all been circulated with background notes. There is even talk of new amendments to accommodate Opposition concerns. The reason for this sudden outbreak of reasonableness is not hard to discern. Namely, that – with the exception of the security services – just about everyone who has been consulted is deeply unhappy with the Bill as it stands. Even the tame committee who are supposed to oversee the work of the security services has registered its unhappiness. The police are furious because it fails to make clear who will be in charge. The definition of what constitutes serious crime is extremely wide. In practice, MI5 will be a law unto itself, as it has always been.

Chris Smith came to the What's Left group in the evening to talk about his plans for pensions and social security. He said that old-age pensions had fallen from 20 per cent of average earnings in 1979 to 14 per cent today. He would like to restore the link with earnings, but Gordon was 'intractable'. He hoped at least to link pensions to inflation, but Gordon would need to be persuaded on this, too. Chris also said he was looking for a way of helping the poorest three million pensioners, but this was difficult given that means testing was politically impossible. He was hoping to restore some sort of benefit for sixteen- and seventeen-year-olds, but only as part of a welfare-to-work scheme. He also wanted to create incentives to tempt people out of welfare dependency. He would like to tax child benefit, which would enable us to pay a big increase for those who really needed it, but there was a danger of alienating Middle Britain. That, of course, is the nub of the problem. The greed and myopia of a large section of the middle classes, their constant baying for tax cuts and the eagerness with which they lapped up shares in the utilities is what has got us into this mess. We are terrified of alienating them so we have to go around pretending that they are the real victims of the Thatcher Decade when in fact many of them did extremely well out of it.

Chris said he was trying to close down talk of Singapore as a role model because it was of little relevance to our situation. In Singapore most people were in work and the family was still intact. In the entire country there were only 2,500 people on benefit. He did talk approvingly, however, of the JET scheme in Australia which has apparently had some success enticing single parents back to work.

Wednesday, 31 January

George Mudie, one of the whips, was working his way round the division lobby in the evening collecting signatures on what, at first sight, appeared to be a harmless little motion calling for MPs' pay to be referred to the Nolan Committee. He had a list of all Labour members and was ticking off those who signed, so it was well organised and appeared to have semi-official backing. At first I refused to sign, then relented on the grounds that the issue needs at all cost to be got out of our hands. Ten minutes later I received a call from a BBC journalist who asked if I had signed the motion for MPs' salaries to be doubled. In a blinding flash I realised what was going on. The Tories behind the motion are using Labour members as cover. Knowing they can't get Labour signatures for a motion calling for salaries to be doubled they have come up with a bland little formula designed to maximise the signatures while, simultaneously, giving an entirely different spin to the media. I went straight to the Table Office and removed my name before it appears on the Order Paper. The clerk said I was not the only member to withdraw, so several people have worked out what is going on. I am absolutely, utterly opposed to any increase over the rate of inflation and I shan't hesitate to say so no matter how unpopular it makes me.

Friday, 2 February
Sunderland

I called on Joe Mills, the chairman designate of the local health authority, who told an amusing story about Tony Blair's receipt of an honorary degree from the University of Newcastle. Apparently Blair's staff arrogantly decided that their master would pick up the degree and depart without sitting through the speeches. Ted Short took offence at this and called at Blair's office to make clear that he thought

Tony should stay for the full ceremony. The youth who managed the diary gave him the brush-off, saying, 'It's all been cleared with the Chancellor'.

To which Ted Short replied, 'I am the Chancellor.'

Blair stayed for the entire ceremony.

Sunday, 4 February

We let Civilised Baby cry last night. She carried on for fifty-five minutes before falling asleep. Hard, but it's the only way. Otherwise she will drive us all potty.

This evening Civilised began howling at 9.30 p.m., soon after Ngoc had gone to bed early to store up energy for the night ahead. I let her carry on for more than an hour. A pitiful little sound, pausing at every creak on the stairs, to see if help was on the way. Eventually I was overruled. Ngoc came down and picked her up. The howling stopped immediately, as if at the touch of a button. Civilised looked over Ngoc's shoulder and gave me a little smile as if to say, 'I won, Dad, so there.'

Monday, 5 February

I wrote to Tony Blair about the proposed increase in our salaries. I said that this was an issue on which there ought to be clear water between us and the Tories and yet we seemed bent on demonstrating that, when it comes to self-enrichment, there was no real difference. The fact that our whips were touting around a motion that implied a large increase made it look as though the campaign had official backing. In government we would have to take some harsh decisions about public sector pay and awarding ourselves a whacking great rise will surely come back to haunt us. I said he should make clear that there is no case for an increase in MPs' wages above the rate of inflation and that if we wanted to link future pay increases to anyone, it should be a cross-section of our constituents' incomes rather than to some mythical civil servant. I copied the letter to Ann Taylor, Bruce Grocott and Doug Hoyle, all of whom will disagree. I am afraid this is going to make me unpopular, but I don't care. It is outrageous.

Tuesday, 6 February

Joe Rogaly of the *Financial Times* came to see me at Brixton Road. He wants to write a profile for the Weekend section. Why me? 'We wanted to talk to a sane left-winger.' I said that I was flattered to be certified sane by the *Financial Times*. He replied, 'It was only the suggestion of one man. We didn't take a vote on it.' We chatted for a couple of hours. His heart didn't really seem to be in it and I sense I was a disappointment. He kept asking where I stood in the political spectrum. Was I 'hard' or 'soft' left? I said labels were meaningless. How would he like to be labelled? He replied, 'Jaded hack.'

Wednesday, 7 February

A handwritten note, marked private and confidential, from Tony Blair in reply to the letter I sent him on Monday. The speed of his response suggests I have touched a raw nerve. He said he agrees. The motion had been circulated before he was aware of it. He was keeping a very (underlined) close eye on the situation.

Jean Corston told me that one of the whips touting for signatures on the wages motion had told her that he wasn't party to any campaign to double our pay. Then he added, 'But we might get £20,000.'

Thursday, 8 February

I travelled home with Derek and Anne Foster. Derek said that at last week's Shadow Cabinet, Tony had announced that Peter Mandelson was to head the new election unit in Millbank Tower. Frank Dobson had said, 'I think I speak for a number of colleagues, when I say that I don't like it but, if it has to be, I hope that the unit will serve everyone equally and not operate in first gear for some, second gear for others and in reverse for the rest.' Tony had said, 'Look, if there are any problems, just come to me.'

Derek says nothing will happen. 'With the best will in the world, Tony hasn't got the time to go sorting out disputes between colleagues when he's supposed to be fronting an election campaign.'

Sunday, 11 February

A huge bomb exploded in Docklands last night, clearly the work of the IRA. Monstrous, but hardly surprising. Major has had eighteen months to start talking and all he has done is fiddle. Whatever the outcome of the election, he might have gone down in history as the Prime Minister who ended the war. Now he's blown it. In the end I guess the Tories decided that, given their shrinking majority, keeping the Unionists sweet was more important than peace.

Wednesday, 14 February

Peter Mandelson asked to speak to me after the meeting of the parliamentary party. He said Tony was worried about reports that Michael Green wants to take over MAI, a media conglomerate with stakes in several regional TV companies. He wants me to keep an eye on it and, if necessary, organise a fuss. Peter also said that there were signs that the *Sun* was reverting to type and the *Express* and the *Mail* were turning increasingly nasty. Cherie was being trailed around the courts by hacks from the tabloids who were looking for trouble. Murdoch was upset about the vote on sports rights in the Lords and was blaming us. Peter said that for the time being he was just monitoring the Tory relationship with the media. When we have enough to go on we will make an issue of it, but it was important not to be seen to be whingeing.

The Security Services Bill had its final stages today. I hadn't intended to say anything, but – prompted by a contribution from Rupert Allason – I got up and said I was unhappy about the whole thing. I thought I ought to put down a little marker, just in case in ten years' time it all goes horribly wrong and someone says, 'Where were you?'

Liz Forgan came to dinner. Afterwards we wandered around the House of Lords and in the Royal Gallery we ran into Bernard Donoughue, who was feeling very pleased with himself for having moved the amendment prohibiting Murdoch from getting his hands on the eight listed sporting events. The first serious resistance Murdoch has ever encountered. Bernard, who was sacked from *The Times* by Murdoch, said 'Revenge, a dish best served cold. I have waited fourteen years.' Does Murdoch know? 'He does. David Elstein said to me, "We know why, but there's no need to go over the top, Bernard."

'The beauty of it is,' he said, 'I never once referred to Murdoch when introducing my amendment.' He really was a very happy man.

Bernard alleged, citing a Tory source, that Thatcher had sent a draft of the 1990 Broadcasting Bill to Murdoch's lawyers and allowed them to make deletions as they saw fit.

Thursday, 15 February

The report by Lord Justice Scott on the sale of arms to Iraq was published today with a great fanfare. The Trade Secretary, Ian Lang, made a statement, the gist of which was that everyone was in the clear and no one will be resigning. William Waldegrave and Nicholas Lyell were seated on the front bench looking unhappy. They obviously knew they were in far deeper trouble than Lang was admitting to. He quoted very selectively from the report, safe in the knowledge that no one else had seen it, except Robin Cook who had three hours to digest 1,800 pages and who responded brilliantly. Even the Scot Nats sitting next to me were impressed.

Friday, 16 February
Sunderland

The surgery lasted until after eight. The last customer was an obsessive who was convicted of beating up his girlfriend and believes he is the victim of a miscarriage of justice. He's been on at me for months. I told him I can't help, but he won't take no for an answer. He wouldn't go so in the end Jacky and I packed up our papers, put on our coats and locked the office while he continued to harangue us. I was afraid he would follow me home and find out where I lived, but fortunately he got tired about 100 yards short.

Sunday, 18 February

Civilised Baby is unwell. She whinged for half the night and much of the day. She never seems to sleep for more than thirty minutes. We put her in the buggy and took her for a walk around Mowbray Park in the morning, which kept her quiet for a while, but she resumed her wailing as soon as we were home. In the afternoon we put her in the car and went for a drive up the coast road to South Shields, which brought some relief, but she howled all evening and is still howling as I write (at 10.20 p.m.). Hanh, Ngoc and I have divided the night into three-hour shifts. My watch is from 1 a.m. to 4 a.m.

Tuesday, 20 February

To London on the 10.50. The only other first-class passenger to board at Durham was a sour elderly woman who, despite wearing what appeared to be a red tracksuit bottom, was unmistakeably grand. A large coat with fur cuffs was draped over her shoulders. She tottered along beside a railway employee who pushed an empty wheelchair. A chauffeur with a blanket over his arm hovered. When the train arrived another BR person materialised to help load her bags. I heard her complain about 'rotten service'. In fairness, I suspect she was referring to the fact that the train was running ten minutes late rather than to the attention she was receiving. I sidled up to her luggage and read the label: 'Viscountess Lambton'.*

Thursday, 22 February

One of the upwardly mobile female members bent my ear in the Tea Room about MPs' wages. She went on about her £100,000 mortgage, the cost of her nanny, her cleaner. She said, 'It cost me ten pounds in taxi fares just to get to the hairdresser and back this morning.' How my heart bled.

---

* Wife of Tony Lambton, the Tory minister who in 1973 was obliged to resign after being photographed smoking cannabis in bed with two prostitutes.

Monday, 26 February

The debate on the Scott report. Ian Lang was hopeless, but then he had a rotten case. Robin was wonderful. He displayed total mastery and, after initial barracking, most of the Tories listened to him in gloomy silence. Those who did raise their heads above the parapet were knocked for six. Robin even managed to get under Heseltine's skin by praising him for being the only minister to refuse to sign one of Nick Lyell's bits of paper. One can always tell when Hezza is upset because a nerve starts to twitch in the right hand side of his face. Alex Carlile said to me afterwards that Cook's was one of the best performances he had seen in years. I had expected the result to be a foregone conclusion since Paisley's men had already said they were abstaining. The other Unionists were in and out of Downing Street all afternoon and eventually voted with us. In the end, there was only one vote in it. Not that anyone would have resigned, had they lost. They really are unembarrassable.

Wednesday, 28 February

We had a little debate on the Carl Bridgewater case. Dennis Turner, who knows nothing about it, came up in the ballot so Paul Foot drafted a speech which Dennis delivered with great aplomb. Roy Hattersley spoke well. He has taken this one on board, unlike the Birmingham Six. There were even a couple of Tories who spoke in favour of reopening the case. The minister, Tim Kirkhope, was dismal. I am certain we will win this one, but not until it is out of the hands of the Home Office.

Tuesday, 5 March

I was number seven at PM's Questions, which were taken by Heseltine. Couldn't think of anything to ask until someone suggested I ask Hezza if on reflection he regretted his refusal to sign a Public Immunity Certificate, given that we now knew (from Scott) that the Attorney General had been right all along? It went down a treat. Hezza, who has absolutely no sense of humour, just stood glaring at me, apparently lost for something to say. In the end he gave a more or less sensible reply. It won't look much when it's written down in Hansard, but it did go down well with the troops. All sorts of people remarked on it afterwards. Pathetic really, that we derive so much satisfaction from such a piddling little sound bite, but such is life on the Opposition back benches.

Wednesday, 6 March

Hugh MacPherson, *Tribune*'s lobby correspondent, berated the left in general and me in particular for not standing up to Blair and co. 'If you were still at *Tribune*, you'd have something to say. You MPs are all the same,' he said, 'once you get in here all you care about is your seats.' In vain did I protest that what I cared about was winning the election and I didn't think anyone would thank me for starting a civil war. Not that I could, even if I wanted to. There aren't enough takers. Dissenters, I argued, would have more influence after the election, when we have only a small majority. 'But supposing Labour has a big majority?' he said, 'Blair won't need you.'

Jung Chang, author of *Wild Swans*, and her husband Jon Halliday came to dinner. They are working on a biography of Mao and Jon is going to Vietnam in search of people who had dealings with him, which is why he contacted me. The Mao project will take three years and they are interviewing everyone who has ever met him including Heath, Bush and Kissinger. Jon said Kissinger was trying to distance himself from his earlier enthusiasm for Mao. Although banned in China, *Wild Swans* has opened a lot of doors including those of the wife of the former President Liu Shao-chi; the daughter of Lin Biao, the former defence minister who disappeared in that mysterious plane crash in Mongolia in 1971; and Mao's last mistress. None of these people have ever spoken out before. We talked about political heroes. Jon reckons that Chou En-lai is the greatest political figure of the century. Jung is understandably wary of heroes, given her experience of China, but she suggested Václav Havel and Gandhi. Mandela we all agreed on. Jon suggested the Dalai Lama, who certainly has my vote. I suggested Ho Chi Minh and Pope John XXIII, both of whom remained humble to the end of their lives. I suspect, however, that a frank account of Uncle Ho's life would reveal that he, too, has feet of clay. History, we agreed, will be kind to Gorbachev but he, of course, is seriously flawed by his neglect of the home front.

Friday, 8 March

Awoke to hear a Labour peer, Meghnad Desai on the *Today* programme saying that the economy is in good shape and that Labour ought to concentrate on something else. I do wish he would keep his mouth shut. He is supposed to be on our side. The Tories – helped by their usual good fortune – are organising an economic miracle to coincide with the election and they might just get away with it. If they win a fifth term, only a world war or an environmental catastrophe will shift them. Even then the election would have to come soon afterwards, so short is the public memory. It is too depressing even to think about.

Wednesday, 13 March

A madman has gunned down fifteen primary-school children and a teacher in Dunblane.

Thursday, 14 March

A school photograph of the children murdered in Dunblane dominates most of today's newspapers. I wept when I saw it. Fifteen beautiful little people, their faces full of hope and innocence, whose lives have been cut short by an inexplicable act of madness. I think of all the years of love and care invested in the bringing up of one small person, wiped out in a single moment.

I ran into George Robertson in the Members' Lobby. He lives in Dunblane and his children went to the primary school. He and Michael Forsyth were at the school yesterday, a few hours after the massacre. George has behaved with great dignity. He said that Thomas Hamilton, the killer, had actually been in his house.

Prime Minister's Questions was given over entirely to Dunblane. Tony Blair was almost in tears as he read his statement. Both he and John Major were heard in absolute silence.

In the evening we debated renewal of the Prevention of Terrorism Act. Having opposed it for the last fifteen years, we are now instructed to abstain. A wholly untenable position. Michael Howard made mince-meat of Jack's attempt to explain this latest volte face. If the object was to make us appear more voter friendly, it has entirely failed. All we have succeeded in doing is alienating many of the chattering classes while failing to appease the *Sun*-reading end of the working class. Twenty-five of us, by no means all on the left, defied the whip and voted against.

Friday, 15 March

Predictably, tonight's *Echo*, for the second time in ten days, carries a page lead headed, 'City's MPs defy Blair over Terrorism Act'. As far as most of my constituents are concerned, it will be yet more evidence that I am a tool of the IRA.

Saturday, 16 March

Today's *Financial Times* carries a profile based on my interview last month with Joe Rogaly. He has tried hard to be fair, but he's too mired in his own prejudices to succeed. A great deal of space is devoted to Ireland and whether or not I think it is right to plant bombs and shoot at British soldiers. When have I ever suggested it was? I am labelled 'obsessive' – by someone who has only ever spent an hour in my company. Even my views on taxation are quoted out of context with the result that they appear to be opposite to those I actually hold. Not that it matters much. Hardly anyone in Sunderland reads the *FT*. Lily at the paper shop doesn't stock it, but she loaned me the one she reserves for the press office at the Civic Centre on condition I let her have it back before Monday.

Tuesday, 19 March

This afternoon, a guided tour of the party's new Media Centre in Millbank Tower (which, ironically, stands on the site of Tony Benn's birthplace). Here Mandelson is king. He gave an amusing little introduction and then we were shown the slogans that will form the basis of our campaign.

ONE NATION
YOUNG COUNTRY
STAKEHOLDER ECONOMY
NEW LABOUR
NEW BRITAIN

Ugh. One has visions of rows of glassy-eyed young zealots chanting 'New Labour, New Britain' cf. China, circa 1966.

Upstairs sixty (rising in due course to a hundred) enthusiastic young spinners are beavering away on state-of-the-art software. The boxes in which their new computers arrived are stacked in piles in every corner. They are divided into units with names like, Rebuttal, Projection and so on. Total cost is said to be about £2 million but I suspect it will be considerably more in the end. If only we had a message worthy of such an expensive delivery system.

Thursday, 21 March

George Robertson told me that more than 600 bullets were found on Thomas Hamilton. I have seen no mention of this in the papers. The suspicion is that he intended to wipe out the entire school while they were at assembly but arrived a few minutes too late. 'So in a sense we must thank God for our good luck,' one of George's neighbours had said. Funerals have been taking place all week. One by one the little white coffins lowered into the Silence. I can't stop thinking about it.

A long chat with Ann Whelan, who says that the lawyer who represented the Director of Public Prosecutions at the Bridgewater trial has written to the Home Office arguing that the case should be sent back to the Appeal Court. Incredibly, the Home Office are still resisting, so in the end he copied the correspondence to the defence solicitor, Jim

Nichol. However much the Home Office wriggles, they will have to give way in the end. It's only a matter of time.

Friday, 22 March

I sent a carefully worded letter to Barbara Mills, the Director of Public Prosecutions, asking what her plans were re the Carl Bridgewater case. I didn't let on that I knew about the letter from the lawyer. This is the moment to turn the screws. Amazing how little they have learned from past disasters.

This evening a Tory Party political broadcast, the drift of which was that the British economy was ahead of Europe in just about every respect. 'Ask our competitors,' the commentator kept saying and then the camera cut to an actor posing as a French, German or Dutch businessman who would duly confirm that they were outclassed by Britain. The effect was somewhat spoiled by *News at Ten*, which followed immediately. 'Europe bans British beef' was the lead. One by one our competitors – this time not actors – were shown demanding an end to exports of British meat – a result of the BSE crisis.

Saturday, 23 March
Sunderland

To the Civic Centre to hear John Prescott open a political education conference. There was standing room only in the council chamber and getting on for half of those present were new members. The chairwoman, a member of the National Executive Committee, started the meeting, saying that under New Labour political meetings did not consist of politicians talking at people. On the contrary New Labour wanted dialogue with its members. Everyone had a part to play. 'Do you believe that?' I whispered to Derek Foster who was sitting beside me and he offered a discreet smile. Whereupon Prescott got up, talked for an uninterrupted forty minutes, and left as soon as the applause had died down without taking a single question.

Monday, 25 March

BSE is turning into a big disaster for the Tories. There is talk of having to slaughter at least four million cattle. Needless to say we are shamelessly exploiting the situation. I feel a little uneasy every time I hear one of our spokesman going on about how incompetent and indecisive the government is. (Actually, the Health Secretary, Stephen Dorrell, has handled the situation well.) Then I imagine what they would do to us if our roles were reversed and I feel happier.

For the first time I begin to think we might have a serious majority at the Election.

Tuesday, 26 March

When I rang home this morning Ngoc told me the following story: Last week the Woodcraft Folk sent a form to be filled in with examples of Sarah's good behaviour and helpfulness. For a week Sarah was on best behaviour. The form was duly completed and dispatched. This morning Ngoc said to her, 'Fold your pyjamas and put them away to show how good you are.' To which Sarah replied, 'But Mum, you've already sent in the paper.'

According to Jack Straw, Michael Howard is being uncharacteristically friendly over the review of gun legislation in the wake of Dunblane. Jack has been invited to the Home Office, his every suggestion treated with respect. 'He wants cover,' Jack says. I only hope we extract a high price.

David Elstein, head of programming at BSkyB, addressed the all-party Media Group in advance of the Broadcasting Bill. To hear him talk you'd think Sky is a philanthropic organisation concerned solely with the improvement of British culture. He claimed they are spending £160 million on original programming. When I asked for a breakdown this turned out to be 50 per cent on sport and 25 per cent on news, virtually nothing on drama or documentaries. What's more they are undermining everybody else; just as the *Sun* forced the *Mirror* to plunge downmarket, so the same is happening to television. He went on about how generous Sky is in allowing other companies access to their channels via the set-top box. 'We would hate to have a war,' he said. Why, I asked, is Sky such an apparently gentlemanly organisation when other parts of the Murdoch empire are so ruthless? The answer – which he didn't offer – is, of course, that they are anxious to do nothing to provoke the regulators. In ten years' time, when they dominate the market, it could be a different story.

Thursday, 28 March

I managed to get in a little shot at Agriculture questions. Some of us, I said, welcomed the collapse of the odious trade in live animals brought about by the BSE crisis. There was a big audience because it was immediately before Prime Minister's Questions. The Tories jeered loudly and a Liberal MP, Charles Kennedy, said, 'You'll get a lot of letters about that.'

Thursday, 11 April

Blair is in New York. He was pictured on the news last night shaking hands with Henry Kissinger. Really, this is too much. What has rubbing shoulders with a clapped-out war criminal got to do with getting us elected?

Friday, 12 April

This morning's news bulletins are full of our leader's speech in New York last night hinting, but not actually saying, that we might cut taxes for the middle classes. I do wish we would stop pandering. We ought to be appealing to the best rather than the worst instincts of the middle class. In any case, we can never outbid the Tories over tax. In the last analysis they will just lie.

Saturday, 20 April

Sarah and I spent a couple of hours distributing local election leaflets in the smarter part of my constituency – 1930s houses and bungalows, neat gardens full of daffodils, tulips and purple aubretia; new and almost-new cars in the drives; two Tory votes in every home, or at least there would have been five years ago. Now, who knows? After lunch we drove to Farndale where the daffodils were in full bloom.

Sunday, 21 April

With Sarah I leafleted in Hendon, Harrogate and Amberley streets where the social fabric has collapsed. A stark contrast to yesterday. What nonsense to talk of a North–South divide. I have only to travel a mile across the constituency to pass from one world to another. Three or four houses were burned out, a dozen others abandoned and unsaleable. Pavements strewn with rubble, litter and dog dirt. Most of the remaining houses have fallen into the hands of absentee land-lords. Every so often one comes to net curtains and dried flowers in the front window, a home where decent people, unable to escape, are clinging on by their fingertips. And only a couple of hundred yards from where we live. How close we are to the abyss.

Monday, 29 April

An hour or more with Tony Blair in the Shadow Cabinet Room. Part of a consultation he is doing with backbenchers in groups of about fifteen. I can't recall any previous Labour leader undertaking such an exercise. Morale among the troops is not high. People feel irrelevant and angry at learning from the media about New Labour's dramatic policy changes. The latest is Gordon Brown's suggestion that child benefit for over-sixteens in higher education should be reviewed. People are very pissed off about that.

Tony opened by saying we could still be brought down by money-in-the-pocket issues. The press was now back in the Tory fold. Tax was the single biggest obstacle to victory. Gordon's child benefit speech had, he said, been misconstrued. Then we had a little briefing from party pollster Greg Cook, who said that we were still vulnerable on the economy. So far we had done little more than neutralise Tory propaganda. The electorate still didn't trust us.

We went round the table and everyone chipped in. Tony sat there in his shirtsleeves carefully taking notes. He knew everyone's name, which was impressive. Dave Hinchliffe complained that we didn't appear to be offering any alternative vision. No one was sure what we are offering. Alice Mahon weighed in on child benefit, saying she had brought two kids through A levels on a low income and she wouldn't have been able to manage without child benefit. Several others endorsed this. Bernie Grant complained about policy being made on the hoof – the change of line on the Prevention of Terrorism Act, for example. Mike Gapes made some trenchant comments about the negative spin-doctoring coming from Blair's office and the damage it was doing.

When my turn came I said the Rebuttal Unit appeared to be targeted against our own side rather than the enemy. On tax, I said we shouldn't pander to middle-class greed but rather we should appeal to their decent instincts. I added that one of the most damaging allegations made against us was that all politicians are the same. There was no better illustration for that proposition than the row over MPs' wages. I was of the view that there ought to be clear blue water between us and the Tories on this issue. As things stood, the only difference was an argument about how much.

Ken Purchase said we must be doing some things right because we were so far ahead in the polls and this was in large measure due to Tony. This was almost the only positive comment anyone made. He added, to some amusement, that he didn't believe in all this modernising and stakeholding 'crap', but it was clearly working so keep at it, Tony.

There were some amusing moments. Tommy Graham announced (not, I suspect, for the first time) that he was giving up smoking and intended to lose eight stone.

Diane Abbott, who waltzed in twenty minutes late, began by referring to Brian Donohoe as 'comrade'.

'Do you mean Brian?' said Tony.

Diane pulled no punches, 'You get the feeling from New Labour that you are being talked at rather than listened to.' She went on, 'I feel like a disreputable single-parent black mother from Hackney being lectured at by someone from the better part of Islington.'

Tony said quietly, 'I used to live in Hackney.'

We had to give hope to our people, Diane went on. We were losing sight of those who traditionally voted for us. Several others made the same point, but rather less provocatively.

There were barbed comments from one or two surprising sources. Eddie O'Hara said people in his constituency were 'incandescent' at the choice of school some senior members of the party made for their children. Tony just looked at the table.

Finally, there was a contribution from Brian Jenkins, the victor of the South East Staffs by-election, who is obviously still on a high following a staggering 22 per cent swing to Labour. People, he said, wanted hope, a dream. They didn't want detail. He reported overwhelming enthusiasm for the Labour message. The public, it seems, is far keener on New Labour than most party members.

We were interrupted by a division and when we reassembled Tony responded. 'Tax is the thing that could kill us stone dead. Believe me, this is a dangerous area. Discipline and self-control are essential.' On child benefit, all Gordon had proposed was a review. It was a fact that child benefit was not paid to people on the dole, but if you had a son at Eton, you would qualify.

At this point Ken Purchase interrupted. 'That won't wash.'

'My argument can be justified intellectually.'

'Your argument is spurious.'

'I can justify my argument, whether or not it is politically possible to do anything about it.'

At which point Diane intervened. 'The spin was coming out of your office.'

'Diane, not everything is centrally controlled. All I ask is for people to distinguish between fact and fiction.'

Diane and Ken kept it up for several minutes. Kinnock would have gone bananas, but Tony handled it with good humour. He will have got the message that feelings are running high, but I am not sure he will have heard much to change his mind. 'I make no apology for trying to broaden our appeal. Labour is the least successful political party in modern history.' He concluded by listing five tests of a Labour government: (1) a significant improvement in education; (2) reform of the welfare state; (3) partnership with industry; (4) decentralisation of government; (5) improved relations with Europe.

No mention of unemployment, which, I would have thought, was the single greatest test of a Labour government, even one that wanted to reduce taxes. No mention either of the power structure. I dropped Tony a note afterwards saying that, if we leave the power structure intact, we won't win a second term.

Tuesday, 30 April

Gordon Brown has made another speech, this time to the Manchester Business School, all but ruling out tax increases for anyone. Full of talk about New Labour's fiscal rectitude. 'We will save money before we spend money.' There is talk of 'across the board efficiency reviews'. If there was any further money to be squeezed out of the public sector I am sure the Tories would have found it by now. What makes Gordon think he will succeed where they have failed? The plain truth is – and I entirely understand why we can't say it – that it is not the highest rates of tax that are too low, although they may be. It is the basic rate. The middle classes are paying too little, given the rate of unemployment we have to sustain. The only way to reduce tax is to cut unemployment. A sad comment on our arid little world, that any politician admitting the truth would become instantly unelectable.

Wednesday, 1 May

Most of the day was spent at the select committee. Judicial appointments in the morning. Dangerous dogs in the afternoon. I overheard two Tories in the Tea Room talking about free lunches. One had just been lunched at Shepherd's, an expensive restaurant in Marsham Street, by the cable TV lobby and had been spotted by the other who was being lunched by a Granada lobbyist. One said, 'I'm in Shepherd's every three months or so and I can honestly say that I have never yet paid for a lunch.'

Wednesday, 8 May

The select committee took evidence on guns. Jerry Wiggin gave evidence for the gun lobby. His line was basically that most gun-related crime involved unregistered weapons and that, therefore, little or nothing could be done about anything. I asked whether it worried him that there were more than 700,000 shotguns in circulation, but it didn't. Neither was he concerned by the fact that it was as easy to acquire a shotgun licence in urban Sunderland as it is in rural North Yorkshire. In the end, I suspect Dunblane is going to make very little difference.

One interesting little New Labour vignette: Paul Flynn proposed a motion at this morning's meeting of the parliamentary party calling for Shadow Cabinet elections to be transferred from October to July. The aim was to ensure that they can't be cancelled in the autumn on the grounds that they are too divisive. I was unable to attend because I was in the select committee, but at about 12.15 p.m. Nick Brown and George Mudie put their heads round the committee room door and beckoned to John Hutton, who disappeared for about ten minutes. When I asked where he'd been, he said he'd been told to go to Committee Room 14 and vote against Paul. Even party meetings are whipped.

Thursday, 9 May

Lunch with Ed Pearce, a lobby journalist; his political instincts are moderate Labour but even he is concerned that Blair and Brown have gone too far. He said, 'We should be talking to the middle classes in the language of Ian Gilmour, not that of Norman Lamont.'

This evening, a free vote on allowing gays into the armed forces. A very British debate. Everyone knows that sooner or later we shall be forced by the Europeans (another stick for the Tories to beat them with) to admit gays, but nobody (including some New Labourites) wants to upset the bigots in the military. Not that there was any suggestion that gays should be excluded from the armed forces when there was a world war to be fought or when there was conscription. Needless to say, the proposition was comfortably defeated. Lucky the armed forces aren't allowed to choose whether they will admit women and blacks.

Monday, 13 May

To the Senior Salaries Review Body to discuss MPs' remuneration. Sir Michael Perry, a former chairman of Unilever, presided, flanked by a large lady who asked the occasional question and another woman who said nothing. Mine, he said, was the only submission based on principle. I had argued that it was unhealthy in a democracy for too wide a gap to grow between the electorate and their representatives and that it was possible to live comfortably on £34,000 a year. All the arguments in favour of a large increase were bogus. All parties were oversubscribed for candidates. We had no great responsibilities. Most of us would not be earning significantly more if we had remained outside Parliament and many of those shouting loudest for more money contributed least to the day-to-day operation of Parliament. He asked how future increases should be calculated and I suggested they should be linked to the average increase in a cross-section of our constituents' incomes – and not to the income of 'some invisible civil servant'. He was courteous and not at all pompous. He asked if I had given any thought to what the Prime Minister should earn. I said it was not a subject I lay awake worrying about, but perhaps he could take an average of EC prime ministers and link it to a multiple of MPs' salaries. We also discussed the mileage allowance, which, I said, was a racket and, if he was looking to save some public money, there was ample scope. I was with them a little more than half an hour. I don't suppose my contribution will make the blindest bit of difference, but somebody has to speak up.

In the evening I went to dinner with James and Margaret Curran in Wimbledon. James said, 'Give me a reason to believe there is a serious difference between us and the Tories.' I gave him several, but it is depressing how widespread this sentiment is becoming.

Thursday, 16 May

Half an hour with Barbara Castle, who is fuming about New Labour's plans to do away with SERPS, the state earnings-related pension scheme, which was her brainchild. Vintage Barbara. There she sat, an aged queen, seething with magnificent indignation, not a hair out of place. Her colours, a subdued yellow, matched perfectly – even her hair. Oh for such energy when I am eighty-five. Or even, indeed, when I am fifty. 'I am as loyal as anyone in this party, but if I am to be rode roughshod over, then the balloon will go up,' she said. As she spoke she banged the table. She had tried to obtain a list of delegates to the National Policy Forum and been told that none was available. She had telephoned the general secretary, Tom Sawyer, to try to discover the timetable for the pensions policy document, but he had not returned her calls. She had talked both to Gordon and Chris Smith. 'No one will put a figure on the cost.' Instead of agreeing to restore the link between earnings and pensions they were looking at every single means-tested alternative. 'I told Gordon I will not go quietly, even if some of us are driven to keep our mouths shut this side of a general election.'

Saturday, 18 May

To Manchester City Hall for the National Policy Forum. In a very surly frame of mind. How I resent giving up a weekend to listen to hours of claptrap. 'Dad, why are you always going to meetings?' asked Sarah. Why, indeed?

I read the documents on the train (they arrived only two days ago). Clare's transport paper and Robin's on foreign affairs were good. Chris Smith's very thin. Just a copy of a recent speech and a consultation paper, asking questions. Barbara need not have worried. Clearly nothing has been decided on pensions. Or if it has, we are not being told. Blair opened with his usual warning against complacency. As ever, he demanded discipline. We weren't going to set out our Budget in advance of the election. 'We'd be certifiable if we did.' He was unapologetic about the proposed review of child benefit for the over-sixteens, but he added that no one was suggesting that we take it away from those who need it. He ended by promising the most radical government since 1945. Despite everything, I am inclined to give him the benefit of the doubt. We have never, in my time at least, had a leader so clear about where he wants to take us.

Gordon Brown was much in evidence, exuding artificial bonhomie. What a contrast to Blair who is so relaxed, confident and above all capable of listening. Gordon is constantly wringing his hands and unable to sit or stand still for longer than a sound bite. He made an unscheduled address to the plenary session in an attempt to damp down the outrage at his review of child benefit, but he was received without enthusiasm. There was the usual talk of not shrinking from tough choices. To be fair, he did say firmly that he was going ahead with his windfall tax on the utilities. A couple of people were allowed questions. Someone asked if we couldn't consider some other tough choices, such as progressive taxation? There is no doubt that Gordon – and Tony (who is obviously in this up to his neck) – have blundered. All that assiduous wooing of the middle classes squandered in a single act of foolishness. At the workshop on foreign affairs I suggested we say something about our alleged commitment to amend the Treaty of Rome to have farm animals treated as sentient beings rather than agricultural products. It beats me why we never make more of this, given the strong feelings about animal welfare among the better elements of the middle classes. Precisely the vote we are anxious to attract. It also has the advantage of being morally right.

The workshop on pensions was dominated by child benefit. There was no sign of Gordon so Chris Smith had to carry the can.

Tuesday, 21 May

To the Home Office to see Lord Lloyd* who is conducting a review of the Prevention of Terrorism Act. The first time I have seen him without his wig. A handsome man with a fine head of white hair, a light tan and a benign, affable demeanour. We spent the first twenty minutes discussing the Birmingham bombings case. I remarked that it was possible to be very intelligent and stupid at the same time. By

---

*The judge who presided at the final appeal of the Birmingham Six.

way of example I cited the trial judge, Lord Bridge. To my surprise, he agreed.

We then discussed the PTA. He said I was pushing at an open door as regards applying the rules in the Police and Criminal Evidence Act and exclusion orders. In any case, he said, the present arrangements won't get past the European Court of Human Rights. Out of the blue he asked for my view of the EC. Generally positive, I said, but before we sign up to a single currency I would want to know about the likely effect on employment.

He said, 'You are one of the most reasonable politicians I have met.'

On that note we parted.

Back at the House I got into the lift with John Patten and mentioned that I had just been with Lord Lloyd.

'How did you find him?'

'He seems a decent fellow; a one-nation Tory, I would guess.'

'Judges these days are all raving lefties. They all want lesbian clerks.'

I ventured that I didn't think it was quite like that. His eyes began to swivel. 'Oh yes,' he said, '*I know.*'

Maria Fyfe, also a delegate to the Policy Forum, told me that at the report back on Sunday morning there was an uprising over child benefit. The convener of the first social security workshop reported that 'concern' had been expressed about Gordon's plans. Whereupon one of those who had attended intervened to say that concern was the wrong word, unanimous opposition had been expressed and he wanted it minuted. At this point people from the other two workshops shouted that they, too, were opposed. So Robin Cook, who was in the chair, formally asked for their opposition to be minuted.

No word of this has reached the outside world.

Wednesday, 22 May

I told one of the committee clerks that I was unhappy with the stand being taken by our front bench on the Criminal Investigations and

Procedure Bill. We discussed the possibility of an amendment at report stage. He said that Home Office civil servants of his acquaintance were surprised that Labour went along with it. 'They are wondering if there is any Bill that this Home Secretary could produce to which Labour will object.'

Sunday, 26 May
Sunderland

A dreadful night with the Tiny Tyrant. She awoke at three-hourly intervals before rising at 5.40 a.m. We are exhausted and bad tempered. How much longer can this go on?

Tuesday, 28 May

Baby Mullin woke at midnight, 3.54 a.m. and 6.40 a.m. Ngoc produced a book entitled *Solve Your Child's Sleep Problems*. Chapter 6, night feeding, seems exactly to describe our problems with Emma. Beginning tonight there will be a new regime: she must be weaned off the bottle, however long the screaming lasts.

Tuesday, 4 June

This evening as I was leaving for Durham to catch the train Sarah came to the door in a bad mood. 'Dad, Dad, come here. Mum says I have to kiss you.'

When I didn't respond fast enough, she stamped her little foot. 'You're wasting my time. I'm supposed to be watching *Sooty*.'

Friday, 7 June

Steve Byers came in the evening. We had dinner in the garden and then went across to the Civic Centre where he addressed my general committee. I like Steve. He is immensely capable and yet entirely without self-importance. It wouldn't surprise me to see him in the Cabinet within three years, assuming of course that we win. I had asked him to talk about the next Labour government. He was surprisingly cautious and stuck closely to the official line. 'Until we have reduced the welfare burden, we will only be able to start spending on health and education when we begin to create wealth.' Work, a minimum wage, devolution of power and regulation of the utilities were his priorities.

Tuesday, 11 June
Brixton Road

A man came to give the boiler its annual check-up. A former employee of British Gas, he was a victim of privatisation. He now worked for a sub-contractor. No holiday pay. No sick pay. He was paid only by the job. If no one was at home, he got nothing. I asked what training the new masters provided. None. There was still a plentiful supply of employees trained by the public sector. What would happen when they ran out? Who knows? He said that the billing people were all temps, employed only two months out of three. No job security. No pensions. No nothing. They live in fear. In fairness, he did say there had been a lot of abuses under public ownership. Take meters, for example. When he worked in the public sector he rarely installed more than five a day. Now he was expected to install up to forty. He lived in Islington, where much of the old nonsense still went on. There was a saying among the Islington workforce, he said: 'One week's work, six months' sick pay.' That's one thing we never face up to on the left. To a large extent the public sector workers are the authors of their own misfortune. I have heard ex-shipyard workers in Sunderland say the same.

Monday, 17 June

After a lot of to-ing and fro-ing we finally managed to persuade Derry Irvine to visit the Civil Liberties Group. He talked at length about incorporating the European Convention on Human Rights into British law. He said very clearly that it should be regarded as a floor, not a ceiling. He spoke up for a security service accountable to Parliament, non-lawyers appointed to the European Court, judicial authorisation for phone taps, freedom of information, a public interest defence for whistleblowers. All good liberal measures. On judicial appointments, he favours an appointments commission to advise the Lord Chancellor. He has already talked to the civil servants about this and says they are resolutely opposed. I bet they are. He said, 'We should not miss the opportunity to alter the attitude and quality of senior judges.'

I was pleasantly surprised by Derry. Contrary to reports, he came across as lucid, radical and amiable. One can't help wondering, however, if someone who has done so well out of the existing system is best placed to take on the legal establishment.

I asked a junior member of our Treasury team what we were proposing to say about our tax plans before the election. 'As little as possible.'

Tuesday, 18 June

In the evening I attended a talk by a New Zealand academic, Jane Kelsey, on the collapse of the New Zealand Labour Party following their total surrender to the market. 'The left abdicated economics to those who understood the subject – who were mainly neo-liberals.' New Zealand has also switched to a PR system which has fragmented the vote and led to the rise of an unpleasant nationalist party. Now Labour are down to 15 per cent in the polls (from 50 per cent ten years ago). According to Dr Kelsey the rifts in the party are irreconcilable and the public no longer trusts Labour because it is indistinguishable from the National Party. The parallels with our situation are not precise. There are, however, enough similarities to ring the odd alarm bell.

Thursday, 20 June

An amusing lunch with Ray Powell, who regaled Audrey Wise and me with tales of his triumphs as the accommodation whip. His greatest was the discovery of three floors of rooms above the Speaker's House which had not been visited since the end of the war. They were sealed at the end of Upper Corridor North, behind a door which Ray insisted be removed from its hinges. The extra space has now been converted into seventeen large offices.

Tuesday, 25 June

The Tories announced the return of the grammar school today. Blunkett responded robustly, but was continually baited about Harriet's and Tony's choice of schools.

Thursday, 27 June

I was drawn fifth at PM's Questions, the third time my name has come up this month. Hezza presided since Major is in Florence. As usual I went along to the little pre-meeting in the Shadow Cabinet Room to find out what the line was. John McFall, who was number one, had an excellent question: 'Was the PM aware that last night's European Football Championship – which had an audience of twenty-eight million – may be the last to be shown on terrestrial TV? What guarantee could he give that the next European Championships would not be kidnapped by pay-TV – audience one million?' To everyone's surprise, Alastair Campbell rejected this. Instead, he said that John must go on devolution. I shook my head and Alastair said, 'I can't see why Chris is shaking his head. It's obvious. If the number two in our Scottish front-bench team doesn't go on devolution, the media will want to know why.' In the end we deferred to Alastair's judgement. So poor John was saddled with a referendum question and I took the one on football. Result – disaster. Hezza – who was on top form – hit John for six. I got smashed, too. Foolishly I inserted a reference to Murdoch at the last minute. 'At least I didn't fly halfway round the world to pay homage to Mr Murdoch …' roared Hezza. Not a good day.

I travelled home with Steve Byers. What does he think Blair would do if we lost the election? Steve says he would go. He has heard Tony say that he only has one chance. What if we only lost by a handful and there was a prospect of another election within a year or two? Steve reckons he would still go. It's all or nothing.

Monday, 1 July

Everyone is talking about a report on the front page of the *Observer* suggesting that our New Labour masters are contemplating a cull of candidates to remove the – quote – disloyal and the substandard – unquote. The report is remarkably free of substance, but it hasn't been denied. I don't think anything will happen this side of an election. After that, who knows? Perhaps they will set up a New Labour cloning factory. The puzzling thing is, given that the back benches are increasingly expected to be seen and not heard, I would have thought they will want more substandard candidates, not less.

Paul Flynn has gone public with his dissatisfaction over the proposed referendum on devolution. I didn't hear, but I gather he was on the *Today* programme this morning and went a bit over the top. Needless to say, the media are lapping it up. I had a message to call Michael Brunson at ITN and when I returned his call the woman who answered the phone shouted across the room to him, 'Michael, are we still looking for people who are attacking the Labour Party ...'

The front bench have adopted the new clause I tabled inserting a quality threshold into the Broadcasting Bill. As a result the Order Paper contained my name followed by those of Mr Tony Blair, Mr John Prescott, Mr Jack Cunningham etc. Worth framing, since I am sure it won't happen very often. Since the territory is unfamiliar, I typed out my speech triple spaced and simply read it out, as ministers do. Although we are supposed to be legislators, we do remarkably little legislating and I am unfamiliar with the procedure. So when the time came for me to reply to the debate I remained in my seat, expecting to hear my name called. Instead the Deputy Speaker simply moved straight to the vote. Not that it mattered. We lost. Home by taxi at about 12.30 a.m.

Tuesday, 2 July

Internal security at the Palace of Westminster appears to have been privatised. Each morning the TV monitors contain a 'Security Thought for Today' straight out of paranoia gulch. Today's fatuous offering is, 'The only way to be safe is never to be secure.'

I showed around a party of about twenty A-level students. Their ignorance and indifference were terrifying. I took them to the Royal Gallery and pointed out Charles I's death warrant and other high-lights. Some couldn't even be bothered to look. In the 'No' Lobby, I showed them the page from the official record on the day the Gun-powder Plot was discovered. Again, some didn't even glance, although the teachers kept saying how fascinating it all was. When we went out on the terrace, they all with one exception refused to have their picture taken with me. I confess to feeling a little hurt, although I don't think it was anything personal. A girl asked whether the outside of the building was cleaned every day and that was that. A teacher said that many of them were more interested in shopping. Is this the future?

In the evening, another foray into the Broadcasting Bill. This time on cross-media ownership. The Bill proposes that any national newspa-per company with more than 20 per cent of the market should not be allowed to buy into television. Incredibly, Jack Cunningham and Lewis Moonie are arguing that all restrictions should be removed and the market should be allowed to rip, subject to a public interest test to be enforced either by the Monopolies Commission (which so far has proved utterly useless) or the Independent Television Commis-sion. This appears to be a piece of opportunism devised on the spur of the moment in committee when a couple of Tories rebelled against the government. The trouble is the rebellion was defeated and we are now saddled with a policy utterly at odds with everything for which we have previously stood. I chatted to Lewis, an intelligent, easy-going fellow. He seems genuinely to believe in the new line. It has a certain logic, even if it does imply a touching faith in the ability of regulators to police some of the mightiest vested interests in the land. I put down an amendment excluding all the tabloids on the grounds that those who have given us junk journalism ought not to be allowed to give us junk TV. After a lot of agonising I decided to press it to a vote in defiance of the official line. Jack asked me – gently, it has to be said – to withdraw. I declined. The whips stood in the lobby telling everyone not to vote for it and I stood beside them urging people to vote. In the event, we attracted about seventy-five members (including half a dozen nationalists).

A chat with a Labour veteran in the Tea Room. 'In government,' he said, 'backbenchers are treated like shit. Until they rebel. Then they get respect.' Moral of story: get your rebellion in early.

Wednesday, 3 July

To a press conference at Millbank to launch my Animal Husbandry (Review) Bill, which aims to phase out factory farming. While I was there news came in that the Senior Salaries Review Body was recommending a truly outrageous £9,000 increase for members' pay and I was asked to do interviews for the lunchtime TV news and the *World at One*. Later, when I returned to Millbank to record an interview on my Bill for *Farming Today*, I was intercepted outside on the pavement by John Sergeant and recorded another sound bite on pay which I gather was used on both the six and nine o'clock bulletins. Meanwhile, my speech on the welfare of farm animals was delivered – at the not inconvenient time of four o'clock – to an almost empty Chamber and an entirely empty press gallery. I doubt whether a single word will reach the outside world. The entire centre of gravity has shifted away from the Chamber to Millbank. I would stand a far better chance of smuggling a message to the nation if I stayed out of the Chamber altogether and hung around outside Four Millbank offering my services as a rent-a-quote.

Thursday, 4 July

Sure enough, today's papers contain not a word about my Animal Husbandry Bill. Not even a mention on *Today in Parliament*. I have spoken three days running, each time on fairly weighty issues, and so far as I am aware not a word has reached the outside world. In the last couple of weeks the *Independent* has scrapped its parliamentary column, the last national newspaper to bother with one. Now all we are left with is sketch writers and the BBC and, as one of the clerks in the Public Bill Office remarked to me this morning, even the BBC is succumbing. Editorialising is on the increase and PM's Questions often occupy five or six minutes on *Today in Parliament* while major debates pass virtually unreported.

The government has decided to recommend a rise of only 3 per cent for MPs – which will save me having to put down an amendment to that effect. People have been badgering me all day about my views on the subject, including one old-timer who sits in the Tea Room going on about his pension (as he has done for much of the last decade – when not asleep in the Library). Several people made snide references to my books, as though they represent some vast source of extra wealth (less than £750 last year). Alex Salmond told me he'd be earning £80,000 if he had stayed at the Royal Bank of Scotland (where he was the chief economist). Someone else gave me a breakdown of his mileage (he reckons he'll lose several thousand if the mileage allowance is reduced as the Review Body have recommended). Why on earth he needs to drive everywhere I can't imagine. This afternoon, a call from Hilary Coffman in Tony Blair's office. She said Tony would also be urging 3 per cent and had requested that I 'put myself about' on the subject. I had only half an hour to spare, but I went over to Millbank and did interviews for ITN and the BBC. None of this is going to do my Shadow Cabinet vote much good, but who cares?

Monday, 8 July

I came across Andrew Mackinlay in the Tea Room, mightily exercised by the proposed cancellation of the Shadow Cabinet elections. He had just been in to see Blair and was not well received. 'He reminded me of my headmaster, in his shirtsleeves, looking disapproving. I was scared of my headmaster, but I'm not scared of him.'

Blair's public position is that he is relaxed about whether or not the elections go ahead, but it is quite clear that he is up to his neck in the attempt to stop them. Andrew said to him, 'If you are relaxed, then be relaxed,' to which Blair apparently replied, 'If they go ahead we will lose the general election.' If that's what he really thinks, he has totally lost his sense of proportion.

Andrew also told Tony to stop the whips pressing everyone for nominations in this year's leadership election in which, of course, he is the only candidate. 'You are behaving like Enver Hoxha,' he said. 'Some of those who have nominated you don't actually like you.'

Tuesday, 9 July

Gordon Brown made a rare appearance in the Tea Room. He has moved office from Millbank to the Cloisters. Word has obviously reached him that he was too remote. 'Now,' he said, 'I can be criticised to my face.' Was that remark aimed at me? He has been told that he will have to vacate his office when the Queen Mum dies, since the Cloisters will be needed as an ante-chamber for the Lying in State.

Wednesday, 10 July

This evening, the long-awaited debate on pay. Mine was the only back-bench speech against. There was great deal of barracking from the Tories, but our side behaved reasonably (although I was told afterwards that there was a good deal of sotto voce heckling). It was clear from the outset that there was a big majority in favour of the full whack. When I got into the 'Aye' Lobby (in favour of 3 per cent) it was almost deserted apart from the Prime Minister who was chatting to Nicholas Soames. Soames was saying that his salary (as a minister of defence) was about the equivalent of his brother's annual bonus. 'Mind you, he works jolly hard.' His brother, needless to say, is a banker.

Major was looking anxiously around. 'There don't seem to be many of us here,' I said.

'They'll be along in a minute,' he said uncertainly. Eventually, people began to dribble in.

It was an odd combination. The leaders of all three parties, a handful of left-wingers and a lot of ministers – but by no means all – most of whom were hoping to be defeated so that they could pocket the full 26 per cent and the credit for having voted the right way.

I said to Major, 'You are in government, we aspire to government – that's why we are in the same lobby.'

He said, 'That's a very cynical remark.' What I meant was no government can afford to be seen encouraging huge public sector wage increases. Alastair Goodlad, the Tory Chief Whip, came along and I remarked, referring to the government members in the 26 per cent lobby, 'There are going to be some kneecaps broken tomorrow.'

'Not tomorrow,' he replied. 'Tonight.'

The big rises went through overwhelmingly, of course. A black day for the reputation of politics and politicians. This will be quoted back at us for years to come.

I shall give away everything over 3 per cent. That's the only way I can retain my self-respect.

Thursday, 11 July

A visit from Nelson Mandela. You have to hand it to our ruling class. They do a wonderful line in state visits. Mandela got the full treatment. State trumpeters, Yeomen of the Guard, Gentlemen at Arms … The Lord Chancellor's procession included species that are all but extinct – the Purse-bearer and the Fourth Clerk of the Table (Judicial). Some magnificent ruling-class specimens on display. The Honourable Corps of Gentlemen, led up the central aisle by a character straight out of central casting with a ramrod back and a hat overflowing with feathers. The Band of the Grenadier Guards playing the South African national anthem.

Wonderfully satisfying to watch all those Tories paying homage to one of ours. Even Thatcher was there, appropriately seated level with the great man's ankles. The Speaker, Betty Boothroyd, rubbed salt, saying how proud she was to have taken part in demonstrations outside South Africa House. I overheard a few Tory wives tut-tutting about her speech, but it was spot on.

Much fallout in the media from last night's vote on pay. I passed Tony Blair's press spokesman, Dave Hill, in the corridor and we agreed it will discredit us far more than the Tories. He said, 'People will say, "You are all the same – but you hold yourselves up as better."'

Friday, 12 July

The *Echo* has gone to town on my opposition to the pay rise. Last night they led on my promise to give away the rise and the leader page was dominated by a feature headed 'Mullin – Voice in the Wilderness'.

The surgery lasted nearly four hours. Customers included several victims of the tightening benefit regulations and a youth who had taken a place on a training scheme only to give it up for the prospect of a permanent job. The job disappeared after two weeks and when he tried to sign on again he was told he must wait six months because he had abandoned his place on a training scheme. Also, an old lady from Plains Farm who was looking after her husband who had chronic emphysema. She had made the mistake of buying her council house and then discovered that she didn't qualify for help with a chairlift, so the old boy was confined to the living room. They had a wheel-chair, but she couldn't get it up and down the steps so he hadn't been out of the house for a year, except to hospital. The poor old soul was at her wits' end and broke down in tears.

Home at 9.15 p.m. My earliest night this week.

Saturday, 13 July

To Durham for the Miners' Gala. Sarah and I marched in with the Wearmouth band from the New Inn. Outside the prison, just as we were entering the County Cricket Ground, the bandmaster dropped dead in front of us. We told Sarah that he had fainted and she seemed to accept that. What a way to go.

Monday, 15 July

Blair has backed down over the Shadow Cabinet elections. Instead of being held in October, they are to be brought forward to next week. New Labour's first ever defeat at the hands of the poor bloody infantry.

Tuesday, 16 July

To Westminster to receive the Dalai Lama. It is twenty-four years this month since our first meeting in Dharamsala. We began with a well-attended press conference in the Jubilee Room, during which he remarked that he was 'to some extent a socialist ...' Not often one hears that word used in the Palace of Westminster these days. He added, '... or even half Marxist'. No thunderbolt came from heaven. Hardly an eyebrow was raised. Wonderful not to have to depend on votes for a living.

After the press conference he addressed a meeting of MPs, peers and diplomats in the Grand Committee Room, which was full, but not overflowing. 'Good to see you are on the side of the angels this time,' Ken Baker whispered as I walked up the aisle behind HH. Jack Weatherill, a former Speaker, presided. HH spoke without notes. He talked of compassion, what he called inner disarmament and reducing hatred. His English remains as imperfect as it was when we first met. Every so often he lapses into Tibetan until an interpreter who stands just behind him supplies the missing word. Asked how we could help, he said simply, 'Encourage the Chinese to negotiate.' There was a Chinese diplomat in the audience so no doubt the message went home. How foolish the Chinese are not to deal with this man. He is the best they are ever going to get. What's more he is the only Tibetan leader with the moral authority to make a compromise stick. As he said when I took him to see Robin Cook later, 'My people follow me with a blind faith.'

In the evening I went to Jack Straw's room for an end-of-term drink. We talked about TB's habit of constantly rewriting key policy statements up until the last moment. Jack gave a hilarious account of the new Clause IV, with Tony in Blackpool scrabbling through his briefcase for a bit of paper containing the latest version. Drafting 'Paths to the Future', the latest polling document, had, said Jack, been a nightmare.

Wednesday, 17 July

At the select committee in the evening we debated the chairman's draft report on handguns. Apart from a bit of tinkering it proposes to do nothing about anything, despite Dunblane. I am beginning to realise the extent to which the Tories are in hock to the gun lobby. It is becoming clear that Michael Howard wants to use our report as a cover for inaction. We can't let them get away with it. I stayed behind after the meeting and discussed with the clerks an amendment which should put some clear blue water between the Tories and ourselves.

This evening to Church House, where Tony Blair was addressing a reception for animal welfare organisations, something I first urged on him a year or more ago. When I asked our animal welfare spokesman, Elliot Morley, if the media was being invited he said, 'Tony's office want to keep it quiet.' Why? Who are we afraid offending? Surely not the farmers? Most of them don't vote for us anyway. It can't be that it would cost too much money, because it would cost little or nothing. Having heard the speech, however, I can well see why we should want to keep quiet. It was Blair at his most bland. Halfway through he lapsed into his familiar refrain about rights and responsibilities, which seemed to be of little relevance to animal welfare. It seemed to be all about creating the illusion of concern while promising nothing.

Thursday, 18 July

It is becoming clear that although the Shadow Cabinet elections are going ahead, they are not going to be free. All those who stand a chance of unseating Harriet Harman are being leaned upon not to stand. It has been made clear that their careers will suffer if they break ranks. The whips are coming on very heavy. 'Why don't you show some loyalty?' one said to Mike Gapes. Dale Campbell-Savours, who is running Ann Clwyd's campaign, says, 'I have heard things that would make your hair curl.' People are being offered next week off, on condition they sign proxy forms and hand them to the whips. Ken Purchase told me that he asked the whips for the night off on Monday and was told that he needn't come in at all next week, providing he authorises one of them to vote on his behalf. All the old corruption is resurfacing. It's all about saving Harriet. New Labour is beginning to look remarkably like Old Labour.

Friday, 19 July
Sunderland

Called on a constituent whose wife was burned alive by a gas leak on New Year's Day. The leak came from 100-year-old pipes under the pavement outside. She went into the kitchen, switched on the oven and was turned into a fireball in front of her family. The poor woman lived for three days after the accident. The children are traumatised, the house was destroyed. The family were left with only the clothes they stood up in. They didn't even have clothes for the funeral. Friends and neighbours rallied round, but not a word was heard from British Gas until, unbelievably, they received a bill for gas – in the wife's name. No sooner had that been sorted out than another came. The inquest was this week and apparently, even after seven months, the Transco engineer was remarkably ill-informed about the causes of the leak and what had been done to prevent a repetition. If I don't get satisfaction, I shall organise a debate.

Monday, 22 July

Everyone is talking about the Shadow Cabinet elections. Irene Adams, who on Thursday was insisting that she would stand regardless, has suddenly withdrawn. What's more, she is nowhere to be seen. One can only guess at what persuaded her not to run.

This evening, sitting in a nearly empty Tea Room, I saw a mouse. It didn't seem at all shy and ran around happily in the middle of the floor for several minutes.

Tuesday, 23 July

I came across Michael Foot sitting on a bench by St Stephen's entrance and spent a while chatting to him. Frail, unshaven, skeletal, long snow-white hair and wearing a pair of dirty old trainers. A lovely old gent. He remarked on my stand on members' pay. 'If the party had followed your lead, the whole country would have cheered.'

Wednesday, 24 July

At the party meeting, a debate about child benefit, on a motion from Jeremy Corbyn. At the end the vote was four to one in favour of Gordon's review. What a supine lot we are. In the current climate, if the regime suggested bombing Vietnam, the parliamentary party would probably vote for it.

At the select committee this afternoon we finalised our report on guns. We divided along party lines. My amendment, calling for a ban on handguns, an end to shotgun licences in urban areas and for airguns to be brought within the licensing system, was lost 6–5. It will, however, stop Howard using the select committee report as an excuse for doing nothing.

The Shadow Cabinet election results are a triumph for the regime. Everyone re-elected by a record margin. Jack Cunningham has taken the vacancy created by Joan Lestor's departure. More than fifty votes separate Harriet from Ann Clwyd, the runner-up. I collected sixty-six, my usual quota. We deserve everything we get from now on.

Thursday, 25 July

First day of the recess. John Prescott was on the *Today* programme denying that any pressure had been applied on the Shadow Cabinet elections.

Later, we heard that Harriet has been swapped with Chris Smith, presumably because she can be relied upon not to offer the slightest resistance to Gordon's plans over child benefit. Clare Short has been moved from Transport to Overseas Development, thereby maintaining the tradition of having a different Overseas Development spokesman every year.

Monday, 29 July

The regime is after Ken Livingstone for claiming that the Shadow Cabinet elections were rigged. He's right, of course, but unfortunately he chose to unburden himself to readers of the *Mail on Sunday*. Irene Adams has been wheeled out to deny that she was leaned upon to stand down. Everywhere the sound of cocks crowing. If Ken is to be deselected, a show trial will have to be organised. Witnesses will have to be intimidated. Perjury will have to be concocted. I foresee months of warfare ahead. The Tories must be relishing the prospect. Is Blair really as insecure and petty as Kinnock, after all?

Friday, 2 August

Rang the Fees Office to find out how much I must transfer to my donations account in order to dispose of the recent salary increase. The answer – £371 a month, after tax.

Friday, 9 August
Chillingham

Jorgen* and I rose early and walked up Ros Hill, from where, it is alleged, five castles can be seen. We managed to spot only four – Dunstanburgh, Banburgh, Lindisfarne and Chillingham. Jorgen recounted the wonderful story of his uncle who telephoned Stalin. The uncle was a communist student in Copenhagen in the 1930s. One evening he and a group of friends were heatedly disagreeing over some fine point of ideology when someone had a bright idea. 'Why don't we ask Stalin?' So they telephoned the Kremlin and asked in a confident tone to be put through to Stalin. The Kremlin switchboard operator, no

---

*Jorgen Oestrom Muller, a senior official in the Danish Foreign Ministry, who married a Vietnamese friend of my wife.

doubt too terrified to argue, put them straight through. Whereupon, speaking slowly in German, which apparently Stalin understood, the youth explained that he was one of a group of Danish students and they wanted the Great Leader and Wise Teacher to resolve an argument. There was a silence followed by laughter as Stalin realised what had happened. Then, '*Sie konnen sagen sie haben Stalin lacheln gehort.*' ('You can say that you have heard Stalin laugh.') After which the line went dead. History does not record the fate of the operator who put through the call.

Tuesday, 13 August

Our much-leaked handguns report is published today. The Tories have dug themselves into a great big pit. No doubt Ivan Lawrence thought he was doing Howard a favour by concluding that nothing could be done about anything only to find that the Home Office is rapidly back-pedalling, leaving Ivan and friends gently swinging in the wind.

The day began at 6.30 a.m. with a trip to Broadcasting House for the *Today* programme and ended with *Newsnight* at Television Centre. During the morning I spent an hour touring the studios at Millbank and then to New Labour's Media Centre for a press conference, chaired by Prescott. I haven't had so much attention since the Birmingham Six were released. In the afternoon I did the *Jimmy Young Show*, a clutch of local radio interviews and wrote an op-ed piece for the *Guardian* which I faxed over at about six.

Earlier this evening, a call from a slightly embarrassed Jon Hibbs, the *Telegraph*'s lobby correspondent. His masters, he said, were drafting a leader on the handgun report which, needless to say, will be sympathetic to the gun lobby and were looking for some way of discrediting me. They wanted to know my view on IRA decommissioning. I replied, 'Tell the bastards to do their worst.'

Wednesday, 14 August

The papers are full of the handgun report. The *Telegraph* seems to have had second thoughts about an IRA smear. There are several articles by Dunblane relatives. For the second time the *Sun* has printed pictures and telephone numbers of the six Tories on the committee. Being monstered by the *Sun* is a new experience for the Tories. They must be cursing Ivan for getting them into this.

Friday, 30 August

Customers at the surgery in the evening included two women complaining about a neighbour who, they said, was threatening to burn them out. Also, a man who had been awarded £1,900 in a routine industrial injury claim. The Unemployed Centre would have handled his claim for a flat fee of £100. However, he had made the mistake of going through a lawyer who had taken him for just about all of it. He showed me the solicitor's statement. It said 'We have pleasure in enclosing £22 ...' and then, adding insult to injury, '... please note this is subject to tax.' I shall threaten this thieving lawyer with publicity unless he drastically reduces his fee.

Friday, 6 September

The vice chairman of Chelsea Football Club, Matthew Harding, has donated £1 million to New Labour. We are starting to attract exactly the sort of people who went for Thatcher in the early eighties. I fear it will end badly.

Friday, 13 September

To Pennywell for a chat with Dave Wilkinson, the embattled headmaster of the local comprehensive. He has taught in inner-city schools all his life. Previous postings include Moss Side and Chapeltown, but this is by far his toughest assignment. As ever he is upbeat, but this time I detect a certain weariness. Although he would never concede it, I suspect that for the first time that he is beginning to wonder whether or not he is fighting a losing battle. Sixty-three per cent of his 1,000 pupils are on the special needs register. Just over half on free school meals. Under 10 per cent leave with five A to C grades at GCSE. There is chronic truancy. He recently wrote to every parent whose child had been absent for one day or more in four consecutive weeks – nearly 400 letters. Beyond the school gates mayhem reigns. Two or three times a week he has to confront intruders. The day after the London headmaster Philip Lawrence was murdered Dave was threatened by a knife-wielding youth who actually referred to the previous day's killing. In June he arrived for work – at the usual time, 7 a.m. – to find the school sealed off by armed police. They were raiding the home of one his pupils for guns and drugs – both were found.

Yet in the midst of chaos there are triumphs. Only yesterday an ex-pupil called in to tell him she had just graduated from the University of Sunderland with a 2.1 in psychology. Several of his school's kids have even made it to university at Durham. Morale among his teachers is, he says, good. Staff turnover is low. Everything is clean and in order. A haven of tranquillity in the midst of a disintegrating social fabric. Every year the ratchet turns a little tighter. Two years ago the school employed the services of two social workers to follow up truants. Since then the problem has got worse, but now there is only one – budget cuts. In the outside world the climate grows increasingly hostile. 'If you've got committed staff, it hurts to be constantly battered by league tables, OFSTED, Woodhead and co. ...' The school has just been 'OFSTEDed'. The inspectors came from Buckinghamshire, another planet. The lay inspector, a former university professor, fell asleep during a meeting with staff. To be fair, however, the report was good. And so it damn well should be. Dave Wilkinson and his team are heroes. Like so many others around here, he clings on desperately, praying for a change of government, hoping it will make a difference, but at the back of his mind suspecting it might not.

This afternoon my annual visit to Vaux Brewery. The managing director, Frank Nicholson, a thoroughly decent one-nation Tory with a real interest in the welfare of his workforce, recounted an exchange with a friend who said, 'I've sold my shares in your company.'

'Why?'

'Because my stockbroker told me that you care more about your employees than you do about your shareholders.'

Saturday, 14 September

Steve Byers has triggered a row at the Trades Union Congress where he dined with four journalists who afterwards reported that, after the election, New Labour is planning to 'dump' the unions. I am sure he didn't use that word, but I am equally sure that Blair plans to use state funding as a way of breaking loose. And why not? Only about a third of the workforce are union members and of those only a little over half even vote for us. I could live with a new relationship. What worries me, however, is that our masters are spending a lot of time sucking up to big business. What is the point of exchanging dependence on one mighty vested interest for dependence on another?

Sunday, 15 September

Kim Howells has written a piece in the *Sunday Times* saying Labour should dump 'socialism'. Coming hard on the heels of the Byers row at the TUC, we need this like a hole in the head. His timing is impeccable – just as people are beginning to realise that the market doesn't offer the solution to all our problems.

Monday, 16 September

This evening to St Chad's branch. By no means full of left-wingers, but people were angry about Byers and Howells. Someone asked angrily whether the discipline that our leaders keep demanding from the members applied to the leaders? Also, a feeling that the leaders view the party as a troublesome pressure group that hinders their pursuit of power. Rightly or wrongly, the impression we are giving is that we don't believe in anything.

Tuesday, 17 September

To the Civic Centre to meet with the senior officers group. I addressed the big picture. So far as I am able to judge my talk went down fairly well. The one thing everyone agrees about is that the principal threat to the social fabric comes from young, unskilled males who, with the collapse of the shipyards and the mines, are useless either as fathers or providers. Twenty years ago they would have gone into apprentice-ships, started mixing with adults and moderated their behaviour accordingly. Now they just wander the streets causing mayhem. To be fair to New Labour, this is a point that has been firmly grasped. Whether we can raise the means to make a difference is another matter. The genie is out of the bottle. Putting it back is going to be difficult. To start with, of course, it means spending some public money and the middle classes simply may not stand for that. Maybe we just have to write off a generation – Thatcher's generation – many of whom wouldn't be capable of work if it became available tomor-row. Instead we must concentrate on making sure that the next gen-eration don't disappear down the same plughole. The alternative is a steady slide into chaos and endless baying for greater and greater ret-ribution, which won't make the slightest difference.

Afterwards, the chief executive, Colin Sinclair said he was opposed to regional government. If there was a referendum, he thought we would lose. 'No one is going to vote for an extra tier of government.' What we had to do was restore democratic control over the Develop-ment Agency and other quangos. We might even like to think about giving local authorities control over the purchasing of health care. Finally, he said, local authorities weren't looking to a Labour govern-ment to write out big cheques. Just for an end to the relentless down-ward pressure on services and the removal of the first C from Compulsory Competitive Tendering.

Sunday, 22 September

To Bishopwearmouth cemetery, where I have never been before. We came across the tomb of John Doxford 'of St Bede's Terrace' and his wife Mary, who died in 1899 and 1912 respectively. The original occu-pants of my house.

Tuesday, 1 October
Labour Party Conference, Blackpool

The big news today is that Neil Hamilton has abandoned his libel action, with the result that the *Guardian* has declared open season. Today's front page is dominated by a large picture of Hamilton, under the heading, 'A Liar and a Cheat'.

I had intended to watch The Speech from my hotel room to avoid the embarrassment of being ambushed by television cameras demanding instant reaction. However, I fell in with Bruce Grocott and Bryan Davies on their way in and sat with them. Some bright spark has cut the seating for MPs and candidates by two-thirds so we queued for half an hour (in front of a sign which said 'Labour will reduce waiting lists') and only just found seats. The Speech was preceded by a five-minute film so vulgar as to make Kinnock's Sheffield extravaganza seem tasteful. Neil and Glenys, sitting one row in front, looked uneasy. The Speech, for the first fifty minutes or so, was good, addressed entirely to the nation rather than to the party and including substantial commitments. The last ten minutes, however, was truly awful – Sheffield going on Nuremberg. A Union Jack was projected onto the backdrop. The Man then delivered himself of a series of carefully worded 'vows', hostages to fortune some of which are bound to feature in Tory Party broadcasts a few years hence ('Read my lips'). There was then a good deal of meaningless claptrap about Labour 'coming home'. Cherie, who had been sitting in the audience with Tony's father (a former chairman of the Durham Conservative Association), rushed up to the platform and planted an awkward kiss on The Man's cheek. There was then a standing ovation, during which the royal couple went walkabout. The ovation went on far too long and reeked of triumphalism. And sure enough, as soon as it was over I was caught by not one, but two camera crews. Of course, I said it was wonderful. Anything less effusive would have been deemed treachery. Next year I shall watch on TV.

Bruce Grocott, incidentally, asked whether I had received a call from Tony at the time of the last reshuffle. I didn't, as it happens, but he said they had talked of giving me Overseas Development. Grateful though I am for the thought, what I am really after is the chairmanship of the Home Affairs Committee. My fear is that some disappointed office-holder or privy councillor at a loose end will, at the last moment, be parachuted in over my head.

In the evening I addressed a fringe meeting organised by the Law Society. Afterwards I was approached by a lawyer who had once been Clerk to the Justices in Portsmouth. He had also worked in the clerks department at Birmingham magistrates court when the Birmingham Six came up on remand. He told me three interesting things: (1) Within weeks of the bombing rumours were circulating among local lawyers that the police had caught the wrong people. (2) Lord Lane had told him twice, once before and once after the convictions were quashed, that they were guilty. (3) When he worked in Portsmouth in 1979, it was discovered that thirty-five of the ninety-six magistrates were Masons. This was considered to be unhealthy and the local Masonic hierarchy was persuaded to agree a five-year moratorium on the appointment of Masons. Despite this, however, more magistrates were Masons by the end than at the beginning – the brotherhood had simply waited until they were recruited before signing them up.

Phil Kelly told me he overheard a delegate chatting up a policeman outside the Imperial. The policeman said, 'Sorry, sir, we are not allowed to talk about politics.'

To which the delegate replied, 'Neither are we.'

Wednesday, 2 October

Another BBC reception. Another talk with Bob Phillis. He remarked, apropos of Neil Hamilton, that only once in his career had someone attempted to bribe him – and that was a former Labour MP. Robert Maxwell, of course. At the time Phillis was managing director of ITN Publications and Maxwell had just bought a printing company. Bob was summoned to Maxwell's suite at Claridge's. The dialogue was as follows:

'Twenty-five – do you want it in used notes or American Express?'
'I'm sorry?'
'I've bought the printing company ...'

'Yes, I had noticed.'

'… and I need your contract. We both know how the world works, so how do you want it, cash or American Express?'

On the way into the *Mirror* reception I passed Steve Richards who used to work for the BBC and is now political correspondent at the *New Statesman*. He said he is constantly harassed by our spin doctors. 'If I write something they don't like, I get a call within an hour or two of publication – from Alastair Campbell or Peter Mandelson. "You don't understand …," they say. It's very effective, I'm afraid. After a while you ask yourself how they will react every time you type a paragraph.'

David Montgomery approached me at the *Mirror* reception and asked if I had seen Polly Toynbee's piece about Murdoch. He said if something isn't done about him soon, it will all be over. He added that he had lunched with Tony Blair today and told him so.

Saturday, 12 October

The surgery at Ryhope in the evening lasted three hours. Customers included a man whose wife kicked him out when she opened a letter from the Child Support Agency and learned that he was supporting a child he had fathered with another woman long before he was married. He is now living with his mother and supporting two families. Another life wrecked by the CSA. He was remarkably lacking in bitterness.

Also two security men from the port. They earn £3.87 an hour plus a small shift allowance and have just been told they are to be sacked and the work put out to tender. It has been hinted that, if they were to put in an in-house tender at about £2.60 an hour, they might get their jobs back.

Tuesday, 15 October

Lunch in the Tea Room with Gwyneth Dunwoody, who is very hostile to New Labour. 'It's about time they realised that a 3 per cent swing is only a 3 per cent swing if you can count upon the other 35 per cent. I spoke at three meetings last week and everyone is saying the same thing – what's happening to the party? I find myself saying, "I disagree with this, with that ..." I'm surprised someone doesn't stick up their hand and say, "Mrs Dunwoody, are you sure you're a Labour candidate?" I hope I'm chucked out a couple of months after the election so that I can sit as Independent Labour.'

Ray Fitzwalter came in for dinner. Afterwards, as we took coffee in the Pugin Room, he remarked, 'The one thing that even Thatcher must regret is that the profit motive has eclipsed the public service ethic.' I doubt whether Thatcher regrets it, or has even noticed its disappearance.

Wednesday, 16 October

Lord Cullen's report on Dunblane was published this afternoon. Michael Howard made a statement saying he will ban most – but by no means all – handguns and weapons storage at home. He managed to make it sound as if this had been his intention all along, but actually it amounts to a total climbdown. He originally intended to do as little as he could get away with. That's why Ivan Lawrence was put up to write his ridiculous report. He was well and truly set up. Basically Howard has accepted the main plank of our minority report. At this afternoon's meeting of the select committee Ivan opened by offering his 'grudging congratulations'. John Greenway did a passable impression of the Vicar of Bray, declaring that he would have no difficulty voting for the new measures. I bet he won't. What fun it will be seeing all those Tories trooping grimly through the 'Ban Handguns' lobby. Jill Knight was upset about the monstering she and her Tory colleagues had received from the *Sun* for opposing action on handguns. As a result she had been deluged with hate mail and even death threats against her grandchildren. Ivan said he had been sent excreta. They wanted our support for a complaint to the Press Commission. We sympathised and agreed to go along with it (a fat lot of good that it will do). The truth is, of course, that most Tories aren't used to being on the receiving end of the sort of hate campaign that is usually reserved for the Arthur Scargills and Peter Tatchells of this world.

Thursday, 24 October

The start of the committee's prisons inquiry. We began with a visit to HMP Doncaster, a purpose-built private prison. As prisons go the regime seemed fairly relaxed. The wings were light and airy, about one-third of the staff were women. With the exception of the top grades all staff have been recruited locally from outside the Prison Service and are paid considerably less. We were allowed to mingle freely with prisoners, most of whom had experience of many different prisons and seemed to think that this was the best – Hull, by common consent, being the worst. Then we drove to Full Sutton at which, although only nine years old, the climate was depressingly institutional. Security is obsessive. We had to take off our shoes and empty our pockets before being body searched. They told us with great pride that Ann Widdecombe had received the same treatment when she visited. We went on one of the maximum security wings housing serious criminals. Big surly men with shaved heads, covered in tattoos. You could feel the suppressed violence as they squeezed past in the narrow corridor. There was no natural light. The cells were untidy and the air stale. We were told that the food budget averages out at £1.37 per head per day. It is hard to believe that much good can come of warehousing human beings like this.

By evening we were in Manchester. We are staying at the Palace Hotel, a magnificent conversion from the old Refuge Insurance building. Ivan Lawrence, a talented pianist, played the grand piano in the dining room after dinner – until a leg fell off and we all slunk upstairs to bed.

Friday, 25 October

To HMP Manchester, formerly Strangeways. A lot of money has been spent since the riot and the atmosphere on the wings seemed far less oppressive than at Full Sutton. The management contract was put out to tender and the in-house bid won. The trouble is, the Home Office keep rewriting the contract. First, they want year-on-year cost reductions. Then they demand that Manchester take more prisoners than it is contracted for within more or less the same budget. At the end of the visit we were addressed for five minutes by the chairman of the Prison Officers Association, a real chip off the old block. His theme was 'we know best how to run a prison', everything would be okay if the government stopped interfering. He did score one bull's eye. Ivan asked about morale among his members and he replied, 'It fell sharply when we were awarded 3 per cent and you got 26 per cent.' When John Greenway and Walter Sweeney attempted to shake hands he demanded to know which party they were from. 'What does it matter?' asked Greenway. 'It does to me,' he said.

Finally, to Buckley Hall at Rochdale, a Category C prison run by Group 4 Security. The local MP, Liz Lynne, has been complaining long and loud about it, but with the exception of a couple of incidents early on I could see no real basis for her complaints. A third of the staff were women. Senior staff were recruited from the Prison Service and the officers were all from outside the service. There were unions, but not the Prison Officers Association. We asked the governor what the main difference was between his establishment and those in the state sector. He replied, 'The absence of cynicism among staff.' The regime seemed as good as anything we had encountered elsewhere. There was a good library. Most prisoners were gainfully employed during the day. Group 4 were naturally keen to impress, since there is big money to be made out of prisons. Every private prison has a Home Office controller. The one at Buckley Hall was a woman in her fifties. She is responsible for adjudicating disciplinary charges and contract compliance. There is an obvious danger that controllers can go native. Indeed, she told me that the controller at Doncaster had left the Prison Service and signed up with the company running the prison.

The purpose of this inquiry, from Ivan's point of view, is to produce a report in favour of privatising. Obviously, we have to avoid being taken for a ride, but we are going to have to accept that the private sector has something to offer. Old Labour's big weakness was to become obsessed with ideologically correct mechanisms of delivering public service. We have to start judging by results.

Monday, 28 October

To Gateshead Civic Centre, in the company of half a dozen colleagues
for a meeting with officers of the Tyne and Wear Pensioners Association. I was taken aback by how angry they were. They really tore into
us. 'You have absolutely nothing to offer us. I've been a party member
all my life, but I'm going to have difficulty giving people a reason to
vote Labour. It's nearly five years since the election and we still don't
know what party policy is.' Dave Clelland did his best to put the party
line: our first priority will be to help the poorest pensioners. This
didn't go down at all well. What they want, of course, is a promise of
an across-the-board increase. A woman who owned her own home
said she had worked and saved all her life and she didn't want the
feckless to be brought up to her level. In vain did we seek to persuade
them that, if we committed ourselves to spending billions – and
putting up the basic rate of tax accordingly – on an across-the-board
pensions increase, we risked losing the election. They came out with
the usual nonsense about how there were eleven million pensioners
and we couldn't afford to ignore them. I pointed out that more pensioners vote Conservative than any other sector of the population and
that recent history showed that the more we promised poor pensioners the more the prosperous voted against us. That upset them even
more.

Wednesday, 30 October

At the select committee in the afternoon we spent the first hour
arguing about dangerous dogs followed by two hours of evidence on
prisons. The governors were sensible and undogmatic but, true to
form, the representatives of the Prison Officers Association dug themselves into a big pit. Ivan asked if anything had improved. They
couldn't think of a single example. No mention of the abolition of
slopping out or the end of three to a cell. No mention of the incentive
scheme for good behaviour, which everyone we met last week said
had been a success. Just total doom and gloom. Whereupon Ivan put
it to them that, given that the private sector was almost universally
positive in its outlook and the public sector almost universally

negative, why should the government opt for those whose outlook was wholly negative? There was no answer to that. At least none that was credible.

Friday, 1 November

On the train from Newcastle to Sunderland I ran into Ashok Kumar. His is one of the seats we must win to form a government, but he didn't seem optimistic. He said, 'The voters like Tony more than they like the party. We must stay above 45 per cent to win Langbaurgh.' We won't, of course.* I felt sorry for him.

Sunday, 3 November

The Tiny Tyrant rose at 4.30 a.m.

I took Sarah out for spin on her new roller skates (a birthday present from Ngoc and me). While she was practising in The Oaks I got chatting to an old boy sweeping leaves from his garden. 'I'm getting too old for this,' he said, wiping his brow. 'Well,' I said, thinking he was about seventy-five, 'you look in pretty good shape.'

To which he replied, 'Not bad, I suppose, for ninety-three.'

Tuesday, 5 November

With the other members of the Northern Group, a meeting with Tony Blair in the Shadow Cabinet Room. It opened with a brief presentation from Greg Cook, the party's pollster. The gist was that, although we did well out of the conference season, the Don't Knows were beginning to drift back to the Tories. Major was scoring well ahead of his party and people seemed more optimistic about the economy. We still score well with the under-thirty-fives, but they were less likely to vote than pensioners, where Tory support is strongest. Tony said there was no point in denying that the economy was in better shape than two years ago. We must emphasise fundamental weaknesses.

---

*In fact he was elected with a majority of 10,607 and held the seat until his death in 2010.

Unemployment, the crumbling social fabric. He said the Tories were planning to spend £7 million on a big negative advertising campaign in January in the hope of frightening the electorate. Their problem was, however, that fear of a fifth Tory government was greater than fear of us. Let's hope he's right.

Half a dozen of us chipped in. Dave Clelland, Bill Etherington and I reported on our meeting with the pensioners last week and said we must have something to offer them. Tony acknowledged the problem but said we could not make big spending promises. 'I am sure that our tax and spending line is right. I remember so clearly in '87 and '92 that what started out as cherished commitments suddenly became liabilities.'

Thursday, 7 November

Bill Clinton has been re-elected by a landslide and there are rumours that one of his spin doctors is coming over to advise New Labour.

Tuesday, 12 November

Terry Davis has asked me to join our delegation to the Council of Europe. 'I don't think you've got much chance of becoming a minister under New Labour,' was how he put it. I mentioned my real ambition and he replied, 'I don't think New Labour is going to want Chris Mullin as chairman of the Home Affairs Select Committee.' I said that I had been doing the job for our side for the last four years. He said, 'That won't cut much ice.' There is no way I am going to join the Council of Europe. All those pointless meetings. All that hanging about at airports. After a decent interval I shall drop Terry a polite note declining.

Saturday, 16 November

Tribune contains an article under the nom de plume Cassandra saying the parliamentary party is deeply disillusioned with the Blair regime and predicting that he will be replaced by Robin Cook, soon after he wins the election. Not a very credible thesis. If we couldn't bring our-selves to remove obvious losers like Foot or Kinnock, it is not very likely that we would sack a leader who had put us back in government for the first time in nearly twenty years. The article is said to be the work of a senior Labour MP with front-bench experience and, they might have added, poor judgement.

Monday, 18 November

Yesterday's *Sunday Times* reported that a clutch of millionaire busi-nessmen were funding Blair's office through a blind trust. Apparently it's all right, providing he doesn't know where the money is coming from. As far as I'm concerned it stinks. How on earth are we going to put clear water between us and the Tories when our arrangements are so similar?

Sandra Sheal, whose husband is serving life for a part he is alleged to have played in a particularly nasty murder in a Belfast club, came to see me. He was convicted almost entirely on the basis of a statement extracted at Castlereagh during three days of unrecorded interviews. Same old story. No solicitor. No tape recorder and, of course, no jury. Incredible, in the light of all that has happened, that the courts in Northern Ireland are still sending people away for life on this basis. There is an appeal pending. I advised her to get as many distinguished observers as possible, to let the judges know they are being watched.

Tuesday, 19 November
Brixton Road

I was number four at PM's Questions (what a run of luck I have had this year). I asked if it were still Major's position that there was a moral case for reducing taxation. If so, what was the moral basis for cutting taxes before an election and putting them up as soon as it was over? It seemed to go down well on our side. Lots of people, including Peter Mandel-son, patted me on the back. I should have asked about the Rwandan refugee crisis in Zaire really but no one would have been interested.

Rang Ngoc. She says the Tiny Tyrant rose at 4.30 this morning.

Wednesday, 20 November

The Tory Lie Machine swung into full gear this morning with an outrageous claim that Labour's spending programme will cost £30 billion. Hilarious really, considering that the complaint from most people is that we are promising little or nothing. Public opinion is obviously being softened up for a big poster campaign in the new year alleging that a Labour government will cost the average family £1,000, £2,000, £3,000 – you name it – in extra taxes. A straight repeat of the line that worked so well for them last time round. Will it work twice? Even if no one believes the figures, enough mud may stick. What a depressing business politics is becoming. Just an exchange of slogans dreamed up by rival advertising agencies.

Thursday, 21 November

We debated air weapons and shotguns in the committee on the Firearms Bill this morning. Doug Henderson moved amendments which would have brought airguns within the licensing system and increased the age – presently fourteen – at which children could use them unsupervised. The Tories were having none of it. They couldn't have been less interested. Mostly they chatted among themselves as our side listed examples of the mayhem caused by out-of-control youths with air weapons. I overheard one Tory regaling his neighbour with an account of his boyhood activities with an airgun. They are determined to do as little as they can get away with and they are seriously out of touch. At last, an issue on which there is clear blue water between us.

Monday, 25 November

I joined Ivan Lawrence in the Pugin Room, where he was entertaining two MPs from Ukraine who wanted to talk about party funding. He went on at length about how our system, while not perfect, had worked well. I let him go on for a while and said, 'There are two aspects of our system which you won't want to copy. One, an upper house based mainly on the hereditary principle. Two, a system of funding elections under which no one knows from where the ruling party gets its money.' With that, I departed.

I spent the rest of the evening watching Alan Bennett's, *The Madness of King George* on Channel Four. Talking of madness, on my way out through the Members' Lobby I noticed what appeared to be a bundle of bags and blankets lying across the entrance to the Chamber. On closer inspection the bundle turned out to contain Dame Elaine Kellett-Bowman. She was sleeping, like a dosser in a shop doorway, with her head resting on a mat in the doorkeeper's box. At first, I thought there was something wrong and went back to the policemen in the Central Lobby. 'She's all right, sir,' one of them, said. 'She just wants her usual seat for the Budget.'

'Her last Budget, you see?' said the other – as though that explained everything. Actually, I don't see. Not at all.

Tuesday, 26 November

Arrived at the House at 7.45 a.m. By now there was a queue of Tory MPs, headed by Kellett-Bowman, stretching all the way across the Members' Lobby. Some must have been waiting for hours. Also, several Labour members – Canavan, Skinner, Lewis – but they had just arrived, or so Dennis assured me. A funny place, this.

At 8.15 a.m., with half a dozen others, I boarded a coach at the members' entrance and set off for BBC Television Centre. Here John Birt and his senior managers – of whom there were many – briefed us. The BBC, far from sticking to what it is good at, has ambitious plans to expand into commercial activity and use the proceeds to subsidise the core business. 'We intend to be a pioneer of the digital age,' was how Birt put it. Murdoch and the licence fee were their chief concerns. 'We are not indulging in hyperbole,' he said. 'We believe we are at a critical moment.' Murdoch had taken extraordinary risks with an untried technology and he had won. He had tied up rights on soccer and movies for years to come. He had a subscription base of four to five million. It was not worth anyone else's while to invest in a set-top box because no one else had the 'drivers' – soccer and movies rights – to make it saleable. Therefore, everyone was going to have to use his system and it was vital that it be properly regulated, particularly the electronic programme guide. Otherwise, how will the consumer find other services in a world where the dominant player controls access? Birt added, 'Every member of the government now regrets that Murdoch was allowed to get into this position.'

The Budget in the afternoon was an anticlimax since most of it has been leaked. The usual pre-election strategy: a penny off income tax introduced with much fanfare. Then, tomorrow, John Gummer will claw it all back with a local authority settlement that obliges big increases in council tax – which can be blamed on us since we control most of local government. Ken Clarke was on good form for the first hour or so, but suddenly started to flag, just at the point where he should have been building to a climax. Blair responded brilliantly. Not only had he managed to master the details, he managed to combine humour with genuine passion. I don't regret having voted for him, despite all the tribulations he has put us through.

Elaine Kellett-Bowman, having queued all night for her seat, dozed for the first half of the Chancellor's speech in full view of the cameras. Foolish woman.

Wednesday, 27 November

To HMP Holloway with the select committee and a BBC television crew. We split into two groups. Ivan, who tends to dominate the proceedings, and John Greenway went one way and the rest of us went the other. Unfortunately the TV crew followed us so it was difficult to strike up much of a dialogue with inmates. I did talk to a woman in the mother-and-baby unit. They are allowed to keep their babies for the first nine months and after that they must part. About a third of the women are of non-European origin and about one-fifth foreign nationals, mostly drug 'mules' who will be deported on release. We traipsed around the wings with the camera crew in tow. There were single and double cells and even four-bed 'dormitories'. Every inmate had a noticeboard by her bed with pictures of children, sometimes – but not often – a picture of a male. Some of the noticeboards were bare. I guess some people have nothing to look forward to outside. There were workshops where women sorted and repaired clothes for charity and some sort of commercial temping service. The woman in charge was reluctant to say what they were paid.

The governor was a clean-cut, liberal man who, like most of the movers and shakers I meet nowadays, is several years younger than me. He has been there less than a year and seems to have turned the place round since the Chief Inspector of Prisons, David Ramsbotham, staged his walkout in protest against conditions at the end of last year.

In the afternoon we took evidence from Ramsbotham and a former Chief Inspector of Prisons, Sir Stephen Tumim. Both good witnesses. Humane, decent, the very best sort of upper-class English gents. Ivan whispered to me that he had a struggle to get Tumim his knighthood because certain people in high places – he didn't say who, but it's not hard to guess – didn't like him.

To Central Hall for a meeting organised by the Campaign for Press and Broadcasting Freedom about digital TV. I shared a platform with Polly Toynbee, who has done her best to alert the world to the Murdoch threat with a hard-hitting series of articles in the *Independent*. She has certainly upset our front bench, accusing them of lacking guts and failing to oppose. The truth is, of course, that neither of the main parties dare take on Murdoch for fear of having his newspapers unleashed against them. No point in going on about it, it's just an inescapable fact of political life.

Thursday, 28 November

Tony Blair spent PM's Questions trying to extract an admission from Major that taxes have increased. Tax, tax, tax, that's all we seem to talk about these days. The trouble is no one believes a word we say on the subject either.

Tuesday, 3 December

With Ann Clwyd, Tony Benn and several others I walked up Victoria to support a demonstration outside the Department of Trade and Industry against the sale of arms to Indonesia. We were preceded by a couple of Buddhist monks banging a drum. En route Tony was nobbled by an attractive young woman in a denim skirt and a jacket trimmed with artificial fur who engaged him in animated conversation all the way up Victoria. Later, after Tony and Ann had addressed the gathering, the same woman stepped forward and read out, with all the zeal of a recent convert, a three-page statement on the wickedness of the capitalist system. People applauded politely. I assumed she was a stray Trot, but she turned out to be the Marchioness of Worcester. Her name is Tracy. Not every day you come across a marchioness, let alone one called Tracy.

Mr Wang, a First Secretary at the Chinese embassy, came to the Tibet Group in the evening. He had with him two colleagues. One a fat commissar, the other a pale intellectual. Mr Wang was smug and self-assured. He wore a smart suit and cufflinks. He could have been a Hong Kong businessman. What a change from the days of Mao suits and slogans. He began by reading a prepared statement, coherent but contentious. It might have been drafted by Peter Mandelson. Then he answered our questions. No, they did not have political prisoners in Tibet, or anywhere else in China for that matter. They had only criminals, just like Britain. Yes, China was willing to negotiate with the Dalai Lama on condition that he gave up his demand for independence. When we pointed out that he already had, he said that you had to judge by actions rather than words. Tibetan exiles in Delhi were still staging demonstrations calling for independence. The Dalai Lama still maintained his own 'government'. Mr Wang made only one concession. The Cultural Revolution, he said, had been 'a nightmare – not only for Tibetans, but for all of us'. I asked if any of them had been to Tibet. Needless to say, none had.

Wednesday, 4 December

At the party meeting this morning we debated the new code of conduct. There were two controversies. The first was over whether we should be obliged to adhere to the 'policy' of the Parliamentary Labour Party. Jeremy Corbyn moved that we delete the word 'parliamentary' on the grounds that the PLP wasn't entitled to a separate existence. Dennis Skinner made a funny speech saying that an announcement on the *Today* programme didn't amount to party policy. It was only if it was repeated on the lunchtime and evening news and, finally, on *Newsnight*, that it could be considered official. Jeremy's amendment was voted down by a margin of about four to one.

The main debate was about clause 1(d), which creates a new offence of 'bringing the party into disrepute'. Incredibly, no one had tabled the obvious amendment, 'delete 1(d)', so the dispute was about whether the code should be accepted or rejected as a whole. Tony Benn reminded everyone that some of our most distinguished members – Stafford Cripps, Nye Bevan and Michael Foot – had the whip withdrawn for allegedly bringing the party into disrepute. If we went down that road again we would turn in on ourselves and provide our enemies with a field day. He should have stopped there, but instead he went on to tell one of his old jokes about Denis Healey being a tax-and-spend Chancellor and lost the attention of the meeting. Attention span in the parliamentary party is notoriously short at the best of times. Most of those present were payroll or prospective payroll. They just wanted to get the vote over and leave. Whenever someone went on too long or came up with an argument the Blairistas didn't want to hear, cries of 'get on with it' broke out all around.

Gerald Kaufman made an effective but chilling speech. The parliamentary party, he said, was not an adventure playground. Our job was to support Labour governments 'right or wrong'. He blamed the fact that he had spent most of his career in opposition on backbench indiscipline. Audrey Wise, who followed Gerald, said that the fact that Labour governments had not been re-elected had far more to do with the actions of ministers than humble backbenchers. She then spoiled her argument by regaling the meeting with her life and times supporting, as she put it, workers in struggle on various picket lines. Cue much groaning from loyalists. Jim Cousins, who, like me, opposed the code, leaned across and whispered that the Old Left were a liability.

Donald Dewar wound up, saying that the ultimate sanction would be used only in extraordinary circumstances. A similar offence existed in the party rulebook. Why should MPs be exempt from rules that applied to ordinary members? That drew a cheer. The code was endorsed by 86 votes to 27. What a gutless lot we are. As someone said afterwards, they were sure Donald Dewar would exercise his new powers responsibly, but supposing he were to be succeeded as Chief Whip by Nick Brown?*

Monday, 9 December

Into town for what turned out to be a rather drastic haircut. New Labour, new haircut. I also bought some new shoes. I need a new coat, too. My present one is frayed around the edges. Jacky says it would be all right in Hampstead, but not in Sunderland. I am sure she is right.

To London on the 18.50, feeling cold around the head, where my hair used to be.

Tuesday, 10 December
Brixton Road

A young man came to repair the boiler, the latest in a long line. He worked at it for two hours, but in the end admitted defeat. When he discovered I was an MP he became quite animated. He was surprised when I informed him that the *Sun* was not a Labour newspaper and seemed to think that one of the reasons for the decline of the NHS was because Indian migrants were buying up our medicine on prescription and sending it to relatives at home. How long had I been in the Labour Party, he wanted to know.

---

*He was.

'About thirty years.'

'Oh, so you really believe in it, then?'

'Yes.'

He wasn't stupid or particularly self-centred. He earned £14,000 a year, had a £40,000 mortgage and a wife who probably earned as much as he did (but would have to give up when they started a family). He had no recollection of life under anything but a Tory government and a low opinion of politicians in general (although I don't suppose he had ever met one before). Exactly the sort of person we must win over, if we are to form a government.

When I got to the House there was a message waiting from Donald Dewar. He showed me a statement about the single currency which he said had been agreed by the Big Four – Blair, Prescott, Brown and Cook. They wanted some 'sensible' left-wingers to endorse it. Roger Berry was also being asked. Would I be willing? The BBC is apparently snooping round trying to demonstrate that Labour is as split as the Tories and Donald was looking for something to show how united we all are. I asked for time to think and discussed the matter with Roger. We agreed that, with the possible exception of a couple of phrases, the statement was unobjectionable. The problem was that it was so obviously a put-up job, designed to paper over cracks, that it was bound to arouse suspicions. Besides which, why me? Roger knows all about economics, but no one has ever asked my opinion about the single currency. I went back to Donald and said that, happy as I was to endorse the sentiments, this didn't seem a very sensible enterprise. The Tories were already doing a good job of self-destructing and we ought to let them get on with it. He seemed to agree and hinted that the idea had come from higher up than him. I left it in his hands and was relieved to hear later that the scheme had been abandoned.

Jack Straw mentioned that he had recently been to see the new head of MI5, Stephen Lander. They had discussed accountability and, needless to say, the new man was against the service being made accountable to Parliament. Among his excuses, the absence of a secure room in the Palace of Westminster which I am sure we could sort out. Jack says he advised him to prepare for the possibility. Everything, of course, depends on our beloved Leader.

A brief exchange with Peter Archer about House of Lords reform, which, he says, could bog us down for months, if not years. He suggests we put Lords reform on the back burner until the Tories give us trouble, preferably over an issue to which our constituents can relate.

Wednesday, 11 December

A cup of tea with Jack Straw, who told a fascinating little tale about the time he was positively vetted. It happened in the late seventies when he was working for Barbara Castle. Jack was summoned to a room in Whitehall. On the desk was his security file which, even at that early stage in his career, was several inches thick. The National Union of Students, of which Jack had been president, was obviously heavily infiltrated. A report was even produced of a pub lunch he had had with a student communist. The information was so detailed that Jack was even able to narrow down the informants to one or two suspects. Years later a Tory MP with close links to the security services remarked out of the blue that the man who had interviewed him had just died. Jack went to the Library, looked up the obituary and recognised him at once. How thick is Jack's file now, I wonder. Perhaps he will get to see it when he is Home Secretary.

Thursday, 12 December
Brixton Road

I was number eight at PM's Questions, but since we rarely get beyond four I didn't spend much time worrying about it. I went off to address law students at Gray's Inn and returned just in time to hear my name called. I decided to ignore all the pettiness about taxes and went on Murdoch instead, adopting a lofty, statesmanlike posture in the hope of heading off any jibe against Tony for his trip to Australia. Afterwards, in the Tea Room, several Tories came over and said how much they agreed. A raw nerve has been touched.

Caught the 18.30 north. David Clark got on at York. I asked if he was looking forward to becoming Secretary of State for Defence. He looked around to make sure no one else was within earshot and then said he was beginning to suspect that he wasn't going to be in the Cabinet. He said he had checked standing orders and they clearly required that the Leader offer a Cabinet place to every elected member of the Shadow Cabinet but, if Tony decided not to, there is nothing anyone could do. 'I know it sounds awful,' he said. 'I trusted Neil Kinnock implicitly. I trusted John Smith. But I don't trust Tony.'

Monday, 16 December

Last night I dreamed that Betty Boothroyd had had a nervous break-down and leapt from the Speaker's chair shouting at everyone and pushing them about. It was extraordinarily vivid. At one point I saw two attendants waltzing with each other across a crowded Chamber.

To Parliament Street to see Jack Straw, as John Gilbert has been advising, to stake my claim to the chairmanship of the Home Affairs Committee. To my surprise, he said he had me in mind for the Home Office. Was I interested? I said I couldn't bear the thought of being an under-secretary. He agreed, I shouldn't accept anything less than being a Minister of State, adding 'Tony owes you' (I have never thought that Tony owes me anything). Jack would speak to him. To be honest, I would much prefer to chair the select committee, but I will have to treat seriously any offer that comes my way because it may be my last chance to achieve anything in politics.

David Clark showed me a newspaper cutting predicting that half a dozen members of the Shadow Cabinet would not make it into the Cabinet. He was one. The others were Michael Meacher, Ron Davies, Tom Clarke, Margaret Beckett and Frank Dobson. The usual anonymous 'informed' sources were cited, but there was clearly an element of speculation.

Several more Tories remarked how much they agreed with my question the other day about Murdoch. Among them Tom King. I asked if they were likely to do anything about him if they won. He said they might. It would depend on the size of their majority. The best way, he said, would be to insist that only EC citizens could own a controlling interest in our national media. Now that is radical thinking. I don't suppose for a moment they would dare, but it does show how worried they are about the monster they have spawned.

Wednesday, 18 December

The Freemasons inquiry finally got off the ground today – after months of prevarication by Ivan and co. Only John Greenway declared an interest (Peter Butler, our other Mason, having left the committee some time ago). Greenway said he had been a Mason twenty years ago, but had long since lapsed. He clearly hoped to get away without mentioning it in public, but Ivan told him that he had to. No big deal, but it does explain why he got so upset when we first discussed the possibility of an inquiry. I noticed Sir Gerard Vaughan, one of the leading Masons in the House, sitting in the public seats. He said to me a couple of years ago, 'If I have any criticism of freemasonry' – and he clearly doesn't have many – 'it is very difficult to resign.'

Martin Short* was our first witness. On the whole he was good. He didn't go over the top. He has a nice sense of humour and dealt well with Gerry Bermingham, who behaved appallingly. Although there is no shortage of evidence about misbehaviour by Masonic police, judges and magistrates are more of a problem. Short was weak here. If we want to change anything, we are going to have to come up with some facts. We have the power, but as ever there simply isn't the will to conduct a serious inquiry. Fortunately, I was able to persuade the committee to let the clerks make some inquiries on our behalf but I'm not hopeful. This is only the opening round of a long struggle.

---

* A former *Sunday Times* journalist and author of *Inside the Brotherhood*, the standard exposé of freemasonry.

Monday, 30 December
Chelmsford*

Dad drew my attention to a leader in today's *Telegraph* in defence of Freemasons in the guise of 'defending our traditional liberties'. With touching naivety, the *Telegraph* declares, 'Masons devote their time mainly to supporting charities and urging each other to behave better; if a disproportionate number are policemen and lawyers, it is because these professions are naturally attracted by an organisation concerned with civic duty.' I am referred to as 'the leader of the parliamentary Mason-baiters'. Nothing like a good denunciation to get things going. My little campaign is taking off at last.

---

*Home of my parents.

CHAPTER FOUR

1997

Wednesday, 1 January 1997

My resolution for the New Year: cut down on pointless activity, of which there is a great deal in my profession. No more nine-hour trips to Oxford and back to address a dozen students in a back room. From now on I shall only attend meetings where my presence will make a difference.

Saturday, 4 January

Spent the morning on a first draft of my paper on what to do about Rupert Murdoch. Seventeen hundred words. They have been on my mind for a long time and spilled easily from the computer. Potentially the greatest contribution I can ever make to British politics or culture. On the other hand, it may come to nothing.* Top secret until after the election, when I will arrange for Bruce to put it personally into the hands of The Main Person. In the meantime I shall show it, on an eyes-only basis, to a few trusted friends.

Monday, 13 January

To London on the 10.49. Everyone up in arms about the Police Bill, which puts phone tapping on a legal footing. Jim Callaghan and Merlyn Rees have joined in, which is a bit rich considering that they

---

*It did. See 3 June.

presided over a regime far less regulated than anything proposed by the Bill. Tony Benn is hawking around a motion opposing the Bill. He appeared unaware that the police have been bugging criminals on the say-so of senior officers for decades and that the safeguards in the Bill, modest though they are, are an improvement on what has gone before. I told him he hadn't done his homework. When I saw him an hour later he said he had now read the Bill and it was worse than he had thought. I declined to sign his motion, which he accepted rather wearily but I can tell he was disappointed.

Tuesday, 14 January

At breakfast in the Tea Room I was joined by Dawn Primarolo. She whispered that Gordon was coming under pressure to rule out any income tax increases. She says Gordon is resisting and no decision has yet been made, adding, 'If you see Gordon, tell him there is a lot of support for holding out.' No one, she said, is opposed to a 50p top rate. It's what the Tories will make of it that terrifies everyone.

At lunchtime Jack Straw came to the Civil Liberties Group to talk about the Police Bill. He started by making the very reasonable point that this was going further than any previous government. However, no one was persuaded. I polled those present and everyone preferred judges to police officers. Today's *Times* has a leader headed, 'A Bill Too Far'. There's a strong leader in the *Evening Standard*, too. Amazing how it's suddenly taken off, but as Jack says, 'That's politics.'

This evening I was sitting in the Tea Room with Tony Benn. We were joined by Peter Shore. Although they were on opposite sides in the civil war, they have been good friends for many years. Tony reminded Peter that he had driven him to his selection conference at Stepney thirty-three years ago. It was rather touching to see these two old gents reminiscing. Both feel alienated by New Labour. Tony, of course is predictable, but Peter is – or was – more on the right of the party, which makes his views more interesting. Peter said, 'I like Tony Blair. I think he is probably right about wanting to put a certain distance between the party and the unions, but I'm offended by New Labour's constant repudiation of our past.' He said that, although he recognised certain practicalities, his basic beliefs remained the same. 'I still believe in state intervention, a good measure of equality, full employment. It used to be the role of politicians to offer leadership. Now we just follow public opinion. We don't challenge anything.'

Tony said, 'Politicians have lost confidence. We no longer believe we have the power to change anything.' He then went way over the top and talked of Tony Blair being the political wing of the *Daily Mail* who would eventually lead us into a National Government. He even speculated that he might one day be expelled by New Labour. I told him he was talking nonsense. Secretly, I suspect, he yearns for martyrdom.

Wednesday, 15 January

Jack Straw nobbled me as I was going into the meeting of the parliamentary party and said he is backing down over the Police Bill. I am sure he is right. All hell has broken loose. Even as we were talking Andrew McIntosh passed and said, 'Message from Jim Callaghan: unless there is movement by this evening, he will put his name to an amendment.' Jack says we will table amendments in the Lords that require a senior judge to authorise any tapping of domestic premises without consent. If Howard won't go along with that, he will accept a circuit judge. You have to hand it to Jack, he may not always be right, but he does listen.

Tony Blair addressed the party meeting. On top form. Passionate, witty, positive. We should never underestimate the capacity of the Tories to fight, he warned. It is possible to have a fifth Tory government. We had plenty to offer and we should make sure people knew about it. He listed commitments – work, education or training for 250,000 young people; an end to the internal market in the NHS; reduced class sizes; an end to nursery vouchers; an extension of protection in the workplace; we will sign up to the EU Social Chapter; the right to join and be represented by a union; a minimum wage; a Freedom of Information Act; the incorporation of the European Convention on Human Rights into law.

He added, 'Disabuse yourselves of the notion that we won't have enough to do. On the contrary, we will need a second term to make a real impact and everyone must work to this end.' He ended by asserting that it was possible to have a society where people are ambitious and want to get on in life, but which was also fair and compassionate. Great stuff. Inspirational even. As Tony Benn might reluctantly have conceded – had he been there. On second thoughts, perhaps not.

Ken Livingstone said that higher taxes – especially corporation tax – were essential. We mustn't make the mistake made by previous Labour governments over devaluation and put off the inevitable until the markets had undermined us. We must strike decisively in the early days. Tony replied that a campaign on the basis of substantial tax increases would be 'a problem'. This drew sniggers from the loyalists who loathe Ken. Tony said he didn't think that his government would be faced with a market panic on the scale that previous Labour governments have had to face. He told Ken, 'If you go around making inflationary promises, you spend your whole time in government trying to convince people that you didn't really mean it.'

He then launched into an ominous little homily. The Attlee and Wilson governments might be held up as icons now, but at the time they were under almost constant attack for selling out. There would be difficult decisions to take in government. If these provoked disunity, then we wouldn't get a second term. He talked several times about tough decisions, dialogue, partnership ... more tough decisions. The message was clear. Dissenters can expect trouble. Maybe Tony Benn will get his martyrdom after all.

I showed Bruce Grocott my Murdoch memorandum. He suggested a few minor amendments. I intend showing it to Liz Forgan and Ray Fitzwalter and then it will go in the bank to await events.

Ivan Lawrence has rumbled my little stratagem for dealing with the Masons. He told the select committee this afternoon that he had ordered the clerks not to pursue the questions I handed in before Christmas. We shouldn't be asking people whether they were Masons or not. It was an intrusion into privacy. This got Jill Knight going. She wasn't in favour of questioning anybody about anything. At this point Gerry Bermingham wandered in late as usual and launched into a diatribe. Over and over again he repeated his view that the inquiry was a waste of time. Attempts by Ivan to persuade him to address the point were rudely rebuffed. On and on he rambled. He did reveal that he had once been a member of that sinister Catholic sect, Opus Dei, until being obliged to leave following his divorce. He had also been a member of another secretive Catholic society, the Catenians, until they had kicked him out too. In the end we agreed to ask the Lord Chancellor, various magistrates' clerks and chief constables to provide us with numbers only of Masons under their wing. Except for the West Midlands Serious Crime Squad. It is to be exempt. By four votes to two (only Jean Corston supported me – John Hutton was in the Chamber and Jim Cunningham, as usual, nowhere to be seen) it was decided that we should not attempt to discover how many members of the squad were Masons. Warren Hawksley said several former squad members lived in his constituency. They had had a hard time and it wouldn't be fair to rake it all up again – especially as none had been convicted of anything.

We will never get anywhere, of course. The inquiry has been neutered. I told them they were not only content to remain ignorant, they were prepared to fight to remain ignorant.

Thursday, 16 January

Today we are accusing the Tories of wanting to put VAT on food. So far as I can see there isn't any serious evidence to support the charge. I suppose we are playing them at their own game: think of a lie and double it. I thought our case was supposed to be that we are better than the Tories, not that we are the same.

Friday, 17 January

Stayed down for Audrey Wise's Cold Weather Payments Bill. A complete waste of time since there was never the slightest chance that the government would let it through.

I whiled away most of the day reading Andrew Neil's book *Full Disclosure*. Essential reading for anyone under the illusion that New Labour can live with Murdoch:

When you work for Rupert Murdoch ... you are a courtier at the court of the Sun King – rewarded with money and status by a grateful King as long as you serve his purpose, dismissed outright or demoted to a remote corner of the empire when you have ceased to please him or outlived your usefulness ... All life revolves around the Sun King. All authority comes from him ... The Sun King is everywhere even when he is nowhere. He rules over great distances through authority, loyalty, example and fear. He can be benign or ruthless, depending on his mood or the requirements of his empire. You never know which: the element of surprise is part of the means by which he makes his presence felt in every corner of his domain. He may intervene in matters great or small: you never know where or when, which is what keeps you on your toes and the King constantly on your mind. 'I wonder how King is today' is the first question that springs to a good courtier's mind when he wakes up every day.

Examples abound of what happens to those who think they can form lasting alliances with Murdoch. He reneged on his deal with the electricians' union to let them organise at Wapping, when they had outlived their usefulness. One of his most loyal and longest-serving courtiers was sacked by fax. Can't say we haven't been warned.

Monday, 20 January

A couple of hours in the office and then to London. Gordon has made his big speech ruling out income tax rises for five years and promising to stick to Tory spending plans for two years. Absolute folly and totally incredible. Gerry Steinberg, the MP for Durham who calls himself a right-winger, was on the train. 'This isn't why I joined the Labour Party,' he said.

Tuesday, 21 January

Everyone is depressed as the extent of New Labour's tax bombshell sinks in. Far from being cautious, Gordon and Tony are embarked on a high-risk strategy. If we have to do something unpopular, then the first two years would have been the time to do it, but that is precisely the period we have mortgaged. After that another election will be looming. In theory, I suppose, Gordon could raise money some other way – by increasing VAT or abolishing mortgage tax relief – but no one believes he will. In any case, before long the Tories are sure to outbid us by promising ludicrous new tax cuts which we shall feel obliged to match. After that, downhill all the way. By pandering to the meaner elements of the middle classes we have mortgaged our future. And for what? We would have won anyway.

This afternoon there was a debate on the health service. Chris Smith made a lacklustre speech full of complaints about the shortage of resources, but what's the point of complaining if we haven't got the funds to do anything about it? Labour, he claimed, would raise £100 million by abolishing the internal market and ironing out inefficiency. Nobody on either side believed it would make much difference. Neither, I suspect, does Chris.

Our Great Leader was all over the news tonight glad-handing business fat cats. Labour is now the party of business, he declared. Pull the other one. Why do we have to suck up to these people? Most of them aren't going to vote for us whatever promise we make.

Paddy Ashdown was on the bus going home. He said he thought Gordon's speech was a big mistake. 'Your party is supposed to be the party of change. If you can't change anything, people are going to say – and, forgive me, we'll say it – what's the point?' Interestingly, however, he added, 'Blair and Brown might be right. They haven't been wrong about anything so far.'

Wednesday, 22 January

The Lord Chancellor, Lord Mackay, came to the committee this afternoon to give evidence on Freemasons in the judiciary. He radiated complacency. Round and round we went. Everything was fine. How did he know? What evidence did we have that it wasn't? Even Ivan grew impatient. 'You're not being very helpful,' he said. 'The trouble with Mackay,' someone said afterwards, 'is that he thinks everyone is as decent as he is.'

Mike and Parvin Laurence came to dinner. I rang Ngoc before they came and she said, 'Give them my regards.' Then Sarah came on the line and asked me to give them her regards, too. There was a pause. Then she said, 'Dad, what is a regard?'

Thursday, 23 January

Alan Milburn was on the train home. He reckons we'll have a majority of about twenty-five. I reckon between minus and plus ten. Alan says a spell in government will cause a sea change in attitudes, even for those on the back benches. 'We've got so used to blaming the government for everything that goes wrong. Now we shall have to change our tune.' He also predicted that a Labour Cabinet will be unrecognisable in two years. We discussed who the new faces would be. The list included: Steve Byers, Tessa Jowell and Peter Mandelson (of course). Alan even suggested that Gerald Kaufman might make a comeback. I'm sure Alan will also be in the Cabinet before long, although he was too discreet to say so.

Saturday, 25 January

Alan Clark has been selected – aged sixty-eight – to fight Chelsea in place of Nick Scott. I can't for the life of me understand why he wants to come back. By the time I'm sixty-eight I shall be long gone. He's got everything – a lovely wife, a castle, 17,000 acres in Scotland. He could have fun just managing his assets. What's more, he has made a far greater impact on the world since he left Parliament than he ever did when he was here. I suppose he just wants material for another volume of diaries.

Wednesday, 29 January

Liz Forgan came to lunch. As always full of good cheer and common sense. Time in her company always passes too quickly. Liz says she's thinking of voting Lib Dem at the election because Labour has 'conspired' with the Tories against progressive taxation. She believes that

Mandelson, whom she does not dislike, has been since the days of Kinnock the single most influential figure in the Labour Party. He recognised early on that he could never hope to be elected to office on his own merits and so he has used others as his vehicle. Initially Gordon, but he soon recognised that Tony was a better bet and so took the hard decision to transfer his allegiance. He recognised from the outset that Tony was a blank sheet upon which almost anything could be written. 'Peter,' she says, 'is a brilliant Machiavelli who understands how to get from A to B without getting lost on the way.' I showed Liz my Murdoch memo and she made some constructive suggestions.

Today's *Guardian* reproduces on the cover of its Review section the magnificent colour photo of the Scotland Yard Masonic lodge, the Manor of St James, set up in defiance of the then Commissioner, Robert Mark. I've had it in my possession for several years, but unfortunately was sworn not to use it. Curiously, although there were half a dozen copies of the *Guardian* in the Members' Tea Room this morning, someone had gone to the trouble of removing the Review section from every one.

Later, at the select committee, we took evidence on Masons from the Association of Chief Police Officers and the Police Federation. ACPO supports a register but the Federation – surprise, surprise – is dead against. Fred Broughton, the chairman, just sat smirking and repeating that there was no evidence of malpractice, which is nonsense. We are awash with evidence on misbehaviour by Masonic policemen. When this was put to him, he just said it was all a long time ago and everything had changed since. I'm afraid I got quite ratty with him, which only made him smirk more.

In the evening Stewart and Jean Valdar came in for dinner to celebrate Stewart's eightieth birthday. He told an amusing story about King Carol of Romania who turned up for the funeral of George V with his masseur just as the procession of heads of state was about to set off from New Palace Yard. As a result the masseur had to march with the crowned heads and was clearly visible in the photographs the next day. Only the *Daily Worker* was indiscreet enough to identify the mystery face. Today he would be all over the tabloids.

Thursday, 30 January

PM's Questions. Worse than ever. Blair baited Major about European Monetary Union – a pointless exercise since we are almost as divided as they are. Major responded by pointing out very reasonably that in 1983 Blair had been elected on a manifesto which called for withdrawal from the EC, which made Blair look silly. He even tried to get up a fourth time, to general groans. We face another three months of this. I look up at the faces in the public gallery and wonder what they are thinking.

Tuesday, 4 February

Jack has got together with Derry Irvine and come up with a party line on Masons. We are in favour of disclosure by judges, police, prosecutors and defence counsel. Better than I could ever have hoped. He wasn't planning to make an announcement until we report, but I suggested he go ahead immediately. A much needed boost for our little inquiry.

Wednesday, 5 February

Gordon Brown was on the radio this morning announcing his latest wheeze – a pay freeze for top salaries, including those of MPs. He had a little package of sound bites that he kept repeating, 'tough decisions', 'firm but fair'. Just when we thought we had finally escaped from having to vote on our own salaries Gordon has devised a scheme that will take us back there. He is a potentially catastrophic Chancellor.

At the select committee in the afternoon, I proposed we have a formal vote on research for our Masons inquiry. I assumed we would lose, but much to my surprise we won. By a clear majority the committee voted to ask Grand Lodge to tell us how many High Court judges and above are Masons, the existing membership (and their ranks in the police) of the Manor of St James. We even decided to make inquiries about the West Midlands Serious Crime Squad, over the objections of Warren Hawksley and Jill Knight. Jill muttered, 'You've done a lot of damage in Birmingham.' Good. I haven't finished yet.

We took evidence from the Police Superintendents Association and then the magistrates. The superintendents were a pleasant surprise; although they both claimed to have heard nothing and seen nothing during their combined fifty-six years of service, they did concede that they would accept a register, providing it applied across the criminal justice system. They didn't want police singled out. Neither do I. That's very helpful.

The lady from the magistrates posed as a friend of openness, but as time passed it became clear that her heart wasn't entirely in it. She did, however, provide us with one interesting snippet. Of the fifty-one male members of the Magistrates Council, eight are Masons and eight others declined to respond to inquiries. In other words, between 16 and 32 per cent (she accepted that it was probably over 20 per cent) are Masons. Not counting, of course, the wives of Masons. We have lifted the carpet, just a little.

Thursday, 6 February

Doug Hoyle, who shares my assessment of Gordon, predicts that he will be swapped with Robin Cook within two years. Too late. The damage will be done by then.

At about 5.30 p.m., just as I was getting ready to depart, a call from Jack Straw. He has just reached agreement 'without prejudice' with Michael Howard on the Police Bill. The police will have to obtain prior authorisation from a commissioner (who will be a High Court judge) for bugging homes, hotel bedrooms and offices. The commissioner will be appointed by the Lord Chancellor. Lawyers, doctors and journalists will be privileged. Confessionals (to trap a priest running a paedophile ring, for example) will only be bugged with the consent of the church. This last point has still to be cleared with Basil Hume.

I told him this seems fine with me. Light years away from where we started.

Wednesday, 12 February

The select committee was cancelled because of the second reading of the Police Bill. Howard has backed down completely on judicial scrutiny and there is a not very holy alliance between the two front benches on the rest of the Bill which drew complaints from all sides. The most worrying issues are the definition of serious crime, which is wide enough to take in just about anything, and the proposed criminal records certificates which are going to make it even more difficult for the underclass to find work. Tony Benn made a brilliant but, as usual, over-the-top contribution. He recited a long list of distinguished people who, he said, had objected to the Bill without once acknowledging that the main source of their objection – the absence of judicial scrutiny – had been conceded.

I made a speech setting out my reservations, all of which can be addressed in committee. About fifteen of our people, including Tony, joined the Liberals in the 'No' Lobby. I didn't. It would have been churlish since Jack has consulted me all the way through. I guess I've traded independence for a little bit of influence. I hope it's not entirely an illusion.

Friday, 14 February

Lunch with Tim Schofield, who will be my Tory opponent in the election. My idea, in the hope of avoiding some of the nastiness of earlier campaigns. A pleasant fellow in his early thirties. Opposed to the death penalty – and abortion. He had read *A Very British Coup* and professed admiration for my role in the miscarriage of justice cases. Like me he has Southerner written all over him. Officer class, but not especially posh. He served seven years in the army and now runs a recruitment consultancy in Durham. He may well be elected in due course – but not in Sunderland.

Monday, 17 February

With Hanh and Sarah for a look round Parliament and then to the Tower of London. Ngoc insists that she should learn from our outings so I did my best to drum a few simple facts into that little head. As we were leaving she asked, 'Dad, have I learned anything today?'

Tuesday, 18 February

A free vote on whether or not to compensate gun-shop owners who will lose out as a result of the ban on handguns. I voted – uneasily – with the government. As I was going through William Waldegrave remarked that we were standing shoulder to shoulder on guns. Then he added quietly 'and on Freemasons'.

Wednesday, 19 February

We had our first Freemason to the select committee this afternoon. Sir Ian Percival, a former Solicitor General. An amiable, complacent old buffer who assured us that everything was for the best in this the best of all possible worlds. I managed to get under his skin and he accused me of being smug, which is a bit rich.

Friday, 21 February

To the High Court just in time to see the three men falsely convicted of murdering Carl Bridgewater walk free. The crowd blocked the Strand. A lot of old friends turned up, including three of the Birmingham Six, Paddy Hill, Billy Power and Gerry Hunter. Later there was a crowded press conference at the St Bride's Institute. I had heard that the men were in bad shape, but they put on a pretty good show. They said they weren't bitter, just angry. They said some nice things about Ann Whelan, the mother of one of them, who is the real hero of the hour. I have only a walk-on part in this one. The day belongs to Ann, the solicitor Jim Nichol and Paul Foot. Jimmy Robinson remarked that Douglas Hurd, the only Home Secretary to take their case seriously, was the only one who wasn't a lawyer. Doesn't that say it all?

I did half a dozen interviews and caught the 6.30 train to the North.

Monday, 24 February

To London on the 17.02. One of the first people I ran into at the House was a senior Tory lawyer. He immediately raised the Bridgewater case. 'You realise, of course, there was another confession ...'

Here we go again. Okay, the confession may be a forgery, maybe the police overdid it, but they are all really guilty. That's clearly what's being whispered in the highest legal circles. I had hoped we might avoid a whispering campaign this time around, but no ... They just can't help themselves.

Wednesday, 26 February

An entertaining two hours at the select committee interviewing one of the chief Masons, Michael Higham. Fluent, unruffled and (almost) plausible. He claimed that they had not a single serving chief constable on their books (surprising, since the Association of Chief Police Officers thought there might be half a dozen). Grand Lodge have also supplied us with figures on the judiciary, suggesting that no more than a handful of senior judges are Masons. The only significant number were on the North East circuit. We are not short of evidence of Masonic skulduggery in the police, but we have very little on the judiciary.

Our evidence sessions are attracting a lot of conspiracy freaks who believe that Masons rule the world. They sit at the back of the committee room twitching and blithering. One even tried to address the committee from the floor. They keep pressing messages into my hands, asking for meetings. I am doing my best to steer clear.

Ivan got a bit ratty towards the end of today's session. Having wasted half an hour with a series of lollipop questions about the charitable activities of the Masons, he then tried to hurry everyone else along. 'In future,' he mumbled, 'one question each and that's it.'

'In future,' I said, 'there will be a general election.' That shut him up.

Friday, 28 February

We have won a by-election at the Wirral with a swing of 17 per cent, a majority of nearly 8,000 on a turnout of 73 per cent. Amazing.

Tuesday, 4 March

The result at Wirral has set everyone talking about landslides. 'They could be out for the rest of our active lives,' Paul Boateng said to me. Personally, I think such talk is premature.

Several people drew my attention to a piece in the *Mail on Sunday* that says I am likely to chair the Home Affairs Committee. I hope so, but speculation in the *Mail* is unhelpful. Not least because the report says that I will cause trouble for Jack.

Wednesday, 5 March

A vote on the Prevention of Terrorism Act in the evening. Jack had been hoping to avoid a division, but the Unionists pressed it. I was one of only thirteen to vote against, which leaves me a bit exposed. Later, I ran into Chief Whip Donald Dewar who was looking grim. 'Off to break a few kneecaps?' I inquired.

'Yes – yours.'

I said I had told Jack two weeks ago that I intended to vote against, if there was a vote. Happily Donald didn't seem too bothered.

And then to *Tribune*'s sixtieth birthday celebration at Brown's in St Martin's Lane. Jam-packed with beautiful people, some of whom had only the most tenuous connection with the paper, but a great success. Among the speeches, one from Robin Cook predicting a Labour landslide.

Sunday, 9 March

Mother's Day. Sarah woke us at 6.40 a.m. She was carrying a tray with a glass of orange juice, a single daffodil in a glass of water and a card with a little poem which she had made at school.

Monday, 10 March

An interview with Paul Linford of the *Newcastle Journal*, who remarked in passing that Tony Blair had a high opinion of me and that I was likely to be in the next government. Several people have made similar remarks in the last few days. I don't know what's caused it, but I'm not losing any sleep. I couldn't bear the thought of being an under-secretary. Signed up to every dot and comma of government policy without having the slightest influence over any of it.

Tuesday, 11 March

Murdo Maclean* stopped me this evening. 'What job will you have in a Blair government?' I said my expectations were not high, but I would be happy to chair the Home Affairs Committee.

'I thought you might be Home Secretary,' he said. 'Jack might have something to say about that,' I replied.

Wednesday, 12 March

At the select committee this afternoon, good progress on our report on prison management. An iceberg is looming, however. Jean Corston and Gerry Bermingham both say they are opposed in principle to private sector involvement in prisons. That's Jack's position, too. The problem is that the evidence points in the opposite direction. Even after all the usual qualifications and caveats have been entered it is inescapable that the introduction of a mixed economy into the prison system has been beneficial. For one thing, privately managed prisons have spearheaded the introduction of women officers who are without doubt a civilising influence in an otherwise macho culture. Even Jean, when pressed, concedes that private prisons have had some beneficial effect. However, she will keep saying she objects 'in principle'. This is classic Old Labour territory. An obsession with mechanism rather than outcomes.

---

*A civil servant whose official title is Secretary to the Chief Whip, behind the scenes a man of great influence.

Thursday, 13 March

Jim Sillars, one of the most amiable Scot Nats, was on the train this evening. He told an amusing story about his seven-year-old grandson who had recently been taken to a posh restaurant for the first time in his life. Next day, at school he gave the dinner lady a 10p tip.

Friday, 14 March

Among customers at my surgery this evening an auxiliary nurse at the hospital employed on a zero-hours contract, one of the most pernicious by-products of the New Orthodoxy. He can be called at any time without notice and dumped at any time. He does not qualify for holiday or sickness pay or any other of the benefits we used quaintly to associate with civilisation. During his first week he had five shifts and went out and celebrated his good fortune. Since then he has had just two shifts in a month. He has disappeared from the unemployment figures and no longer qualifies for benefit. He can't chuck in his 'job' because he would be considered to have made himself unemployed deliberately and disqualified from benefit. Instead he is dependent for survival on his mother, a pensioner.

Monday, 17 March

As I was delivering Sarah to school this morning I heard a woman shout at an angelic little boy, 'Ashley, come here – I'm going to smash your face in.'

Spent the morning in the office and caught the 12.43. Richard Caborn got on at Doncaster. He reckons we're in for a big majority. 'I used to say forty, but since the Wirral who knows … ?' I remain sceptical.

Richard, who used to work with Barbara Castle when he was a Euro MP, said her advice to a new minister entering his department for the first time was, (1) remember that you are not important – the department would continue to function if you never even crossed the threshold; (2) only aim for two major achievements – any more and you will lose your way.

The Chief Whip, Donald Dewar, took me aside. 'Have you heard about tomorrow's *Sun*?'

'No.'

'Murdoch is coming out for us. I know you've got strong views on Murdoch, some of which I share, but I would be grateful if you could refrain from commenting.'

I agreed – until 2 May.

Tuesday, 18 March

Sure enough, today's *Sun* is covered in 'We back Blair'. Inside there are two pages of justification. Every word reeks of cynicism. Murdoch is just protecting his assets. If we had the guts, we should keep quiet until 1 May and strike with deadly force in the first week. We won't though. We haven't neutralised Murdoch. He's neutralised us.

Wednesday, 19 March

The select committee lasted seven hours, with two adjournments. We completed the prisons report in less than an hour and then went on to Freemasons. Ivan Lawrence presented an extremely bland draft and I spent most of the day drafting amendments. Everyone was grumpy. At one point I lost my temper with Walter Sweeney who reverted to his usual theme, that the inquiry was a waste of time. By about 10 p.m. we had reached impasse. I moved a vote. Ivan, knowing he was in a minority, refused to take it. He started waffling about how unfair it was to Jill Knight and John Greenway who were absent. I pointed out that even with both of them present he would still be in a minority. He then proposed adjourning until tomorrow morning, by which time of course they would both be present and several of our side would have disappeared. I again insisted on a vote. Again he refused, this time claiming outrageously that Jill and John hadn't had notice that there was going to be a vote. The ground was immediately shot from under him by the clerk who read out the notice which made it perfectly clear that votes might take place. Again I moved the vote. Again Ivan refused. I was on the point of moving that he be removed from the chair when he suggested an adjournment of an hour. When we reassembled at 11 p.m., Jill was present but there was still no sign of Greenway. The vote – on whether or not to legislate for disclosure – was six–three (four counting Ivan, who can only use his vote in the event of a tie) in favour. One of our number, an absolutely useless specimen, was angry with me for stringing things out. 'No change without struggle,' I said cheerfully, but he was not amused.

Thursday, 3 April

The Man was interviewed at length on the *Today* programme this morning. He was on top form, but there is no disguising the fact that every word he utters is designed to pander to the meaner elements of the middle classes, the Sierra owners, as he calls them. Do we really need to appeal to every last *Daily Mail* reader? There must surely be a few one-nation Tories left. They can't all have been murdered or brainwashed by Thatcher.

Friday, 4 April

Our lives are ruled by the Tiny Tyrant, Emma Mullin, aged eighteen months. When she is happy we are all happy. When she is in a foul mood – which she often is – we sink into depression and become irritable with each other. Her every whim has instantly to be gratified for fear that failure to do so will provoke a terrifying tantrum. When she runs we chase after her in case she falls and injures herself, as she has done several times. Reminiscent of the scene from *The Last Emperor* where the young Son of Heaven amuses himself by racing around the Forbidden City pursued by anxious courtiers.

For the past week the Tiny Tyrant has had a streaming cold, which has made her mood worse than usual. She indicates her requirements by a series of one-word commands repeated, at a gradually increasing volume, until she has our attention. Because her vocabulary is limited, a single command can mean many things. Thus 'Up' can mean 'I wish to get down from the feeding chair', 'I wish to get out of the car' (regardless of the fact that we are travelling down the A1 at 70 mph) or 'Open' indicating the dressing-up box (usually when it is long past bedtime). Most of her commands relate to food or drink. Often they are in Vietnamese. 'Banh', screamed hysterically, means 'I want a biscuit NOW'. 'Ou' means likewise for orange juice. Sometimes 'banh' and 'ou' are accompanied by the word 'please', repeated endlessly in a pathetic little voice intended to induce sympathy. If she does not get satisfaction from one adult she appeals immediately to whoever else is available. Thus 'Hanh, Hanh', 'Dad, Dad'. Recently she has mastered her first sentence: 'I want crisps.' For all that, however, she is a lovable little monster.

Sunday, 13 April

With Kevin Marquis, my agent, and Sarah to one of the more difficult parts of my constituency, a ward recently inherited from my neighbour, courtesy of the Boundary Commission. A handful of party members had assembled in a local social club. Kevin and I had hoped that by going in person we might at least embarrass the local oligarchy into some form of activity. However, we had underestimated them.

Six or seven unhealthy looking men were seated in twilight around tables in an empty function room. Most were smoking. There was no natural light. The air was stale. Only one of the three councillors showed up and he had only come to tell me in person that he proposed to take no active part in the campaign. 'My days of walking the ward are over,' he said amiably, in the manner of a great statesman taking a well-deserved rest from public affairs.

'At least you can take a poster.'

'Not necessary, Chris. I live in a close.'

'You are a councillor. You must set an example.'

'There are only eight houses.'

'So?'

He did not actually refuse to put up a poster, but he would have done had I pressed him. It was nothing personal. On the contrary, he exuded goodwill. It is just that this is how it has always been. Welcome to the land of the 10 per cent turnout. And no wonder.

Tuesday, 15 April

To Tynemouth, one of the North East's few marginal seats. We were sent to knock on doors in Monkseaton, an area where the social fabric was entirely intact. Streets of middle-class houses, gardens full of tulips and aubretia. Two cars to every household. Not our natural territory, but I was pleasantly surprised. We found several former Tories who were coming with us this time. Contrary to what the newspapers are saying, they showed no sign of wavering. One woman said the gap between rich and poor had grown too great. I came away heartened.

Wednesday, 16 April
Sunderland

A man in Grindon this evening asked if I was a socialist. I said I was. He asked me to define socialism and I gave a not very adequate answer, to which he responded, 'You create scenarios, don't you?'

'I'm sorry?'

'Scenarios.'

'What do you mean?'

'You go in search of a bit of poverty and then you launch a crusade about it.'

Monday, 21 April

I saw my first Tory poster this evening. On the car of one of the Conservative candidates, parked outside the Ewesley Road Methodist Church where we held one of the few public meetings of the campaign. The apathy is so appalling that I feel like carrying a bundle of Tory posters and handing one out every time I come across a Conservative voter in the hope of provoking our people to get their fingers out.

Tuesday, 22 April

Tonight's news reported two new polls – one giving us a 21 per cent lead and the other 9 per cent. Followed by the rider, 'Each poll is subject to a 3 per cent margin of error'. Obviously they can't both be right. I don't believe either. Whatever it is, the gap is bound to close during the next week as the 'don't knows' turn back into Tories. I'd be amazed if we have a majority of more than twenty. We could even lose.

Thursday, 24 April

We're going to lose. Blair knows it, too. I can see it in his eyes every time he appears on the TV news. The magic is fading. He looks exhausted. Major, by contrast, is as fresh as a daisy. The massive rubbishing to which our man has been subjected is paying off. The Tories have succeeded in turning him from an asset to a liability. To be fair, some of it is self-inflicted. We have spent too much time apologising for the past and it has undermined our credibility. BRITAIN IS BOOMING, DON'T LET LABOUR SPOIL IT, shout the Tory hoardings. They are everywhere, eclipsing our pathetic little promises which no one believes anyway. Who needs the *Sun* when you can advertise on this scale? And of course, the Tory message is not entirely a lie, only half the truth. Middle England *is* booming. Every day the papers are full of the latest huge handouts from demutualising building societies. Not to mention massive tax reliefs on various government-sponsored saving schemes. By comparison the repossessions, negative equity and even the corruption are a fading memory.

Tuesday, 29 April

In the morning, with the other candidates to the Bede Sixth Form Centre. About eighty students attended. They didn't seem particularly enthusiastic, but the questions were intelligent. I told them there was nothing complicated about the choice they had to make. There was only one major issue – the huge gulf that had grown up between the fortunate and the unfortunate. If they wanted it to widen, they should vote Conservative. If they wanted it to narrow, they should vote Labour.

This afternoon Kevin and I went down to Tory-held Stockton,

where about twenty of us 'blitzed' an estate of middle-class housing containing exactly the sort of people who voted for Thatcher in the eighties. This time they nearly all seemed to be with us. We came away greatly cheered. We will win, after all.

Thursday, 1 May

Polling day. Bright sunshine, a good omen (but then it shone in '87 and '92 as well). A pleasant day touring in an open-top bus bedecked with balloons, posters and a loudspeaker to blast away the apathy. The natives were, on the whole, friendly. People sitting on their door-steps giving us the thumbs-up. The occasional V-sign from the rougher end of town. I did my best to insert a little humour into the sloganis-ing, 'VOTE EARLY, VOTE OFTEN, VOTE LABOUR', 'VOTE LABOUR AND WE'LL BRING YOU MORE SUNSHINE' and 'VOTE LABOUR AND KEEP SUNDERLAND IN THE PREMIER LEAGUE'.* And as we passed some old boys doing their allotments, 'VOTE LABOUR TO MAKE YOUR LEEKS GROW'.

In the evening we poured people into the Ford estate in an effort to drive up the turnout. When that was done we went into Pennywell and, finally, Thorney Close. Our strategy seemed to be working. There was a steady trickle of voters and by the end of the evening most of those on whose doors we knocked claimed to have voted. Kevin thought we would win by thirty seats. I stuck to my original estimate of not more than twenty. How wrong we were.

I went home for a bath and a bowl of soup. At ten I turned on the news. The exit polls were predicting a landslide. I still didn't believe them. Not until I reached the count at around 10.30 p.m. and glanced at the table in the centre where the votes were laid out in bundles of a thousand did I realise that something astonishing was about to happen. The Tory vote had collapsed. Their candidate was on 7,000 against my 27,000.

Once again we were the first to declare, at 10.46, having shaved ten minutes off the previous record. The media were out in force: BBC, ITN, Sky. I had instructed everyone to look cheerful, regardless

---

*The team was relegated ten days later – our first broken election promise.

of the result, but in the circumstances there was no difficulty. We had a swing of over 10 per cent. For about twenty minutes I was the only MP in the country. I could have formed my own government. My victory speech was shown live on all channels. 'From now on,' I said, 'Britain will be governed on behalf of all its people. Not merely on behalf of the fortunate.'

By the time we went to bed five Cabinet ministers – Ian Lang, Michael Forsyth, Malcolm Rifkind, William Waldegrave and Michael Portillo – had gone. We waited up until Neil Hamilton went down to Martin Bell at Tatton at about 3.30 a.m.

Only one little fly in the ointment: the turnout has collapsed – here it is 8 per cent down on last time. In some parts of Sunderland less than half of the electorate voted, which means that many of those who claimed already to have done so when we knocked on their doors last night were lying. The alienation is massive. Especially among the young.

My thoughts on this, the night of the greatest ever Labour victory, are: (1) that we would have won without making our Faustian pact on tax – but that, of course, is hindsight; (2) that Blair is not a moderate, he is a radical and has the capacity to be a great Prime Minister; (3) that such a large majority is neither healthy, nor fair; (4) that we must urgently find a way of redistributing some wealth; (5) that victory is not when our side get the red dispatch boxes and the official cars, but when something changes for the better.

Friday, 2 May

Up at 6.30 a.m., after three hours' sleep. The sun is shining – we have delivered on our first promise. There are only 165 Tories left. We shall have a majority bigger even than Attlee in 1945. Extraordinary scenes on the telly. The Man is back in London, pressing the flesh at a huge party in the Festival Hall.

By lunchtime he was entering Downing Street. Most of the crowd seem to be waving Union Jacks. (No detail too trivial – or tasteless – for our new masters.) No matter, this is a wonderful day to be alive. Even the hardest Old Labour hearts cannot fail to have been moved.

Saturday, 3 May

To town with Emma. The mood is upbeat. People were hooting, waving and coming up and shaking hands.

The first six or seven names in the new government were announced today. Donald Dewar is to be Scottish Secretary, George Robertson Defence Secretary (displacing David Clark, who has long laboured under the New Labour black spot). Nick Brown, who is not famous for his tolerance, will be Chief Whip. Unlikely that I shall receive a call, but you never know. I have taken the precaution of carrying a mobile phone, borrowed from a neighbour.

This evening I examined the detailed results for the first time. They are truly astonishing. The landscape has changed beyond recognition. We have taken seats we never dreamed of – Scarborough, Shipley, Shrewsbury, Rye and Hastings – on swings of up to 18 per cent. Ann and John Cryer have both been elected. Sir Marcus Fox has gone to spend more time with his directorships. Ivan Lawrence has also gone.

Monday, 5 May

Rain all night which shows no sign of stopping. By this evening most of the junior appointments will be made. Although I am affecting disinterest, the truth is I am ever so slightly on edge. Why I should want a job, I cannot think. Most of the junior jobs are sheer drudgery. In any case, in five years' time no one will ever be able to recall who was Minister of State at the Home Office. Why sacrifice independence and self-respect for a few baubles? I suppose I just want to be asked. The truth is that I am a rather less significant figure than I – or my friends – like to pretend.

The evening news reported that Tony Banks has been made sports minister. He was filmed attempting to walk along a straight white line. He looked very happy, but if someone had said fifteen years ago that his career would peak at Minister for Sport, we would have laughed derisively. I guess we must all adjust to lower expectations. Still no word of the Home Office appointments.

Tuesday, 6 May

To the office to find a message waiting from Joyce Quin who has been shadowing the Europe job at the Foreign Office for which she was admirably qualified, only to find herself Minister of Prisons, about which she knows nothing.

To London on an evening train. I have only two remaining political ambitions: the chairmanship of the Home Affairs Committee and an office with a window.

Wednesday, 7 May

Attention has now turned to the Tory leadership struggle. Wonderful to wake in the morning and hear leading Tories on the *Today* programme talking of the need to make their party electable again. It seems like only yesterday that they used to talk pityingly about how unelectable we were.

To the first meeting of the new parliamentary party, which bears little resemblance to the old one. There are so many of us that we have had to hire Church House, over the road, because there is no room in the House of Commons big enough to accommodate everyone. As with all New Labour events the choreography was brilliant. Just five people on the platform – Chief Whip Nick Brown (who acted as chairman), Ann Taylor, Alan Haworth (secretary of the parliamentary party), and John Prescott. The Man arrived to a standing ovation. The media were allowed into the upper circle for his speech. Above, a wooden plaque which read, 'The spirit of the Lord shall rest upon him ...' Around the inside of the dome in large gold letters were the words 'Holy is the true light and passing wonderful. Lending radiance to that which endured in the heat of the conflict ...' I sat between Jean Corston and Dawn Primarolo, now a Treasury minister. Dawn saw me taking notes. 'For your diary?' I just smiled. A carnival atmosphere, but no triumphalism. The Man on top form. 'We are not the masters. The people are the masters. What the people can give they can take away. We won't forget that.' Just the right tone.

After the press had left, there were contributions from the floor. Dennis Skinner complained about Gordon Brown's decision to give the Bank control over interest rates. Discipline, he said, went two ways. 'I can't recall an occasion when we discussed handing over power to the Bank of England. We get into power in order to keep it.' Several others took up the theme. Ken Livingstone said the Federal Reserve in America had shafted Carter during the oil crisis. At which point Dawn whispered that we had a reserve power to take back control over interest rates if it didn't work out. A point no one seems to have picked up. Alan Williams spoke up for Gordon and said he may well have headed off a run on sterling. The Man gave no quarter. 'Those of you who believe that it is your job to make a list of demands and our job to deliver, get that idea out of your heads. Your job is to explain ... We sink or swim together.' Even he referred in passing to the *Shadow* Cabinet. It is so hard to get used to the change in our fortunes.

I saw Jack Straw, our new Home Secretary. Loving every minute. He has the great advantage of knowing the brief inside out, having shadowed it for so long. According to Jack, there is great relief among the civil servants – except among the anti-terrorist brigade – that Michael Howard has gone. After a discussion on prison numbers the other day, a senior civil servant remarked to Jack, 'We haven't had a discussion like that in eighteen months.' He said he expected me to get the chair of the Home Affairs Committee and even asked if I wanted to go on the Intelligence Committee – I said yes, but only if the two were compatible.

The atmosphere is extraordinary. The Members' Cafeteria ran out of food. Upper Corridor South has been swept clean of Tories. Fiona, who used to work for David Mellor, was clearing out his office. I dropped notes to George Mudie and Janet Anderson (who are in charge of accommodation) listing vacant rooms with windows. They have absolutely no excuse for not giving me one.

New faces everywhere – and from the most unlikely places. I have to keep peering at their passes to see if they are members or researchers (which some were until recently). I met a woman who claimed to represent Castle Point in Essex. When I last looked Castle Point had a Tory majority of 17,000. What a time to be alive.

Thursday, 8 May

Called on Anna Haggard, one of my Stockwell neighbours, who is overjoyed by the result. 'Colonic irrigation', she calls it. She described how, on the morning after, on the way to her cottage, she called at a farm shop in Virginia Bottomley's Surrey constituency, full of the joys of spring, only to be met with frosty stares. Shades of the scene in the bar at the Savoy on the night of the 1945 victory. (*'They've elected a Labour government. The country will never stand for it.'*) Someone had amended one of Virginia's posters so that it read 'Virgin Bottom', so there is at least one dissident in that part of Surrey.

A hilarious story about Brian Donohoe. Apparently he was a minister for eight seconds. Downing Street rang him by mistake, confusing him with Bernard Donoughue. He was actually put through to The Man.

This afternoon we were sworn in. The Speaker, Betty Boothroyd, was as cheerful as ever. 'Wasn't it good, our winning Basildon?' she whispered. 'You're supposed to be impartial,' I replied. Good old Betty.

Still no office. I put my head around George Mudie's door to find out what was going on. About a dozen people were camped outside, waiting – but no sign of George. Later, Janet Anderson spoke to him for me and he told her that the offices on Upper Corridor South are still in dispute. This must be nonsense. At least three of the vacant ones were ours to begin with and we are not likely to end up with less than we started with. Janet said some of the new members were getting stroppy about their lack of an office. So will I, if something doesn't move soon. I've been five years in an office without natural light, and I'm not having any more of it.

Alan Milburn, now Minister of State at Health, was on the train home, working his way through the contents of a red despatch box, looking for all the world like someone who had been in the job for years. There is, he says, a huge black hole in the budget. The Tories got through last winter by allowing trusts to run up deficits and using capital as revenue. He reckons we could be short by as much as £500 million. The whole place is booby-trapped.

Monday, 12 May

George Mudie rang to say I can have David Young's old office on Upper Corridor South. At last, a room with a view – a glimpse of the Victoria Tower – and fresh air, or what passes for it in central London. The news has put a spring in my step. Who wants to be a minister anyway?

Then a call from Nick Brown. 'Chris, I have a job for you.' What can this be? I thought all the jobs had been allocated. I am being asked to second the Queen's Speech. Gerald Kaufman is to propose. We come before the Prime Minister and the Leader of the Opposition and are thus assured of a packed house. Delighted, I say, but in truth I am apprehensive. Gerald will be a difficult act to follow and the House has a notoriously short attention span. Nick hands me over to Murdo Maclean. It is, he assures me, a great honour. There will be an invitation to the Prime Minister's eve-of-session reception at Downing Street tomorrow evening and to the one at Speaker's House on Wednesday lunchtime. Gerald and I are to present ourselves at 12 Downing Street as soon as possible where we will be given, in strictest confidence, an advance copy of the Gracious Speech.

Immediately I rushed home and changed into a suit. Had the call come twenty minutes later, it would have been too late. I would have been on my way south and my one and only suit would have been at the wrong end of the country.

Tuesday, 13 May

With Gerald Kaufman to Downing Street. The gates swing open as if by magic. No one asks to see our passes.

What I notice first about Number 12 is the silence. The only sound is the ticking of clocks. Tranquillity in the midst of bedlam. The top people, I have noticed, always dwell in silent places. I was struck by this when I went to see Mary Robinson at the Irish presidential residence in Phoenix Park. I'll bet even the Congolese President Mobutu lives in a silent place, while about him everything disintegrates.

We take tea with Murdo Maclean on a green three-piece suite at the far end of an L-shaped room, dominated by a conference table. The walls are adorned with landscapes in oils on loan from the Tate. Murdo presents both of us with a blue folder containing the Speech. Highly confidential, numbered in red so that leaks can be traced. Mine is number 26. Our folders also contain copies of speeches by movers and seconders past and a list of members who have been previously accorded this honour back to the beginning of the century. The only name from Sunderland is Fred Willey in 1945. Gerald says, 'There is obviously a tradition that whenever there is a Labour landslide a Sunderland member seconds the Address.' That line will come in handy.

On the way out we pause in the entrance lobby, which is hung with photos of governments past and whips past, back into the last century. Murdo points out two sepia prints, taken on the Commons terrace, of Lord Curzon and friends. They are identical, except that in the top picture, someone – I can't recall who – has been removed without trace. The photo was taken in 1899, thirty years before Stalin perfected the technique.

For five hours I labour in my windowless room, tapping words into my processor. A little self-deprecating humour is the key to holding everyone's attention. I will start by reading out my *Sun* headlines, 'Loony MP backs bomb gang' etc.

Back to Downing Street for the pre-Speech party at Number 10. Official cars are disgorging new ministers, boys and girls who can hardly believe their luck. Humphrey the Downing Street cat is sitting outside the front door preening himself. There have been ugly rumours that the Blairs want him reshuffled, but yesterday's papers are full of pictures of Humphrey with Cherie assuring the world that he is safe in her hands.

Inside, at the foot of the stairs greeting all and sundry with much hugging and back-slapping, is Neil Kinnock. Has there been a coup?

Not at all, he is a guest like the rest of us. It is the Kinnock of old. Life and soul of the party. Not the slightest sign of resentment that the tide of history has swept past. Secretly, I suspect, he is relieved.

The state rooms are hung with Turners and Constables. I was last here in March 1970 when I came to interview Harold Wilson for *Student*, a magazine run by a budding entrepreneur called Richard Branson.

People eye me as if to say, 'What are you doing here?' One says, 'Is there something I don't know?' Instead of maintaining an air of mystery, I blurt out the truth.

Everyone is so happy. They are the masters now. All these people who used to sit around gossiping in the Tea Room are suddenly running the country. Or are they? How long is Banksie going to last? He really has to make up his mind whether he is going to be a serious politician – of which he is perfectly capable – or a court jester. On that issue the jury is still out. All future requests for media interviews now have to go through Alastair Campbell. Appearances on *World in Action* and the Frost programme have already been vetoed, although he was allowed on Jimmy Young. Today Banksie is in the news for crossing his fingers while swearing the oath of allegiance. I fear it will end in tears.

A pleasant chat with John Gilbert who is back in his old job at the Ministry of Defence after an absence of eighteen years. He could not be happier if he had died and gone to heaven.

I went over my speech with Bruce Grocott, taking care to say that I was seeking his advice as a friend rather than the Prime Minister's Parliamentary Secretary, but he soon switched into official mode. The Murdoch paragraph must go. He even wants rid of my *Sun* headlines, which leaves a damn great hole in the joke section. I consulted Alastair Campbell who says keep them, so I will.

Brief speeches from Tony Blair and Betty Boothroyd. Ideology is out, ideals are in. That was the evening's sound bite. Prescott made a little show of noting it down. Betty said this was her sixth Queen's Speech reception, but at the others she had felt like 'Ruth amid the alien corn'. Goodwill was everywhere, but she did strike one discordant chord, referring to a bygone era 'when comradeship had been distinctly patchy'. On this glorious evening, however, we are overflowing with comradeship.

At chucking-out time, I left with David Clark, now Chancellor of the Duchy of Lancaster, who took me out through the door that leads into the Cabinet Office, which operates with a high-security switch card. This is the door Sir Peregrine Craddock used when he came to give Harry Perkins the bad news.* David has a room on the third floor, overlooking the Number 10 rose garden. If he is disappointed about not being given Defence, he is not admitting it. He will be responsible for the Freedom of Information Act. He's also in charge of the new food agency which, thank heavens, is being taken away from the Department of Agriculture, Fisheries and Food. David pointed out Peter Mandelson's office, on the same floor and opening directly into the room where some of the main cabinet committees meet. A matter about which, according to David, there is some concern.

Wednesday, 14 May

The day of the Big Speech. Mine, that is, not Her Majesty's. I went in early and ran my draft through the word processor for the umpteenth time. The words are okay, but how will they sound? If only I had the self-confidence to address the House without notes, but I don't. It could go either way. Triumph or humiliation beckons.

At noon I went to the Speaker's reception and chatted briefly with Cherie Blair. She said they had been to Chequers at the weekend and the children loved it. The staff were glad to see them because the Majors hardly ever went. I mentioned that I had seen Humphrey the cat on my visit to Number 10 yesterday. 'Give him a kick from me,' she said. So the rumours are true.

The moment came. The Chamber was packed. I sat trembling between Tony Benn and Andrew Bennett, while Gerald spoke. His hands were shaking, too, which was reassuring. Gerald was brilliant. Wickedly funny about Mandelson, who sat smiling wanly on the steps by the Speaker's chair.

My turn. I decided at the last minute not to use notes for the jokes, which I knew by heart anyway. This meant I was able to look

---

*In *A Very British Coup*, p. 208.

around as I spoke, which made all the difference. I even addressed a few words to Neil Kinnock, who was in the gallery. A wonderful and rare feeling to be (however briefly) in total command of a packed House. Afterwards, everyone was kind. John Major held up a copy of *A Very British Coup*. From the gallery Neil gave me the thumbs up. All evening people were coming up saying how good it was. Jacky says we have had several calls from people who saw it on TV. My finest hour.

Later, back to Downing Street for a reception at Number 11. Humphrey the cat was in his usual place. According to Nick Brown, he has been murdering ducklings in St James's Park and Alastair is briefing against him. We stood on the upstairs terrace looking down into the garden. A walled garden in the centre of London. The manicured lawn in luminous health. Not a weed, or a human being, in sight. Almost too good to be true. Will the young Blairs be allowed to kick a ball around down there? The only sign of a life was easy chairs on the lower terrace behind the Cabinet Room. A good place for breakfast – and the walk to work is short.

The Man called in briefly, in shirtsleeves, jacket slung over one shoulder. He was kind about my speech. Everybody was. The first family are living above the shop in an apartment that spans Numbers 11 and 12. A door leads into it from the first-floor landing. Nick Brown says that, from his office, he can hear one of the boys practising the piano. He said he called round the other day and Cherie came into the living room wearing nothing but a bathrobe. 'I could have been naked,' she said.

Quick as a flash, Nick replied, 'It could have been worse. *I* could have been naked.'

Westminster is a series of fortified villages. Once you have passed the armed policemen on the gate an air of informality prevails. The doors of Numbers 10 and 11 are ajar. The cat sits preening himself. The family car, a Ford Galaxy, is parked among a handful of others. The privileged people who live and work there are all on first-name terms. The entire terrace is linked by corridors and doorways. With the right switch card, it is possible to pass from Number 12 to the Cabinet Office on Whitehall without setting foot outside.

There are other villages, of which Parliament is the biggest and least exclusive, although Parliament, too, has its secret places and degrees of access. The most exclusive village (unless you count MI5 and the SIS) is, of course, the Palace. Many people have access to one or other of these secret worlds. Very few have access to all. Those who do, move effortlessly between them, until the dread day dawns when they pass back through the looking glass. The passes, the security men and the official cars (unless you have been Prime Minister) disappear. Suddenly you are on the wrong side of the gate and can return only by invitation. The Queen, Murdo Maclean and Humphrey the cat are the only permanent fixtures.

Most of this, of course, will be lost on Gordon. I bet he's too busy crunching numbers in the Treasury to admire the view.

Monday, 19 May

To London in time to watch Ann Widdecombe putting the boot into Michael Howard, about whom she said there was 'something of the night'. She did it skilfully and with uncharacteristic humour, but didn't quite land a knockout blow. All she succeeded in doing was adding to the general impression that he is not entirely trustworthy – which most people had already realised. In the end I almost felt sorry for her. She has inflicted as much damage on herself as she has on him. And he, unlike her, will live to fight another day.

Tuesday, 20 May

Diane Abbott told me she has advised Tony Banks to acquire gravitas and on no account to resign. We both agreed that Banksie is capable of great things, providing he can shake off his court jester image. The big wasted talent is, of course, The People's Ken but, according to Diane, he is beyond redemption.

Just about everybody I pass mentions my speech last week. I am in serious danger of being labelled 'a good House of Commons man'. Then I will know that I have been rendered utterly ineffective.

Thursday, 22 May

A depressing aura of self-congratulation hangs over this place. I suppose it will wear off in time, but there is no sign so far. Scarcely a backbencher – on either side – rises to ask a question without first congratulating the minister on his or her elevation. On our side just about every question is asked from a kneeling posture. John Hutton was holding mock auditions in the Members' Lobby, 'Repeat after me, "May I congratulate ..."'

This was rejected by Bruce Grocott as being, in Gerald Kaufman's memorable phrase, 'suspiciously lukewarm'. Bruce came up with the winning formula, 'May I trouble the Prime Minister to list his three greatest achievements ...'

Sunday, 25 May
Chillingham

Paradise. Dad and Mum are in the Lookout apartment. We are in the Grey. Our good friends David and Marie Lorraine Fraser are in the Dairy wing. Sir Humphry Wakefield, the laird, is in residence and can be seen rushing hither and thither. Today he is hosting a banquet in the Minstrels' Hall for members of the Irish Georgian Society. They arrived in a fleet of immaculate vintage Rolls-Royces and parked in a semi-circle along the front of the castle, like something out of *Brideshead*.

We picnicked by the lake and then drove in convoy to the manor at Etal, where we spent a pleasant afternoon wandering amid the rhododendron and scented azaleas.

By the time we returned to our castle the Irish Georgians and their Rolls-Royces were nowhere to be seen. Maybe we imagined them.

Thursday, 29 May

To Mellerstain, an Adam mansion in the Scottish borders. As we were leaving I was buttonholed by Sir Humphry.

'What's a socialist doing staying in a place like this?'

'I'm sure my money is as good as anyone else's.'

'Oh,' he said, 'these apartments are awfully underpriced.'

At this point he mellowed and proceeded to deliver a little lecture, the drift of which was that he was prevented by government regulations from requisitioning unemployed labour to help restore his castle. He talked endearingly of his desire to help the 'yobs'. In this world, he said, everything went to those whom God had blessed with grey matter. The poor yobs got nothing. He had had youth trainees in the past, but there were all sorts of rules about what he could and could not ask of them. He couldn't ask them to pick up heavy things for fear that the poor dears would strain themselves. He couldn't send them out in cold weather for fear they would catch cold. He couldn't pay them pocket money without jeopardising their unemployment pay. Then he started on about English Heritage. Their grants were hedged around with all sorts of unreasonable conditions to the point where it was hardly worth his while to apply. This was clearly a well-worn theme. At one point he said self-deprecatingly, 'Don't worry, the lecture ends in a minute.' Actually, he was angrier with the Tories than he was with Labour. I wasn't clear why. Probably because, despite their talk of deregulation, they hadn't delivered.

Monday, 2 June
Sunderland

Today's post brought a pleasant surprise – a photo of John Doxford, the first inhabitant of 7 St Bede's Terrace. It was discovered by local antiquarian Douglas Smith who, at my request, trawled a box of glass slides, the work of a High Street photographer in Victorian times which has lain uncatalogued for years. He took the plate to a local photographer and there, out of the darkness into which he receded over 100 years ago, emerged John Doxford. A lean, ascetic man with grey whiskers and a stiff collar. Not, I imagine, a bundle of laughs. I shall have him framed and hung upon the wall of our hall from where he will watch over future generations in the house that he inhabited for nearly fifty years.

Ngoc took me to Durham for an evening train to London. I had forgotten that there was a vote at ten o'clock and arrived twenty minutes late. Never mind, we had a majority of 260 and no one seemed to care.

Tuesday, 3 June

Lunch in the Members' Cafeteria with Brian Donohoe, the man who was a minister for eight seconds. He said there hadn't just been one call from Downing Street, but three or four and in the end he was actually put through to The Man who believed throughout that he was talking to Bernard Donoughue. When the plug was pulled he was told that there was a fault on the line and they would reconnect him as soon as possible. He didn't become aware of the truth until he read it in the paper the next day.

A brief chat with Bruce Grocott about my Murdoch memorandum. I was relying on Bruce to put it in The Man's hands come the summer recess, but Bruce says I should give it to Chris Smith, which will be a fat lot of use. Bruce says he has raised the subject with The Man several times. 'He listens impassively, but does not respond.'

Unwisely perhaps, I penned a piece in *Tribune* the other day about sorting out Murdoch. I should really keep my head down until after the select committee chairmanships are resolved.

Dinner with my old friend Claes Bratt. He gave me two nice quotes, one from a laid-back poet friend: 'It's not in every incarnation that you feel like doing something.' And one from a Thai woman of his acquaintance: 'Unlimited growth is the ideology of the cancer cell.'

Thursday, 5 June

I have been elected to the executive of the Parliamentary Labour Party, a token male among five women: Jean Corston, Sylvia Heal, Ann Clwyd, Charlotte Atkins and Llin Golding. Charlotte, who has only been here a month, polled 109. Obviously there is an unseen hand at work. New Labour leaves nothing to chance. Alice Mahon told me that the whips had a slate though I don't think I was on it. Lindsay Hoyle, who has an office opposite me, said that last night he overheard five new members in the office next to his, organising a canvass.

As for me, I polled 105 out of a possible 274 – 21 ahead of the next highest male, a good but not an enormous vote considering the alleged brilliance of my speech the other week.

A brief chat with Elliot Morley, who is attempting to civilise the Min of Ag's attitude to farm animals. He is making life as difficult as possible for the live exporters and has just ordered bailiffs to be sent in to one particular villain who hasn't paid his bills. Jack Cunningham, he says, is pretty laid-back and lets him get on with it, but the officials are fairly hostile. They've been in the pocket of agribusiness for so long that they just can't adjust. He fears that they will start running to Jack behind his back. There are exceptions, however. One official whispered that the change of tune is a liberation and has started tipping him off when he is not being given the full picture.

The Foreign Office, he says, were nearly persuaded to sign up to an agreement on imported fur caught in leg-hold traps that even the Tories had rejected. He suggested I put down a question about it, which I did immediately.

Thank heavens for Elliot. He's the only one who cares about animal welfare. And, unlike the others, who are just reading from briefs, he knows what he's talking about. He talks of changing the whole ethos at MAFF. I pray he gets a chance. My fear is that he will be isolated and reshuffled.

The Tories have been filibustering the Education Bill which abolishes the assisted places scheme. Nothing like the defence of a little bit of privilege to get them going.

Saturday, 7 June

Channel Four is reshowing *A Very British Coup*. Two episodes this evening, one next week. A little dated, but still good fun.

Sunday, 8 June

Tony Benn rang at 8.15 a.m. to say how much he enjoyed seeing *Coup* again. He takes it all so seriously. 'Of course,' he said, 'they killed Kennedy, didn't they.' I hadn't the heart to tell him that I don't think 'they' did.

Monday, 9 June
Sunderland

To the Civic Centre to discuss plans for the new town centre with William Ault and Eric Holt.* They seem sensible enough. Basically, we are destined to spend the next thirty years trying to undo the work of the planners during the previous thirty. Dynamite, I remarked, was the appropriate solution for Crown House, a 1960s tower of stunning ugliness recently abandoned by the Department of Social Security. 'Yes,' said Eric, 'with the people who gave the planning permission inside.' My sentiments precisely.

I worked in the office all day and caught an evening train to London. Stuart Bell was on the train. He is among the Disappointed. Eight years on the front bench, much of it spent wooing the City, and the call never came. So confident were the civil servants at Trade and Industry that he would be appointed, that on the Saturday he had a called from a senior official asking if he wanted the private office staff to come in on the Monday (which was a bank holiday).

At the ten o'clock division Jack Straw took me aside and said that The Man had agreed I should chair the Home Affairs Committee.

Tuesday, 10 June

The first ballot results of the Tory leadership contest were announced this evening. Ken Clarke, who clearly has overwhelming support in the country, leads William Hague by a mere eight votes while the right – John Redwood, Peter Lilley and Michael Howard – have about seventy votes between them. Clarke has clearly had it.

---

*Environment Director and chairman of the Environment Committee, respectively.

Wednesday, 11 June

Tom Sawyer, the party's general secretary, addressed the parliamentary party this morning. There had, he said, to be a new relationship between the government and the party. We had to develop a new mindset. Active members, or stakeholders as we are now called, had to see themselves as representatives of the community and not of warring factions. We had to move away from resolutionary politics. The role of MPs, he said, would be 'to explain and persuade'. Tom was careful to say that this brave new world would, of course, require a new approach by both sides – party and government – but I noticed that he devoted only a sentence or two to what was expected of our leaders. All the rest was about the changes expected of the led. Afterwards we were treated to a little slide show by a sharp-suited New Labour apparatchik. Diane Abbott pointed out that, for all their talk about inclusiveness, our masters still overrode the Policy Forum when it suited them. She mentioned the debacle at Manchester over Gordon's plan to do away with child benefit for sixteen- to eighteen-year-olds. Yes, replied the apparatchik, there would have to be a place for minority views. He entirely missed the point. Diane was talking about accommodating the majority, not the minority.

I am sure it makes sense to try and avoid the conflicts which have bedevilled all previous Labour governments. Success, however, will require an air of humility and some give and take on the part of the leaders as well as the led – and right now I don't see much sign of it.

To the first meeting of the new parliamentary committee. We met in the Prime Minister's room off the corridor behind the Speaker's chair. The first time I have penetrated that particular inner sanctum. Jean and I arrived five minutes early to find it as deserted as the *Mary Celeste*. It showed no sign of being lived in. Not a flunkey or a piece of paper in sight. We sat around a table big enough to hold a Cabinet meeting. The ceilings are miles high. The walls oak panelled for the first six feet, after which acres of yellow wallpaper. Gilt everywhere. Huge gilt-framed mirrors at either end. A gilt stationery holder, a gilt clock on the mantelpiece that struck five ten minutes ahead of time.

Clive Soley was in the chair, the government was represented by

John Prescott (who looks exhausted), Mo Mowlam, Frank Dobson and Nick Brown. Margaret Jay, Charles Williams and Denis Carter attended from the Lords.

The main business was sorting out the backbench and the select committees. Nick announced that a letter soliciting expressions of interest would be circulated with this week's whip. Jean and I made the point that only those willing to pull their weight should be put on select committees and Nick confirmed that he intends to take an interest in attendance records. I said that they didn't give the full picture since some people only attended for ten minutes to get their names on the record. Nick said that he would be open to representations on particular cases.

Thursday, 12 June

Home on the 20.00 train with Derek Foster, who related the inside story of the deal that preceded his resignation as Chief Whip. According to Derek, The Man persuaded him to stand down in return for a promise of a place in the Cabinet. A promise which was reiterated several times in the intervening eighteen months. When Derek told Gordon Brown what had been promised, Brown had replied, 'I'd make sure you have that in writing.' John Prescott was sceptical, too. 'You and I understand what is meant by a deal,' he said, 'but this guy doesn't.' An interesting insight into the degree of trust at the highest level. In the event, Derek was offered only a lowly job in the Cabinet Office from which he resigned after a couple of days. He is very bitter.

Sunday, 15 June

To the Allgoods' wonderful garden at Nunwick, opened in aid of the Red Cross. In the walled garden I counted nine different types of potato as well as nectarines, apricots, figs and grapes. 'These people don't have to go to Asda when they want fruit or vegetables,' I said to Sarah.

Quick as a flash she replied, 'What about ice cream?'

Wednesday, 18 June

The Tory leadership contest grows more bizarre by the hour. Redwood has come out for Ken Clarke. Thatcher for Hague. She was sighted in the Tea Room this afternoon for the first time in years. No one knows what the outcome will be. Even a dead heat is possible. Grim-faced Euro-sceptics are to be seen everywhere in urgent little conclaves.

Thursday, 19 June

A chat with Mo Mowlam in the Tea Room. Northern Ireland, she says, is a very enclosed world. Wherever she goes she keeps running into the same thirty or so top people who appoint each other to everything. She has decided to go outside the province in search of a new Permanent Secretary and the local establishment has done everything possible to dissuade her.

At five o'clock I went upstairs to the Committee Corridor to await the result of the Tory leadership election. Police had sealed off the area between Room 12, where the votes were being counted, and Room 10, where the Tory backbenchers were awaiting the result. Beyond, in all directions, journalists, groupies and assorted hangers-on. When the moment came, a silence descended on the assembled multitude and the towering gloomy figure of Archie Hamilton appeared. Accompanied by a single policeman he walked towards the small group of us standing by desk in the Upper Waiting Hall. I suddenly found myself face to face with him and said, 'This could be your big moment, Archie,' whereupon his face lit up. '*You* certainly aren't going to be the first person I tell.' And with that he disappeared.

In the event, Hague won easily. They have probably made the right decision. Had Clarke won, they would have been irrevocably split. Some of our lot think this is an ideal result for us, but I wouldn't bet on it. Hague is smarter than we imagine, and time is on his side. We now have a Leader of the Tory Party who was born two years after I had failed my eleven-plus …

Incredibly – and against all expectations – Blair has decided to go ahead with the ludicrous Millennium Dome at Greenwich. Absolute madness. The last thing we need, as we close down hospitals and collapse the voluntary sector with year-on-year spending cuts, is a big black hole in Greenwich into which we pour money.

Eric Martlew, MP for Carlisle, was on the train. He agrees about the Dome, but added, 'Maybe Tony's right. He has been right about so much that I am beginning to doubt my own judgement.'

Tuesday, 24 June

A message from a fire officer asking me to ring him at home. He was ringing about a recent BBC2 programme about the select committee's Masons inquiry. A clip from one of Grand Lodge's promotional videos had been shown and in it, decked out in his Masonic regalia, he had spotted the Chief Fire Officer for the Palace of Westminster. I bet this place is riddled with them.

Wednesday, 25 June

I was number three at PM's Questions. At the briefing, Bruce and Ann produce the usual list of lollipop questions, all of which I declined. They asked what I had in mind. Fox-hunting and Lords reform, said I. Bruce, as amiable as ever, seemed to think it might prove too upsetting. 'What's your fallback?'

'Murdoch.'

'In that case, Chris, I'd stick with the Lords.'

Moral of story: if you're planning a difficult question always have a worse one up your sleeve. In the event it went smoothly. The Man confirmed that he was still planning to do away with the voting rights of the hereditaries, although he didn't sound very enthusiastic about taking on the fox-hunters.

Hague's first Question Time and he did well, getting under the wire with a succinct inquiry about an allegation that Ron Davies was leaning on Welsh members to toe the line over devolution, and he followed up well. A smart issue to choose. It taps the rich vein of unease on our side about New Labour intolerance. Blair's reply was ambiguous. Any backbencher could speak his mind, providing he kept within party rules.

Friday, 27 June

Among the customers at the surgery an elderly man who is one of the last inhabitants of Pickhurst Road, Pennywell. The four houses on either side and all of those behind are derelict. After dark, marauding bands of youths wreak havoc in the ruins. Fires are started, walls demolished, cars attacked. The police appear to be impotent. The old boy is terrified. His wife died in December and on the day of her funeral the cars of mourners were attacked outside his home. A casualty of the right to buy that the Tories are so proud of. Having purchased his council house (where he has lived for more than thirty years) he cannot now be evacuated. The only way out is for the council to buy it back, which, understandably, they are not keen to do since the house is valueless. I promised to do what I can but I am not confident.

Wednesday, 2 July

Budget Day. Gordon has hit the utilities for over £5 billion, more than expected. Some of it he is putting into schools but most is going to fund Welfare to Work.

Thursday, 3 July

To dinner with the Woollacotts. The guests were journalists and their spouses. A woman who runs a bookshop in Wandsworth told an amusing story about the musician Sir Thomas Beecham.

Shopping in Fortnum & Mason just after the war, Beecham was approached by a woman whom he vaguely recognised.

'Sir Thomas, how are you?'

Sir Thomas replied that he was fine and, still unable to put a name to the woman, fished for clues. How were her children?

'Fine.'

'And your husband?'

'Yes, he's fine, too – still King.'

Martin told a story about Noël Coward who introduced a female friend to an imposing-looking gentleman, 'This is the King of Sweden.' The man took her hand and bowed and as he did so whispered, 'Norway.'

Friday, 4 July

The Americans have landed a computer-driven vehicle on Mars. It made a flawless landing after a journey of 308 million miles. Mind-boggling.

Monday, 7 July

The papers are reporting that Cherie paid £2,000 to fly her hairdresser to the Denver summit two weeks ago. It comes hard on the heels of reports that the Blairs have just paid £3,000 for a bed. No one seems bothered now, but it will come back to haunt them when things start to go wrong. People will ask if they have any understanding of how ordinary folk live. 'In Republican Rome,' writes Anne McElvoy in today's *Telegraph*, 'when a successful general was celebrating a great triumph, he would be borne back to the capital in a chariot, to receive the victor's laurels with the wild applause of the plebs ringing around him. Standing next to him would be a slave whose job it was to whisper into his ear: "General, remember you are mortal." This is one appointment Mr Blair has yet to make.'

To London on the 17.02. Archie Norman boarded at Doncaster. I asked why he'd gone into politics from Asda. 'To do some good,' he said. Far be it from me to suggest that the Tory Party is not the obvious home for do-gooders. He'll be bored stiff on the back benches after the life he's led. However, Archie is not short of things to do. He's been asked by Cecil Parkinson to help modernise the Tory Party, a task which he readily admits will be a severe test of his considerable talents.

Wednesday, 9 July

At the parliamentary committee in the evening I inquired about our plans for holding the security services to account. The truth is that we haven't got anyone with the requisite weight or experience to take over as chairman so Tom King is going to be left in place for at least two years. I said, 'The security services have run rings around all previous Labour governments and I hope this one will be the exception.' I also reminded those present that it used to be our position that the Security and Intelligence Committee should be accountable to Parliament and not to the Prime Minister. With the best will in the world The Man couldn't be expected to keep tabs on them. I suggested we invite him to discuss it with us. To my surprise, no one threw up their hands in horror. Clive Soley and Nick Brown said they would talk to The Man and report back.

To Lancaster House, for a reception hosted by Clare Short. I had a lively discussion with one of the new intake, Derek Wyatt, about the future of television. Derek, a likeable, laid-back fellow who used be head of BSkyB's computer channel, declared that 'television is finished'. The internet is the future and we should forget about trying to tame Murdoch or enforce minimum standards. There was, he conceded, a slim hope that we might preserve the BBC as a public service broadcaster, but it was only likely to be of interest to about 15 per cent of the population and there wasn't much hope of persuading the rest to cough up the licence fee. All deeply depressing, but he seemed very cheerful about it. He has just been put on the Heritage Committee, but obviously can't be counted on to put up a fight. We walked back through St James's Park and almost the whole way he was talking into his mobile to his stockbroker in San Francisco.

Tuesday, 15 July

John Major, who now occupies Michael Martin's old room at the end of the Upper Committee Corridor, invited me round for a chat. After congratulating me on my chairmanship of the Home Affairs Committee he said, 'I was hoping you'd chair Heritage so you could sink your teeth into our common enemy.' Murdoch, he said, had done great damage, both here and in Australia. 'Look who owns our media: Harmsworth, Black, Murdoch. They all live abroad and pay little or no tax.' John was as passionate as I have ever seen him get. He clearly loathes the press barons, prompted no doubt by their treatment of him. He said we should move against foreign ownership. 'If there is one thing the Great British Public hates, after politicians and estate agents, it's foreigners owning their newspapers. You'd be surprised how much support you would get from our side.' We should also go for cross-media ownership, he said. The EC would probably be helpful. 'You will have forgotten,' said I, 'but I had a little ten-minute-rule Bill on precisely these points. Indeed, I raised it with you once at Question Time.'

'I have not forgotten. That's why I'm raising it with you now.'

I asked if he had ever mentioned the subject to Blair. 'No, because I couldn't trust him. The spin doctors would have been all over it. I could have trusted John Smith.'

Thursday, 17 July

The select committee met at last and I was duly confirmed as chairman, the only survivor of the *ancien régime*. The Tories have appointed Douglas Hogg, who is going to be a pain, Humfrey Malins, a wet retread lawyer, and Gerald Howarth, who is said to be fearsomely right wing. Our side includes Robin Corbett, David Winnick, Bev Hughes, Ross Cranston, Martin Linton. There is also, for the first time ever, a Liberal, Richard Allan. We agreed two inquiries: a review of police complaints and discipline and a look at alternatives to prison. Jack Straw is to be invited before the House rises. I also obtained the approval of the committee to ask the questions about Masons that Ivan blocked in March. So far, so good.

Friday, 18 July

Ngoc and Sarah are off to Vietnam next week. This evening Sarah asked, 'Dad, do aeroplanes have accidents?'

'Not very often.'

'Then why do they have parachutes under the seats?'

Monday, 21 July
Sunderland

To London in time to attend the Arms Export Control Group, which Ann Clwyd convenes. We had an excellent presentation from two academics who argued that, far from being a vital part of our economy, the arms trade was in serious decline, that it was sustained by levels of public subsidy that were not available to other industries and that the government should instead promote investment in such obvious growth areas as alternative energy and clean technology.

Wednesday, 23 July

Once again the Prime Minister was absent from the parliamentary committee. A feeling is growing that we aren't being taken sufficiently seriously. The more so, because we all knew he was down on the terrace, mingling. Later, when he returned, instead of coming in he waited in the outer office for us to leave. I am beginning to get annoyed. So, too, are Jean Corston and Ann Clwyd. For the third week running I raised the accountability of the security services. Once again Clive promised to raise the matter with The Man, but time is running out. In the end it was agreed that Clive, Jean and myself should seek an audience. Questions were also asked about the news – which we read in the newspapers, of course – that Liberals are to be added to the cabinet committees dealing with electoral reform. Neither Nick nor Ann Taylor was able to give an authoritative response. They both referred to The Man who, of course, was absent.

Fifteen minutes after the meeting ended I received a call from Anne Coffey asking me to return at once to the Prime Minister's room. When I got there The Man was sitting with Clive Solely in the easy chairs. Sally Morgan was the only other person present. Clive was delicately expressing the view that he should show up at the committee at least twice a month. Tony was saying that 'maybe he could pop

1. The Tiny Tyrant and her Dad: Emma Kim Van Mullin, born 18 June, 1995.

2. Sarah with Joan Maynard, former MP and close family friend who died in March, 1998.

3. 'I'm voting for my Dad … I think', Emma on election day, 1 May, 1997.

4. On holiday in North Yorkshire with Granny and Grandpa.

5. Sarah with Tony Benn at Stansgate.

6. Jacky Breach, my friend and secretary, died March 1999.

7. *CM and friend: I invited him to help out at my surgery.*

8. *In Vietnam with George Galloway, an agreeable travelling companion who harboured a number of illusions about the joys of life under the Stalin system.*

9. *'A new dawn has broken, has it not?'*
Tony Blair succeeds
John Smith.

10. *'He's behind you.'*
The Man and his
shadow.

11. The Sun *shines on New Labour … up to a point, Lord Copper.*

12. *Send him Victorious: Blair enters Downing Street on the day after the Labour landslide.*

13. Finest hour? 14 May, 1997: CM seconds the Queen's Speech. 'A wonderful and rare feeling to be in total command (however briefly) of a packed House …'

14. '… for a moment I even had the attention of the New Labour top brass.'

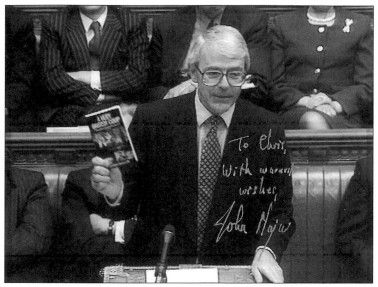

15. Queen's speech debate continued: John Major brandishing a copy of CM's first novel, A Very British Coup.

16. The parliamentary committee which met weekly with the prime minister. Front row (1to r), Jean Corston, Ann Taylor, John Prescott, Tony Blair (aka The Man), Clive Soley, Chris Mullin, Mo Mowlam; back row (1to r), Margaret McDonagh, Denis Carter, Charlotte Atkins, Syvia Heal, Ann Clwyd, Alan Haworth.

17. *The Man campaigning (through gritted teeth) for the People's Ken, having moved heaven and earth to prevent him becoming Mayor of London. Moral of story: you can fix the party, but you can't fix the electorate.*

IN COMMITTEE, ON THE SQUARE

© Steve Bell 1998 — 1069 · 20 · 2 · 98 —

18. *Cartoonist Steve Bell's take on CM's memorable confrontation with Commander Higham, secretary of the freemasons' Grand Lodge. 'As each elephant trap opened he duly fell in.' (19 February, 1998)*

in for ten minutes or so', although it might be necessary to bring forward the meeting time by forty-five minutes. Sally was saying this was impossible because 3.45 p.m. was the time he reserved for seeing individual members. It really isn't good enough.

On the security committee, The Man said the names would be announced any day. Three or four of the names would be people with a track record of scepticism towards official pronouncements. I said it was important to get the details right because the security services had run rings round every previous Labour government without exception. The Man replied that the days when they bugged trade unions and the Labour movement were over, but he seemed rather vague about the present set-up, saying he had only had one meeting with representatives of the security services since taking office. I said that proved my point. Namely, that with the best will in the world he wouldn't have time to give them the attention they deserved. When I suggested they should be accountable to Parliament and not to him, he laughed and said, 'I suppose that was the line we took in opposition.' It was indeed.

I put it to him that the end of the Cold War had taken away a large part of the security services' *raison d'être*. If there was a settlement in Ireland, they would have serious problems. There was a strong case for downsizing and saving some public money, even amalgamating MI5 and MI6. The Man laughed at this and said it would meet stiff resistance. Finally, I said that, if he wasn't minded to make the security services accountable to Parliament, he should at least keep the possibility hanging over them to encourage good behaviour. Clive suggested an annual debate on the security services. The Man said he didn't see why not.

Finally, we talked about the decision to put Liberals on cabinet committees. 'It was,' The Man said, 'the continuation of a strategy. We don't want them forming a bloc with the Tories.' It was more of a problem for Paddy Ashdown than it was for us. It makes it easier for Liberal voters to switch to us in the West Country and, if we lost a few votes to the Liberals in places like Richmond, so what? He added that he appreciated that local Labour parties in Liberal areas might not see it that way.

At this point someone came in and said that he had to go and see the Queen and the meeting, which had lasted about twenty-five minutes, broke up.

Thursday, 24 July

A quiet word with Bruce Grocott about The Man's attendance at the parliamentary committee. 'Why Tony?' he asked. 'Won't Prescott do?' No, I said. Prescott isn't in the loop. Besides, the country appears to be being run by only about four people – Alastair Campbell, Mandelson, Jonathan Powell and Tony. Of those, only Tony was eligible for a place on the committee. Bruce didn't dispute any of this, although he did suggest Gordon (Brown) as a possible addition to the inner circle. Pressure on time, he said, was tremendous. Bruce is just about the only person in Number 10 who appreciates the importance of maintaining links with the party in Parliament. He was also worried about Tony's attendance at the weekly meeting of the parliamentary party – only twice since the election and on both occasions to speak rather than to listen. I said trouble was being stored up for the future. He promised to pass on the message 'with knobs on'.

Tuesday, 29 July

To the Liaison Committee where, as usual, most of the talk was about overseas travel. If the credibility of a select committee chairman is to be measured by the number of foreign trips he can organise, I am going to prove a severe disappointment to my colleagues. Several times Dave Hinchliffe, my only soulmate, rolled his eyes heavenward. I didn't utter a word. The only useful contribution was made by Bruce George, who said that our committees were among the least effective in the developed world. He was deputed to come back with a paper setting out what should be done.

Wednesday, 30 July

To the High Court for the Carl Bridgewater judgment. A place had been reserved for me in the jury box where I sat in splendid isolation throughout. Not a bad judgment. Names were named and referred to the Director of Public Prosecutions. The trial judge, of course, was exonerated. Regret was expressed. There was even a passing reference to 'lessons for all of us'.

Mike Mansfield remarked afterwards that he was ready to eat his words about Jack. 'He's proving a much better Home Secretary than I expected.'

At the parliamentary committee I asked why we weren't making time for a hunting Bill; several others joined in. Nick Brown replied that it would become bogged down in the Lords and derail our entire programme. He added, 'I assume we will deal with this in the next session. That is my working assumption.'

Llin Golding asked about the pending Uxbridge by-election. People were uneasy, she said, that the candidate who had been thought good enough to represent us at the recent general election, was not considered good enough for the by-election. Charlotte Atkins made a lame attempt to defend the by-election panel, but the truth is that our masters have overreached themselves and it's going to cost us the seat.

Thursday, 31 July

With Ruth Winstone to Hughenden Manor, once the home of Disraeli, set in 500 acres on the side of a wooded valley just outside High Wycombe. When Disraeli contested High Wycombe in 1832 there were just thirty-two electors, which must have made canvassing easy. His financial arrangements wouldn't have got past Lord Nolan. The House was purchased for £25,000 – a colossal sum in the 1840s – with the help of a loan from a friendly aristocrat. When the loan was called in ten years later, Disraeli was saved from ruin by a wealthy widow who bequeathed him £35,000 on the very odd condition that she be buried in his family vault.

Ruth told a hilarious story related to her by Alan Clark, whom she went to see yesterday to discuss the possibility of writing his biography. He told her he is hosting a fund-raising do at Saltwood for the Chelsea Conservative Association. The organisers first suggested an entry fee of £100 a head which, he protested, was too much, where-upon, after much discussion, they agreed a £50 concessionary price for anyone with property worth less than £1 million. Even Clark, with all his millions, could see the joke.

Friday, 1 August

We lost Uxbridge by nearly 4,000 votes. Which only goes to show that you can fix the party, but you can't always fix the electorate.

Tuesday, 5 August

A letter from the Secretary of Grand Lodge, Commander Higham. On behalf of the select committee, I had sent him a list of those involved in the Birmingham Six case and asked him to say which are Masons. I intend to do the same with the John Stalker case. Sure enough, Higham is quibbling about our right to ask. He always used to say how keen the Masons were to cooperate with Parliament, but now we are getting down to the nitty-gritty his enthusiasm has suddenly evaporated. Well, if they want a confrontation, they can have one. I cannot think of a better issue.

Thursday, 28 August
Berden, Hertfordshire*

A dreadful night. The Tiny Tyrant, whose nose was blocked, rose at 2.30 a.m. Her screaming woke the whole house and no doubt the neighbours (the walls are paper thin). Nothing for it but to evacuate. We put her in the car and drove round the villages at dead of night. Although she soon fell asleep, we didn't dare return for fear that she would start her nonsense all over again. So we drove to Much Hadham, parked in front of the church and tried without much success to doze. A milk cart passed at around 5.30 a.m. At seven precisely, the gate of the old vicarage swung open and a large Volvo sped out. Between

---

*Home of my sister, Elizabeth.

seven and eight two dog-walkers passed. That was the total sum of activity in five hours. The Tyrant slept soundly throughout.

Saturday, 30 August

To lunch with Tony and Caroline Benn at Stansgate, an ungainly, rambling 1920s house in a stunning location on an Essex river estuary, several miles wide and dotted with small sailing boats. Eccentricities abound: a Victorian postbox, presented to Tony after his stint as Post-master General; a disused red telephone box; a monument to Rosa Luxembourg, basically a brick wall with a hammer and sickle in the middle. We did our best to keep straight faces as Caroline explained that the original was one of the first monuments to be torn down by Hitler. I forbore to say that in this instance Hitler and I are in agreement.

Stansgate explains why the Benns are such a close, happy family. Three generations have spent holidays and weekends here for eighty years. Tony says he can recall his father shouting down the telephone in the hallway to Lord Halifax in India. An air of amiable chaos pervades. The furniture consists mainly of cast-offs from other Benn houses. Vacuuming is intermittent. The rooms are cluttered because little has ever been thrown away.

Tony entertained the children with his full repertoire of party tricks. The highlight, an imitation of a steam train achieved by reciting a menu backwards at increasing speed – 'Biscuits and cheese, biscuits and cheese, beef and carrots, beef and carrots, suet pudding, suet pudding …' and then a high-pitched 'S-O-U-P'.

After lunch I was taken on a tour of the archives. A converted stable and half a dozen prefabricated sheds which accommodate the Benn papers, all neatly arranged in carefully labelled boxes. Caroline showed us her nature reserve, eight acres of wasteland planted with young oaks and other trees. I reminded Caroline that, some years ago, at the height of the anti-Benn hysteria, the *Guardian* had offered a prize – which I won – for the most spiteful news story about the Benns. The winning entry was a report in the *Daily Telegraph* after she had rescued two men in a boat who got into difficulties in the estuary.

She had swum out to them, pulled the boat in, given them tea and taken them back to their caravan site. Had they been rescued by anyone else there might have been talk of an award, but the *Telegraph* chose to lead on her failure to report the incident to the coastguard. Caroline said that she had recently met the coastguard concerned and he had said, 'I've been waiting all these years to apologise.'

In the evening we drove back to Sunderland, arriving after midnight. As I was getting into bed I switched on the radio to hear Alun Michael talking about Princess Diana. At first I couldn't understand what the story was and then I noticed he was referring to her in the past tense. She is dead.

Monday, 1 September
Sunderland

Back to the office – and a mountain of mail. The pile on Pat's desk was 11.5 inches high – I measured it with a ruler.

It has emerged that the driver of the car in which Diana died (an Al Fayed employee) was three times over the drink limit and travelling at way over the speed limit. Until now everyone had been blaming the paparazzi, but it seems to be the curse of the Al Fayeds. First they bring down the Tory Party and now this ...

Tuesday, 2 September

A huge, overwhelming outpouring of grief for Diana. Flowers piled high outside the royal palaces. The queue to sign the condolence books at St James's Palace stretches down the Mall and back again. On television, hour after hour of eulogy. All sensible editorial judgement abandoned. Perhaps it is better that she went this way. Had she lived she would have proved a disappointment to her admirers. Reality never matched the image and, as the years passed, the gap would have widened. The affair with Dodi was always destined to end badly. She might have gone down as a lonely, self-indulgent, well-meaning woman with a disastrous taste in men. Instead she will be remembered with affection for ever. Right up there with the all-time greats, struck down in the prime of life, JFK, Marilyn Monroe ...

Wednesday, 3 September

Sarah's first day at Grangetown School. 'Mum, I love it,' she said when she came home in the evening, 'I've already got SIX friends.'

Friday, 5 September

To town at lunchtime. Flowers for Diana are piled high around the war memorial in Mowbray Park. There must be the best part of a thousand bouquets and more are arriving all the time. Each with a little message. One says,

> To Diana,
> Born a lady,
> Became a princess,
> Died a legend.

Outside the Library, a queue about a hundred yards long of people waiting to sign the condolence book. It's the same all over the country. We are in the grip of hysteria. Even the party meeting in the evening started with a minute's silence for Diana, causing one of our number to walk out in a huff.

Saturday, 6 September

Diana's funeral. London looking beautiful in the sunshine without cars. Parliament Square a village green, overlooked by St Margaret's, the parish church. That's how it should always be. Parliament Square free of vehicles? Now there's a little project for the millennium instead of that stupid dome ...

Compulsive viewing. We sat riveted in front of the TV from the moment the gun carriage bearing the coffin left Kensington Palace until the hearse, strewn with flowers, reached the motorway four hours later. Crowds lined the streets all the way. Highlights: Elton John singing 'Candle in the Wind' (Sarah asked, 'Why couldn't they have the Rolling Stones?') and Charlie Althorp getting stuck into the paparazzi. The attitude of the crowds towards the senior royals was distinctly lukewarm. When the Queen left for the Abbey a big round of applause went up from the crowd. Only as the camera panned away did one realise that the applause was not for the Queen, but in response to the Union Jack that was being run up to half mast on the Palace flagpole. Another little victory for the people over the stuffed shirts. In death, as in life, Diana has upstaged them all.

Tuesday, 16 September
Sunderland

To the local Jobcentre. Bright and modern. Light years away from the old dole office stereotype. Most of the jobs advertised were in private security and care work at anywhere between two and three pounds an hour. All subsidised by the taxpayer through family income supplement and earnings top-up. Trust the Tories to devise a system where the state is subsidising the worst employers. The national minimum wage should put a stop to this, but it won't be of much benefit to the low paid if it is set so low that it simply replaces the existing subsidies. Someone estimated that it would need to be set at about £3.75 an hour to make a difference to the poorest wage earners.

Monday, 29 September
Labour Party Conference, Brighton

The sun shines on New Labour. The climate is positively Mediterranean, not a cloud in the sky, people lounging in deckchairs on the beach, everywhere pavement cafes.

Security, as befits a party which for the first time in a long while is worth blowing up, is tight. A security 'village' has been created, incorporating the conference centre, the Grand and Metropole hotels. Entry is via a tunnel under the road leading from the promenade. The unwashed and their banners are kept at a safe distance, separated from the shiny New Labourites by metal barriers, their slogans barely audible across the stream of passing traffic.

Inside our New Labour condominium a great calm prevails. The pamphleteers, leafleters and assorted agitators of previous years are scarcely to be seen. In their place sharp-suited young men and women pace up and down talking urgently into mobile phones. Never in my twenty-six years of annual conferences have we looked so respectable.

At the shop, the range of books and videos available has narrowed. Half the covers depict Our Leader in triumphant mode. His face is everywhere – on posters, dust jackets and in every newspaper. Never have we gone in for leader worship on this scale. Never has a Labour leader had such an unrivalled grip on the levers of power, within the party and without … and yet, deep below the surface, all is not as it seems …

At about five o'clock I was in the bar when from the conference hall there came the sound of unscripted cheering. Suddenly the doors opened and Ken Livingstone, looking extremely pleased with himself, swept past pursued by cameras and reporters. He has, by a handsome margin, defeated Peter Mandelson for a place on the National Executive Committee. The first stirrings of rebellion or the last gasp of the old order? Most likely the latter.

Tuesday, 30 September

All over Brighton one runs into people chortling over Ken's great victory – or, to be more precise, Peter's defeat. It has made a lot of people happy. And not just the usual suspects. There are two particularly satisfying aspects. One, the margin of victory – Ken won by more than 20,000 votes. Two, far from being elected by an unrepresentative elite, Ken was elected by a ballot of the entire New Labour membership. A point that seems to have been lost on the hacks. Elinor Goodman, on the Channel Four news last night, ascribed Ken's victory to 'activists', and one of the BBC's many commentators remarked on the breakfast news this morning that he hadn't realised there were so many left-wing delegates present, as if the delegates had anything to do with it. The whole point is that this was a victory for the inactive over the active.

The Speech. I was in two minds whether to attend. The MPs' pen is very exposed and you never know who is watching for signs of irreverence. And then, of course, there is the embarrassment of being caught up in that silly standing ovation. I sat in the back row between George Galloway and Paddy Tipping. Alastair Campbell lurked in the background, looking grim and throwing occasional glances in our direction. George, who has a soft spot for dictators, has perfected the art of maintaining prolonged applause with a minimum of exertion. 'Under Stalin,' he whispered, 'no one wanted to be seen to be the first to stop clapping.'

It was a good speech. Witty, positive, relatively low on claptrap and addressed primarily to the nation and not to the party; lots of references to 'hard choices', which had been widely trailed in advance. It does slightly worry me that most of those being called upon to face these hard choices are the very people who suffered under Thatcher. When, I wonder, will the middle classes be called upon to face hard choices?

At the end The Man left the stage to a long ovation accompanied by the music of Saint-Saëns. So heady was the atmosphere that no one would have been at all surprised had he been assumed into heaven. As the applause died down Robin Cook, who was in the chair, remarked that it was 'one of the best' leader's speeches he had heard in his thirty-one years of conference-going. Suspiciously lukewarm, I thought. Mandelson, no doubt, will have taken note.

Wednesday, 1 October
Tony Banks is in trouble for a tasteless gag about William Hague. The evening news bulletins lead on it. An apology has been issued, but it may not be enough. I fear the worst.

Monday, 6 October

I caught Emma raiding the sweet jar. Thinking she was unobserved, she dragged a chair as big as she is across the kitchen, climbed up on it and opened the cupboard. At which point she noticed me, standing by the door. Far from being embarrassed she waved her arm in a southerly direction and said loudly and firmly, 'DAD – GO TO LONDON.'

Monday, 13 October

Derry Irvine came to the select committee. Like most expensive lawyers he speaks ponderously and at length. There has been some backtracking. The judicial appointments committee is on the back burner and he clearly isn't going to take on the judges over freemasonry. He does, however, have plans for making the law cheaper and more accessible and seems genuinely committed to widening the social base of the judiciary.

Douglas Hogg and David Winnick gave trouble, demanding to ask questions on everything, interrupting when I wouldn't let them. Hogg in particular is difficult; having been minister of just about everything he has opinions on everything.

Dinner with Bruce Palling and his wife Lucinda. Lucinda told a tale about the September issue of *Tatler*, which doesn't seem to have seen the light of day. Two years ago the magazine predicted that Diana would fall in love with a playboy and go to live abroad. In view of the affair with Dodi, they commissioned a big 'we told you so piece' for September. The edition had already gone to press when disaster struck. In top secrecy, all 90,000 copies were taken to a barn in the countryside where a gang of immigrant labourers had been hired to excise the offending piece from every copy. The only clue as to what the magazine had once contained was a trailer on the spine.

Tuesday, 14 October

A call from a journalist to say that Neil Hamilton, one of the Tories accused of taking money from Al Fayed, has, while giving evidence to the Privileges Committee, compared himself to me – as someone who was vilified and eventually vindicated. Asked to comment, I said, 'Grateful though I am for any friendly reference, the parallels between Mr Hamilton's career and mine are not precise.' I then hurried upstairs to Committee Room 15, arriving just in time to hear Hamilton rounding off his two-hour submission with the claim that he was the victim of a miscarriage of justice equal to that of the innocent people convicted in the Guildford, Birmingham and Carl Bridgewater cases. Afterwards, in the corridor, I said that I could not recall his help with any of those cases. He readily owned up, adding that at least he was not one of those who had done the jeering.

Wednesday, 15 October
Sunderland

A visit to the County Durham Masons, who have an office just up the terrace from mine. Lord Barnard, the Grand-What-Have-You, a pleasant old gent in a brown three-piece, came in person all the way from Raby Castle. The others were the provincial secretary, a rotund cheerful man, a retired doctor who is about to succeed Lord Barnard, and a tall, bald, red-faced, sinister-looking man whose name I didn't catch and who seemed more on edge than the others. As ever, they were at pains to assure me that their purposes were charitable and social and their rituals harmless. They said they were doing their best to overcome public suspicion by holding open days and being generally more forthcoming. I replied that my only interest was in doing away with secrecy, particularly as regards public servants and people doing business with the public sector. There were two ways of resolving the problem which – as they readily conceded – is doing them great damage. Either they could be open about their membership or Parliament could require that certain categories of public servants who were members of secret societies should disclose. This gave rise to the usual guff about golf clubs and rotary clubs being similar organisations, but they didn't make much of it. They mentioned Catholics and I agreed that the Catenians appeared to be in a similar category, but pointed out that there were only 30,000 Catenians whereas there were 400,000 Masons and they didn't argue with that. They argued that publishing the names of members would be an infringement of their liberties to which I responded that since they already publish – in their handbooks – the names of the 10 per cent or so of their members who hold office, I couldn't see what the problem was. At this, the red-faced man said they were worried that Masons would be discriminated against. Indeed, he alleged, this was already happening. There had been a number of resignations, particularly of policemen who thought that membership of the Masons could damage their career prospects. 'So,' I said, 'the tide is beginning to turn.' At this they shifted uncomfortably, not quite willing to acknowledge that when it came to career prospects, the tide had long flowed in their favour. I added that I would be glad to speak up on behalf of anyone who could demonstrate that he had been discriminated against on the grounds that he was a Mason. If they were open about membership, the problem would melt away.

At this it seemed to dawn on the doctor that no amount of open days or charitable donations could resolve the problem. I confirmed that this was so. The issue was secrecy. If Masons were worried that they were the subject of a great deal of unjustified paranoia – and they are – they had only themselves to blame. They looked uncomfortable, but didn't offer much resistance. The penny, I suspect, is dropping. The brighter of them are smart enough to know they have a crisis on their hands. Masonry, like the Conservative Party, no longer attracts the ambitious. Recruitment is drying up. They are increasingly elderly. Their influence is drying up, too.

They gave me a tour of their little museum, full of banners and medals, and then their hall, which is marginally less sinister inside that it looks from outside. We parted on friendly terms.

Tuesday, 21 October

To lunch with John Gilbert at the Reform Club, where he told me the extraordinary story of his translation from the back benches to, aged seventy, the number two job at the Ministry of Defence.

When the House was dissolved in March, John had been intending to contest the election. Characteristically, he informed his party that he did not intend to start campaigning until the Monday after Easter. On Thursday, 3 April, three weeks into the official campaign, he was relaxing at home in Earls Court when he received a call from Tony Blair's chief of staff, Jonathan Powell, asking if he would like to go to the Lords. He replied that he was not in the least interested in going to the Lords unless he was given something useful to do. On Saturday came a call from The Man himself, saying that he was intending to offer John a place in the government, although it might be difficult finding him a place in the Cabinet. At which, says John, he fell about laughing. He quickly recovered, however, and named his price. It was high. ('I have,' he says, 'always worked on the principle that others will place the same value upon you as you place upon yourself.') He wished either to be Paymaster General, Ambassador to Washington or chairman of the Civil Aviation Authority. Somewhere along the line he added that he might combine whatever job he was given with the deputy leadership of the Lords. There was also talk of having Cabinet rank, even though he would be outside the Cabinet. As to what his responsibilities as Paymaster General might entail, he suggested that these might include coordinating the intelligence agencies. It was left that Jonathan Powell would ring back. By Sunday evening, no call having been received, he called Powell to say that he must have an answer forthwith since he was due to launch his election campaign the following day. Powell went to consult and then rang back saying that The Man agreed to John's terms.

On Monday, 7 April, his election address already printed, John travelled to Dudley, under strict instructions not to reveal that he had been offered any sort of inducement (there was, after all, the formality of an election to be won). Instead, he told his constituency party that he had to go because the seat was marginal and, although it would be won this time round, it might be more difficult next time if they had a new candidate. No one, he says, believed him.

At this point John left the meeting and the regional organiser outlined the emergency procedure for finding a new candidate – they had just five days. Would the selection be open or was it already fixed, she was asked. She assured them that it would be entirely open. On this basis the party chairman Alan Harvey, a well-respected trade union official, put his hat in the ring. He was told to report to Labour Party HQ in London for an interview by the by-election panel of the National Executive Committee, the following Friday. The interview duly took place. The next day's newspapers carried the outcome of other last-minute selections, but no mention of Dudley. That evening word reached Dudley Labour Party that their candidate would be Ross Cranston, an academic lawyer with no local connections and who was not among the candidates who had been interviewed the previous day. Cranston later told John that on the Friday evening he had received a call from the New Labour command centre saying that, if he could get himself up to Edinburgh (where the by-election panel was convening to resolve the last-minute selections in Scotland) by noon next day, the seat was his. At this point, says John, he received a call from Party HQ asking for his help in persuading the Dudley party to accept Cranston, which he declined to do on the grounds that they hadn't bothered to consult him in the first place. Meanwhile, the hapless Cranston was already en route from Edinburgh to Dudley to be crowned. A crisis loomed. Only at the last moment, with the adoption meeting already under way and the deadline for close of nominations fast approaching, was the party persuaded to endorse Cranston. Understandably, there are some very angry people in Dudley.

No doubt there are similar stories to tell at Newport, Hull West, Warrington and in all the other places where incumbents were prevailed upon to stand down at the last minute in return for peerages or other inducements. A last-minute attempt was also made to remove Derek Foster in Bishop Auckland, although that failed when Derek refused to budge. The new masters just can't stop fixing. Even when it doesn't matter.

The question arises, of course, why go to all this trouble to install an obscure academic lawyer with no very obvious New Labour credentials? The answer is that this was not the original plan. The purpose of the exercise was to find a seat for The Man's friend, Charlie Falconer, but only on condition that he withdrew his children from their expensive public schools, which he refused to do. Not that it made much difference. Within weeks, Charlie Falconer was wafted into the Lords* and appointed Solicitor General, without the bother of having to get elected.

Monday, 27 October

Parliament resumes after a scandalous eighty-seven-day recess.

Tuesday, 28 October

To the Environment Department as part of a delegation to see Angela Eagle about leylandii hedges. Denis Howell came with a man who had spent years of anguish and thousands of pounds fending off rogue neighbours who sued him after he had cut back their hedge because it was excluding his light. The problem seems easily resolvable. Either bring hedges within the planning laws or extend the law of nuisance. Angela was accompanied by a young civil servant, with a 'can't do' mentality who raised objections to every suggestion.

Later, a statement on reform of magistrates courts, which comes firmly within the remit of the select committee. I rose, but Betty ignored me. When she called Ross Cranston, a member of my committee, ahead of me, I walked out in disgust. I received similar treatment yesterday in Home Office questions. At one point I was the only member standing and she just glanced at me and moved on. I am not having it. I shall make a fuss.

---

*Where, it must be admitted, he turned out to be a great success.

Wednesday, 29 October

The first meeting of the parliamentary committee in three months. The Man graced us with his presence for half an hour. (Alan Haworth said he had bent The Man's ear on the need to treat the committee seriously when they were up a mountain in the Pyrenees in the summer.)

We raised the row over plans to impose PR and a list system for the next Euro elections. I said that, speaking as someone who would have been in the high six-hundred-and-forties had a list system been in operation for Westminster, I wasn't very keen on lists.

Nick Brown reported that he was collecting evidence on the systematic heckling of women members by some of the adolescents on the other side. They've even been harassing some of the women on their own side. Much of it is pure smut. Nick said he was having the audio tapes checked and the whips were taking notes. If he can gather enough evidence he is going to take it up with the Speaker.

Thursday, 30 October

John Farr, a ruddy-faced knight of the Shires with whom I formed an unlikely alliance over the Birmingham Six, has died. He dropped dead while out grouse shooting, which I am sure he would regard as a good way to go. I once asked whether his stand on the Birmingham bombings had caused problems with his Conservative colleagues. 'Only from the lawyers – and they are all arseholes,' he replied.

Tuesday, 4 November

Came across Nicolas Bevan, the Speaker's Secretary, in the Library and inquired why I did not seem to be accorded the same degree of precedence at Home Office questions and statements as my predecessor, Sir Ivan Lawrence. He was slippery at first but eventually I pinned him down. 'I think people are having difficulty adjusting to your new status,' he said.

'Well I'm not,' I replied.

'Point taken.'

We'll see what happens. If there is no improvement I shall go over his head.

This evening, the long-awaited showdown with the senior Masons, Commander Higham and John Hamill. I want the names of the Masons on the West Midlands Serious Crime Squad and those involved in the Stalker affair. They are refusing to provide them. 'I'm not looking for a confrontation,' I said, 'but I am prepared for one if you insist.' What better issue on which to test the powers of the select committee? They agreed to go away and recommend cooperation to their board. We shall see.

Wednesday, 5 November

Breakfast in the Members' Tea Room which, even at that time in the morning, stank of cigar smoke. The House of Commons Tea Room is surely just about the only restaurant in the country where people can sit puffing their foul weeds in the midst of diners.

The Man addressed the parliamentary party. All the usual watch words, 'unity', 'discipline', 'hard choices'. The euphoria, he said, was over. 'We are now in a period when people want results.' He rang a lot of bells: 'The last Labour government spent its first two years with the purse wide open and the last three years with its purse tight shut. That was crazy.' He made an ambiguous little joke about sycophancy. 'It may not go down well elsewhere, but it goes down well with me.' We laughed, but was he joking?

Happily there was no hint of sycophancy in the comments from the floor. Paul Flynn said we appeared to be soft on fox-hunters and the tobacco industry, but hard on students and pensioners. Up to that point he had a lot of people with him. He then blew it by talking of 'treachery and political incompetence'. Rhodri Morgan talked of the growing culture of leaks and off-the-record briefings, with particular reference to the hunting Bill – that drew a round of applause. Dennis Skinner advised Tony to 'wean himself off this Tory budget'. David Winnick, referring to yesterday's suspension of four Euro MPs, called for tolerance. The Man replied calmly but robustly to each point, advising everyone to keep their eye on the big picture. The only hint of annoyance was at Paul Flynn's contribution, which he described as 'drivel'.

Hunting came up again at the parliamentary committee. The issue was getting us a very bad press, The Man acknowledged. We were being blamed even though it was (mainly) Tories who were planning to derail it in the Lords, where there was danger that our entire programme would become bogged down. A chance, I ventured, to mobilise public opinion for when the time came to reform the Lords. Until now I thought this was something we were definitely going to take on in the next session, but suddenly I'm not so sure. He said, 'If you look at the history books ...'

'You've been reading a lot of history recently,' I whispered. (This morning he was alleging that disunity sunk the Attlee government.)

'If you look at history, you'll see that the 1906 government was totally derailed by reform of the House of Lords. Everyone says today that the 1911 Act was the right thing to do, but it took five years to get through.'

Why not offer the hereditaries a deal, I suggested. Life access to the club facilities in return for going quietly. To which Margaret Jay responded that most of them cared more about hunting than they did about the survival of the Lords.

Several people raised the proposed cut to the Lone Parent Premium, to which Ann Clwyd added the cut in Reduced Earnings Allowance. The Man sighed and said the problem is that social security is more than one billion over budget and there were half a dozen other problems in the pipeline.

I pointed out that the plan to cut single-parent benefits didn't square very easily with our policy of encouraging single mothers back into work, since – if they lost their jobs – they would have to re-register at the lower rate. Jean Corston added that Harriet Harman had confirmed that this was so. I wasn't sure that The Man had grasped this point, but Jean reckoned that he had – and it had appeared to come as a surprise. Foxes and single parents have got him worried. He's obviously getting similar messages from several quarters.

Thursday, 6 November

To the Liaison Committee, which contains some very self-satisfied and comfortable people with a highly developed sense of their own importance. The clerk (a large, pink man) positively glows with self-satisfaction. He would have been at home in this building any time in the last 300 years. For all I know, he may have been here all that time.

Seven chairmen had submitted applications on behalf of their committees for foreign excursions. Five had found urgent reasons for going to the United States. They all specified the best hotels and club- or business-class travel. Someone remarked that the dignity of Parliament required nothing less. In every case they had budgeted the attendance of every committee member plus a minimum of two retainers. Costs per trip varied between £50,000 and £70,000. They were all approved just about on the nod, although Nick Winterton did query an item on the International Development Committee's budget for a trip to Africa which allowed a staggering £1,200 a day for two locally recruited interpreters. Bowen Wells undertook to make inquiries. I remarked that we seemed to be scrutinising the activities of the American government rather more vigorously than our own. Beyond that there was no resistance.

We then went on to discuss a paper drafted by the clerk suggesting that the travel budget for next year be increased from £710,000 to £1.2 million, a rise of 55 per cent. The main justification was that the number of committees had increased. It was also argued that 'forcing committees to travel in inappropriate conditions and to stay in inadequate hotels redounded to the disadvantage both of the ability of members to work and also to the reputation of Parliament'. 'Our reputation' in this instance appears to mean in the eyes of fat cats from other parliaments rather than in the eyes of those who elected us, who, I suspect, would take a wholly different view. It's not more resources or even powers that select committees most need. Those we already have are underused. Our status will only improve when committee members start to take their work more seriously – by reading their briefs, turning up on time and learning to ask simple, relevant questions. I sometimes think we'd get a better turnout if we convened in a luxury hotel in Washington rather than in a room on the Committee Corridor.

The government is becoming accident prone. First, the botch-up over the hunting Bill. Now cigarette advertising. Tessa Jowell announced yesterday that Formula One racing was to be exempt from the much-heralded ban on cigarette advertising. The decision seems to have come from Downing Street after a visit by a powerful lobby of motor racers. As if that wasn't bad enough, we learn this morning that Tessa's husband has some sort of commercial relationship with the Formula One team. Not that Tessa is at fault. She apparently declared the possible conflict of interest months ago. This being so, why on earth was the decision left to her? Surely we could have found someone in the Department of Health who has no connection with motor racing?

Jean Corston told today me of another cock-up. Scottish ministers apparently went ahead and announced their own, more generous, formula for student funding without informing the Secretary of State for Education, David Blunkett. Result: English and Scots students with different funding regimes will be studying alongside each other at universities all over the country. The Tories have already seized on the point. One intervened on Blunkett in a debate on Tuesday and David simply replied that Brian Wilson would deal with it in his summing-up. 'What else could I do?' he said to Jean afterwards. Needless to say, when the time came to reply Wilson skated round the issue. What else could he do?

Monday, 10 November

A call from Jack Straw, who says that the judges are absolutely refusing to cooperate with any kind of disclosure re membership of secret societies and Derry Irvine declines to face up to them. Part of the problem is that it is difficult to recruit judges because they are making so much money at the Bar and so Derry can't afford to alienate them. I fear we are in for disappointment.

Tuesday, 11 November

Everyone is talking about the £1 million donation to the Labour Party by the Formula One magnate Bernie Ecclestone. We have returned the money, but the Tories won't let it drop and who can blame them? 'Of course, he bought access,' remarked Margaret Hodge when I passed her in a corridor. The truth is we are now in hock to the same sort of people – in some cases precisely the same people – who were funding the Tory Party. A big mess. The only good to come out of it is that people are starting to talk seriously about a cap on what political parties can spend on election campaigns. About time, too.

Wednesday, 12 November

To the meeting of the parliamentary party, where for the first time in my life I found myself on the platform delivering what will become regular report-back sessions from the parliamentary committee. About 100 members attended. The gist of my contribution was that our masters ought to bear in mind that 'the judgement of the led is some-times superior to that of the leaders', a sentiment that led to a little round of table banging. The issue that arose most in the discussion that followed was the planned cut in Lone Parent Premium, part of our inheritance from the Tories which we indignantly opposed in opposition and which we now propose to implement. There is wide-spread unease, even among the loyalists. If we can't head it off, this will be the subject of my first rebellion.

Single-parent benefit came up again at the meeting of the parliamen-tary committee in the evening. Someone asked if it would come up on the floor of the House, to which Chief Whip Nick Brown replied, 'Not if I can help it.' Later, Andrew Bennett suggested a resolution to the next meeting of the parliamentary party with lots of signatures which could be shown to our masters before it was tabled in the hope that they would have second thoughts.

Tom Sawyer reported that – as a result of returning the Ecclestone donation – the party was now £5.5 million in the red.

PMQs – the liveliest so far – were dominated by the Formula One fiasco. Not a total disaster. There is, after all, no shortage of ammunition to fire back at the Tories and The Man made a good job of it. Unfortunately, just when he seemed to have got away relatively unscathed, up got Martin Bell to put the boot in, which he did skilfully. The public, of course, will just say that we are all as bad as one another. The quicker we sort out party funding, the better.

Tony Benn reports that he came across Rupert Murdoch this morning, while waiting for a lift at the Queen Elizabeth Centre. 'Rather like meeting the Queen at a bus stop,' was how he put it. They had last met, Tony had reminded the Great Oligarch, twenty-five years ago when he had come to solicit Murdoch's support for a referendum on the Common Market. Tony said, 'You listened courteously and then you rubbished me in your newspapers.'

Thursday, 13 November

Ran into John Major by the photocopier at the end of Upper Corridor South. We had another conversation about Murdoch, whom he clearly loathes. He talked of 'the damage he did to your party in the early eighties and mine in the early nineties'. I asked what could be done, given that the Tyrant would unleash the full force of his empire against anyone who tried to tame him. 'The only way is a two-party alliance,' he said. Time to dig out my great – unsent – memorandum.

On my way to the BBC at Millbank, to talk about party funding, I came across Sir Patrick Neill emerging from the Lord Chancellor's office and took the opportunity to bend his ear. He was affable and open to the idea of a cap on election spending. I also drew his attention to the little racket that we uncovered when the select committee looked at the subject. Namely, that the drinks and tobacco industry have all the best poster sites permanently booked and at elections they make them available only to the Conservative Party. He said he wasn't aware of that. I promised to send him a copy of the select committee report.

I did a turn on *The Week in Westminster* with a dreadful man called Shaun Woodward, who replaced Douglas Hurd at Witney. Before that he was a Tory apparatchik – and it showed. He arrived clutching a pile of briefing notes and spent ten minutes scribbling furiously. As soon as the microphones were switched on he launched into a tirade about the wickedness of Blair and the Labour Party over the Ecclestone donation and refused to be diverted into any discussion of practical measures to resolve the problem. The Liberal Democrat, Nick Harvey, and I looked on in amazement at such a bravura display of shamelessness in one who has only been in Parliament six months. Who would have guessed that this was a man who represented the party of Mohammed Al Fayed, Asil Nadir, Neil Hamilton, Jonathan Aitken, to mention but a few? He will go far.*

Monday, 17 November

To London. Derek Foster was on the train, still smarting from the disgraceful way he has been treated. We talked about Mandelson. Derek said that, in opposition, Peter was in the habit of strolling into the Leader's room, taking off his jacket and settling down behind the desk as though he owned the place. 'I used to complain to Tony about Peter week after week. Tony would say, "What do you want me to do? Hang him from a yardarm?" Doug Hoyle, who was present on one occasion, said, "I could sell tickets for that."'

Derek also had some harsh things to say about The Man. We agreed that he has been seriously damaged by the Ecclestone affair. Not least because the truth has only been squeezed out of him bit by bit. Derek, referring to his time as Chief Whip, said, 'I soon discovered that nobody believed a word he said.' He spoke slowly, emphasising every word. Derek added that he had recently attended a social in Spennymoor and someone remarked to him, 'You've been here a long time. Blair usually leaves after the soup.'

---

*He did. He defected to Labour and was appointed Northern Ireland Secretary.

Tuesday, 18 November

A big row brewing about the proposed cut in Lone Parent Premium. No one is happy. Jean Corston says that about seventy members had written to Gordon protesting. Maria Fyfe produced a copy of the briefing note which Harriet Harman put out before the budget debate, when the Tories announced the cut last November. 'Abolition', she wrote, 'will make working lone mothers worse off and will discourage work amongst this group.' In the debate on 28 November she said that the proposed cuts 'will make hundreds of thousands of the poorest children worse off'. Now she's proposing to do just that. About a dozen people, including several new members, attended the What's Left meeting in the evening. I drafted a motion calling for the cuts to be postponed until the Welfare to Work strategy is up and running and – a nice touch this – until Peter Mandelson's much-trumpeted Social Exclusion Unit had had a chance to study the impact. We agreed to see how many signatures we get before deciding what to do.

Wednesday, 19 November

A big turnout at this morning's meeting of the parliamentary party to hear Harriet justify the cut in Lone Parent Premium. She gave a competent but shameless performance, starting with an upbeat account of her plans to get single parents off benefit and into work. The cuts, she said, were regrettable, but unavoidable. No stone had been left unturned in an attempt to find an alternative. There was the inevitable talk of hard choices, a phrase which always seems to precede some new assault on the poorest. No sooner had she sat down than up got Caroline Flint, one of the new upwardly mobile women who, despite having been part of a single-parent family herself, proceeded to justify the cuts. It was as though someone had pushed a button. The mood, however, was overwhelmingly hostile and, as Ian Davidson pointed out, it wasn't just the usual suspects. I decided that it was time to come out: I told Harriet it was a mistake and that I wouldn't support her. Later, Nick Brown told me he had proposed to Gordon that the cut be put back a year, but Gordon was resisting. Incredibly, neither

Gordon nor any other member of the Treasury team bothered to show up. Harriet is being hung out to dry.

At Questions, the Tories were still harping on about Bernie Ecclestone's donation, but The Man hit back cleverly by saying that he had invited Sir Patrick Neill to examine all Labour donations back to 1992 and the Lib Dems had agreed to do likewise. He challenged the Tories to do the same. That wiped the smile off their faces. Suddenly it dawned on even the stupidest of them where all this is leading.

Thursday, 20 November

Awoken at seven by a call from *Today* wanting me to talk about the uprising over Lone Parent Premium. I didn't respond. When I got to the House there were several more messages waiting, but I declined all offers. The only time I ever get invited to appear on *Today* is to attack my own side.

George Mudie, a whip, told me how worried he was about the single parent row. He said that Nick Brown and he had been trying to convey a message to our masters for some time, but that they were starting to shoot the messenger. I rang Clive Soley to find out what happened at yesterday's meeting of the parliamentary committee (which I missed). He said The Man had attended for about twenty minutes. Everyone had pressed him about Lone Parent Premium and he went away promising to reflect. The committee had agreed to send a delegation to talk to Gordon about it. Clive seemed hopeful that we could at least get a postponement. However, no sooner had I put the phone down than a journalist told me that Downing Street was saying that there would be no change. It is no longer a question of resources, but of virility.

Monday, 24 November

To London, arriving in time to show my face at Home Office questions. Derek Foster was on the train. Tony, he says, has practically abandoned cabinet government. All key decisions are taken by the small cabal around him – Alastair Campbell, Jonathan Powell, Peter Mandelson and (sometimes) Gordon Brown. He'll live to regret it, says Derek, because when things go wrong – as they did with Ecclestone – he'll be glad to take refuge in collective responsibility.

After questions, the latest Tory defector, Peter Temple-Morris, took his seat on our side, to loud cheers and much back-slapping. Obviously it was carefully choreographed. The episode left me cold. It's only six months since he was elected with the word 'Conservative' after his name on the ballot paper. If he's no longer a Tory, the only honourable course is to stand down and fight a by-election under his new colours.

Later, Jack Straw took me aside and explained the problems he is having with Derry Irvine over Masons. Derry apparently sided with the judges and says there is no way they will be signed up to any register. So vehement was his opposition that Jack was obliged to remind him that as recently as March this year he (Derry) had agreed to a register which covered judges and magistrates as well as the police. Jack had then produced a copy of Derry's letter signing up to a register. Whereupon Derry had apologised, but still refuses to budge. Jack is, therefore, proposing a voluntary register which non-Masons would also be requested to complete, with a threat of legislation if that fails. The key point is not to isolate the police. It has to apply to everybody. A poor substitute, but I suppose it's worth a shot, although I fear the Masons will boycott anything which allows them the slightest discretion.

At seven o'clock there was a well-attended meeting of the backbench Home Affairs Committee at which Jack outlined his European Elections Bill and the proposed list system which is upsetting a lot of people. He made no attempt to hide the fact that he is opposed to PR, which, he said, could lead to 'an effete political elite who don't know what is going on'. Ann Clwyd, who supports PR, said a list system was the one sure way to discredit PR. Merlyn Rees, a former Home Secretary, said he was instinctively against lists. Jack left the impression that the matter was not yet resolved and said that the party must be consulted. Although no doubt the final decision will be taken by someone in our effete political elite.

Tuesday, 25 November

A brief chat with Chris Smith about Murdoch. I asked what the chances were of bringing Sky within the licensing and quality regime that applies to other commercial channels. He said he had included this in a list of options to Downing Street (through which all decisions affecting the interests of Murdoch have to be cleared), but that 'the smoke signals are not good'. The regime, he says, is 'terrified' of Murdoch.

Gordon delivered his pre-Budget statement. Mostly a restatement of aims, but there was some welcome help with pensioners' heating bills and some adjustments to the proposed cuts in Lone Parent Premium. Afterwards Gordon's henchmen were putting it about that this solved the problem, but it doesn't. Later, Gordon made a rare appearance in the Tea Room and Ann Clwyd said to his face that she had 1,400 single mothers and only 200 job vacancies in her constituency – where were the jobs going to come from?

Gordon Brown has been made Parliamentarian of the Year by one of the political magazines. An odd choice, considering he rarely sets foot in Parliament and on the few occasions he does, he talks at, rather than to, us. He is hardly ever seen in the division lobby, let alone the Tea Room.

I have been collecting signatures on a motion calling for the single-parent cuts to be postponed until after Welfare to Work is up and running. Hard work at first although it got easier when it became clear that we have friends in high places. The sheer gutlessness of many of the new members is depressing. Not much hero material among this lot. The new, younger women are the worst. All style, no politics. Jean Corston recounted how she overheard one of the new women sounding off about the wickedness of the cuts, but as soon as she was offered a copy of the motion to sign, she made an excuse and left. Many of those who signed did so only after carefully cross-examining me about the chances of their name leaking and what would happen if the whips found out. As it turned out, we appear to have some sympathisers in the higher reaches of the Whips Office. George Mudie, one of the senior whips, stopped me and said he was quietly encouraging people to sign. By close of play we had 120 signatures.

Wednesday, 26 November

To the House, where I wrote a covering letter to Gordon for the petition on Lone Parent Premium. I made a point of saying that forty members had signed since Gordon's statement and that the signatories included six select committee chairmen. I made five copies and addressed the others to the Prime Minister, the Chief Whip, Harriet Harman and the chairman of the parliamentary party, Clive Soley.

At 3.30 p.m., Jean, Sylvia Heal and Ann Clwyd went with Clive to see Gordon at the Treasury, where they handed over the letter and petition. An hour later, as we assembled in the Prime Minister's room at the House for the parliamentary committee, I handed The Man his copy. I said that feeling was running high, but that we had all gone out of our way to avoid making a fuss in public. Clive said he was in no doubt that a significant minority of single parents would lose out seriously. Sylvia said the change would act as a disincentive to single parents to find work, since they risked having to sign back on at the lower rate if they lost their job. She added, it was not true to suggest – as some of the apologists have been – that no one will lose out. In response The Man said that he appreciated the distinction between public and private criticism – and contrasted our approach with Ken Livingstone addressing firefighters outside the NEC this morning. He expressed concern that news of the uprising would leak and I said that the only copies in existence, apart from mine, were now in the hands of the most senior members of the government, to which he smiled and said, 'We won't leak this one.'

There was discussion about an article in this week's *Sunday Times* which suggested that, within hours of the election, Mandelson had been compiling dossiers of unflattering material on the new members. The party's press officer, David Hill, didn't, however, deny that some sort of dossier had been compiled or even that some of the wilder comments had been made. Nick Brown was at pains to assure us that the whips kept no details of members' personal lives – only notes on speeches, attendance records at select and standing committees and 'press highlights'. The Prime Minister added, 'Contrary to speculation, I don't desire to lobotomise the entire parliamentary party.'

'Not entirely,' added Ann Taylor to laughter.

As we were leaving, David Hill – who had left earlier – reappeared and said that the Press Association was running a piece about the petition and other journalists were snooping round. We agreed to say nothing.

On the way out I was waylaid by Don Touhig (Gordon Brown's Parliamentary Private Secretary) who asked if I had another copy of the letter because Gordon had 'mislaid' (did he mean junked?) his copy. Why did he want it? 'Because he is meeting the Prime Minister – now.'

Thursday, 27 November

The day passed with no word from on high. Then, in the evening, I was sitting with friends in the Pugin Room when George Mudie came in and said that the Chancellor wanted to see me immediately, in the Chief Whip's office. When I got there Gordon, Nick Brown and a little group of advisers were sitting in the anteroom with long faces. Gordon and I retired to the inner sanctum. He did most of the talking. He was amiable, but unbending. He said that the order authorising the cuts had already gone through and could not be reversed. He didn't seem entirely certain of this point and summoned his assistant, Ed Miliband, who confirmed that this was so. He did, however, concede that the issue had been badly handled.

I responded, saying that the unrest arose from the fact that we are going ahead with Tory cuts and that he, or at least members of his team, should have been at the parliamentary party meeting instead of leaving Harriet gently swinging in the wind. He replied disingenuously that it was Harriet's decision and he didn't want to embarrass her by making it look as though he were breathing down her neck. I said he was in danger of becoming out of touch and needed to be seen in the Tea Room more often and also get into the habit of voting at least once a week. This he appeared to concede.

Basically, he wants me to damp down the rebellion. I told him that this was not within my power but it might be helpful if he were to provide a letter setting out his position which I could then circulate. The danger of this, of course, is that the press will get it. He said he would think about what to do and that Ed Miliband would call me in the morning.

Friday, 28 November

Four messages from the *Today* programme, all of which I ignored, inviting me to discuss single-parent benefit. At the House, a message from Ed Miliband awaited. Gordon has decided to circulate a briefing. He gave me Gordon's mobile number and suggested I call, but I didn't bother. Gordon only wants to hear me agree that he has met the concerns of the objectors and the truth is, he hasn't.

Unless I am mistaken, the atmosphere is turning ugly. Although Nick Brown and George Mudie have handled this little crisis sensitively, the same cannot be said of the lance corporals, several of whom have been ringing round signatories to Audrey Wise's motion, inviting them, with varying degrees of menace, to withdraw. It may have been my imagination but Jim Dowd, who is normally amiable, cut me dead when I passed him in the 'Aye' Lobby. Later, I heard that he is one of those threatening 'consequences' for those who signed my letter. It all made sense, however, when I saw the *Telegraph*, the front page of which is headed, '120 MPs Defy Whips Over Single Parents'. I suppose it was too much to hope that the uprising could be kept under wraps for long. There is a danger, I fear, that the messenger will be shot.

Tuesday, 2 December

I sat with Audrey Wise in the Tea Room opposite a pleasant, bright young fellow who was recently elected for a seat in the Midlands. After he had gone Audrey said that she had shared a platform with him at a May Day rally last year where he had made a speech to the left of her. 'Don't worry,' he told her afterwards, 'I'm no Blairite. We defeated the Blairites here.'

Lo and behold, eighteen months later he has popped up as one of the silent New Labourites on the standing committee that was supposed to scrutinise the cuts in Lone Parent Premium. Audrey says that, when challenged, he came out with all the usual New Labour claptrap. Audrey reckons they've had microchips inserted in their brains.

Wednesday, 3 December

Awoke at 6 a.m. with a terrible pain. So excruciating that I had to get up and walk around, massaging my stomach. After about an hour and a quarter, when I was on the point of calling an ambulance, it faded.

Wayne David, Leader of the European Labour Party, addressed the parliamentary party. He appeared to have no opinions of his own and was clean bowled by a question inviting him to express a view about a single currency. Then came David Blunkett, who described the new arrangements on student fees as 'the nearest thing to a graduate tax without using the word "tax"'. He had an easy ride. As Doug Hoyle remarked, 'The heat has gone out of it.' The truth is, of course, that the new arrangement is far superior to anything that has gone before and much more likely to attract students from poorer backgrounds.

The mood at the parliamentary committee was sombre. The Man opened by saying that the lesson he had learned from the row over single parents was that you had to arrive at a view quickly and then stick to it. In other words, he concedes nothing. By all means, I replied, take decisions quickly, but for heaven's sake consult first. Ann Clwyd said she had visited single parents in one of the more depressed areas of her constituency over the weekend. There was an air of hopelessness and cynicism about the proposed childcare arrangements. She said she would be abstaining in the vote next week. I said I would, too. The Man seemed hurt and said, 'We've got to be clear. A three-line whip is a three-line whip. Once you lose control, you lose control. We can't have people abstaining on every difficult issue.'

Later, after Tony had gone, Nick Brown read out the passage in the party standing orders which forbids votes against the whip and recognises the right to abstain only on matters of 'deeply held personal conviction'. The core issue, he said, was what constitutes a 'deeply held conviction'. He had always taken it to be things like abortion and capital punishment, but he agreed the wording was ambiguous. However, there was a limit to the number of deeply held personal convictions he could tolerate. I said that he and George had handled the problem very well so far. It was important not to over-react. Christmas is coming and the story will soon disappear. He asked what we were going to do on third reading and seemed to think that, if the Tories and the Liberals piled in, there was a chance of losing the entire Bill. There is not the slightest danger of that. My main fear is that the rebellion will fizzle out at the last moment, like most Tory rebellions used to, leaving those of us whose heads are above the parapet exposed. Some of those who were talking tough last week can already be overheard making excuses. Ann Clwyd said some of the junior whips were making threats whereupon Nick demanded chapter and verse which Ann declined to give. Nick said he had specifically instructed the whips not to make threats and he would come down hard on anyone who was caught doing so.

After the meeting the backbench members of the committee – Ann, Charlotte, Llin, Sylvia and myself (minus Jean, who is in Saudi Arabia) adjourned to Ann's room. I was anxious to find out how the others were intending to vote since it is important that Ann and I don't become isolated. Charlotte and Sylvia said they hadn't made up their minds between abstention and reluctantly toeing the line, but it was clear that they will vote with the government. Charlotte said maybe she would vote against 'next time'. Llin Golding said with refreshing candour that she would vote for the government come what may – 'once a whip, always a whip'. As I suspected, Ann and I are on our own. When the music stops, I'd be surprised if there are more than forty dissidents. Later, Clive Soley tried to talk me out of abstaining, saying that he was sure Tony and Gordon had learned lessons for the future. I doubt it. The only way to be sure is to fire a big enough warning shot.

The paperback edition of Andrew Neil's *Full Disclosure* contains an interesting chapter on Murdoch and New Labour. Neil writes: '... like everyone else who deals with Rupert, there comes a time when you are past your sell-by date ... If the Tories become solidly Euro-sceptic with a clear post-Thatcher agenda, then Rupert will be tempted to return to the fold.'

Can't say we haven't been warned.

Thursday, 4 December

Awoke after only an hour of sleep with an excruciating pain in my left side. So bad that I dressed and took a taxi to the Casualty Department at St Thomas's. Despite my being doubled up with pain, a dead-eyed woman on the reception showed far more interest in the paperwork than my condition. An electronic sign on the wall indicated an average waiting time of four hours and fifteen minutes. Clutching the paperwork, I was directed to the casualty ward where an equally unsympathetic nurse took my blood pressure and demanded a urine specimen which I was unable to produce, having been to the toilet shortly before coming out. By way of punishment she just walked away and left me sitting by the blood-pressure machine without offering any clue as to what would happen next. I sat there for about an hour, watching her go back and forth, but she didn't offer another glance. Eventually, a pleasant young nurse directed me to an examining room, asked me to get undressed, drew the curtain and left. She returned once, at about 3.15 a.m., to say that there were three more patients ahead of me.

By now the pain was fading, although it seemed to return whenever I lay down. Beyond the curtain I could hear various comings and goings. Other customers included a chef who had sliced off part of his finger, a woman with a bad fracture, an older man wheeled away wearing an oxygen mask, his wife trailing after him carrying his clothes. Somewhere I could hear a woman weeping and moaning.

At 4 a.m. my doctor appeared. A pleasant young woman of Croatian origin. By now the pain had completely faded. She prodded and poked me and diagnosed either a blocked bowel or kidney stones, for which she prescribed laxative and painkillers. When she discovered I was an MP she started lobbying about junior doctors' pay. She spoiled her argument by saying that some of her contemporaries who had gone into finance or accountancy were already earning big bucks.

'They laugh at us,' she said. I didn't feel like arguing. She was diligent and took an interest in my problem. By the time I got back to bed it was 5.30 a.m. I slept soundly until 8.15 a.m. and then went to the House, where I chaired a select committee session with Sir Paul Condon which lasted the best part of three hours, during the course of which I staged a miraculous recovery. By afternoon the pain was back. Home on the 19.00. Ngoc met me at Durham.

Monday, 8 December

A call from Jack Straw, who wanted to know how our report on police complaints and discipline is going. He wants us to be as tough as possible – and preferably unanimous. Also, he has given up trying to negotiate with Derry Irvine on the Masons and decided to go for the toughest option. There is no love lost between him and Derry, whom he referred to as 'the Cardinal'. 'He possesses none of the qualifications required by a politician. Fortunately others are beginning to notice.'

'But he has got one very important friend,' I said.

'Watch this space,' said Jack.

Tuesday, 9 December

The lone-parent rebellion is shaping up nicely. Glenys Kinnock has put her name to a letter in today's *Guardian* calling for the cuts to be scrapped and the Tories have announced that they will be voting with the government – a smart move calculated to cause maximum embarrassment. 'Hard times,' I remarked to Malcolm Wicks in the division lobby. He replied, 'It'll be all right when we get a Labour government.'

My pain comes every few hours, usually in the evening. Always in the same place – the area of my left kidney. Usually it lasts about an hour, but tonight I was plagued for five hours.

Wednesday, 10 December

The debate on the Lone Parent Premium was kicked off by Steve Webb, one of the new Liberals, who was impressive, not least because he has only been here six months. He was followed by Audrey Wise, who was brilliant, and later by Alice Mahon, also good. Ken Livingstone, on crutches, sounded as though he were placing himself at the head of a rival camp – a point that will not be lost on our masters. He criticised not only the policy on single parents, but the entire economic strategy. A few people spoke up for the government – Patricia Hewitt, with great competence and utter insincerity. It can only be a matter of months until she is assumed into government. Indeed, the person sitting next to me remarked that he could see Patricia and Harriet changing places before long. Harriet and her team were left to stew alone on the front bench. With the exception of Clare Short, who looked as though she had been press-ganged, no other Cabinet minister turned up to support her. Harriet stuck closely to her script.

Interesting to note that her line has changed over the last few weeks. When she addressed the parliamentary party last month she suggested that it was all about resources and that no stone had been unturned in the search for alternatives. Today she seemed to be saying that bashing single mothers was an essential part of our Welfare to Work strategy and they'd all be better off in the long run. She was repeatedly challenged to say how it could possibly be an incentive for a single mother to take part-time, seasonal or insecure work when she knew that, in the end, she would have to sign back on at the new, lower rate. To that she had no answer. Indeed there is no answer and that was perfectly obvious to everyone. So unconvincing was she that several people who came along with the intention of abstaining ended up voting against the government. A rare example of people being swayed by what they hear in the Chamber. The result when it came was a pleasant surprise – forty-seven of our side against and another fifteen (myself included) ostentatiously abstaining. We could see the journalists crowding into the gallery to note down our names.

Three parliamentary private secretaries lost their jobs and one minister resigned. A totally avoidable crisis. Our masters have brought this entirely on themselves. They have had months of warnings. Will they learn any lessons? And, if so, what?

The omens are not auspicious. Jean, who attended the parliamentary committee, said The Man was in a belligerent mood. 'These people have got to be told ...' Then he started going on about the lessons of history. A familiar refrain. The real lesson of history is perfectly clear: governments that don't listen come unstuck.

Thursday, 11 December

Awoken by my pain, just after six. Gordon was on the radio digging the pit deeper. No alternative. Plough on. The dissidents were only the same people who had been wrong about everything else – Clause IV, for example. That man is so isolated. Does it happen to all Chancellors? I remember Denis Healey's special adviser saying that he once counted about sixty meetings in Denis's diary with journalists and bankers, but none with fellow MPs.

To the Customs House, a lovely early-nineteenth-century building overlooking the Thames near Tower Bridge where the Chief Investigator and his deputy briefed me about their work tracking drug dealers, pornographers and VAT evaders. They have their own investigators, powers to tap telephones at home and abroad. Domestic bugging is done from the building and the rest by GCHQ on warrants, all of which have to be authorised by ministers. Every so often, he said, Lord Nolan comes and trawls through the warrants to see that the rules are being followed. Unlike the police, I was told, they have never had a serious case of corruption. In passing, the Chief remarked that the change of government had been a breath of fresh air. 'So good to have ministers who listen, instead of pretending to know everything.'

'Long may this continue,' said I.

Afterwards I was taken to the basement, which was crammed with confiscated drugs of every kind – cannabis, cocaine, amphetamines, heroin by the ton, all expertly packaged, stored in transparent plastic bags, labelled with code words according to the operation which led to its capture: Chatsworth, Apache ... Outside there was a lorry, rented in Liverpool, which only yesterday had yielded five tons of cannabis. The cannabis smelled sweet, but I came away with a headache from the hard stuff.

Back at the House everyone is talking about the retribution, if any, to be meted out after last night's uprising. There are reports that four people – Ken Livingstone, Brian Sedgemore, Bob Wareing and John Marek – are to be singled out and that everyone else will get a letter. I can't believe the regime will be daft enough to create martyrs, but you never know.

Archie Norman was on the train. I asked how his master plan to shake up the Tory Party was going. He said it was meeting resistance from the Old Guard who wanted everything done as it had always been, despite their dire predicament. Sounds very Old Labour, circa 1983. He said the quality of their councillors was poor and it was getting harder to find volunteers. The Liberals, he said, were attracting better people. We mustn't gloat. It's a crisis that afflicts not just the Tories, but the entire body politic.

Friday, 12 December

My fiftieth birthday. My active life is now two-thirds over. I suppose I have made moderately good use of my limited talents. I have also been lucky. My political career, however, has peaked. Most of my remaining ambitions lie outside politics. I want to do several of the great walks – from Holy Island to the Lakes, the Southern Upland Way – while I still have the energy. I have at least three more novels in my head. I want to write the story of Ngoc and myself, so that our children will have something to remember us by. Above all, I want to restore a walled garden and leave it for my children so that they will have a haven of tranquillity to which they can retreat from a world that will grow increasingly inhospitable. None of these things are compatible with my present incarnation and yet I can't afford – or I am not bold enough – to simply pull stumps and go back to writing.

My worst fear is that, having a young family, I shall have to go on working to support them until the day I die.

Talking of dying, I went to hospital in the hope of discovering the source of my pain. After scanning, injecting (with dye), X-raying, prodding and poking, the surgeon declared that I had a stone in my left kidney. The X-ray appeared to show an irregular object, almost but not quite blocking the ureter. The consultant said it might clear naturally, but he was not optimistic. They wanted to keep me in, but I declined their kind offer and was instead sent home with a bottle of painkillers and instructions to come back if the pain became unbearable.

Sunday, 14 December

My pain has returned. After lunch we went to buy a Christmas tree and set it up in the living room. All the time clutching my side. By the time Malcolm and Helen came around for tea at four it was unbearable. I was practically in tears. Helen took me to the hospital, where I was injected in the backside, whereupon I promptly vomited and fell asleep. I was kept in overnight.

Monday, 15 December

Awoke at 5.30 a.m. The pain had gone. I sat up writing Christmas cards until breakfast when the consultant came and said that he had examined the X-ray taken after my admission yesterday and could find no trace of the stone. It seems to have disappeared naturally, which was what caused yesterday's prolonged pain. I am so relieved. Yesterday they were talking a week in hospital and possible surgery. A long list of engagements would have had to be cancelled. Christmas wrecked. Even my annual walk in the Lake District was in jeopardy.

I went home, bathed, lunched with Ngoc, spent the afternoon in the office and by five I was on my way to London. Suddenly there is a spring in my step.

Tuesday, 16 December

We wrapped up our report on police discipline and complaints. Not quite as tough as I would like, nor is the committee unanimous on all points, but it should make a modest impact.

Audrey Wise waved a motion on disability benefits under my nose after the ten o'clock division. It was moderate, but I hesitated. I don't want to manoeuvre myself into a ghetto. In the end, however, I signed.

Wednesday, 17 December

The Man addressed the parliamentary party. He looked and sounded very relaxed, in shirtsleeves even though outside there was a blizzard. No sign of last Wednesday's pique. His theme was familiar. Tough decisions, hard choices, difficult times ahead – at one point he actually said, 'Things can only get tougher.' Someone whispered that we should set it to music. No apology for the events of last week, although he several times said, 'I'm not saying we haven't learned any lessons.' As to what the lessons were, he didn't say. On disability benefits, he offered no reassurance. On the contrary. Welfare, he said, was costing more than the education and law and order budgets combined. Welfare reform was at the heart of what we are trying to do. 'I will listen, but in the end the government has got to make choices.'

Some good contributions from the floor, several from people who voted with the government last week, but who weren't happy. Phyllis Starkey said, 'If we aren't taken into the government's confidence, we are not able to explain its policies.' Bob Blizzard said that, as a former local authority leader, he had spent six years having to stay within spending limits set by a Tory government, but had he usually found that it was possible to avoid doing things that he really wanted to avoid. The events of last week he described as 'politically suicidal'. Most contributions were low key. There was very little applause and no one was jeered. The only jarring note came from George Turner, a grey authoritarian, who used to lead a council in Norfolk. 'New Labour,' he said, 'had got to say to Old Labour, "If you don't like what we're up to, go elsewhere."' That drew a few desultory claps from a solitary ultra-loyalist and a couple of hear hears, but most people just looked at the floor in embarrassment. Turner obviously thinks he's New Labour, but actually he is just another Old Labour machine politician. We've got lots of them in the North East.

Malcolm Chisholm (who resigned from the government) said he accepted that the social security budget had to be reformed, but that was not the issue. The point was that cutting the Lone Parent Premium was utterly counterproductive from a Welfare to Work point of view. He added, 'Can Gordon stop going around television studios saying that people like me were against all change?'

We were repeatedly enjoined not to leak the contents of the meeting to the media, but when we got outside, there was David Hill surrounded by a huge scrum of lobby hacks. Tony Benn filmed the scene with the little camcorder he carries everywhere. About twenty minutes later I ran into Bob Marshall-Andrews, who said he had already received a couple of calls from the media asking what happened. Was it true, one of the journalists had asked, that the dissidents had received a bollocking? That, of course, is how leaks occur. The spin doctors declare an enormous triumph. No one in the lobby believes them, so they start ringing round to find out what really happened.

Later, I was approached by Tony Colman, who replaced David Mellor at Putney. He had missed the meeting and wanted to know what happened. On paper, archetypal New Labour – a successful businessman – but even he seemed nonplussed. 'In local government,' he said, 'we discussed decisions before we made them. Here it seems almost a point of principle to make decisions in advance and impose them.'

I rang Audrey and asked her to take my name off her motion about disability benefits. She wasn't pleased, but I really ought to give the inside track a chance before I start addressing the government through a megaphone – although, of course, the day may come when there is no alternative.

The Man was absent from the parliamentary committee in the evening. Prescott came instead. There was much talk of avoiding another crisis over disability benefits, but in the absence of the only person who counts, the discussion was deflated. Jean and I suggested that the government issue a Green Paper on reform of welfare, signalling its intentions while there was still time to influence debate. Nick Brown said he thought one was planned for the summer – not the last week in July, I hope.

Margaret Jay warned that the single-parent problem was not over. The Social Security Bill would be in the Lords after Christmas and Jack Ashley and Alf Morris would be lying in wait. Nick Brown said he was conscious of the climate. He was well aware that no previous Labour government had ever served two full terms. That in the past the parliamentary party had divided into those who were in and those who were out and everyone ended up quarrelling. 'I look at the pictures of my predecessors on the wall and realise that they always ended up demented. I want to avoid that fate.'

Thursday, 18 December

As I was leaving the House I found myself following a young man carrying what appeared to be a wedding present in the direction of the Opposition Leader's office. Dennis Skinner was coming in the other direction. 'Have you been invited?' I asked cheerfully. Without a flicker of a smile Dennis replied, 'I don't believe in organised happiness.'

Monday, 22 December

The single-parents fiasco continues to reverberate. It has done enormous damage. Out of all proportion to the sums involved. If everything goes wrong, we will look back on this as a turning point. There are reports of a steep decline in party membership renewals. Everyone fears the worst over benefit cuts. Goodwill is evaporating: there is a general climate of suspicion. Giles Radice told me that he had written to Tony saying how unhappy he was. He said: 'What have things come to when I find myself more in agreement with Audrey Wise and Ken Livingstone than I do with the government?' He added, 'We have used up an awful lot of political capital.'

To Downing Street, where Gordon and Nick Brown laid on Christmas drinks. The doors between Numbers 11 and 12 were open and we could roam at will. The walls of the halls and staircases are lined with sepia prints of Chancellors and Chief Whips past. Many of the names do not even ring a bell. A constant reminder to the governing classes of how ephemeral they are. Murdo Maclean is the one permanent fixture. He has been in Downing Street since the late sixties and Private Secretary to all Chief Whips since 1978. He proudly showed me a passage in Andrew Marr's book *Ruling Britannia* which refers to him as one of fifty most influential people in the country. One of Murdo's predecessors held the post from 1919 to 1961. At the heart of government for forty-two years and yet his name rarely, if ever, appeared in print. So far as we know he kept no diaries and wrote no memoirs. His secrets died with him. His only memorial a modest photo on the wall of what was once his office which, in due course, will be joined by a photo of Murdo.

I had a long chat with Sarah Macaulay, a close friend of Gordon's. She denies that Gordon is a workaholic and says he is capable of switching off completely. They had been on holiday to Cape Cod for three weeks in the summer and were unmolested, apart from a couple of calls about devolution. On one occasion Gordon had suggested they visit a supermarket. When they got there she asked what he wanted to buy and he had replied that he didn't want to buy anything. He just wanted to see what it was like. Something he can no longer do in England.

I said he was in danger of getting out of touch with the back benches. 'He knows,' she said, and suggested I talk to Gordon's assistant Lizzie 'and get her to build more Tea Room time into his diary'. I shan't bother. There are plenty of people telling Gordon that he needs to mix more. It's up to him to take control of his life. As for 'building in more Tea Room time', ugh.

Clive Soley nobbled me after the vote and said he was worried about leaks from the parliamentary committee. Like the rest of us, he has his suspicions. He had received a call from someone on the *Mail on Sunday* who appeared to be aware of something Prescott had said at the committee. He asked what he should do. Nothing, I said. Under no circumstances raise the problem with The Man because that will merely provide him with an excuse for not taking us into his confidence.

Wednesday, 24 December

A morning in the office signing letters, leafing through piles of corporate Christmas cards and throwing bumf into the recycling box. The *Echo* is full of the usual stories about families who have had their Christmas presents stolen. One in particular, with a photo of a sad young single mother and her five young children whose presents had been looted. Usually when such things happen generous readers send in money, but this one I suspect is too close to Christmas. I rang the news desk. Sure enough, only £25 had been received. On impulse I put £50 inside a Christmas card and, like Good King Wenceslas, set off for her house in a blighted part of the constituency. There was litter in the garden, the house next door was boarded. I knocked, someone shouted 'come in', the front door opened directly into the living room. A woman of about thirty was sitting smoking, in front of a TV set. She did not get up. 'Are you sure?' she said, when I handed over the envelope. 'I've managed, you know.' I was glad that she at least had the dignity to offer token resistance. It was all over in less than a minute. Did I do right? Who knows? Anyway, I expect she can make better use of the money than I can.

The wind was howling as we went to bed. Gales so loud that it was hard to sleep. I was afraid we might lose more trees in the terrace or one of the chimney pots. Sarah was concerned that Santa Claus might be blown off course.

Thursday, 25 December

As the children opened their presents, Ngoc told a touching little story from her childhood in Kontum, in the central highlands of Vietnam. She had a doll, her only toy, to which she was very attached. Somehow its head was crushed. She was dreadfully upset and organised a funeral. She put the doll in a box, dug a hole in a small plot of public land and buried the box, scattering petals. For some time afterwards she visited the grave.

CHAPTER FIVE

1998

Thursday, 1 January 1998

My resolutions for the New Year are as follows:

As before – avoid pointless activity.

Recognise that my future lies with the select committee and to abandon all thoughts of ministerial office – which is in any case incompatible with a young family and a capacity for independent thought.

Never forget that there is life outside politics.

Awoke to blue skies, but wind and rain forecast. We decide to risk a picnic in Castle Eden Dene.

Emma fell asleep halfway round and I had to wheel her in the pushchair along muddy tracks. As we walked, Sarah said to Ngoc, 'Mum, why are you only nice to me when Emma is asleep?'

It's true: when Little Monstrous is awake she rules our lives. 'Sarah, hold her hand', 'Sarah watch out, she might fall'. Later, the Tiny Tyrant awoke and insisted on running along the muddy path which falls away steeply to a stream on one side. Hypertension all round. Home just as rain and wind are setting in.

Friday, 2 January

For several days I have been receiving messages from the *Today* pro-gramme and *World at One* inviting me to express indignation at the refusal of the courts to allow the naming of a Cabinet minister whose seventeen-year-old son has been the victim of a cannabis 'sting' organised by the *Daily Mirror*. No one has told me but I suspect the unfortunate parent is Jack Straw, who has a son in the right age bracket. Didn't I think the public had a right to know, asked a woman from *World at One* in today's message on my answerphone.

Why, for heaven's sake? I detect no great issue of principle. There is no suggestion that the minister concerned has behaved with the slightest impropriety. On the contrary, on being told the bad news, he immediately delivered his son to a police station. The law that pre-vents his son being named was designed for the protection of juve-niles and, until recently at least, had the support of all parties. Why should the son of a Cabinet minister be treated differently from the son of any other citizen? What a sanctimonious bunch of hypocrites our hacks are – those from the BBC are as bad as any.

Wednesday, 14 January

The newspapers are full of stories about bickering among ministers. For reasons that no one can fathom Gordon Brown seems to have cooperated with Paul Routledge on a biography which makes no secret of his resentment at having been eased out of the leadership race by Tony Blair. Nick Brown, who ran Gordon's campaign, has also (unwisely) talked to Routledge. The media are making much of it. An odd time to be writing memoirs – on the strength of only six months in government. Ian Davidson put it nicely at the party meeting this morning. 'We are repeatedly asked to exercise self-discipline and yet every day in the papers we read that this minister hates that minister and that they all hate Peter Mandelson.'

Talking of Mandelson, the Dome is becoming a public relations disaster. Every day more bad news. Today's episode is that the exhibits may include Japanese-made cars. A fitting symbol of British industrial progress. It is essential that, whatever new responsibilities he may assume, Mandelson is left in charge of the Dome until the end.

To the parliamentary committee. The Man, hotfoot from Japan, in fair shape considering he cannot have had a decent night's sleep for a week. The burden of office is beginning to take its toll. Hairline receding, cheeks hollowing and the bags under his eyes growing more pronounced with each passing week. No matter, he still has a ready smile and a relaxed manner. John Prescott and Mo Mowlam, however, look exhausted. For much of the meeting JP sat with his head back, eyes closed. The bags under his eyes extend over his cheekbones. Mo was wearing a scarf wound round her head like a turban. She sat, head in hand, eyes closed, nodding occasionally.

Clive Soley kicked off with a little warning about plans for welfare reform. There was a feeling, he said, that we didn't have a strategy. That the reforms were Treasury-driven. We needed to adopt a listening approach. The Man responded that we had to keep focused on the big picture. We had clear principles. Help for the poorest and help into work for those capable of work. The row over the Lone Parent Premium was unfortunate because it had got us off on the wrong footing. He was about to embark on a series of meetings designed to win over the party and public opinion – starting tomorrow.

Ann Clwyd said she hoped the meetings would be open and no attempt would be made to exclude likely dissenters. At which point Sally Morgan from the Number 10 political office assured everyone that nothing could be further from her mind. No one believed her.

Ann also said she had attended the backbench social security committee, addressed by Harriet, at lunchtime and there was great deal of unease. 'Regard this as an early warning.'

I said we had to make the world of work more attractive. The minimum wage was a good start, but we also needed to introduce some elementary job security and reduce benefit tapers. Llin Golding backed me up and Tony seemed to take it seriously.

There was a brief discussion about other recent crises – Robin Cook's love life, Straw Junior's run-in with the law and Geoffrey Robinson's tax arrangements. The Man said he wouldn't be browbeaten. 'The media are bullies. Under the last government they got used to the idea that if they ran a big enough campaign against a minister, he will go. That is not how this government is going to be run.'

Thursday, 15 January

A crowded press conference to launch the select committee report on police discipline. I remarked that the existing discipline process had been subverted by a minority of dishonest officers who had exploited every conceivable loophole in the rulebook. The BBC ran the clip. Alun Michael, a Home Office minister, later said that he'd had the chairman of the Police Federation on the phone, huffing and puffing.

Friday, 16 January

Customers at the surgery in the evening included a poor old soul who has spent her life caring for two mentally handicapped daughters. One, aged forty-nine, has a mental age of three, she is incontinent and wakes twice a night with fits. The other, aged forty-one, has a mental age of six. The mother had just received a proforma letter telling her that her benefit has been cut off on the grounds of an alleged 'recent improvement in her daughter's condition'. There's been no improvement whatever. Nor will there ever be. What's more, she says, no one has been out to assess the situation.

She was a dignified woman. Still with a little spark of life in her, but I could see she was distraught. She's sixty-nine and all she has to look forward to is more of the same until the end of her days. Never again will I complain about being woken up by Emma.

Monday, 19 January

A letter from Fred Broughton, chairman of the Police Federation, demanding that I apologise for my remarks at the press conference last week. Way over the top. Passages are underlined. You can almost see the green ink. He's copied it to all sorts of people. The Shadow Home Secretary Brian Mawhinney received his copy before I saw mine. He remarked that it was very intemperate and didn't seem inclined to exploit it.

Tuesday, 20 January

Another Catholic murdered in Ireland last night. 'Things not going too well on your side of the water,' I remarked to one of the more obscure Unionists who was doing his ablutions in the gents washroom on Upper Corridor South.

He looked at me and growled, 'That's what you get if you talk about peace.' An illuminating insight into the Unionist psyche.

This afternoon the Police Federation have put out a press release questioning my suitability for the chairmanship of the select committee. They have also written to Brian Mawhinney and Alan Beith demanding that they persuade their members of the committee to disown me. What a bunch of headbangers. I saw Jack in the division lobby, who was amused. They have been on to him as well and he has sent them a bland reply.

Wednesday, 21 January

The welfare review dominated the parliamentary committee in the evening. We have opened a can of worms. The fiasco over single-parent benefits has created a climate of mistrust. The government has started a debate without any clear idea of where it will lead or even what they want from it. Even the Green Paper – promised for the end of February – is likely to contain little more than generalities. The Man replied there would be no big bang. Changes to pensions, for example, would take decades. On disability, all we had done so far was give out extra money. He said – quoting Prescott – that there was a tendency in the party to pocket the good news and focus on the bad. This needed to be countered. He added that he was worried about the capacity of the party to cope with difficult issues, given the recent fuss over single parents – 'What will happen when we hit a really rocky patch?'

To my surprise I notice that The Man is given to mild name dropping. We usually exchange courtesies before we get down to business. This week he mentioned that in Holland yesterday he had called on the Queen. I remarked that the Dutch Royals were much less stuffy than

ours and he began to agree before seeing an iceberg looming and trailing off in mid-sentence. The other day he quoted something Hillary
Clinton had said to him. On another occasion he quoted the president of Brazil, on another, that he was off to see the Queen. Only
when you add them up, a pattern emerges. Even after eight months,
he can't quite believe he's made it, which I find endearing.

Tea with Alan Keen and Jean Corston. Jean remarked that the whips
had been touting a slate for the elections to the Policy Forum – the
results of which were announced this morning. All save one of the
official candidates had been elected. Alan added that he'd seen a whip
handing out a list. Does New Labour have to fix everything? Surely
something can be left to chance? The problem is they just can't stop
even if they want to. It's compulsive.

Monday, 26 January

The papers are full of stories of alleged Labour sleaze which the Tories
are exploiting for all they are worth. Mainly it's trappings of office
stuff: Derry Irvine's wallpaper, Margaret Beckett's grace-and-favour
apartment, Tony Blair's new kitchen, Robin Cook's mistress. Individually they don't amount to much, but cumulatively they give the
impression that New Labour in office is not so different from the
Tories. The mud is beginning to stick.

Tuesday, 27 January

Today's *Mirror* carries several pages by Robin Cook's ex-diary secretary
alleging that he got rid of her in order to replace her with his
mistress.

Dinner in the Cafeteria with Jack Straw. He says my remarks about the
Police Federation defending the indefensible touched a raw nerve
because I was telling the truth – and they know it.

Jack agrees we have a problem over the way in which some of our
colleagues are adjusting to office. He calls it 'limo fever'. He has

declined the grace-and-favour residence in Belgravia to which the Home Secretary is entitled, in favour of remaining at home in Lambeth. Alice and the children flatly refused to go, despite strenuous efforts by the security men to persuade them. As a result his home has been turned into a fortress. The windows have been replaced with bulletproof glass. Armed detectives are based downstairs. At their cottage in Oxfordshire steel sheds have been erected in the garden to house protection officers and in Blackburn they have moved into the offices below his flat.

I asked about the much-delayed response to our report on Masons. Derry and John Morris are causing problems. Jack is sound on this issue. He wants me to write him a stiff letter demanding reasons for the delay. I shall be happy to oblige.

Wednesday, 28 January

Robin Cook addressed the party meeting. A fair turnout, but not enormous. EC enlargement, he said, was a chance to reform the Common Agricultural Policy since not even the French would argue that the EC could offer Polish farmers intervention prices without going bankrupt. On Bosnia, he claimed, we had made a difference, stepping up the arrest of alleged war criminals and increasing the pressure for multi-ethnic, plural politics. However, he added with a smirk, there was still work to be done democratising the Foreign Office – a recent work experience scheme had taken on fifteen pupils of whom only one came from a comprehensive. The rest were from private schools.

He ended by thanking everyone for their solidarity over his personal difficulties. The applause was polite, but not ecstatic. There is a widespread feeling that he has been foolish.

At lunchtime Ann Keen approached me in the Library. I had last seen her in a lift at 10.30 a.m. yesterday, en route for the standing committee on the Minimum Wage Bill. She had just emerged – after twenty-six hours. The Tories had been trying to wreck the Bill so our side just let it run all night. It came as a shock to the Tories, who had been expecting to filibuster for a few hours and then draw stumps at midnight. Instead they got a stiff dose of their own medicine. After a while they ran out of amendments and the committee got through seventeen clauses. Our side just sat quietly while the Tories ran themselves ragged.

The Man was on devastating form at Question Time. Hague led off on alleged New Labour sleaze and was duly nailed to the floor. As The Man pointed out, the Tories keep trying to pretend we are as bad as they are, but no one on our side has accepted cash for questions, money in brown envelopes. That shut Hague up. He looked shaken. Rarely have I seen misfortune turned to advantage with such devastating effect.

Later, at the parliamentary committee, The Man said he was surprised the Tories hadn't attacked him on what the Confederation of British Industry were saying about our plans for union recognition. 'They are a brain-dead Opposition.' He was asked about rumours that we are on the point of caving in to the CBI and it was clear from his answer that we are. He talked of 'a balanced package', 'arguments both ways', 'listening carefully'. Compulsory recognition, he said, was a big step which even the Wilson government had shied away from. Another iceberg looms out of the mists.

I asked why it was thought necessary to have an official slate in last week's elections for the Policy Forum. Nick Brown said blankly, 'I am not neutral,' as though that explained everything. There was an embarrassed pause and, realising that further explanation was required, Nick added that there were other slates besides his (actually, I am not sure there were). Charlotte Atkins said that, as a result of interference by the whips, four of those elected came from Yorkshire while other regions are unrepresented. I said that I hope to live long enough to see an election in which market forces were allowed to prevail and, on that note, the subject was dropped.

Afterwards some of us had a meeting with David Pitt-Watson, the recently appointed Labour Party finance officer who is said to have given up a huge salary in the City to come and dig the party out of the financial black hole into which it has fallen under New Labour management. The party, he said, was in deep financial trouble. Worse than ever. He had been negotiating with the bankers and advertising agencies and disaster had been narrowly averted. Our masters had been spending money like water in the run-up to the election – what with all those fatuous posters and helicopters for the Leader – to say nothing of Excalibur, an expensive computer program. Presumably the hope was that the taxpayer would bail us out with state funding, but Sir Patrick Neill (with a little help from Bernie Ecclestone) may put a stop to that. Next time round, said David, we must have strict limits on election spending – which applied to all parties.

Thursday, 29 January

To Sunderland on the 20.00, with Derek Foster. As ever we discussed The Man. Although it pains him to admit it, Derek agreed that Tony has the makings of a great leader. Devolution, Lords reform, freedom of information, welfare reform are all things which, if they come to pass, may award him a place in history. However, said Derek, there was one serious flaw: 'I'll only be convinced that he is truly great when I see he is not dependent on Peter Mandelson.'

Friday, 30 January

An invitation to lunch at the *Daily Mail*. One of a number received recently from political correspondents. Must be down to my new status as a 'senior' backbencher. I replied: 'I can see no advantage, either for the Labour Party or myself, in lunching at the *Daily Mail*.'

Monday, 2 February

Anne Perkins has written a tongue-in-cheek profile of me in today's *Guardian* … 'Rebel on the Fringes of the Establishment'. No harm done, although a few people have pulled my leg. The picture makes me look a bit wizened. An anonymous colleague (who I suspect was Roy Hattersley) is quoted as saying, 'I happen to believe that Parliament corrupts most people, but he has actually been improved by it.'

Tuesday, 3 February

The bad habits of the past are beginning to resurface at the select committee. Only four members arrived on time for today's session and
several went AWOL during the sitting. It looks so bad when half the
seats are empty. If we don't take the inquiry seriously, why should
anyone else? There is one blessing. Douglas Hogg has disappeared to
Ireland for three weeks' barristering. I intend to take advantage of his
absence to sort out the Masons, who are still giving us the runaround.
I proposed we summon Commander Higham to explain why he has
not answered our questions. Ross Cranston asked for another paper. I
replied that it was not a paper we needed, but a decision. In the end I
carried everyone except the Tories and they didn't make a fuss.

According to the *Mail on Sunday* Commander Higham has been
given notice of dismissal. The reasons are unclear, but I suspect they
may have something to do with this dispute. Maybe the hardliners
think he has conceded too much. What better way of testing the
powers of the select committee than taking on the Masons? I had a
word with the Chief Whip Nick Brown and he is all for a fight.

At Environment questions I asked Prescott an off-message question about the government's ambiguous attitude towards the green
belt. It drew a little cheer from the Tories and was taken up by Norman
Fowler. Later, one of the whips, Graham Allen, collared me. 'Do you
like being cheered by the Tories, Chris?'

'I don't care where the cheers come from. It's the outcome that
interests me.'

'Why don't you come in and see us, if you're worried about something? We're the government now, you know.'

I turned on the radio when I got back to the flat and just caught the
presenter of *Today in Parliament* saying that 'a senior backbencher'
had attacked the Environment Secretary. Nonsense, of course. I – ever
so gently – criticised the policy, not the man. No harm in occasionally
tugging at one's ball and chain.

Wednesday, 4 February

To the Prime Minister's rooms for the weekly meeting of the parliamentary committee. The Man was off to Washington as soon as our meeting was over. The outer office was crowded with retainers awaiting his pleasure. Among them Alastair Campbell, lounging in a chair by the window. 'Hello, Alastair', I said. 'What time does your plane go?'

He looked at me pityingly. 'It's not like that, Chris. The plane goes when we arrive. You'd love it.'

Trade Union recognition and Tom McNally's amendment to the Competition Bill – designed to stop Murdoch sinking his competitors with predatory pricing – were the two main items. On the unions, I pointed out that the CBI proposal requiring a majority of all eligible union members, not just those who voted, appeared to mean that a ballot which resulted in a 70/30 vote in favour of recognition would result in defeat. The Man replied that whatever happens we must not allow the debate to deteriorate into unions versus business. We had built up a big coalition in order to win and we mustn't blow it.

On the McNally amendment, I said that Murdoch was out to sink the *Independent* by predatory pricing and the odds were that he would succeed. The present situation was indefensible. If the Bill came to the Commons without the McNally clause, someone – 'myself perhaps' – might be tempted to try and put it back again. Nick Brown gave a dry little laugh. Denis Carter offered a couple of lame reasons for resisting the amendment, one of which was that the Office of Fair Trading already had powers to deal with the problem and didn't need any more. 'In that case', I asked, 'why is Gordon Borrie* supporting the amendment?'

To that there was no clear answer.

With that The Man stood up, lifted his jacket from the back of the chair and put it on. Someone made a crack about discussing affairs with Bill Clinton to which he replied lightly, 'That is one subject we will not be discussing.' Then he walked to the door, closing it behind

---

*A former director general of the Office of Fair Trading.

him, and with that he was gone. Down in Speaker's Court the convoy was waiting, engines running. A detective will have phoned ahead to the gate so the traffic can be stopped. Jean Corston whispered, 'Lifting his jacket off the back of the chair is the only action he has to take to get himself from here to Washington.'

Sure enough, when I turned on *Newsnight* there he was in Washington coming down the steps of Concorde, same jacket, same tie as he was wearing sitting opposite me a few hours earlier.

Thursday, 5 February

Growing unease about our slavish addiction to the American line on Iraq. I asked Ann Clwyd, who has long taken a close interest, what she would do. 'Back the opposition,' she said. 'They are organised inside the country. They are capable of killing Saddam – and came within a whisker of killing Uday. It would be much cheaper than bombing and much more effective.' There had been two big missed opportunities in the aftermath of the Gulf War when, with outside help, the Kurds could have overthrown the regime. The CIA and MI6 had both been represented inside Iraq. The Kurds had been told to expect help, but it never came. She said that, on a visit to Washington, she had put this to the Iraqi desk officers in the State Department. They didn't attempt to dispute it. Just looked embarrassed. Had she put this to Robin? No point, she said. 'He's so arrogant. He doesn't listen. He thinks he knows it all.'

Monday, 9 February

To the Lords for the debate on Tom McNally's amendment to the Competition Bill. Debates in the Lords are very different from those at our end of the building. Everyone is terribly polite – no heckling, speeches are short and to the point. Several of the older peers appear to be gently snoozing. They seem to know which order they are to speak in without waiting to be called. When one sits another rises. Apart from the minister, the only people to speak up for Murdoch seemed to be in his employ – two non-executive directors of *The Times* and a columnist. The amendment was comfortably carried, with many rebels on our side. Now the government must decide whether or not to remove it when it comes to us. A nice little crisis brewing.

Wednesday, 11 February

Iraq and Murdoch topped the bill at the parliamentary committee. I kicked off. 'People are saying that they knew the political but not the military object of bombing Iraq.' The Man, who had a heavy cold, said the aim was to stop Saddam developing chemical and biological warfare capacity and to destroy his guidance systems. Some of the so-called presidential sites, from which UN inspectors were excluded, were huge. One is the size of Paris. It wasn't true to say we were alone in supporting America. Australia, Canada, New Zealand and Poland favour the use of force. He had also spoken to the Italian and Spanish Prime Ministers and they would go along with it. He added that King Hussein was not as opposed to force as his public pronouncements suggested.

On Murdoch, The Man was adamant that the McNally amendment would have to go. The Competition Bill was intended to bring our law into line with that elsewhere in Europe. There was no case for going further (except, I said to myself, that we've got Murdoch and they haven't).

At about eleven this evening I came across John Major letting himself into his room and asked what he thought of the McNally amendment. He invited me in and opened a bottle of wine. I was there for more than an hour. We talked about everything from Saddam Hussein to welfare reform.

On Murdoch, John said that he didn't think we could attract the Tory right, who didn't like Murdoch but believed in unfettered competition. As to what he would do, he was non-committal but promised to keep his ear to the ground. He did say he wasn't really interested in taking on Murdoch 'unless we could inflict a fatal blow'.

On welfare reform, he said that he had looked at all the main possibilities and there was very little scope for savings. He spoke passionately against taxing child or disability benefits, describing himself as 'a Macleod Tory'. At times he sounded like Ken Livingstone: 'We are the sixth richest country in the world. Existing levels of benefit are affordable.'

He was also strongly against tuition fees. Working-class families – like the one he came from – were terrified of debt and it was bound to deter poorer people from higher education. He added that the biggest mistake the Tories had made was greatly to increase tuition fees for overseas students. British education had been respected around the world. Many foreign leaders had been educated here. The big increase in fees for overseas students had done us enormous damage.

The one area where he did think we could raise serious money was by increasing the National Insurance ceiling in line with earnings. In Gordon's position, that's what he would do.

On Saddam, John said that The Man (who had consulted him) was right to go along with the Americans. 'He will know things that we don't. He will know, for example, that Saddam may now have the capacity to deliver chemical or biological weapons.' During the Gulf War we were terrified that he would use them against us. We now know that he hadn't then had delivery capacity, but he might well do now – or he will have before long. Supposing he were to deposit a missile on Tel Aviv? The Israelis would reply in kind. The Russians, the other Arab states, everybody could be dragged in. A huge conflict could be ignited.

He spoke of Neil Kinnock with surprising warmth. He had always found Neil straight. Neil had never reneged on any private understanding. Allegations of windbaggery were unfair. He was up to being Prime Minister. John Smith, with whom he also had good relations, was very cautious and, had he been elected, would not have changed much. As for The Man, he couldn't work him out. He often made commitments he didn't need to make – on not raising tax, for example. John was incredulous that The Man appeared to be wobbling on trade union recognition. Anyone with a majority our size could do it without fuss. 'In any case,' he added, 'today's unions don't worry me.' (Is it possible that the last Conservative Prime Minister is more radical than the present Labour one?)

By now our mood was extremely convivial. He refilled my glass a couple of times. At one point he was sitting with his leg over the arm of the chair. We ranged far and wide. Had he won again, he would have released local authorities from the spending restraints imposed by central government. As things stood, local authorities were entirely in thrall to the centre. Several times he said we had inherited a strong economy. To which I responded that we had also inherited a huge benefit culture and that in some areas civilised life had broken down.

On an easel in a corner of the room, facing towards the door, there stands a large portrait of Norma and himself painted by someone whose name I didn't catch, a pupil of Annigoni. 'All you need now is a stately home to hang it in,' said I.

'I can't afford one'.

'You'll have to do a few more of those lectures.'

On that note we parted, he promising to keep in touch over Murdoch, 'but don't talk about our alliance'.

Back to the flat at 2.30 a.m., after a day which began in Manchester at 6.30 a.m.

Thursday, 12 February

A chat in the Tea Room with a member of the Cabinet. Cabinet meetings, he said, rarely lasted above an hour (about the same as the parliamentary committee). Today's, at which there was a discussion on Iraq, lasted thirty minutes. Cabinet government, he said, ended with Thatcher and has never recovered. The point has been made to The Man that if he wanted people to share responsibility, they would have to feel included, but there is no sign that the lesson has been heeded. Ministers, he said, frequently learned of major government decisions via the media.

He sits on about ten Cabinet committees where, he says, substantial work is done. However, it was hard to get Cabinet ministers to attend. They often sent juniors.

Jack Straw, he said, had fought hard to water down the Freedom of Information Bill, but had been seen off, thanks to Derry Irvine.

Irvine, he said, had been surprisingly radical. The first time I have heard anyone put in a good word for Derry. It helps explain why he and Jack don't hit it off.

He also spoke well of Gordon Brown. 'He has a serious social agenda. He actually intends to do something.'

Saturday, 14 February
Sunderland

'Is anyone down there going to speak up for the 44 per cent of us who don't believe in bombing Iraq?' asked a man in the corner shop. A question that's been worrying me all week. Do I vote for American bombing or not? Tuesday is Make Your Mind Up day.

To Sowerby to see Joan Maynard. Tears welled in my eyes when I saw the state she's in, nothing but skin and bones. She hasn't eaten a proper meal in nine months. I stayed a couple of hours. Her morale is good, all things considered. We chatted about Iraq and New Labour and watched a documentary about Clare Short. She is due back in hospital in ten days. They are going to open her up again to see what's wrong. I fear the worst.

Monday, 16 February

Jack Straw invited me to his room after the ten o'clock division and showed me the statement he's proposing to make on Masons at the select committee in the morning. Better than I expected. He's persuaded Derry Irvine and John Morris to agree that all new appointments to the judiciary, the Crown Prosecution Service and the police should, 'as a condition of employment', disclose membership of the Freemasons and that those in post should be invited to volunteer. He is also intending to write to Grand Lodge asking them to assist in establishing a voluntary register. If not, he will consider legislating.

Tuesday, 17 February

I went in for Robin Cook's speech on Iraq. He made a good case. There is no doubt that Saddam has the ingredients (some of which we sold him) for making all sorts of unpleasant weapons and within a year or two he may have a delivery system. Nor do I need to be convinced that Saddam is a monster and that his overthrow is desirable. I just can't see how bombing his infrastructure will help. What are we going to do for an encore when he pops up afterwards and says, 'Ha, Ha, I'm still here?'

On the other hand, can we afford to blink first? Tony Benn spoke passionately against. He was in tears at the end. As usual, he went a bridge too far, saying that those who voted for the government would have blood on their hands. George Galloway made a brilliant speech. Passionate, well informed and without a single note. The trouble with George is that – although he was careful to put in a bad word for Saddam – one can't help suspecting that he has a soft spot for tyrants of the Stalinist variety. Indeed the memory of his trip to Baghdad last time round still lingers. I agonised all evening about how to vote. This time round there is no One Truth Path. Just about everyone is uneasy. I wobbled back and forth all evening. In the end, when the bell went I simply stayed in my room and didn't vote. Not a very heroic posture.

Wednesday, 18 February

The Man wasn't present at the parliamentary committee. We met in a downstairs room. Nick Brown reported that he hadn't yet decided what action to take against those who failed to support the government on Iraq last night. He would be discussing the matter with The Man on Monday. He hinted that not much was likely to happen since this was clearly an issue of conscience, reluctant though he was to concede the existence of too many such issues.

Later, in the Tea Room, Audrey Wise remarked that, since both Robin Cook and George Robertson had compared the free debate in our Parliament with any that may be taking place in Baghdad, it wouldn't look good if we were seen to be repressing dissidents.

Thursday, 19 February

The confrontation with the Masons went off magnificently. As each elephant trap opened up Commander Higham duly fell in. At one point he claimed that it would have been perfectly possible for two Masons in the West Midlands Serious Crime Squad to work alongside each other and not to know that they were both in the brotherhood. To which I responded, 'So you are a secret society,' thereby triggering another bout of sophistry. A disastrous performance from his point of view. David Winnick, who started out wobbly, came over to my side when he saw what we were up against. We warned Higham that he would be in contempt if he continued to defy the committee and issued an order requiring him to come up with the information we are seeking within fourteen days.

Friday, 20 February

Today's papers are full of yesterday's row with the Masons. *The Times*, *Guardian*, *Express* and *FT* all lead with it. Jon Hibbs in the *Telegraph* describes me as someone who prefers conspiracy to cock-up – which is nonsense. Simon Hoggart portrays me as an obsessive who 'thunders' and 'storms'. I am also the subject of a Steve Bell cartoon in today's *Guardian*. Nice though it is to be noticed, I must take care to avoid playing into the hands of those who wish to portray me as some sort of swivel-eyed obsessive.

Monday, 23 February

Joan was operated on today. She is said to have come through it well – but there will be no news of what they found until tomorrow.

Tuesday, 24 February

To Oxford to see restorative justice at work, courtesy of Thames Valley Police. Charles Pollard, the chief constable, is one of the more enlightened and held in high regard by Jack. A soft-spoken, self-effacing man, he reminded me more of a priest than a policeman. We passed the morning being briefed by several extremely civilised policemen who seem to have learned all the correct sociological jargon. Then Richard Allan and I were driven to Aylesbury to sit in on a session. The protagonists were two fourteen-year-old schoolgirls, one of whom had seriously assaulted the other. The victim had four studs in her left ear, rings on most of her fingers, unwashed hair and a pasty complexion. The aggressor was an angelic, attractive girl of mixed race, immaculately dressed in a red anorak and white trousers. Which only proves that appearances can be deceptive, or else there was more to the story than met the eye. Both the victim's parents were present along with the aggressor's father. The session was skilfully chaired by a police sergeant. Everyone behaved reasonably. The aggressor admitted the error of her ways and apologised. The apology was gracefully accepted. The aggressor was formally cautioned and everyone went home. As the sergeant teased out what had happened there was a real air of tension. It was an event that all concerned are likely to remember. To work, of course, restorative justice requires the consent of all parties. It would never do for some of the serial villains in my neck of the woods.

The news about Joan is bad. The cancer has spread. Nothing can save her. She will fade away like Uncle Terence. I can hardly think of her without crying.

Wednesday, 25 February

Lindsay Hoyle told me that, the other day in the Strangers' Bar, he was asked to become a Mason. He doesn't know the identity of the man who asked him, but says he is an officer of the House. That they should still be trying to recruit Labour members at a time like this suggests a certain self-confidence – or downright stupidity.

John and Sheila Williams came in for supper. On the way home we ran into Clare Short, walking alone from the direction of Millbank. Clare was in a good mood. Things were looking up, she said. The party was beginning to reassert itself, 'Otherwise Tony would have been away with the Tories by now.' She added, 'We've begun to have real discussions in Cabinet. Before it was, "Hello, I'm in charge. Who are you?"'

Thursday, 26 February

Good news from Sunderland. Barclays Bank is setting up a call centre in the Doxford Business Park. Two thousand full- and part-time jobs are expected. A huge boost. A council official told me that Barclays had been looking at fifty other possible locations. One of the reasons they chose Sunderland was the local accent, which is thought to be customer friendly. She added that the council tax payers of Sunderland were also paying Barclays a subsidy of £3 million, or £1,500 per job, for the pleasure of their company. In addition, Barclays have screwed a £3.3 million rent holiday out of the landlords. We should count ourselves lucky, she added; Dublin was offering even more. This seems to be the way modern corporations do business. They are not entrepreneurs at all. They just tout their jobs around the country demanding subsidies, renting not buying, so that when the subsidies dry up they have the option of upping sticks and relocating to Bangladesh, leaving us with 2,000 unemployed and a derelict site. Meantime, however, it would be churlish not to rejoice.

Found on the photocopier at the end of the corridor:

Dear Jonh Madger,

My famliey and freinds want you Back! actsept my mother. We are fed-up of Tony Blare we want you Back. So we are asking if their will be another vote. You are a wonderful primmister and we want you Back! I hope you will win if their is a vote.

love
from
Juliet
Bedford

Friday, 27 February

A call from Tory MP Tony Baldry, who describes himself as 'the only surviving member of Grand Lodge in the House since the carnage of last May'. He said he was trying to persuade the Masons to cooperate with a voluntary register. Higham had told no one about his undertaking to recommend cooperation following our meeting in November. 'If he wasn't already going, he would be over the way he has handled this.' Promising.

Saturday, 28 February

The media are full of tomorrow's so-called countryside march. It's really just a front for the blood sports lobby, financed mainly by landowners. The Duke of Westminster alone has put in £1 million. Realising they are in a minority, even in the countryside, the hunters have skilfully exploited a range of other issues. The Tories, spotting a window of opportunity, are cynically trying to pretend that some great disaster has overtaken the countryside since 1 May last year. The *Telegraph*, abandoning all pretence of serious journalism, has been placed at the disposal of the organisers. Even the BBC has joined in, leading with the story for days.

Meanwhile, New Labour is running around like a headless chicken. One minute we hear that no ministers will be attending. Now it appears that Michael Meacher is to be present. The whole thing is nauseating. The people who brought us BSE and factory farming, who turned East Anglia into a grain prairie, grubbed up all our hedges and polluted the water table with pesticides have come to London to complain that it's all the fault of a government that has been in office for less than a year – and no one is mounting any serious resistance. My blood boils.

To Northallerton to see Joan, who is recovering from another operation. Sarah made her a card depicting a house surrounded by flowers, a few small clouds and a sun in dark glasses. Joan was asleep when I arrived. I sat quietly for five minutes before a nurse woke her up. Awake, she was remarkably cheerful. The blockage in her bowel has been removed and she should now be able to eat again, albeit in small quantities.

Mark and Helen, the young couple who live locally, turned up. We talked about the so-called countryside march and Joan became animated. If I closed my eyes, she might have been the old Joan I have known and loved for so long, instead of the shrunken, dehydrated figure she has become.

Monday, 2 March

The papers are full of the government's confused response to yesterday's descent on London by the hunting fraternity. The *Telegraph* brags that it was the biggest demonstration in more than a decade, carefully avoiding any reference to the fact that CND turnout in the early eighties was just as big. We should take as much notice of this lot as the Tories did of CND.

However, there is an unfortunate whiff of appeasement in the air. The papers talk of compromise, which is ludicrous. There can be no compromise. Either we are for hunting with hounds or we are against. Supper with Alan Meale in the Strangers' Cafeteria. He says The Man had intended to go along with the CBI on union recognition until JP put his foot down. JP said firmly that he wouldn't go along with it and Blair has apparently backed down. 'The CBI isn't going to be on our side come the election whatever we give them,' said Alan. The unions, he added, were initially complacent, content to sit back on the strength of the assurances they were given before the election. It wasn't until JP got word out that all was not well that they began to campaign seriously.

Alan is convinced that Gordon still believes he will become Prime Minister. According to Alan, Gordon may be suffering from the delusion that Tony will stand down halfway into his second term so that Gordon can take over. Incredible that someone of Gordon's intelligence could be so daft. Quite apart from which, if Tony fell under a bus tomorrow, Gordon wouldn't necessarily be the favourite to replace him. It could be JP. Lord save us.

John Major put his head round my door. 'I see they've arrested Al Fayed,' he said, 'ten years too late.' He spotted the picture of himself on my noticeboard, brandishing *A Very British Coup* during the Queen's Speech debate last year, and autographed it for me.

Wednesday, 4 March

For the second week running I had question six to the Prime Minister. I went on Murdoch, though without mentioning his name. A light touch. It went down well, but Donald Dewar remarked afterwards that I am beginning to look too pleased with myself.

An interesting talk with Chief Whip Nick Brown about Mike Foster's hunting Bill. Nick said his priority was to get rid of the hereditary peers. It was essential that this was tackled separately from other reforms otherwise the whole process would become bogged down and we would end up with nothing. Unfortunately some people hadn't grasped this simple point even though, as a glance at the Crossman diaries confirms, the lessons of history are clear. We asked to whom he was referring. Derry? No, Derry was fine. He was proving an extremely effective chairman of cabinet committees and had saved the government a lot of trouble. Derry is progressive on social issues and not at all authoritarian. Jack? No, Jack was sound. Ivor Richard and Denis Carter were a problem, although Denis would come round in the end. On the rest he wouldn't be drawn at first. As we were leaving, however, he added cryptically, 'Some people around Tony are mixing in extremely exalted circles – circles that are happy with the hereditary principle.' Once again the finger points at Mandelson. According to Jean, he is friendly with the Prince of Wales.

Thursday, 5 March

Lunch in the Attlee Room at the Lords with Kalon Tsewang Tethong, a member of the Tibetan exile administration. About twenty people attended. Jack Weatherill sat on one side of our guest exchanging vacuous pleasantries, I on the other, attempting to engage him in serious conversation. The Kalon said that groups of Tibetan children, often unaccompanied by adults, were starting to appear in Nepal. Some as young as seven or eight. They were coming from the rural areas of Tibet. Their parents were sending them in the hope they would be educated, paying unscrupulous guides to see them through the Himalayas, but the guides sometimes abandoned them well short of the frontier with the result that they were left wandering in the wilderness where some die of cold. Once in Nepal or India, the children didn't want to go back. Many would never see their families again. Imagine being so desperate that I would kiss Sarah goodbye and send her, with a little rucksack on her back, into a hostile wilderness, knowing that – whether or not she survived – I was unlikely ever to see her again.

This afternoon Tony Baldry and Gavin Purser (chairman of the Board of General Purposes at Grand Lodge) turned up to respond to the select committee's ultimatum. The Masons have waited until the last minute to comply. We met in the select committee rooms at the end of the Committee Corridor, an inner sanctum which I never knew existed. The clerks, Crispin Poyser and Tom Goldsmith, sat at the table with me, Steve Barrett was at the back taking notes.

Baldry was relaxed, but Purser uptight. He seemed anxious to travel over ground we had been over many times before. After a lot of huffing and puffing he eventually produced a large manila envelope from which he took out a letter making clear that they were coughing up under protest. Then, one by one, he slid two lists of names across the table. The first, relating to the West Midlands Serious Crime Squad, listed seven Masons.

The second contained two of the seven names we inquired about in the Stalker case. One was said to have resigned from his lodge in the mid-seventies, but that of course is not the point. Once a Mason always a Mason.

A disappointing haul – and not entirely believable. One member of the West Midland Serious Crime Squad was not listed, even though he recently admitted on television that he had been a Mason. Mr Purser said that all of those named had been asked to consent to their names being released and every one had refused, but the Board of

General Purposes decided to go ahead anyway. The Masons blinked first. That's the important point.

Friday, 6 March

The hunting Bill was talked out, of course. *The Times* is running a front-page story saying that the government will not lift a finger to save it. Jack is painted as the villain, though – from what Nick Brown was saying the other day – he was willing to add it to one of his Bills. Tony Benn was livid. I actually heard him use the F-word for the only time I can recall. 'People have been conned. They were promised a free vote, but what we didn't say is that, whatever the result, there will be no change.' George Mudie is going around saying that all that is needed to defuse the crisis is a clear statement from The Main Person that the matter will be dealt with within the life of this Parliament. From that quarter, however, comes only a deafening silence.

Saturday, 7 March

With Sarah to Stadium of Light to see Sunderland beat Stockport 4–1. The Jarrow MP Steve Hepburn, who was at the match, told me that the shoot-out with the Masons had gone down well in the pubs and clubs of South Tyneside. Everyone was talking about it.

In the evening I drove down to Sowerby to see Joan, who is now back at home. She was lying on the settee in the front room, looking very frail. When I held her hand I could feel every bone. She's eating better than she has for weeks and determined to put up a fight. Mind over matter, she says. If she can put on some weight, she might just see another summer. Her friends Mark and Helen were there. We talked about the gardens we will take her to when summer comes.

Sunday, 8 March

Yesterday's *Telegraph* contains the results of a Gallup poll taken in the wake of the so-called countryside march. It triumphantly records that

– 'with one exception' – the protest increased awareness of country-side issues. The exception? The answer is buried six column inches deep on an inside page. Fox-hunting (the pollsters didn't dare mention deer), of course. By 78 to 18 per cent those questioned disapproved. This was the key issue as far as the organisers of the march were concerned. On this basis it was a colossal failure. That didn't stop the *Telegraph* headlining the story, 'Propaganda Victory for Country March'. I suppose it was, in a manner of speaking. You have to hand it to them.

Tuesday, 10 March
Upper Corridor South, 5.30 a.m.

Outside the dawn chorus has started. A small band of Tory zealots are filibustering the Minimum Wage Bill. Morale on our side is good, however. This is old-fashioned class war on an issue where we know we have overwhelming public support.

8.30 a.m. Finally, the vote. We have been here all night. At various times the Tories called votes, waited until we had staggered down to the Chamber and then cancelled. Object of exercise – to make sure no one dozed off. That's how sadistic they are. Most Tories went home to bed and returned about 7.30 a.m. after a good night's sleep. About two hundred of our side had to stay. No one complained. As it was, we all felt we were doing something worthwhile, historic even, fighting for a minimum wage. Puzzling that the Tories should choose this issue – which is supported by most civilised people – on which to make a stand. 'We fought for poverty pay' won't make a good election slogan. There was a spring in my step as I walked through the 'Aye' Lobby. I even found myself humming 'The Red Flag' until Steve Hepburn called out, 'A bit early for that yet, Chris. We don't know the rate.'

Most people went home to bed, but I had to chair the select committee at ten. Sir David Ramsbotham, Her Majesty's Chief Inspector of Prisons, gave evidence. A former general and a toff. He made a good impression. Humane, enthusiastic and dynamic. If Michael Howard appointed him in the hope of a quieter life, he made a big mistake.

I was finally allowed home at 9.30 p.m. – after more than thirty-six hours. I saw a fox cross the Brixton Road in heavy traffic.

Wednesday, 11 March

Lunch with Pat Kavanagh, my literary agent. I am flattered by her continued interest in me since I must be very small beer from her point of view. I revealed the secret of the diaries. Besides Ngoc, she is the only person who knows. My spirits dimmed briefly when she said that she hated dealing with politicians because she found them so patronising and arrogant. Me, she regarded as a writer rather than a politician. That cheered me up considerably.

She added that she was glad Tony Blair was a practising Christian because it meant that he must have some sort of value system. There must, therefore, be some limits to his pragmatism.

To the Cabinet Room at Number 10 for the parliamentary committee. The front door was open so we walked in, unchallenged.

The Man was meeting a delegation from Northern Ireland so we hovered at the door of the Cabinet Room. Eventually the door opened and John Hume emerged in evident good humour, shaking hands with several of us, like a politician working the crowd. A compulsive flesh-presser.

We went in. The Man was at the table in his shirtsleeves, Prescott, besuited, at his side. I took the seat directly opposite him. 'That's where the Chancellor sits,' he said. There was a little light banter along the lines of, 'just trying it out for size'. I remarked that JP wasn't looking too happy at the thought, to which Prescott responded cruelly, 'Your tie looks like a brownfield site,' a reference to my perfectly respectable red tie. Obviously our recent exchanges about his decision to allow Newcastle to concrete over its green belt found their mark.

The Man opened, saying that he had 'overcome combined resistance' and decided to grant our request for an annual debate on the security and intelligence services. Nick Brown intervened, saying the debate would be 'regular' rather than 'annual', to which The Man, looking at the paper before him, said, 'It says 'annual' here.' No one quibbled. A nice little victory.

As ever, we discussed hunting with hounds. This was going to do us tremendous damage with the middle ground, I said. The Man replied that we must be robust. We had to make clear that it was the Tories, not us, who were talking it out. Charlotte Atkins said, 'We can say that until we are red in the face, but no one will believe that a government with our kind of majority can't deliver.' Clive chipped in, saying there was a total lack of understanding outside as regards who was to blame. The debate was just getting interesting when the division bell went. As we went out Jean overheard Clive telling Tony that being robust wasn't good enough.

Three of us piled into Frank Dobson's car. As we swept out of Downing Street we passed Prescott, outside the gate, looking around forlornly for his car. Serves him right for insulting my tie. A brownfield site, indeed.

We resumed at the House twenty minutes later, in the absence of both The Man and JP. Margaret Jay said that on her way out of Downing Street she had been accosted by a woman protesting about the hunting Bill. She had tried out Tony's line, being 'robust' and blaming it all on the Tories, and it had cut no ice. Rarely in the history of focus groups can a policy have been market tested so soon after leaving the Cabinet Room.

Another long night. I am writing this at 2.42 a.m. This time it is the Wireless Telegraphy Bill, though goodness knows why the Tories feel so strongly about it.

Thursday, 12 March

We were here until after 3 a.m. I learned later that the filibuster had nothing to do with wireless telegraphy. It was to give their colleagues time to draft amendments to the Hunting with Hounds Bill. In an attempt to outwit the huntsmen, Mike Foster had submitted an entirely new Bill just before close of business. Since amendments had to be in by close of last night's business the Tories had to keep talking while the hunting lobby frantically drafted amendments to the new Bill in time for the deadline. What foolish games we play in the name of parliamentary democracy.

Saturday, 14 March

In the park, on my way back from town, I passed Gladys, a single parent who works as a part-time cleaner. 'I'm not voting for Tony Blair next time,' she said.

What she means, of course, is that she's not voting for me. A bit sickening considering that, along with 250 other Heroes of the People, I stayed up all night last Monday to vote through the Minimum Wage Bill, precisely so that people like Gladys could have a better life. It's the legacy of the lone-parent fiasco, of course. It will take years to repair the damage.

Monday, 16 March

Ben Bradshaw was on the tube from King's Cross. Had I seen the front page of today's *Sun*, he inquired. Mandelson allegedly spent the weekend at Sandringham with Charles and Camilla. Ben added that his sister, who lives near Peter in Notting Hill, had seen Camilla going into Peter's house. Later I saw Peter talking quietly with Nick Soames at a desk in the 'Aye' Lobby. From the fragment I overheard they were discussing Camilla's coming out. I heard Soames saying something about, 'If he can get away with it ...'

Not content with being New Labour's spin doctor in chief, the Great Manipulator now seems to have placed his talents at the disposal of the royal family.

Tuesday, 17 March

I came across Mark Seddon, the editor of *Tribune*, who told me that he was in Downing Street on the day of James Goldsmith's memorial service and who should he see being ushered into The Presence? Rupert Murdoch.

Mark says that Murdoch, not the CBI, is the main problem over union recognition. 'He won't have unions back at Wapping under any circumstances.'

When I went to consult Bridget Prentice, the duty whip on the Treasury bench, about the timing of the adjournment, I noticed she had open on her lap a red folder. Each page was divided into four or five parts into which was entered the name of each speaker. There were then a series of categories, with boxes to be ticked. I only noted two: 'Generally supportive' and 'A good constituency speech'. Then there was a section labelled, ominously, 'Other comments'. We are being watched.

Wednesday, 18 March

Gordon's first Budget seems to have gone down well with just about everyone. Contrary to rumour, the middle classes emerged virtually unscathed, apart from an increase in tax on petrol which everyone was expecting. Business seems happy with a cut in corporation tax. A large number of low-paid workers are to be taken out of tax altogether, which ought to make the world of work more attractive – a far better strategy than cutting benefits. Single parents are compensated for the fiasco last autumn with a big increase in child benefit and a generous contribution towards the cost of childcare for those who want to work. And just to make sure it can't be billed as a U-turn, it applies to everyone. The only people missing are the poorer pensioners. There is nothing for them – and we have to do something. As for the Tories, they have been left on the sidelines, spluttering about betrayal of Middle England. A sound bite clearly concocted before the Budget. No one believes them. Not even the *Telegraph*.

Friday, 20 March

A call from Joan Maynard's neighbour, Carol. Joan has been readmitted to hospital and is going downhill fast. I am due to visit tomorrow evening, but Carol suggested I come in the afternoon as it may be the last chance to see her.

Saturday, 21 March

To Thirsk with Sarah. Joan is in the cottage hospital, about half a mile from her home. The very room in which her brother Roy died. She was lying with her eyes almost closed, attached to a morphine drip. Her skin yellowy. The room warm and airless. On a table by the bedside, a bowl of ice. Every few minutes she reached for a piece, wrapped it in tissue, and pressed it to her parched lips. She spoke quietly but with absolute lucidity. I tried to be brave, for Sarah's sake, but my lower lip trembled. I managed to hold out for a while, but when she said, 'I want you to say a few words at the funeral,' I caved in. Sarah just sat there bemused. Joan said that she had always intended to be buried with her family at Thornton-le-Street, but had recently come round to cremation so that her ashes could be divided between Thornton and Sowerby, where she has lived for forty-five years. We talked about the abolition of tied cottages which she did so much to bring about. She became tearful when she described how, on the very day of the third reading,* she had been sidelined by the old right-wing establishment in the agricultural workers' union. When we were leaving, she said there was an Usborne children's book which she had bought for Emma and a hardcover notebook for Sarah on the desk in her living room. Would I go and get them and bring them back so she could sign them?

We went back to Joan's house for tea with her niece Anne and Anne's husband Jack, who will be there until the end. Sarah and I went out into the garden. We sat in the little arbour, where we had tea with Joan last summer, a few days before her big operation. I said quietly, 'Aunty Joan is going to die soon.'

'Don't say that, Dad.'

'She is going to heaven and will be with the angels.' I don't know why I spout such nonsense, but I daren't tell her that after life there is nothing, only silence.

We both cried and I hugged her.

I found the books and went back alone to the hospital. I knew this was

---

*Of the Rent (Agricultural) Bill, 1976.

the moment to say 'Goodbye'. When I produced the books, Joan came to life, propped herself on an elbow and signed and dated each one. Then I produced a photograph of us taken in her front room when I last visited two weeks ago. I found it on a table in the living room and asked her to sign it for me. She wrote, 'To Chris, with warmest love and many thanks for everything' and then the date. I moved the trolley out of the way and then leaned over and embraced her. 'I want you to know,' I could hardly get the words out and had to repeat them, 'that knowing you has been one of the great privileges of my life and I will never forget you.' We both cried. After about a minute I disengaged, manoeuvred the bedside trolley back into position and walked to the door. As I closed it behind me she turned on her side, raised her arm and gave me the thumbs up. That was my last sight of her.

Monday, 23 March

Good news. Jack Straw announced that he is accepting most of the select committee's proposals for reforming police complaints and discipline. There was no fuss, not even from the Tories. Several, starting with Ken Clarke, welcomed Jack's proposals. Even the Police Federation, realising the way the wind is blowing, were muted.

To the Lord Chancellor's office to see Derry Irvine. About ten members present, mainly lawyers. Derry has finally realised that he has to make friends at our end of the building and this meeting, belatedly, is part of that effort.

We sat around an oblong table in his cluttered office. Life-size stone busts of ancient Greek philosophers stare down from a bookcase of Halsbury's Statutes. At either end there are massive paintings. One of a naval bombardment. The other of Queen Victoria being transferred by royal barge between the British and French fleets. The Lord Chancellor's wig stands on a dummy beneath, staring the full length of the room.

On a table, beside a grey marble fireplace, a bowl of oranges surmounted by a single plum. Unlike other ministers, whose offices are antiseptically clean, the main impression of Derry's office is one of clutter. One cannot walk a few paces without colliding with a chair or table – one piled high with newspapers. At the far end of the room there is a screen behind which he presumably gets into his ridiculous uniform.

The man himself was on his best behaviour. He greeted us all with a warm handshake and looked straight into our eyes when he talked. He listened. Not a hint of pomposity. He talked frankly of his 'PR disaster' – a reference to the affair of the wallpaper. He pointed out that what is going up in the Lord Chancellor's apartment is exactly the same as that which already covers many other walls in the building, including the Members' Tea Room. Why, for God's sake, haven't I read that anywhere? A couple of minutes' skilful spinning in the early stages and disaster could have been averted.

He gave us a brief rundown of his responsibilities. He chairs five or six cabinet committees, including that which decides the contents of the next Queen's Speech. On Lords reform, he was clear that we are not going to be sidetracked. We will sort out the hereditaries first and nothing else. By way of incentive for good behaviour, the Tories will be offered life peerages for twenty or thirty of their more active hereditaries if they cooperate and nothing if they misbehave. He estimates that it will be done and dusted by the summer of 1999, unless the Parliament Act has to be invoked.

On his relationship with The Man, he said: 'It's not my fault that Tony Blair happened to be a pupil in my chambers.' Adding, 'with all due modesty', that he would have been Lord Chancellor in a Kinnock or Smith government. A fair point. In any case, he shows every sign of being to the left of his protégé.

I came away encouraged. Derry Irvine is a serious player and once the press realise that he is a feature of the landscape they will lay off him.

Wednesday, 25 March

Crawled into bed at 7 a.m. The Tories had agreed to draw stumps at midnight, but reneged. About forty – the friends of John Redwood – kept us up all night.

I slept until about 1.30 p.m. and then went back. The editor of *The Times*, Peter Stothard, and the chairman of Rupert Murdoch's News Corporation, Les Hinton, came in to see Giles Radice and me with a view to putting our minds at rest over predatory pricing. I asked how much it had cost and Hinton replied deviously, 'I have seen a figure of £150 million quoted. In fact it is substantially less than half that amount.' Why can't he be precise, I wondered. Surely he must know.

Murdoch came up again at the parliamentary committee. The papers are full of stories alleging that The Man has been ringing up the Italian Prime Minister on Murdoch's behalf. I asked: (1) Who initiated the call to Prodi? and (2) What is our relationship with Murdoch? The Man was visibly irritated. 'I don't reveal the details of private conversations,' he said testily. I replied that I just want to know who initiated it. He seemed to say it was Prodi, adding, 'The story in today's *Telegraph* is a load of balls.' Then he relaxed and said, 'My relationship with Murdoch is no different from that with any other newspaper proprietor. I love them all equally.' He added forcefully, 'I have never discussed media policy with Murdoch.'

Jean raised hunting, saying it had become an issue of trust. 'I do understand the strength of feeling,' he said, not very convincingly. The longer this goes on, the more convinced I am that the problem is Mandelson and his friends in high places. Jean approached me in the Tea Room afterwards and reported that Nick Brown had told her that the advice from the Palace is that the Royals are not merely opposed, they won't have it. Won't they, indeed? I thought Mandelson was supposed to be trying to brush up the Prince of Wales's image. If so, the most useful advice he could give his new-found friend is not to side with the Unspeakable.

Joan is home again. A bed has been set up for her in the front room, facing the window so she has a view of the church. I spoke to her briefly. She sounds very weak. My eyes fill with tears every time I think of her.

Thursday, 26 March

Awoken at five by a pain in my side. Another kidney stone. This one seems to be halfway down the tube. After an hour the pain became too great to lie still and I got up and paced around, feeling very sorry for myself. Apart from the stone, I've also got a stinking cold and I'm feeling feverish. I would have gone home, except that I am supposed to be taking a party of schoolchildren to Downing Street this afternoon and I can't let them down. I went to Dr Berlyn's surgery feeling absolutely rotten and he gave me a couple of injections which killed the pain. I lay down for twenty minutes and then caught a cab to the House and resumed business as usual.

The kids – two girls and a boy – and three teachers arrived at 2.30. None had been to London before, let alone Downing Street. We messed about for a while taking photos on the doorstep of Number 10 and then went upstairs to the State Dining Room where Cherie entertained us to tea. She was brilliant, working her way round the room, chatting amiably with everyone, not at all the awkward append-age that she appears to be at party conferences. The kids gave her a plate with local landmarks on and a glass paperweight. Halfway through, The Man turned up with Neil Kinnock and they worked the room in the opposite direction to Cherie. This was the Kinnock that I used to know and admire. The life and soul of the party. Amusing, relaxed. He shook my hand warmly and said, 'Who'd have thought?' and suddenly I realised how far we'd both come since those far-off days sitting round his dinner table in Dysart Avenue, Kingston upon Thames.

Later, as we were about to leave, he said to me quietly, 'It's not enough to be in power. We have to make a difference.'

We were given a little tour of the premises. As the kids were being shown the Cabinet Room The Man came in with the President of Poland, to whom he introduced them as 'the delegation from Sunder-land'. That made their day. Mine, too.

Friday, 27 March
Sunderland

No sign of the pain, but the cold has gone to my chest and I feel generally lousy. Back on the 9.30 and then to hospital, where I was X-rayed. The X-ray showed a stone lodged two-thirds of the way down the urethra. Mr Mellon reckons it is the one I had before Christmas. It hasn't flushed away after all. He favours surgery, which will put me out of action for the best part of a week.

Saturday, 28 March

Awoken in the early hours by the pain. By breakfast it was serious. At 8.30 a.m. Anne rang to say that Joan died last night at about 11.30. She slipped away peacefully in bed in her living room, just as she wanted. I had a little cry, but it's hard to be sorry, she was in such a state. I rang Tony Benn and told him the news. Joan Lestor also died yesterday, which was unexpected. I spoke to her only last week and she was talking about attending the Lords.

Helen, a neighbouring GP, came round and gave me another injection which took away the pain. I spent the morning working on Joan's obituary for the *Guardian*. I also rang the Press Association and put out a short statement. Important to get in first before they start using all that bile from Andrew Roth.

Sunday, 29 March

Another bad night. Our neighbour was holding a party. The music was so loud that there was no hope of sleep. At about five o'clock I went round to plead for mercy. I had to ring the bell for fifteen minutes before establishing contact.

When I got up (again) I found a message on the answerphone from Mr Mellon, the consultant, who said that if I could come in by lunchtime he would operate this afternoon. I packed a bag and Ngoc drove me to the hospital. At four I was wheeled down to the operating theatre. My first general anaesthetic. As they wheeled me along I kept thinking, this is how it must be to die by lethal injection. When I came round the stone had gone. They flashed it briefly in my face. There was a tube sticking out of my waterworks, attached to a bag on a little hanger full of blood and urine. A drip was attached to my arm. Ngoc and the children came to see me in the evening.

Monday, 30 March

Not a bad night considering all the things sticking out of me. A male nurse came in every two or three hours to replace the bags and offer painkillers. When I complained about the bag he said drily that some people had to live with such a contraption for life. Mr Mellon, a softly spoken Irishman, a real gent, put his head round the door at nine and said that if progress continued I might get home by tomorrow.

At two o'clock Pat came in with two big files of correspondence. We cancelled all engagements for the week except Joan's funeral on Friday. After Pat left I started on the correspondence and, with short breaks for an evening meal and a visit from Ngoc and the children, continued until 11 p.m.

The *Guardian* published my obituary of Joan.

Tuesday, 31 March

Mr Mellon called in just after nine and pronounced me fit enough to go home. Ngoc came for me about eleven. I went home, had a bath and a light lunch and then spent the rest of the day at the office. I am very tired though, at one point dozing off for half an hour.

Thursday, 2 April

A card has arrived signed by everyone on the parliamentary committee. On the front a sketch of four pigs about to stick their noses in a trough. Inside Jean has written, 'For the sake of the pigs and many others, get well soon'.* Underneath Tony Blair has written, 'I had no idea about this pig thing – interesting.' Nick Brown wrote, 'Get well

---

*A reference to my Welfare of Pigs Bill.

soon – though you are probably better off where you are – note the green ink,' and sure enough he has used green ink.

Friday, 3 April

To Sowerby for Joan's funeral. The churchyard was a sea of daffodils. The vicar had rigged up amplifiers outside in case of an overflow, but in the event we all just about squeezed in. A good turnout from Parliament, considering the logistical difficulties. Tam Dalyell and his wife drove down from Scotland. Tony Benn, Dennis Skinner, Audrey Wise, David Blunkett, Gavin Strang and Jeremy Corbyn. Arthur Scargill was standing at the back. Several Tories, including Michael Jopling, a red-faced squire and a lot of local folk. Before setting out I had a call from Sir Richard Body, who apologised for being unable to attend. I said that Joan had frequently remarked that they often found themselves in agreement on matters agricultural. 'Not often,' he said, 'always.'

We began with Mozart's Clarinet Concerto. Then a hymn, 'He who would valiant be'. Then tributes. Tony Benn went first and made us all laugh. One of Tony's functions in life is to cheer us up at times of sadness. Then it was my turn. I was afraid I'd break down, but I got through, just about. Audrey Wise said afterwards that mine was one of the best tributes she had ever heard, which cheered me up because Audrey does not dispense praise lightly. As with all left-wing occasions, there was a speech too many – five in all. No matter, it was a good day. Joan had planned it all as she lay dying. A soloist sang, 'I know that my redeemer liveth' from the *Messiah*. There was a rousing chorus of 'Jerusalem' and then Joan was carried out through the daffodils to the strains of the Nunc Dimittis.

Tony Benn and I went with the family to the graveyard at Thornton-le-Street. Joan is the last of her immediate family and they are all there, buried side by side: Mum, Dad, Elsie, Edric, Rowy and now Joan. All within a few yards of the little post office they once managed. The wheel of life has come full circle.

Monday, 6 April
Sunderland

Out early for the breakfast launch of the New Deal, Gordon's plan to get the young unemployed into work or other useful activity. Corporate breakfasts are not really my scene, but the cause is good and Diane Hedley, who runs the local employment service, is so full of energy and enthusiasm that I am anxious to please. The personnel director of Nissan remarked to me that the company was being hard hit by the strong pound which hangs like a great cloud over everything. Then to the Civic Centre to see a planning supremo about the preservation of Victorian Sunderland and finally to London – Sarah came with me, which meant that I did not get any work done on the train.

Tuesday, 7 April

On my way to the House, from the top deck of a 109 bus I espied Lord Waddington at a bus stop in Kennington Road. He was wearing a drab raincoat, pulling a little suitcase on wheels and looking slightly anxious. Things can't be all bad with the state of our democracy when a former Home Secretary and Governor General of Bermuda is to be found, *sans* plumed hat, waiting for a bus in Kennington. He was complaining in the Lords the other day about what he alleged was a witch hunt against the poor Freemasons. Had he boarded, I might have engaged him in dialogue on the subject, but he didn't.

With members of the select committee, I spent the day touring 'projects'. Part of our Alternatives to Prison inquiry. The morning in Bermondsey. The afternoon in Dalston. We met some impressive people who assured us that what they were doing worked. Whether or not it did was hard to tell since there was a marked shortage of 'clients'. In Bermondsey we talked to four youths, three of whom – all black – defied the stereotype. They were reasonable, articulate, personable; they appeared to come from more or less stable families and had all held down jobs. The fourth, a malnourished, insolent white youth, lounged in front of us swigging pop and smoking. At Dalston the sole available 'client' was a shy black youth who was being successfully taught to spell diarrhoea backwards by a right-on young woman in a figure-hugging cat suit. Humiliation was narrowly avoided when Ross Cranston, on our behalf, managed to spell diarrhoea correctly.

Thursday, 16 April
Sunderland

Customers at this evening's surgery included a couple from deep within the benefit culture whose son had found work only to discover that they had lost most of their housing benefit and would now be required to pay £5 a week in council tax. They huffed and puffed about the wickedness of it all, complaining that the boy – who lived at home – would 'only' have about £40 a week left for himself and how wrong it was that an eighteen-year-old should be expected to support his entire family. The more they went on the more my sympathy faded. In most parts of the world it would be taken for granted by a poor family that, when one of their number had the good fortune to find work, his income, or most of it, would have to support the family. Here it is considered an outrage.

Monday, 20 April

Today's post brings a letter from a member of United Grand Lodge complaining about the sale of a Masonic hospital in Cheshire and alleging – would you believe – that the Charity Commissioners have been improperly influenced by Freemasonry. As so often, truth outpaces fiction.

Wednesday, 22 April

The mood at the parliamentary committee was upbeat. The Man, fresh from his triumphs in Ireland and the Middle East, was relaxed, enquiring genially about my health and my interest in the welfare of pigs. Amazing. In the three weeks since our last encounter we have glimpsed him on our TV screens sorting out Ireland, holidaying in

Spain, touring the Middle East. One day inspecting a guard of honour with the Saudi King, another with Arafat in Gaza, yet another with the Israeli Prime Minister and so on. Yet here he is sitting directly across the table, unchanged apart perhaps from a light tan, his hairline having receded another millimetre or two, picking up the conversation exactly where we left off three weeks ago. We call him by his first name. He never pulls rank. There are no bodyguards or flunkeys. For forty minutes he is one of us and yet, when he goes out of the door, he is Prime Minister again. I can't get over it. I wonder if he can?

Wednesday, 29 April

Giles Radice and I have tabled an amendment to the Competition Bill, outlawing predatory pricing. John Hutton, Margaret Beckett's Parliamentary Private Secretary, says our masters are getting twitchy about it. He asks whether I had received a call from Number 10. I haven't, but I can't speak for Giles.

Tuesday, 5 May

Our masters, having spotted that Giles and I are unlikely bedfellows, are trying to drive a wedge between us. On Friday, with a European summit and Middle East peace talks about to commence, The Man found forty-five minutes to see Giles in an attempt to persuade him to get back on message. He even tried that old line, 'Would you be interested in a job?' but it doesn't play so well these days. Giles told him he was a year late and claims to have conceded nothing. Unwisely, however, he did hand over a copy of a letter from the Library suggesting a couple of possible amendments.

A call from Margaret Beckett's office. Would Giles and I care to stop by this evening to discuss the Competition Bill? And by the way, the Solicitor General will be present. We really do have their attention. John Hutton told me that Nick Brown has advised the government that a rebellion led by Giles and me could be a big problem. At the appointed time we duly presented ourselves at the Department of

Trade and Industry and were shown up to Margaret's office. A big turnout. Margaret on an armchair, her legs folded under her, the Solicitor General Charlie Falconer (the man the regime tried to parachute into Dudley) and a phalanx of officials. The mood was relaxed. Wine was served, but I stuck to water. Margaret opened by saying that the clause inserted by Tom McNally in the Lords wouldn't work and would have to go. She said, 'If you are out to get Murdoch, this is not the way.'

Our object, I replied, was not to 'get' Murdoch. We were interested in outlawing predatory pricing, whoever indulged in it.

Charlie Falconer was clutching a faxed copy of the letter from the Library, which Giles had left with Number 10. Charlie drew our attention to Clause 60 of the Bill, which no one had previously mentioned. This, he said, incorporated the Tetrapak judgment (the basis of European competition law) without referring to it by name.

'Why not,' I asked, 'for the avoidance of doubt include the European Court's precise form of words in our Bill?'

'Because European case law is bound to develop and we risk narrowing rather than widening the scope of the Bill.'

Neither Giles nor I could think of an answer to that, though we made noises about going away and consulting. That is how the matter rests.

Later, a brief chat with David Clark about Mandelson. Poor David has a haunted look. For weeks, indeed even before he took office, the papers have been running stories about how he is for the chop. One of his staff in the Cabinet Office had been loaned to Mandelson for three weeks and reported, on her return, that he is keeping notes on ministers (which she typed). According to David, Mandelson sees The Man every day. David and he are on several of the same cabinet committees. 'He never speaks. Just scribbles.' Eerie.

Friday, 8 May
Sunderland

To the university to bear witness to the installation of David Puttnam as Chancellor.

This evening, the monthly meeting of the party's management committee. A number of people from addresses in London and Scotland had written asking to be considered as our candidate for the European Parliament. This triggered a discussion about whether candidates from outside the region should be considered. Someone, trying to be helpful, said she didn't see why we shouldn't look at outsiders. 'After all, if we hadn't considered non-local candidates for the parliamentary nomination, we wouldn't have Chris as our MP, would we?' This was received in stony silence. .

Monday, 11 May

To London in good time for the debate on the Competition Bill. Alan Milburn, a minister in the Department of Health, was on the station at Durham carrying nothing but a red dispatch box. Alan says he is surprised by the extent to which the Treasury has its fingers in every department. 'I used to take the view that once they had handed over our money it was ours to do as we liked with. Not a bit of it. They question everything.'

We talked of The Man. 'Ruthless' was one of the first words Alan used. He added, 'One of Tony's great strengths, which comes from having a good family life, is that he is capable of detachment. You have to be able to walk away from the job. After all, it is going to end one day.'

Alan was one of a handful of ministers accorded the privilege of accompanying The Man on his recent expedition to Washington – a sure sign that he is destined for big things. He described a surreal scene in the White House Cabinet Room. Bill Clinton, who had been up all night, dozing off at intervals, leaving The Man to dominate the discussion. The Man, Jack Straw and Alan opposite the President and his men discussing matters of high policy, way outside Alan's brief; he was terrified that someone would ask his opinion. Out on the lawn Elton John was rehearsing for that evening's concert.

The debate on the Competition Bill went off well enough. Margaret gave a competent speech. Giles and I, both called early, expressed reservations, but the truth is that our little rebellion is turning into a damp squib. The Bill is a great deal better than we had originally thought, giving the regulator great powers to address the Murdoch problem, if anything will. The only mystery is why no one mentioned Clause 60 to us before last Tuesday. I asked Margaret and she said she didn't know about it until Charlie Falconer pointed it out.

Tuesday, 12 May

A chat with a Home Office minister, full of praise for Jack Straw, whose handling of officials, he says, is masterful. Jack never gets into rows, listens carefully to advice, lets them fire all their bullets and then announces his decision. On Masons, he came under tremendous pressure and Jack outmanoeuvred both the officials and Derry Irvine.

Wednesday, 13 May

To the Neill Committee to give evidence on the funding of political parties. My theme was that the main problem with British politics is that there is too much money swilling around, rather than too little. I argued for disclosure and a spending cap to be set at levels far lower than the Labour Party is proposing. They were gentle with me, although Anthony King pressed hard on the practicalities of enforcement. I replied, a little sharply, that I refused to accept that nothing could be done. Lord Neill appeared to nod in agreement. This must have stung Professor King because he came back saying that he was not necessarily expressing a view, merely testing my evidence.

At the parliamentary committee there was a lively discussion on trade union recognition. The Man said it was his aim to come up with something that both the CBI and the trade unions could live with. He then reeled off a list of measures that ought to make life easier for working people – the minimum wage, our signing up to the EU Social Chapter, the forty-eight-hour working week, minimum holiday entitlement, extended protection against unfair dismissal ... As I listened I began to think he may be right. As he says, we do have this terrible habit in the Labour Party of pocketing whatever is on offer, homing in on the bad news and, before we know where we are, we are back to the language of betrayal.

Wednesday, 20 May

A row at the party meeting about the role the whips are playing in internal party elections and reports that candidates for the Scottish Assembly are being vetted. Also, rumours that the whips are going to interfere in the next round of parliamentary reselections, which could get us into a lot of trouble. 'We are becoming a democratic centralist party, like the old communist parties in which it is assumed that the top people always know what is best,' said David Winnick. Nick Brown responded unapologetically, with the same little speech that I have heard him give on two or three occasions, the gist of which is that he is not neutral. It sounds less convincing each time I hear it. By the time we got to the parliamentary committee, however, Nick's tone had changed, apparently due to the intervention of John Prescott, who was overheard to remark that what has been going on as regards elections to the National Executive Committee was unacceptable. Jean, Ann, Charlotte and I all chipped in, saying the whips had no business interfering in party matters and they should stop doing so. Nick said contritely that he obviously hadn't appreciated the strength of feeling. There the matter rests for the time being.

Thursday, 21 May

Fairness at Work, the long-awaited White Paper on industrial relations, was published today. Margaret Beckett made a statement in the House. As expected, at least 40 per cent of the eligible workforce will have to vote for unions before recognition is enforced. Companies with fewer than twenty employees will be exempted. The news was received in silence by our side, but there was good news as well. People employed for more than a year – the present minimum is two years

– will be entitled to claim unfair dismissal. That drew a cheer. The Tories seemed upset so it can't be all bad.

Monday, 1 June

A question to Chris Smith about the rapidly declining quality of commercial television and what, if anything, he was going to do about it. The answer – that it was all a matter for the Independent Television Commission – was pathetic. I told him so when I ran into him in the Post Office and he grinned sheepishly. I asked what plans he had for bringing Sky within the existing regulations, such as they are, on quality and domestic production. There were, he said, technical difficulties given that Sky was based in Luxembourg. I replied that this shouldn't be a problem since most of the assets were located here. At this point his tack changed. 'There is also a prime ministerial interest in the matter. But I haven't told you that last part.'

I saw Jack in the Members' Lobby and indicated that I wanted to talk about freedom of information. 'Why don't you come to my Monday lunches?'

'They are not the appropriate forum.'

'No, but we could discuss it afterwards.'

I suspect he is unhappy about my semi-detachment, but I am unrepentant. I am supposed to be scrutinising the executive, not representing it.

Wednesday, 3 June

My attention wanders. So much of our work is drudgery. I find myself day-dreaming about where I was this time last week – by the lake at Duns, by the river at Paxton … At the same time I am wracked by guilt at terrible events elsewhere in the world and my absolute inability to have the slightest influence upon them. Today's *Daily Express* devotes the first three pages to the story of a man and his family in the south of Sudan who, already starving, walked for six days to a feeding station. On the way he buried three of his four children and, on arrival, he too died, leaving his wife and one small child alone in the world. There are harrowing pictures of the exhausted woman, her sole surviving child at her breast, beside his shrivelled body. That awful journey took place last week, while we were enjoying ourselves at Duns. Each morning, when my family's only problem was how to amuse ourselves, that little family were crawling towards an aid station, the children begging their dad and mum to help them, the parents looking on helplessly. I feel so ashamed, so helpless. Everything I do seems pointless by comparison. If I didn't have a family to support I'd pack it all in and become a recluse – or go and work for Joe Homan.*

The party meeting was well attended. A lively debate on the regime's plans to reform the parliamentary selection procedure – a subject always guaranteed to attract a crowd. David Gardner, a senior official, was at pains to assure us that no skulduggery was afoot. 'It won't be like Scotland,' he said. Whereupon a number of Scots rose and described what was going on there, where several sitting members of the Westminster Parliament have been ruled ineligible for the candidates' panel for the Scottish one. Joe Ashton made the same speech he has been making for the last twenty years – opposing any form of accountability. Various people expressed concern at plans for the Chief Whip to supply constituency parties with details of voting and attendance records.

At Prime Minister's Questions Andrew Mackinlay bravely suggested to The Man that he should use his influence to reduce the sycophancy which increasingly demeans Question Time. The Man was not amused. The gist of his reply was that Mackinlay should never expect advancement of any kind. The truth is, I am increasingly coming to realise, sycophancy is exactly what The Man wants. Understandable were he mediocre, but that is simply not the case. He is a star. Potentially one of the all-time greats. Of what is he afraid? Can it be that under the relaxed exterior there lurks a deep insecurity? I can't quite bring myself to believe it, but the possibility can't be ruled out.

---

* A former teacher at my old school who runs several villages for destitute children in southern India.

Yet more evidence of control freakery. At last week's meeting of the parliamentary committee Nick Brown had appeared to be in full retreat on the question of interference by the whips in the elections to the party's National Executive Committee. The minutes of the meeting, normally bland, refer to 'disquiet'. Today, however, Nick appeared to be back in bullish mode. He reported that the promised discussion with John Prescott had taken place and that 'John now understood the issue'. JP, unfortunately, wasn't present and so the extent of his understanding could not be explored. I said the issue had been clear for some weeks. It was whether government should be interfering in party elections. For The Man's benefit I explained that the whips had been standing in the lobbies handing out green nomination forms with the names of the official slate already typed in. The Man replied that he appreciated the sensitivity but – and I quote – 'It would be wrong to imagine that I don't have an interest in the composition of the NEC.' He added ominously, 'Or for that matter in the composition of this committee.' Jean said afterwards that Nick had looked meaningfully at her at this point, as if to say 'Now do you realise what I am up against?' The good news is – and this is a little victory for our committee – that The Man indicated that he had no objection to a secret ballot, which should take some heat out of the issue. All the same it is worrying. This is a regime that can't leave anything to chance. Nothing at all. Everything has to be spun or fixed. Sooner of later they'll come unstuck.

Thursday, 4 June

The main discussion at the Liaison Committee was about whether members who were entertained by British missions abroad should also be allowed to claim the usual meal allowance, i.e. whether or not the taxpayer should pay twice over. Nick Winterton, not for the first time, huffed and puffed about how hard done by MPs were in general. John McWilliam treated the committee, several times, to an account of a meal of egg and chips that he enjoyed yesterday with the British forces in Germany – worth, he claimed, only 30 pfennigs. Round and round they went, some members contributing two, three or (in

McWilliam's case) four times. In the end it was decided not to allow claims for meals that members hadn't had to pay for, mainly on the grounds that this would not look good in the tabloids.

Friday, 12 June
Sunderland

To Pennywell for the launch of the Single Regeneration Budget Programme – £17.8 million to be invested in restoring the damage to the social fabric caused by the Thatcher Decade. I had been given to understand that I was the main speaker, but as I went in the door my eye was caught by a free sheet headed 'Bishop to launch SRB programme'. Sure enough the main speaker was the Bishop of Durham. He spoke very well. Although not as flamboyant as David Jenkins he is every bit as decent. The Bishop did put his finger on a rather sensitive spot when he asked how many of those present actually lived in Pennywell. Six or seven hands went up in an audience that consisted mostly of movers and shakers who don't even live in Sunderland, never mind Pennywell. To be sure, they are well motivated, but there is not much sign of a change in the long tradition of telling people what's good for them. Already there are warlike rumblings from the Ford side of the Hylton Road over the division of the spoils.

Wednesday, 17 June

Gordon Brown addressed the party meeting. Relaxed, confident, credible. Being in government has improved him. Gone is the glazed expression and that mindless chanting of slogans which characterised the last few years in opposition.

Every Labour government, he said, had been brought down by failure to manage the economy. Our challenge was to be credible and radical. He had four aims – stability, increased investment and productivity, Welfare to Work, and better public services. On public services he was upbeat. His aim was a sustainable rise in public spending – 2.5 per cent in real terms over each of the next three years. 'We must get away from the false choice – that the only test of prudence is cutting public spending.' He would be happy to fight the next election on health and education spending. 'It suits me that my statement [on public spending] the other day was interpreted as tough – but you can be prudent and invest. I want to move away from a world where 20 per cent of the population are written off.'

There were complaints about plans to part-privatise air traffic control. Gordon replied that it needed a billion pounds of new investment over the next ten years and there was no way that could come from the public purse. Gordon Prentice said he was dismayed that the parliamentary party was regarded as a stage army; we had been spectators at last week's announcement of an economic policy that will lock us in for years to come. He asked what our target was for redistributing wealth. Gordon replied that he had already raised £5 billion from the utilities and another £7 billion from advance corporation tax – the biggest changes in the taxation of dividends since the war. Lynne Jones said that Gordon's plans to increase public spending were modest compared with what the previous Labour government – and even Thatcher – had spent. Ken Livingstone said there was no support for the privatisation of London Underground and that this would be an issue in the campaign for the Mayor of London – a clear demonstration, if any were needed, of why the government feels it can't afford to allow Ken to run.

Thursday, 18 June

Margaret Beckett made the long-awaited and much-leaked announcement of the minimum wage rates – £3.60 for adults, £3.20 phased in for eighteen- to twenty-one-year-olds. Nothing for those aged under eighteen. A review after the first year. Despite some disappointment the mood on our side was generally upbeat. Not least on seeing the passion with which the Tories remain committed to poverty pay. Some excellent sport was had at their expense. Everyone knows they will not dare go into the next election promising to abolish the minimum wage, but of course when they are re-elected they will run it down.

Monday, 22 June

Alan Clark nobbled me in the Library Corridor and asked whether I would be voting against the proposed restrictions on convicted football hooligans. 'I was relying on you,' he said. 'They can't travel, their benefits are to be investigated, they are to be thrown out of their jobs. It's fascistic.' I didn't really know what he was talking about. But when I looked at the monitor, I noticed that the clauses in which he was interested had passed without a vote, so he hadn't been paying attention either. He did say he was under a 'heavy three-line whip' to keep his mouth shut after his 'outburst' on the *Today* programme the other morning. I squirmed when I heard Tony Blair saying that he hoped the troublemakers would lose their jobs. Will unemployment make them behave any better?

Tuesday, 23 June

Ludo Kennedy called in for twenty minutes this evening. Elegant as ever, with his silver-topped walking stick, a little more fragile than when I last saw him, but otherwise unchanged. He's taking an interest in the case of two guardsmen convicted of shooting a man in Belfast. They are likely to be released soon anyway, but he's convinced they are innocent. He thinks the judge might have been leaned on by the IRA and wanted to know how he could go about checking whether this was the case or not. I told him that my instinct was that his theory is extremely improbable. He went off saying that he 'might give Gerry Adams a buzz'.

An unhelpful piece in the *Financial Times* by Liam Halligan, with whom I lunched the other day, suggesting that I am placing myself at the head of a revolt on the Competition Bill and quoting from our conversation at lunch last week, which I had thought was off the record. He rang yesterday and said he was proposing to quote me. When I protested he said that he would not quote what was said over lunch, only what I said as we walked back over Westminster Bridge. Never trust a lobby correspondent, not even one who works for the *FT*.

This evening Giles convened a meeting of interested parties to discuss a possible amendment to the Competition Bill. The turnout consisted of Bob Sheldon, David Winnick, Clive Soley and Bob Marshall-Andrews. We had to choose between a weak amendment which would incorporate into the Bill sentiments which are probably there anyway and a more robust amendment which singled out predatory pricing in the newspaper industry for special treatment. To my pleasant surprise Bob Sheldon was the most robust. 'It's time to hang out the banners,' he said. 'July is a good month for unrest.'

Clive Soley agreed but said he could not sign because of his position as chairman of the parliamentary party. Winnick, Marshall-Andrews and I also favoured the tough approach, although Winnick said he would want to know how many were coming with him before he went into the division lobby against the government. Giles, who has all along made it clear that he would be reluctant to vote against the government, said hastily that he would have to think about it, whereupon Bob said he would only sign if Giles did. At which point it all seemed to unravel. In the end it will be just Marshall-Andrews, the Liberals and myself. Back to the land of token gestures – and just when it was looking promising.

Wednesday, 24 June

The *Sun* has turned on The Man. Under a ludicrous front-page headline 'Is This the Most Dangerous Man in Britain?' it criticises him for going soft on the euro. The end of a beautiful friendship or a warning shot? Either way, no bad thing. From here on in no one will be under any illusions.

Thursday, 25 June

Someone in a position to know whispered that my insistence that my select committee be allowed to interview the head of MI5 had upset the Intelligence and Security Committee. 'They are paranoid about you,' he said. My purpose, of course, is to force the government's hand and make the security services accountable to Parliament. I wrote to Jack Straw on 25 April asking for an appointment to discuss the matter and the Committee Clerk has been chasing Jack's office ever since. It's clear from the long silence that something is going on, but I'm not sure what.

I've decided to go ahead with an amendment to the Competition Bill, if necessary without Giles and Bob Sheldon. There is a healthy little rebellion in the making. Derek Foster, Martin O'Neill, Andrew Bennett and Bruce George – all select committee chairmen – have signed. All I need now is the Liberals.

Tuesday, 30 June

David Winnick and I met with a delegation from the Russian Duma, three women and a man. Winnick was at his most unctuous, insisting on lecturing them about the Great Terror and the rule of law. They had come to talk about youth justice, but on almost every point Winnick came in with one of his fatuous little speeches. The Russians were visibly irritated. They could hardly wait to escape, rising on the dot of five and disappearing down the corridor, leaving the interpreter trailing. 'They are all hardliners,' she said. Where Winnick is concerned, I am becoming a hardliner, too.

Wednesday, 1 July

At the parliamentary committee Clive Soley drew attention to a story in last week's *Sunday Express*, which has caused a mild flurry among the troops, predicting that Paddy Ashdown was to be offered a job in a coalition. It was sourced to 'senior Liberal Democrats', presumably Ashdown's enemies. Margaret Jay said the report had gone down badly with our people in the Lords, where the Lib Dems were particularly obstructive. The Man said he recognised there were two types of Lib Dems, one kind he wanted and the other kind he didn't. As for the story in the *Express*, it was on page seven, which suggested that those who concocted it didn't believe it either. 'People needn't worry,' he said. 'With a majority of 178 seats I do understand that it wouldn't be wise. However I don't want the Lib Dems going back to equidistance. It was helpful to have them leaning in our direction at the last election and it will be helpful at the next.' Which suggests that something is on offer, though not necessarily a coalition.

Talk then turned to rumours of a split between himself and Gordon. The Man became quite passionate. 'Complete rubbish. I don't know where it comes from.' He had read recently that Gordon was interfering in Scotland in some alleged bid to undermine him. 'It was at my suggestion. I asked Gordon to intervene. I feel bad about the way it's been used against him.' He added that he only usually read the newspapers on Wednesdays, in preparation for questions, and never ceased to be amazed by what he read.

Jean said we had to remind our people that they were not obliged to criticise the government just because the media said they should. The Man replied that he had sat through fourteen years of uncritical questions addressed to Tory Prime Ministers from their own back benches and no one in the media had made a fuss. We had to be robust and take on the media. It was part of coming to terms with being in government.

'Remember Harold Wilson,' I said. 'He became paranoid about the media. Stay above it.'

The master strategists at Millbank, many of whom have never knocked on a door in their lives, are dreaming up more pointless activity to take our minds off mischief. Everyone had been sent a glossy brochure, crammed with useless inserts, to help celebrate the fiftieth anniversary of the NHS. Among them a list of so-called campaigning ideas. Sample:

> Have a photo-op outside a local hospital with a large syringe with the words 'Labour's £2 billion cash injection for the NHS' written on it. Your regional press officer has a four-foot model syringe that can be used for this picture.

> Arrange a photo-opportunity with a long-serving local NHS worker who is celebrating their own fiftieth birthday this year.

> Arrange to spend a morning on a normal working day with an ambulance crew. Invite the media, but get your own photographer anyway so you can do a retrospective press release.

And so on ... It is as though our masters have set up a vast play scheme to keep us amused while they get on, unhindered, with the serious business of government.

Monday, 6 July

The papers are full of stories about Derek Draper, one of Peter Mandelson's protégés, who has been ambushed by the *Observer*, boasting about his lobbying contacts in government. Grotesque, crude stuff ('I just want to stuff my bank account at £250 an hour ...'). Peter Hardy, a Labour Peer, was on the train coming down. 'We won on sleaze, we can lose on sleaze,' he said.

Wednesday, 8 July

PM's Questions were all about the fallout from the Draper fiasco. Hague went on and on about cronyism. At last he's found a word – unlike sleaze – that has the ring of truth without reminding everyone of life under the Tories. The Man responded well enough but he is rattled. He knows the mud is beginning to stick. We are going to be hearing a lot more about 'cronyism' in the weeks ahead.

When we filed into The Man's room an hour later he was looking twitchy. Later, I learned that Clive – who had gone in ten minutes ahead of us – had been telling him what everyone is saying, that the trail leads to Mandelson. A slow fuse is burning. Clive also said he was intending to see The Man again and tell him that it would not be a good idea to put Peter in the Cabinet for the time being.

The first hour was taken up with Draper et al. The Man did most of the talking. We should, he said, be in no doubt that he was taking this seriously. He had looked carefully at the evidence. There was no truth in Draper's boasts. No ministers were involved. There was no point in getting hysterical. There was a feeding frenzy and we just had to keep our nerve. All the while The Man was sitting with his hands joined, resting on the table. When other people were speaking he drummed the fingers of one hand on the other and, at one point, on the table itself. I've never seen him so restless.

There was a brief exchange about the impending reshuffle, prompted by Draper's bad-mouthing of certain ministers. The Man said he hadn't discussed the reshuffle with anyone except John Prescott (and Peter, I thought to myself) yet he was continually reading reports of what was supposed to be in his head. Michael Meacher, he said, was a very good minister (an assurance worth banking). Margaret Jay said that she had heard that Derek Draper was about to make a third career publishing his memoirs. The Man said he didn't think there was any more to come. All the same, the possibility must be worrying him. At about quarter past five Sally Morgan indicated for the umpteenth time that he should go. He seemed to be in a daze as he got up, put on his jacket and followed her meekly out of the room. I suspect it is just beginning to dawn upon him that there is a problem with Peter and his friends.

The mood in the Tea Room is upbeat, not to say gleeful. The perception that Mandelson's star is waning is widespread. As Andrew Bennett said, this is going to make it very difficult for Tony to put Peter in the Cabinet this summer. Even poor David Clark is starting to look safe for the time being.

In the evening we debated the Competition Bill. Despite rumours, the government conceded nothing. Giles moved his amendment and then withdrew it. I pressed mine to the vote. There ensued some good-natured banter as I stood at the entrance to the division lobbies calling 'friends of Murdoch this way' (indicating the 'No' Lobby) and 'free press, that way' (indicate the 'Ayes'). Several people went into the government lobby holding their noses. We got about seventy votes, mainly from Lib Dems and Nationalists; only twenty-five from our side, not even all the usual suspects. I suppose I should have done some organising but I haven't had time. Not that it would have made much difference. Nick Brown and George Mudie were relaxed, but as usual Tommy McAvoy took it personally. 'Next time you come and ask to go home early on a Thursday you'll need fifty references,' he snarled. Sod him.

Thursday, 9 July

Derek Foster was on the train going home. We discussed the Draper crisis. 'A good week for democracy,' he said. He predicted, however, that The Man would still put Peter in the Cabinet. I am sure he's right. Not to do so would be seen as a sign of weakness and The Man must never look weak.

Monday, 13 July

Gordon Brown made a statement setting out his spending plans for the next three years. All good stuff on the face of it. Billions being splashed out. Education to rise 5.1 per cent of GDP in real terms. Health by 4.7 per cent. Transport by 16 per cent. A minimum income guarantee for pensioners. Overseas aid up (modestly). The mystery is where it is all coming from. There will be cuts in Defence and at the DTI. Also Gordon has – as the Tories allege – slyly raised taxes, but none of this begins to explain the apparent largesse. No one is quite sure. For the time being, however, doubts are churlish. All hail to the mighty Gordon, worker of miracles.

Wednesday, 15 July

Gordon addressed the parliamentary party in the wake of yesterday's triumph. He is a man reborn. No more hiding behind tired slogans and sound bites. Every question directly answered. His calculations, he said, were cautious. The possibility of a downturn had been allowed for. We would not be blown off course by recession. As for the Tories, we must rub their noses in it. When they complain about our spending plans we must ask which hospital, which school they want closed. Joy was mainly unconfined. Even Dennis Skinner applauded, albeit modestly. For the moment Gordon can do no wrong. To suggest, as the Tories and other malcontents do, that a certain amount of sorcery has been employed is to appear ungrateful. We must await events.

Tuesday, 21 July

A talk with David Clark. He says he's won the battle over the content of the Freedom of Information Bill but he's outnumbered on the committee that will decide what goes in the Queen's Speech. Officials, he says, are wholly opposed. The loyalty of the private office is to the Permanent Secretary, not to their minister. The switch to performance-related pay has greatly increased the hold of the Permanent Secretaries because they now personally approve the performance pay of their juniors.

Senior civil servants, says David, spend a lot of time at conferences, symposiums and seminars in exotic locations. They travel business class and often go out several days in advance to 'acclimatise'. Gordon Prentice had recently tabled a question asking how many trips the civil servants in each department had been on. Most resorted to the standard brush-off – that the information could only be provided at disproportionate cost – but David refused to endorse his draft – because 'it was a lie' – and ordered an honest reply to be prepared. Later his political adviser found on a photocopier an instruction that the answer should refer only to conferences, not symposiums and seminars. Nevertheless it came to about 140. David, of course, is isolated. Everyone is waiting to see whether he will survive the reshuffle. If he survives, his authority will be enhanced and he'll win on freedom of information. If he goes, the Bill may go too.

Wednesday, 22 July

To Downing Street for the official photograph of the parliamentary committee, which I had hoped would be in the garden, but we were shown up to the state rooms on the first floor. Afterwards we assembled in the Cabinet Room for our weekly meeting. Tea and biscuits were served. The Man carefully dabbed a finger on the crumbs that fell from his biscuit. Nick Brown summarised a letter that he is sending to the National Executive Committee in response to the review of reselection procedures. It contained a reference to an age of retirement for MPs. My ears pricked up at this. What did he have in mind? A number of the older members weren't pulling their weight, said

Nick. 'There is a correlation between age and recidivism.' Llin Golding said that on no account must we lay down an age of retirement. Ann Taylor said it wasn't only older members who weren't pulling their weight. The discussion ended inconclusively.

Nick also reported that he was sending a letter 'one step below the disciplinary procedure' to Dennis Canavan – he didn't mention Dennis by name – for criticising George Robertson in public, and asking for an apology. What will happen if he refuses?

Thursday, 23 July

Rover have announced 1,200 job losses. The high value of the pound is being blamed, although there may be other factors. Ken Purchase is steaming. He reckons the decision to hand control of interest rates to the Bank of England was disastrous and will lead to ruin. Ken started his working life as a toolmaker and, when it comes to manufacturing, he knows what he's talking about. He says we are pursuing precisely what we once criticised the Tories for – a one-club policy. The bankers are behaving in the same way as they have always done. He claims that Gordon told him twelve months before the election that he expected the Bank to make a mess of interest rates and that, when they did, he would take back their powers. I find it hard to believe that Gordon put it quite like that. He may have said *if* rather than *when*. By then, of course, it'll be too late. Ken says that if we carry on down this road we'll collapse our economy, or at least the manufacturing side. I asked if he'd been to see Gordon and he hadn't. If he feels so strongly – and he obviously does – he ought to start mobilising. I told him so.

Monday, 27 July

Reshuffle day. Poor David Clark was on the train. He received a call from Downing Street last night saying that the Prime Minister wanted the Cabinet to be in London by nine o'clock this morning. David replied that, with the best will in the world, he couldn't get down by that time since the last train and plane had already departed and the first ones tomorrow wouldn't get him there by nine. Instead, with admirable cool, he caught the 10.30 a.m. from Newcastle. Why hurry to the scaffold? While waiting on Newcastle station The Man himself came through on a mobile and asked for 'his dispositions', which David took to be code for resignation. He hastily agreed and boarded the train, after arranging to see Tony at 2.15 p.m. When I saw him at King's Cross he was about to take his last ride in an official car.

The changes were fairly predictable. Indeed they have been predicted for some months now. David, Harriet Harman and Gavin Strang are out. Peter Mandelson has replaced Margaret at Trade and Industry. So much of the recent unpleasantness has been caused by the need to find Peter a job. First it was going to be David's, then Chris Smith's and in the end he got Margaret's. It will be interesting to see if, now he has emerged from the shadows, the negative briefings cease. The basic message arising from Peter's elevation is 'Two fingers to the lot of you'. The Man has reacted exactly as Derek Foster predicted at the time of the Draper crisis: by carrying on regardless. Happily, Peter has retained responsibility for the accursed Dome.

Frank Field has resigned after being passed over for Harriet's job. Steve Byers becomes the first of the '92 intake to reach the top table (as Chief Secretary to the Treasury). The one big surprise is Nick Brown's replacement as Chief Whip by Ann Taylor. Nick goes to Agriculture, about which he knows nothing and where he will have absolutely no influence on the operation of government. This is The Man's revenge for Nick's unwise cooperation with Paul Routledge on the Gordon Brown biography. Confirmation, if any were needed, that despite his apparent affability The Man is ruthless.

Tuesday, 28 July

The shake-up of the junior ministers is much wider than expected. Details have been dribbling out all day. The lobbies and the Tea Room are full of the expectant and the disappointed. I feel rather detached, though it might have been otherwise. Don Macintyre says in today's *Independent*: 'Blair ... considered bringing in the able and distinctly left-wing Chris Mullin into the government. He was advised that

Mullin is at present too good a Home Affairs Select Committee chairman to make it worthwhile.' I have been affecting an air of nonchalance all day but, if truth be told, it would have been nice to have been asked.

The Friends of The Man are consolidating their grip on the machinery of government. Charles Falconer has replaced Peter Mandelson at the Cabinet Office. A Sainsbury has appeared at the DTI. Margaret Hodge has forsaken the Education select committee for a job at Education. Geoffrey Robinson has survived unscathed at the Treasury. Joyce Quin has been moved to the European slot at the Foreign Office, the job she should have had in the first place. As usual the drivers were the first to know who was out. Tony Banks said his driver informed him yesterday morning that he was safe, but that Tom Clarke's and Mark Fisher's drivers had been told to leave their mobiles switched on all day. Sure enough, Tom and Mark have both been given the push. Mark is very upset.

Although he is trying to put a brave face on it, David Clark is very bitter and who can blame him? He has been reading stories in the press about his impending demise since even before he was appointed. Tomorrow he has to go and see the Queen to hand back the seals of office of the Duchy of Lancaster and the officials won't even let him have the use of a car for the ride to the Palace. The senior civil servants, he says, shamelessly abuse the use of official cars – in stark contrast, he says, to the zealotry with which they enforce the use of cars by ministers. 'If I've learned one thing,' he says, 'it is that Parliament must be sovereign.'

We had two meetings of the select committee and completed our Alternatives to Prison report. A little on the bland side, I'm afraid. I bent over backwards to keep the Tories on board – although most of the time it's hard work persuading them to turn up, let alone do any work.

Wednesday, 29 July

To the Home Office to try to persuade Jack Straw to make oversight of the security services a responsibility of Parliament – which used to be our policy when we were in opposition. Humfrey Malins and Bob Russell came along to demonstrate that this was an all-party job. Jack, in shirtsleeves and red braces, listened courteously but sceptically. I don't think he is opposed in principle. It's just that he thinks the existing system is working and doesn't see it as a high enough priority for legislation – at least not in the foreseeable future. The Permanent Secretary, David Omand (who used to run GCHQ) chipped in that the security services might not trust – he actually used the word – a select committee in the same way as they did the present committee. The 'spirit' of the two processes was different. I said I took it for granted that the security services would be implacably opposed to any change, but that we were engaged in a process of evolution. We left it that Jack would discuss the matter with The Man, which is exactly what he said when I last raised the subject with him two and a half years ago.

Thursday, 30 July

Janet Anderson, who until her recent promotion had the job of keeping the Queen informed about what goes on in this place, has been to the Palace to bid farewell. Janet told HM that her fellow whips were in the habit of using the official billiard cue (which comes with the post of Lord High What-have-you) to switch the television on and off in the Whips Office. When Graham Allen, who succeeded Janet, went in to pay his respects the Queen asked him if it were true. Graham replied tactfully, 'I am sure my colleagues would not be so disrespectful, Ma'am.'

Saturday, 1 August

Siemens, the German microchip giant which set up on Tyneside with much fanfare a year ago, have announced they are pulling out. They blame the collapse in Asia. The Koreans are said to be dumping microchips on the market at a fraction of the cost. It was always inevitable that the globalisation bubble would burst sooner or later. Rotten luck if it happens on our watch.

Monday, 10 August
Sunderland

Grove Cranes have announced that they are closing. A bad, bad blow – 670 well-paid industrial jobs down the swanny. The Tory spokesman, John Redwood, immediately blamed closure on the strength of sterling even though the statement from Groves talks of heavy losses for the last six years and makes no mention of sterling.

Tuesday, 11 August

To Grove Cranes with Bill Etherington to meet the unions and management. The senior steward opens by saying he doesn't want to sour the meeting ... but ... The workforce, he says, are up in arms about a remark I made during a television interview last night in which I said that the closure was 'a setback, but not a disaster'. I was, of course, referring to Sunderland's track record in recovering from the closure of the shipyards and the pit, but they have chosen to interpret the suggestion that the closure is anything less than a disaster – which obviously it is for those who will lose their jobs – as a personal attack. One of the others present said I had lost 2,000 votes, which is nonsense of course, but feelings are running high. Perhaps I should have chosen my words more carefully, but I decided not to be too apologetic. There was, I replied, always a tendency at a time of crisis for people to turn on each other rather than point their guns outwards. We had to decide whether we were going to concentrate on trying to save jobs or slag each other off. At which point they backed off.

The company vice-president, John Wheeler, was a big, self-confident, soft-spoken American who exuded authority. Everyone called him 'John', but the truth is that he comes from another planet to ours. He cut through all the crap the media and the Tories are peddling about exchange rates. The plain fact was that the market for cranes had dried up. The strength of the pound might be 'an aspect', but the big issue was the collapse of the market. He emphasised that he had no criticism of the workforce, who had done everything asked of them. He was, however, not so kind to management, two of whom were present. 'When I first came to Sunderland twenty months ago this was the most unproductive plant I had ever been in. Management had failed to look the workforce in the eye and tell them what needed to be done.' He held out hope that some jobs could be saved, but made no promises. He was talking to several companies interested in operating some kind of manufacturing facility on at least part of the site. The matter is complicated by the fact that Grove do not own the property and the lease is shortly due to expire. So any new arrangement will have to be squared with the freeholders, whose interests will not necessarily coincide with those of the workforce.

As Bill remarked when we were leaving, we are just spectators. The idea that MPs have the slightest influence in a situation like this is an illusion and some of our colleagues do us no service by pretending otherwise.

Saturday, 15 August
Gamekeeper's Cottage, West Sussex

A huge bomb has gone off in the centre of Omagh. Many dead. The work of one of the republican splinter groups. Ireland is going to haunt us for years to come.

Friday, 21 August
Brixton Road

Much talk of recalling Parliament to push through a new bout of anti-terrorist legislation in the wake of Omagh. It's even being suggested that we should imprison terrorist suspects on the word of a single police officer. If we are not careful the whole dreary cycle of repression and revenge will start again.

To the House, eerily deserted. I spent most of the day in the Library dictating replies to a pile of letters. Only a handful of other members around: Brian Sedgemore seated at his usual table. Gerald

Kaufman drifted by during the late afternoon. Frank Longford looking ever more cadaverous, wandering about like a ghost left over from a pre-war regime.

At lunch in the Westminster Hall cafeteria I ran into Clive Soley and Andrew Mackinlay. Andrew, to my surprise, remarked that he was 'not sure I'll have the courage in the present climate' to oppose the anti-terrorist legislation. It made me realise that opposition is going to be a very lonely business. Probably just a handful of usual suspects.

Clive, who has not been consulted, said he hadn't yet heard whether Parliament was to be recalled. He expressed concern about the proposed new measures but said he had no problem with bringing our anti-terrorist legislation into line with that of the Republic, but it would be foolish to repeat the mistakes of the past. He was preoccupied with moving house and completely lacking any sense of urgency. 'I'll give Mo and Tony a ring next week,' he said. 'Do it now,' I replied.

Bill Clinton, who is in deep trouble at home, has bombed an alleged terrorist training camp in Afghanistan and a pharmaceutical factory in the Sudan. Needless to say, within the hour The Man was on the airwaves professing his total support. So humiliating. We are the Bulgaria of western Europe. Or at least we would be, if Bulgaria was still a Soviet satellite.

Tuesday, 25 August
Chelmsford

It's becoming clear that the Americans have no serious evidence that the pharmaceutical factory which they destroyed last week had been used for producing nerve gas. What it undoubtedly did produce was half the pharmaceuticals for one of the world's poorest countries. The Sudanese are pressing for a UN inquiry. The Americans, of course, are stonewalling and we are going along with them. There's been silence from Robin Cook, although I imagine he's not best pleased.

Wednesday, 26 August
Chelmsford

Parliament is to be recalled next week. I feel a growing sense of depression, as the realisation dawns that I have no choice but to oppose the Bill – or at least key parts of it – if I am to retain my self-respect. I can't claim to be representing my constituents since most of them would happily boil alleged terrorists in oil on the word of a single police officer, so I am going to have to spend a lot of time justifying myself. The hate mail will start again. I can't bear to think about it.

Friday, 28 August
Sunderland

Back to the office, where a mountain of paperwork awaits. There were messages from Mo Mowlam and Jack Straw, wanting to talk about the proposed anti-terrorist laws. I returned their calls, but they were both unavailable. An official in Mo's office undertook to pass the word that I would be available all day if Mo wanted to ring back. Later, the official called back and said that Mo had been after my fax number so that she could send an advance copy of the Bill. After I'd put the phone down, it dawned on me that I was being fobbed off. I rang the woman back and said that it seemed to me unlikely that the Secretary of State would ring in person to ask for my fax number and would she kindly pass on my message. She undertook to do so, but I heard no more.

Dave Clelland (a whip) rang to check that I would be attending next week. I said I would, but not necessarily to vote for the government.

Saturday, 29 August

Tony Benn rang to say that he would be voting against the Bill. As ever he had no doubts. I wish I saw everything as clearly as he does. He said, 'Anyone can be sound on civil liberties when there is no trouble. The real test comes when times are difficult.'

There has been a vicious racialist attack on an Asian boy three streets away from us. Last night's *Echo* had a front-page picture of the poor lad. His eyes are so swollen that they are closed. About twenty youths were involved. All the blows were aimed at his head. I talked to a local Asian shopkeeper. No doubt the perpetrators are some of the youths who make her life a misery. She said, 'I live in fear. They are not afraid of anything. The police seem powerless. Yet if we touch them we are in trouble ...'

Monday, 31 August

August Bank Holiday. The answerphone is full of messages from journalists asking for comments on the Terrorism Bill. I'm ignoring them all, until I see it.

Tuesday, 1 September

To the office. The Home Office had faxed through a draft of the Bill. It's bad, but not quite as bad as everyone has been predicting. Members of specified terrorist organisations – the ones not signed up to the ceasefire – can be sent down for up to ten years, but no longer on the word of a single policeman. There will have to be corroboration, but that might take the form of a refusal to answer questions. In addition, several clauses have been tacked on making it an offence to conspire against foreign governments from British soil. A number of flimsy safeguards have been built in. The Attorney General will have to be consulted, but the definitions are very wide. Like all panic measures, it is a botched job. I rang Andrew Bennett, who is laid up after a hip operation, for some advice. He recommended amendments rather than outright opposition. I faxed a copy of the draft to John Wadham at Liberty and he promised to study it overnight and fax me some suggestions. I also spoke to Roger Sands, the clerk who will be dealing with it. He said he wasn't expecting to see a final copy of the Bill until the early evening and amendments have to be in by noon tomorrow to stand any chance of selection. What a way to do business.

Later Jack rang, full of reassurance, pointing out the various safeguards that had been inserted since the Bill was first mooted. I asked what plans the RUC had for recording interviews. The police in Northern Ireland were resisting the introduction of safeguards which had long been accepted elsewhere in the UK. 'Soon, but not immediately,' he said. Would a solicitor be present during interrogations? 'Probably, I'll know by tomorrow.' The more I hear about this, the less I like the sound of it.

I called Rosemary Nelson,* a solicitor in Lurgan who could be in the front line when the Bill has gone through. She said the existing powers of the RUC were already widely abused and the new measures could only make matters worse. Old scores would be settled. Court proceedings, under the terms of the Bill, would be farcical. A police officer who fingered a suspect would be asked the basis for his information and would reply that he couldn't say. Defence would be impossible. Some of her colleagues were talking about refusing to defend people lifted under the Bill. Thirty had already put their names to a statement condemning it. She said, 'If internment was going to be reintroduced, I'd rather they had done it in a more honest way, instead of giving it a judicial stamp.'

To London on an evening train. Patrick Cormack, a Tory MP who was on board, remarked that all legislation done in a hurry worked out badly. He was concerned about relying on the evidence of a single police officer. There would, he said, be unease among all serious people, but no one would want to rock the boat.

Wednesday, 2 September

An extraordinary day. I went in early, picked up the amendments which John Wadham had faxed over and tabled most of them. The unease about the Bill is widespread. I saw David Davis outside the Tea Room and he said we were in danger of helping to provide the Real IRA with a political base, 'just as we did for the Provisionals with internment on the last occasion the IRA split'. In an upstairs toilet I ran into John Major. He was scathing. The first part (the Irish bit) was

---

*Murdered by loyalist paramilitaries in March 1999.

unnecessary and the remainder could have waited until we had got it right. He added, 'I bet neither Robert Carswell nor Ronnie Flanagan* were consulted.' I said I was sure they must have been. 'Informed, maybe, but not consulted,' he replied.

Another Tory, John Butterfill, told me that he'd vote for the Bill, but he'd be holding his nose. That's how most people seem to feel. No one wants to be seen as soft on terrorism, but everyone knows it stinks.

To Number 10 for a meeting with The Man. We met in the Cabinet Room. Ann Clwyd, Sylvia Heal, Llin Golding and I on one side of the table. The Man, flanked by Clive and Sally Morgan on the other. The Bill was the only item on the agenda. Clive kicked off saying a lot of people were worried about the possibility of mistakes. Nelson Mandela might have been convicted under Clause 5. This could all go badly wrong, I said. A lot of doors were going to be kicked down as a result of this Bill and many of them would be the wrong doors. I went over the problems of corroboration in a jurisdiction where interviews were not recorded and where solicitors (it now emerges) will not be present. I mentioned internment and the round-up of Iraqis after the Gulf War, where it was clear that the quality of intelligence was very poor. Ann quoted a letter from Amnesty expressing concern about the effect on exile communities here, like the Kurds and the Iraqi opposition. The Bill was far too vague, she said.

The Man, looking relaxed and mildly tanned after his sojourn in France, said there were two dangers. One was that we could forget the lessons of the past; the other was to imagine that the situation today was the same as it had been twenty-five years ago. We were talking about a small number of people, probably thirty to forty, most of them in the Republic. There could easily have been other atrocities like Omagh, several other huge bombs had been intercepted. We were virtually alone in having no means to deal with members of terrorist organisations. The Republic were taking action and it would look very odd if we did nothing. It had been made very clear to the Chief Constable that this must be handled sensitively. We would be working

*Lord Chief Justice of Northern Ireland and Chief Constable of the RUC, respectively.

closely with the Republic. The powers in the Bill would not be greatly used – if more than fifty people were picked up, he'd be asking what was going on. He was strongly aware of the lessons of history.

He said the so-called Mandela issue had been taken care of, incitement was not an offence in the Bill and so Ann could rest assured that we weren't going to start picking up people trying to overthrown Saddam.

There was some discussion of what might constitute corroboration. The classic example, said The Man, was if you had been photographed carrying a coffin wearing paramilitary gear. He added that he had been under pressure to include a presumption of guilt, but this had been rejected. (It's becoming clear how Draconian the original plans were.)

I pressed the point about recording interviews. The RUC, I said, could do it tomorrow if they wanted to. Why not make it a condition of the Bill? His lips curled down sceptically at this point. He went off promising to look into it and come back to me.

As we were leaving Ann raised the American bombing of Sudan. Where was the evidence that the factory had been making ingredients for chemical weapons? Foreign Office ministers were saying (before the bombing) that they knew of no evidence. 'The UN are looking into it,' The Man replied, adding significantly, 'The Americans say they've got evidence.' In other words, his unequivocal support was offered without a shred of evidence – and none has turned up since.

At 2.30 p.m. The Man made a statement to the House. I was called first. I put the point about audio recording and received a vague response. Tony Benn made one of his lofty interventions about the lessons of history and got short shrift – 'We must learn from our history, but not be mesmerised by or live in it.' John Hume complained about the haste. (A journalist from Ulster Television stopped me in the street earlier and said that even one or two of the Unionists were concerned about it.)

Jack's second-reading speech was peppered with sceptical interventions from all sides. Bob Marshall-Andrews complained that parts of the Bill were gobbledegook and that, anyway, it would fall foul of the European Convention on Human Rights. I pointed out that the facilities to record interviews were already installed in several RUC holding centres so there was no practical reason why recording couldn't begin tomorrow. Jack continued to insist that there were practical difficulties, but he didn't sound as though he believed it. I intercepted him as he was leaving the Chamber and he ushered me towards the gents loo in the 'Aye' Lobby. 'Between you and me,' he said, looking back at me over his shoulder as he relieved himself, 'I haven't got a leg to stand on.' He added cheerfully, 'Keep up the pressure.' When I ran into Jack again later he said that new assurances would be forthcoming by committee stage in a couple of hours' time. I asked if he had seen the wording. 'It's changing all the time,' he said. There was obviously a row going on behind the scenes. Part of the problem is that Adam Ingram is standing in for Mo, who is in Belfast entertaining the Clintons. Adam is a decent fellow, but he lacks the weight to stand up to the vested interests in the way that Mo or Jack would. I had an hilarious exchange with Adam over audio recording. 'I can't instruct the RUC,' he said indignantly. 'We are not running a police state.' What a topsy-turvy world Northern Ireland is.

Later, I had a call from Sally Morgan in Downing Street to say that audio recording would start on 1 January, in other words too late to apply to most of those arrested under this Bill. I faxed her a page from the report by the Commissioner for the Holding Centres saying that taping facilities already existed in Gough Barracks, Armagh, and that similar facilities were being installed in other holding centres and would be used 'as soon as authorised'. It was dated March this year. I asked her to show it to The Man. (I also passed a copy to Jack.)

By now it was clear we were going to go all night. At 1.45 a.m. I moved the first of my amendments – to allow a solicitor to be present during interrogations. Jack gave a very feeble reply. It was obvious to everyone that his heart wasn't in it. Roger Berry intervened and said that he had yet to make a single point against the amendment (Jack said to me later in the Tea Room that he had wanted to say to Roger, 'I entirely agree'). I pressed it to a vote. At which point things began to go wrong. Brian Sedgemore and Ann Clwyd had volunteered to be tellers but, come the moment, there was no sign of Sedgemore. Roger Berry, who was sitting next to me, reluctantly agreed, saying that he had never done it before. What did he have to do? I had forgotten (if

I ever knew) that the tellers are supposed to present themselves to the chair. Instead I directed Roger to the door of the 'Aye' Lobby and followed him outside to direct the traffic. The 'Aye' Lobby was filling up nicely when, from behind me, came the awful cry, 'Division off.' I stormed back into the Chamber to see what had happened and everyone was shouting at me, 'Where are your tellers?' Too late, humiliation beckoned.

The next amendment – on audio recording of interviews – was also mine. The chairman was on his feet calling my name, but I was caught up in the chaos. Tommy McAvoy, who couldn't believe his luck, was bawling 'not moved, not moved'. I just made it back in the nick of time, grabbed my papers and started babbling, but the hubbub around me was so great and my morale so shattered that I was in danger of drying up. Norman Godman came to the rescue with an intervention and I managed to recover. Jack went out of his way to be helpful. He couldn't accept the amendment, but he could assure me that everything possible would be done to bring forward introduction of audio recording.

At this point I ought gracefully to have accepted what was offered, but having once led my troops to the top of the hill and down again, I didn't feel I could do it twice so I insisted on a division – and this time tellers were in place. I could see from his expression that Jack was peeved (although he was perfectly decent when I explained the dilemma afterwards). In the event we got forty-five votes. Respectable, but not brilliant. There were also a lot of abstentions. The whips had been leaning hard on the new people, who are very timorous. We might have done better but for the previous cock-up. Winnick muttered that I had damaged my position by pushing it too far and I fear he may be right. Several whips (lance corporals, not officers) were unpleasant. Tommy McAvoy was still smirking about the screw-up. Kevin Hughes was shouting that I had no right to be 'touting for business' in a vote against the government (I was standing outside the division lobby during the division, saying 'Audio recording this way', 'Silent videos that way'). I did my best to be good-humoured, but Kevin couldn't see the joke. 'I'll put in a bad word for you,' he was shouting. I caught the bus home at 6.30 a.m. feeling slightly demoralised. I had been doing fine until the cock-up over the tellers. My trouble is that I haven't yet learned to distinguish between a futile gesture and a well-aimed blow. I allowed myself to be talked into voting against the government over the timetable motion, which was completely pointless. I might just as well have voted with the regime and chalked up some credit. On everything else I abstained. If I'm not careful I shall find myself isolated and picked off.

Thursday, 3 September

Up at 10.30 a.m., feeling rotten after only three-and-a-half-hours' sleep. I ran into Dale Campbell-Savours, who remarked, 'Yesterday was a day for your diary.' (Has he guessed?) I explained my fear that I am in danger of becoming isolated, but he would have none of it. 'People would have been amazed if you had done anything else, given your track record.' He added, 'The people the whips are pissed off with are those who are on the media every five minutes slagging off the government.' I said I had ignored about thirty offers. 'Make sure the whips know that,' he replied. I saw Clive later. He didn't seem worried either. I feel a little more cheerful.

12 midnight

The Bill has gone up to the Lords, who are giving it a real pasting. We are under instructions to hang around in case they amend it, which is unlikely since both the main parties are signed up. I propose to ignore the whips and go home to bed, since I'm sure Tommy McAvoy would much rather I was safely tucked up in bed than hanging around here to vote against the government.

12.45 a.m.

Crept down to the Tea Room, intending to buy a half-pint of milk and then sneak off, and ran into Ann Taylor (wan with fatigue), who said there was to be no going home. Instead I went and stood at the Bar in the Lords to see how they were getting on. Jack Straw was there. He whispered that, as a result of last night's fuss, audio recording was to be brought forward to 1 October. 'A good night's work,' he said.

1.30 a.m.

As expected, the Lords have let the Bill through without amendment, though not without shredding it verbally. We are allowed out at last. I'm desperate for sleep.

Tuesday, 8 September

Reports in today's papers say that Marks & Spencer – which has hitherto prided itself on having its clothes made in Britain – is putting pressure on its suppliers to relocate to cheap-labour economies: Indonesia, Morocco and Sri Lanka are mentioned. Bad news for Dewhirst workers, of whom I have about 1,000 in my constituency. It comes on top of the proposed closure of Grove Cranes, Fujitsu and Siemens. If this process goes on all the progress of recent years will be destroyed, along with our hopes for the future. The only difference is that this time round there is no Tory government to blame it on.

Thursday, 10 September

Up early for an interview with the *Today* programme about 'Alternatives to Prison'. *Today* is now based at White City. They sent a car, but it took almost an hour to get there and I almost missed my slot. I crept into the studio during the sports round-up. Everyone was looking very grim. After about a minute Jim Naughtie, thinking the sports man had switched to tape, said 'Good morning, Chris.' To which I responded, 'Good morning, you're all looking very miserable today,' only to be greeted by frantic waving from the sports man. We had gone out live.

Monday, 14 September
Sunderland

Bad news is coming thick and fast. Today it was announced that Vaux is putting its brewing business on the market in order to concentrate on hotels and other more profitable interests. The company has been under pressure from the institutions for some time and has finally succumbed. It is not that the brewery is unprofitable. It is just that it doesn't make enough money to satisfy the greedy spivs in the City. The danger is that it will be bought up by another brewery and closed. At around midday I took a call from Paul Nicholson, who asked if we could speak off the record. 'As chairman, I have to be seen to be neutral,' he said, 'but I'm not.' He wants all the support he can get for a management buy-out. I asked what chance of a successful buy-out were, 'Sixty per cent,' he said.

When I got to the office there was a faxed press statement put out by the Vaux PR person. The sell-off, it said, would be 'cash-enhancing'. A vulgar phrase that perfectly encapsulates the spirit of the age in which we live.

Wednesday, 16 September

To Doxford Business Park where The Man is paying a flying visit to open the new headquarters of AVCO, an American finance company. The visit has been arranged in great haste because he wants some good news to offset against the Siemens and Fujitsu disasters. A clutch of workers from Grove Cranes awaited him, holding up placards saying 'Don't forget Groves'. I made a point of talking to them. I don't want to give them an excuse for alleging – as they are – that no one is interested in their plight.

When The Man arrived I took aside Alastair Campbell – who, unlike everyone else in the entourage was looking relaxed and cheerful – and asked if he could arrange for Tony to spend five minutes with a delegation from Grove's. He said, 'There were shouts of "scab" and "wanker" when we arrived just now.' Even so, he assented.

'Shouldn't we ask Tony?'

'It won't be a problem. Tony's all right about that sort of thing.'

I went outside and asked for three volunteers. There were no stewards present so I took the first three to step forward. They were in their working clothes and totally unprepared for a meeting with the Prime Minister. A Special Branch man asked who I was as I whisked them inside. A room was found for them and I went upstairs to listen to the speech. The media were out in force and the speech dominated the bulletins all day. 'We must keep our nerve', was the theme. Sure, there was bad news about, but there was also good news – witness the new jobs at AVCO and Nissan. 'If' interest rates had peaked, then we were through the worst. He was careful to say 'if' and he repeated it several times, but he clearly believes they have.

I sat uneasily throughout, dreading that he might be whisked away at the end and that the lads from Grove would be forgotten in the rush, which would be disastrous. But, no. Alastair was as good as his word. The Man, I sensed, was not overly happy about having his agenda hijacked by Yours Truly, but this is no time to be squeamish.

The meeting with the Grove's lads went well. There were just the three of them, the Prime Minister, a Private Secretary and myself around a table in a room with walls made entirely of glass. Alastair and the rest of the entourage were pacing up and down outside in the corridor. The men were surprisingly articulate and didn't seem at all overawed. They were feeling forgotten, they said. Everyone was talking about Fujitsu and Siemens and no one had been near them since the closure was announced. Mostly they were in their fifties. They had worked there all their lives and were unlikely ever to work again.

The Man responded by explaining that, since Fujitsu was in his constituency, it was inevitable that his attention should be focused there. With the best will in the world he couldn't wave a wand and make the market for cranes reappear, but he would see what else could be done to help. In the meantime he suggested a meeting with Peter Mandelson, perhaps at Blackpool during the party conference. It was over in less than ten minutes. When we went outside the media were waiting and I whispered to the lads to be as positive as possible; there is nothing worse than being kicked in the teeth when you are trying to help.

Friday, 18 September

To Easingwold in North Yorkshire to deliver the Joan Maynard Memorial Lecture. I arrived at 7.15 p.m. only to discover – oh, horror – that the letter from the organiser which I brought with me did not specify the location (my fault, her earlier letters did). I rang the number on her letterhead and the phone was answered by her husband, who told me confidently it was at the Galtres Centre in the market square. I soon found it, but there was no sign of life. I rang the organiser's number again, this time to be greeted by an answerphone. By now the clock was ticking. Somewhere in Easingwold sixty or seventy people were sitting anxiously awaiting my arrival and I hadn't a clue where they were. I drove around looking out for schools and church halls. No luck. In desperation I rang Jacky, intending to ask her to go to the office and look up the correspondence. She was out. Practically tearing out my hair (or what remains of it), I stopped a man in the street who vaguely recalled seeing something advertised in the local free sheet. We went into the nearest pub and begged a copy behind the bar and there it was – at the local secondary school. By the time I arrived – twenty-five minutes late – a lynch mob was forming (they had been let down earlier in the year by John Battle). No matter. My apologies were gracefully received. My talk – 'The Labour Government – A Report on Progress' – was more or less on message.

Saturday, 19 September

Oh dear, I am in trouble. Foolishly I released the text of last night's speech to the press and most of them have maximised the bad news and minimised or completely ignored, the good. Headlines vary from a friendly 'Give Blair a Chance, Says Mullin' (*Guardian*) to 'New Labour "has sold its soul"' (the *Echo*). The *Journal* (Newcastle) is by far the worst. A piece on the front page describes my speech as 'a sensational attack on Tony Blair', which is complete crap. Inside, across two pages, the political editor, Paul Linford, has a piece headed 'Senior North MP Attacks Pact with the Devil and Rupert Murdoch'. A wilful misrepresentation. Every positive comment (and the balance was overwhelmingly positive) has been carefully excised and the negative ones blown out of all proportion. All deeply damaging. Friends on the left (who mainly read the *Guardian*) will see it as further evidence that I have sold out to the Establishment, while the Establishment will see it as evidence that I'm not to be trusted. I've been around long enough to know that the average British journalist lacks the maturity to cope with a balanced argument. Why didn't I have the sense to extract the key paragraphs, type them out triple spaced and fax them over to the idle hacks, instead of entrusting them with the whole thing? How could I be so daft?

Monday, 21 September

Bill Etherington and I have sent a letter to Peter Mandelson about the sale of Vaux, warning of the possibility that the proposed management buy-out will be outbid by a rival brewery which will then close Vaux down. 'Were that to happen, we cannot overstate the anger that would be aroused.' Important to fire a warning shot now – before a new disaster strikes.

To the local branch of the Federation of Small Businesses, a motley collection ranging from shopkeepers to small engineers and even a chiropodist from Morpeth. I had assumed that they would all be complaining about the minimum wage and the Social Chapter. There was a bit of that, but to my surprise the main enemy turned out to be the big corporations who treat them like dirt, demand huge subsidies and, when it suits them, evacuate to the Far East to avoid their social responsibilities. The more I reflect, devising some method of mitigating the excesses of big business is going to be an important issue in the next century and there will be a broad support for any government with the nerve to take it on.

Friday, 25 September

A call from the personnel manager of Dewhirst's. He confirmed that the company had just opened a factory in Bandung, Indonesia, but offered what he called a categorical assurance that Sunderland jobs are safe for the foreseeable future. I asked him to put it in writing.

Sunday, 27 September

Four of the six places on the constituency section of the National Executive Committee have been taken by the left, despite a frantic campaign by the regime on behalf of the New Labour slate. These are the people Neil Kinnock was denouncing as 'Trotskyites and parasites' last week. There is life in the old party yet.

Monday, 28 September
Labour Party Conference, Blackpool

Blackpool is seedier and more depressing than ever. The only bright spot is the trams which rumble along the promenade. Drivers and conductors alike are courteous, good-humoured, and never baulk at changing a fiver, in contrast to some of the dead-eyed androids on London Transport.

Nita Clarke, who works in Number 10, bet me £5 that I would be a minister by the end of this parliament. Somehow I doubt it, after last week's fiasco. In any case, do I really want to end up answering for the Prison Service?

Tuesday, 29 September

The ballot papers for election to the National Executive Committee were numbered, which caused a great upset. As usual, the regime is claiming a cock-up by an over-zealous junior. This may well be true, but it is a measure of the fear and mistrust that New Labour inspires that no one – right or left – believes them. Later, Jean Corston went in and snipped off the numbers, which upset the new general secretary, Margaret McDonagh, who was threatening to resign (she hasn't even taken over yet). One of the office staff whispered to Jean that she was wise to remove the numbers 'before Margaret gets her hands on them'.

Everyone is saying how dull the conference is. Apart from the upset in the election to the constituency section of the NEC there has been scarcely a whiff of dissent. Most MPs are just wandering about feeling useless and unloved. 'I'm not coming next year,' said Keith

Hill, a loyalist. Derek Wyatt was saying the same. Joy Johnson said, 'Why don't they just hold a rally instead?'

This afternoon, the Big Speech. The Man, as ever, was on top form. Forward-looking, confident. Every word addressed to the nation. No shooting at his own side (save for a passing reference to oppositionists). On the economy he was particularly strong. Whatever happens there will be no going back. The Man is not for turning.

Thursday, 1 October
Blackpool

To the Stakis Hotel – which is surrounded by a massive security cordon – for a meeting with Peter Mandelson about Grove Cranes. Bill and I attended together with four representatives of the workforce who have been here most of the week. On Tuesday they were in betrayal mode, demonstrating outside conference with placards saying they had been sold down the river by Blair, which did not bode well. By this morning, however, they were in a sober frame of mind and put their case with dignity. They want help to be made available to anyone who is willing to buy all or part of the plant. Failing that, help to bring other manufacturing work to the area (by reopening the Pallion shipyard or building one of the proposed new aircraft carriers at Swan Hunter). Peter, accompanied by Ian McCartney, listened courteously but made no promises. Indeed it is hard to see what promises he could have made. We are all just going through the motions. It will end badly, I fear.

Monday, 19 October

General Pinochet, the former Chilean dictator, has been arrested on an extradition warrant issued by a judge in Spain. Peter Mandelson denounced him in the most virulent terms to the Frost programme yesterday. Overnight New Labour has been transformed into a champion of human rights. Rejoicing is unconfined.

To the House, where a message to ring Bernard Donoughue awaited. He wanted to know if I had seen Woodrow Wyatt's diaries, which are being serialised in the *Sunday Times*. I hadn't but I went to the Library and looked them up. The passage to which Bernard was anxious to draw my attention was one in which the old rogue boasts of persuading Thatcher not to refer Murdoch's acquisition of *The Times* and *Sunday Times* to the Monopolies Commission on the grounds that they weren't profitable, when in fact they were. Bernard, who was a director of Times Newspapers at the time, says that this is the first time this has been admitted and he wants to find a way of putting it on the record. He can't, of course, being a government minister. I promised to look for an opportunity. The Competition Bill will be coming back shortly and that might provide a chance. Tom McNally is re-tabling his amendment (to enable Murdoch's use of predatory pricing to be referred to the Monopolies Commission). 'Regrettably,' says Bernard, chuckling, 'I can't be there to support the government tomorrow.' He is recovering from an operation on a toe.

David Clark has been given an office on Upper Committee Corridor South, opposite mine. It hasn't even got a window. His last office looked out on the rose garden in Downing Street. A cruel business, politics.

Tuesday, 20 October

Dinner with Jack Straw in the Millbank Room. He said, 'I tried hard with Tony on the security services but he wasn't having it. He's been got at.' Jack doesn't think MI5 or GCHQ are likely to get up to mischief but he says the SIS are a different kettle of fish. 'The difference is that the others go home to their families every night whereas the SIS people are out in the field and there's no telling what they might get up to.' I asked about amalgamating them but Jack thought they were best kept separate. 'That way they keep an eye on each other.'

We discussed the Criminal Cases Review Commission. Jack said that Louis Blom-Cooper would have made a better chairman than Frederick Crawford. I remarked that Blom-Cooper had blotted his copybook by writing a silly book suggesting that the Birmingham Six were really guilty. To my amazement, Jack said, 'Well they might have been.'

'But they weren't.'

'There may not have been evidence, but that doesn't mean they didn't do it.'

I said I was well aware of the distinction between innocence and insufficient evidence but I happened to know who carried out the bombings and none of the six whose convictions had been quashed were involved. He didn't pursue the point, but I was taken aback.

We talked about Cabinet meetings. Jack confirmed what others have said, that little in the way of serious debate takes place there. 'Too early yet. Wait until the shite hits the fan over the economy.' The important work, he said, is done in sub-committees. All policy initiatives have to be cleared with a committee chaired by Prescott which operates mainly by paperwork. 'If Tony trusts you, he lets you get on with it.'

I bounced a number of issues off him, part of my mission to civilise the inner cities: air weapons, dog licences etc. He's sympathetic but says there's a problem over legislative time. He did suggest they might be possibilities for the next manifesto. We talked about the funding of the Fire Service. He said there were all sorts of scams and management issues that needed to be addressed. The Fire Service was one of the last unreformed redoubts of white, macho, sexist males.

We walked back from Millbank trailed at a discreet distance by Jack's bodyguard, a little man called Carl in a pinstripe suit with a red poppy in his lapel. I like Jack. He listens, he consults, he's got a very good grasp of his brief and a clear idea of what he wants to achieve. He's also a great deal more liberal than he makes out whereas I'm less liberal than my reputation suggests. That's probably why we hit it off.

David Clark has managed to get himself moved across the corridor into Patricia Hewitt's old room, which has a window.

Wednesday, 21 October

Today's bad news is that the Germans are threatening to pull out of the Rover car plant at Longbridge. They are blaming poor productivity which, they allege, is one-third lower than at their German plants. The exchange rate must also be a factor.

I raised the Freedom of Information Bill at the parliamentary committee later in the afternoon, remarking that Derry Irvine now appeared to be its only friend in the Cabinet. The Man laughed and said, 'That's a calumny on Derry.'

Jean Corston, who has just returned from Chile, said that the arrest of Pinochet was going to cause big problems for the left just when it was starting to recover. There was a danger that the Christian Democrats, who are part of a fragile coalition with the social democratic left, would be pushed back into the hands of the far right. We should stick to the line that Pinochet's arrest was a judicial and not a political matter (although our cover on this has rather been blown by Peter Mandelson's incautious outburst on Sunday).

I ran into Tom King in the lift on the way down to the parliamentary committee. His annual report on the security services is published today and there is to be a debate on 2 November. He told me confidently that the debate was a result of his representations. I gently mentioned that Clive Soley and I had pressed the matter, too, but Tom was certain that it was all his own work and I didn't disabuse him. When, at the parliamentary committee, Ann Taylor was reading out the forthcoming business she mentioned the debate on the security services with a nod in my direction. To general amusement I reported that Tom King seemed to think it was all his own work. Clive then revealed that, some months back, Tom had tried to persuade him not to press for a debate. The old rogue.

Lunch with Bruce Grocott in the Millbank Room. Bruce is refreshingly uncorrupted by his proximity to power. We spent a little time lamenting the depredations of globalism. Like me, he firmly believes it's all going to end in tears and that, sooner or later, the government is going to have to terminate its love affair with the market.

Monday, 26 October
Sunderland

Paul Nicholson, chairman of Vaux, came to see me. At his request, he came to the house rather than the office. The atmosphere at Vaux, he says, is poisonous. 'I've lost control.' There is a new chief executive who is determined to sell off the brewing side of the business and is placing obstacles in the way of the proposed management buy-out. 'He has no commitment to the North East and refuses to come and live here. He's only interested in maximising profits in the short term. This is how the City thinks.' Paul is afraid that the company, which is viable, will be bought by one of the big four brewers, anxious to eliminate competition, and closed down. If that happens he wants political pressure for an inquiry by the Office of Fair Trading. We agreed that I should write to the OFT. I will copy the letter to the chief executives of the breweries concerned, whose names he gave me, by way of a warning shot. Paul says none of them will want a monopoly inquiry. I have to fight on this. There will be all hell to pay if Vaux goes down.

A pathetic reply from Barbara Roche to the earlier letter I had sent to Mandelson about Vaux. She hasn't altered even a comma of the official draft. The drift is that the government is powerless and that nothing can be done about anything. If we're powerless, what's the point of being in government? It's so shameful that I dare not copy it to Paul Nicholson. I shall pursue her.

Tuesday, 27 October

Ron Davies has resigned as Secretary of State for Wales following a bizarre incident on Clapham Common in which he ended up being robbed at knifepoint. Alun Michael is to replace him.

Saturday, 31 October
Sunderland

A Halloween bonfire in the Terrace. A neighbour recounted a joke he had heard on the radio. Tony Blair, Gordon Brown and Peter Mandelson go fishing. Without waiting for the boat to pull up on the shore,

Tony steps out and walks across the water. Peter does the same. Gordon steps out and goes straight down. 'We should have told him about the stepping stones,' says Tony. Asks Peter, 'What stepping stones?'

Monday, 2 November

Our long-awaited debate on the security services. The first ever. Robin opened. Jack closed. For the first time the arguments about the status of the Intelligence and Security Committee were brought out into the open. Dale Campbell-Savours and Yvette Cooper made excellent speeches calling for it to be placed on a par with a select committee. It was especially pleasing to hear Yvette, whom everyone says is destined for great things, going slightly off message. Alan Beith was pathetically cautious, saying it should be a process of evolution. The chairman, Tom King, who is carefully watching the direction of the wind, confined himself to asking for power to investigate, which the government said it will think about. Robin, who is supposed to be the great radical, was dismissive of calls for select committee status, but Jack went out of his way to say that the door was not closed.

Tuesday, 3 November

Gordon made his pre-Budget statement. His estimate of growth has been revised downward, but he was still brimming with confidence. His great spending plans will go ahead. Despite all his monetarist rhetoric, Gordon is at heart a Keynesian. If there is going to be a recession it makes sense to try and spend our way out and, at the same time, give the public services a long-awaited boost. Francis Maude, for the Tories, was full of phoney indignation. The gulf between us is as wide as it has ever been.

Wednesday, 4 November

To the Pugin Room for a drink with John Biffen. Subject for discussion: Woodrow Wyatt's suggestion that Murdoch had been allowed to take over *The Times* and *Sunday Times* without a reference to the Monopolies Commission, even though the papers together were profitable. Biffen, who was Secretary of State for Trade and Industry at the time, said he had searched his attic and dug out his pocketbook for the period in question. There had been one meeting of a cabinet committee, which Thatcher had chaired, but she hadn't said much. He had no recollection of any pressure from Downing Street, although he couldn't rule out the possibility that the Cabinet Secretary had been in touch with his Permanent Secretary, Sir Kenneth Clucas. He recalled a meeting at which Clucas had said, 'Do you want *The Times* to go bankrupt?' but so far as he knew everything had been above board. His accountants had examined carefully the figures supplied by Times Newspapers. Murdoch had been interviewed and behaved very professionally. He hadn't tried to bully or cajole the Department. He agreed that his decision to let Murdoch go ahead was a seminal moment which led to Murdoch's dominance of the British media. One of the difficulties was that the only other buyer in sight was Maxwell and nobody wanted him. 'Two things surprised me: the fact that there was no select committee inquiry; and that Harold Evans signed up to it.'

At the seven o'clock division I spoke briefly to Peter Mandelson about Vaux. He muttered something about a reference to the OFT and said, 'We haven't spoken.' It is a depressing fact that in eleven years representing Sunderland I have neither created nor saved a single job (apart from those of the two people who work for me). For the first time, there is a chance to make a difference. I must seize it.

Frank Dobson, hotfoot from Washington, is regaling anyone who will listen with the latest poor-taste Clinton jokes. Sample: 'What was Clinton's only mistake? Not asking Ted Kennedy to drive Monica home.'

Jean Corston capped that as follows: 'Have you heard about the new landing procedure on Air Force One? "Please return the hostess to an upright position."'

Thursday, 5 November

At the Liaison Committee Archie Kirkwood circulated a paper suggesting that the Review Body on Senior Salaries be asked to consider paying select committee chairmen. The reaction was surprisingly hostile. Gerald Kaufman, Peter Brooke, Andrew Bennett, David Marshall and Peter Luff were all opposed. Gerald said that chairing a select committee was an honour and required no further reward. Someone said it would only lead to more stories about MPs lining their pockets. Someone else said it would be divisive. The only person who spoke in favour was Rhodri Morgan. I'm in favour, too, on the grounds that the status of select committee chairmen needs boosting if they are to stand up to the executive. We need to develop a separate career structure and to make it attractive. Thoughts which, I'm ashamed to say, I kept to myself since there were clearly no takers. Archie said he would, in any case, pursue the matter with the Review Body.

Under any other business I inquired whether we were happy that, in reality, the government, not Parliament, decided on the composition of select committees. Mild unease was expressed, but no one wanted to make an issue of it. Gerald Kaufman, who made clear that he was perfectly happy with the present arrangements, remarked, 'We could be seriously damaged by a superfluity of democracy.'

Monday, 9 November

To London, arriving in time for the debate on the Neill report on party funding. A miserable little affair. Jack set a low tone by spending a lot of time deriding the Tories for having changed their tune and the debate never recovered. Patrick Neill was in the gallery, looking disdainful. No doubt the mud-slinging confirmed his low opinion of politicians. The plain truth is that the report is a watershed. British politics will never be the same again. Instead of carrying on down the American road, we have a chance to return to issue-driven rather than money-driven politics. Norman Fowler and John Greenway spoke for the Tories. It's just five years since Fowler, as Tory Party chairman, gave evidence to the select committee opposing any form of regulation. And as for Greenway, then a member of the committee, he fought tooth and nail to prevent the subject even being discussed. Yet here they were today meekly recommending acceptance of everything Neill suggested. As Tony Benn likes to say, radical reform has three stages. First, those in favour are virulently denounced. Then it all goes quiet as it gradually dawns on the denouncers that change is inevitable. Finally, a year or two from now, no one will even be able to recall that they ever held a different view.

Tuesday, 10 November

A pathetic pile of office equipment and personal effects belonging to Ron Davies has appeared in the corridor outside my room. It's been brought over from the Welsh Office and unceremoniously dumped. He's destined to end up in one of the windowless rooms that David Clark rejected.

Wednesday, 11 November

What a mess we are getting into over devolution. Dennis Canavan has announced that he will run for the Scottish Parliament as an independent. In Wales the regime is desperately attempting to block Rhodri Morgan from stepping into Ron Davies' shoes as Leader of the Welsh Assembly and in London Ken Livingstone is talking for the first time about running for Mayor as an independent. At the parliamentary committee this evening Jean and Ann raised Wales, where we are getting a very bad press. I raised London. The Man, unfortunately, was absent. A pity, because we urgently need to engage his attention before it's too late.

Monday, 16 November

With Bill Etherington and a delegation of Grove Cranes workers to see the Employment Secretary, Andrew Smith. Pointless, really, although Andrew handled them well. So far we have arranged meetings for the Grove workers with the Prime Minister, Peter Mandelson and the head of Government Office North East and all that happens is that they denounce us for doing nothing as soon as we are out of the door. Their frustration is understandable, but I do wish they'd stop taking it out on us. The plain truth is that Grove is owned by an American multinational and there is nothing we, the government or anyone else can do to stop them closing the place down.

While entertaining a delegation of firefighters in the Strangers' Bar, I had the following exchange with a Tory backbencher:

'I disagree with you about Masons. They are not some sinister conspiracy. They're all mad … insane.' His father, he added, had been 'a reluctant Mason'.

'What do you mean by reluctant?'

'He was in business. He wouldn't have got any contracts if he hadn't joined.'

'I rest my case.'

Wednesday, 18 November

An interesting little spat about The Man's dalliance with the Lib Dems at this morning's party meeting. Gordon Prentice criticised what he called the 'disdainful' way in which The Man had treated the party. Lib Dem MPs appeared to be better informed on the subject than we were. 'A sad state of affairs. I'm fed up to the back teeth with these *ex cathedra* pronouncements that I know nothing about.' He added, 'In Pendle, we don't have the cuddly kind of Lib Dems. We have a particularly nasty strain. Tony should say where he's taking us.'

Dennis Skinner said we ought to have learned from experience that the Lib Dems were totally unreliable and would pull the rug when it suited them. 'Somebody's got to get a message to Blair. Whatever he's playing at isn't going to do us any good.'

Prescott made no attempt to hold the line. He said only that, contrary to rumour, he had been consulted. 'I expressed my view – and you can guess what it was.' And that was that.

The results of yesterday's election to the parliamentary committee were announced. Andrew Mackinlay replaced Llin Golding. I topped the poll – 182 votes out of a possible 223 (12 of which were spoiled).

At lunchtime I went to address the Labour Club at the LSE. About thirty-five students attended. There were some complaints about student fees, but – as one of them said – the heat seems to have gone out of it. Today's students are surprisingly normal. Short-haired, studious, civil. My, how times have changed.

I managed to get in at PM's Questions, to ask about the sell-off at Vaux. I had gone to some trouble to make sure that The Man was briefed. The last thing I wanted was a reply that said we were powerless. I faxed Bruce Grocott a draft of the question and the kind of answer I was looking for. At 12.30 p.m. Bruce rang to say he hadn't seen the fax so I went over it again on the telephone. To my dismay, when I was on my feet I could see Bruce whispering urgently in Tony's ear. Obviously he was unprepared. In the event he ad-libbed. His reply was all right, but didn't strike quite the tone of urgency for which I had been hoping. Afterwards Bruce was apologetic. He had put a note in The Man's file but it had been overlooked. The best-laid plans …

Later, at the parliamentary committee, Clive Soley raised the unhappiness over the pact with the Liberals, but The Man was unapologetic. Those who are complaining, he protested, were not looking at the big picture. 'There is no hidden agenda. I want the Lib Dems to say at the next election: "Vote to keep the Tories out." It will be to our advantage.' The public did not mind us getting closer to the Liberals. It was just a problem in the party. He understood that people who had to fight the Lib Dems at local level were upset, but in the long run it would work to everyone's advantage. 'I'm doing it because I honestly believe it's in our interests.'

There was a spirited but good-humoured exchange about Ken Livingstone which I triggered off. 'I know he's a difficult customer and that you don't want him setting up a rival government on the other side of the river …'

'I'm with you so far,' The Man grinned.

'… But stopping him running for mayor is going to rebound badly.' I reminded him of other famous fixes that had rebounded. 'This will be messier.' I added that to some extent we were at Ken's mercy. 'If he chooses to run as an independent, he will probably be elected anyway. Remember you heard it here first.' I beamed at him. One should always smile when delivering an unpalatable message. The Man's lip curled.

'I hear you, but at the end of the day it's a matter for the selection board.' Then, realising that no one would swallow this, he added hastily, 'I can't pretend I don't have an interest. It's a bigger issue in the party than outside. As long as we get the economy right, the public won't remember any of this by the time the election comes.'

I begged to differ. 'Ken is a rare example of a politician who is more popular with the public than he is with the party.'

'So what would you do?'

'Open a line to him.'

At this point Prescott came crashing in. He had been to launch his public-private partnership for investment in London Underground and found Ken standing outside with the pickets.

The Man asked light-heartedly if I'd like to be a candidate. And that's where the matter rested.

'He's not listening to us,' Ann said afterwards, 'on anything.'

Friday, 20 November
Sunderland

To a primary school in one of the more prosperous parts of the constituency to talk to a group of nine- and ten-year-olds. I had gone prepared to talk about the environment, animal welfare and various other issues they had tipped me off about, but all they wanted to discuss was teenage gangs. It was amazing. One after another they told tales of bullying or violence at the hands of local yobs. One girl said she had been singled out for not wearing Reeboks. Another because she had been seen coming out of the library carrying books – *books*, for heaven's sake. It was shocking the extent to which violence or the threat of it plays a part in their lives. Not as a result of something they had seen on television or read about in the *Echo*. They were speaking from experience. They couldn't stop talking about it. Even the teachers were surprised.

Wednesday, 25 November

Martin Grant, the chief executive of Vaux and widely regarded as the villain of the piece, came in to see Bill and me. How satisfying it would be if all our villains turned out to have horns growing out of their heads and to eat little children for breakfast. Alas, Mr Grant was charm and sweet reason personified. At pains to assure us that he understood all about the pain of redundancy. His father had been made redundant three times and he once. The situation at Vaux was, he suggested gently, a wee bit more complicated than we imagined. We should not imagine that, were the management buy-out to be successful, there would be no redundancies. On the contrary, venture capitalists who would be funding a management buy-out had minds like steel traps. If the venture wasn't profitable they would pull the plug just as surely as any big brewery would. If he hadn't acted to hive off the breweries, Vaux would have been vulnerable to takeover. There were one or two predators sniffing round and they were still out there. If that happened Sunderland could kiss goodbye to the whole company, hotels as well as breweries. He departed saying that, if the difference between the two bids was marginal, the board could go with the buy-out, but if not …

John Prescott earned himself a round of applause at the party meeting this morning when he made clear that we are deadly serious about sorting out the Lords. We don't have any choice, he said. If we don't do it now, they will murder us in years three and four. Jack Dormand, a Labour peer, said there must be no wobbling, no concessions, and he was applauded too. This is going to be one issue that unites us all.

Thursday, 26 November

A call to Paul Nicholson, who was more optimistic than in any of our previous conversations. Apparently there was a meeting of a board sub-committee yesterday afternoon which did not go well for Martin Grant. The bids from Carlsberg, Tetley and Mansfield Breweries are lower than expected and the management buy-out is looking more attractive. He went on, 'With any luck we will be able to send this chap back to the Midlands.'

'How soon?'

'Within the next two or three weeks if the directors have got any balls.'

Wednesday, 2 December

Extraordinary scenes at PM's Questions. Up got Hague and revealed that The Man has quietly done a deal with the Tory Leader in the Lords, Robert Cranborne, that would allow 10 per cent of the hereditaries to remain until agreement was reached on the future of the Lords. This was news to us and Hague clearly calculated that it would cause havoc on our benches. Instead it rebounded. The Man neatly turned it round by demanding to know whether Hague was backing Cranborne and it soon became clear that he wasn't. By the end, our side was cheering and the Tories were looking distinctly unhappy.

At the parliamentary committee immediately afterwards, The Man explained that he had intended to announce the deal (which Cranborne apparently made without consulting Hague) later today. He had been taken by surprise when Hague led on it. We now had an opportunity to reform the Lords without a fuss. We could even get a couple of extra Bills through – we might even have our Royal Commission and wrap up stage two of the reforms, in this Parliament.

Later, it was announced that Hague had sacked Cranborne. The entire Tory front bench in the Lords had apparently offered their resignations. Still later it emerged that the Tories would be accepting the proposed deal after all. Presumably because Hague has realised that he has lost control of his troops in the Lords. Remarkable.

Thursday, 3 December

Hague has a bad press this morning. It isn't clear whether, when he raised the compromise over Lords reform at PM's Questions yesterday, he was even aware that Cranborne had already signed up to it. If he was, why didn't he sack Cranborne earlier in the day?

The Tories' discomfort, in which we are all revelling, has disguised some unhappiness on our side. Ted Short remarked, 'We didn't need to compromise. Abolition would have gone through anyway.'

John Spellar is cock-a-hoop. 'Hague's big mistake,' he says, 'was to go for the Tory leadership too early. There is no way the Tories are going to win the next election. He should have waited.'

As for the Lords, John says we should do nothing once we have completed the first stage of the reforms. Just turn the ninety-one remaining hereditaries into life peers and let them die out.

Monday, 7 December

Dinner in the Churchill Room with Chris and Annie Price and Helen Jackson. Helen revealed that Mo Mowlam had been against the emergency Terrorism Act in the summer. So was the RUC chief constable, Ronnie Flanagan. 'There are no operational reasons for it,' he had advised. So it was, as I suspected, entirely presentational.

Saturday, 12 December

My fifty-first birthday. A new pair of slippers and one of Ngoc's magnificently unhealthy carrot cakes with six candles – five and one – which had to be repeatedly re-lit and blown out for the benefit of the small people.

After lunch we bought our Christmas tree. When Ngoc and I carried it into the living room the small people sat on the sofa applauding, their little faces alight with excitement.

Wednesday, 16 December

David Miliband, who is in charge of the Policy Unit at Number 10, addressed the parliamentary party. His appearance arose out of my query as to how backbench MPs could influence government policy. He was at pains to assure a sceptical audience that the Policy Unit is not run by, as he put it, twelve-year-olds in red specs who had never attended a party branch meeting. An assertion belied by his youthful appearance. Someone asked about the public finance initiative and

David replied, 'If the government's made a decision, that's it.' What he ought to have said is, 'Please let us know how it's working.' I asked why I had received no reply to a letter I'd sent on 13 November. He apologised, saying he had been on honeymoon for the last two weeks, which was his best answer. Not an impressive performance, although I am sure he is very bright and personable.

After the meeting I walked downstairs with Jack. 'David's a very good guy,' he said, 'but there are others in the Policy Unit I would happily tip over the banister. They forget that, unlike them, we are elected.'

We talked briefly about control freakery. Jack raised the subject. In Wales, he said, we should let events take their course. I said London would be the real test. 'The selection will have to be very crudely fixed if Ken is to be stopped.'

Jack is no fan of Ken's. 'He reduced the GLC to such a point that the Tories thought they could win votes by abolishing it.' He spoke with passion. 'Ken only picked up support when he knew he was going anyway and started spending oodles of public money – your money and mine – on public relations.'

He was so passionate that I could see there was no point in disagreeing – although I do. 'Ken is not the issue,' I said. 'The issue is, will stopping him cause more trouble than it saves?' Jack said he took the point, but his influence was limited.

The Americans have tonight launched a massive attack on Iraq.

Thursday, 17 December

The Man made a statement about the attack on Iraq which is being billed as an Anglo-American operation, though we only have a walk-on part, in keeping with our satellite status. One of those occasions when the House of Commons was at its worst. A huge bout of me-too-ism. Much odious hear-hearing from the Tories, who never had a bad word to say about Saddam when they were happily doing business with him. George Galloway and Tony Benn were the only two dissidents called. They both pointed out that we lack the support of the other three permanent members of the Security Council – France, Russia and China. George was rudely heckled by some on our side and had to point out to them that he was entitled to his say in a free Parliament. That provided Blair with an opportunity to point out that he wouldn't have enjoyed the same opportunity in Iraq. George, of course, is fatally hobbled by the impression he gives that he is really on Saddam's side. I was tempted to ask what we are going to do when, after the bombing stops, Saddam pops up and declares a huge victory, but decided upon discretion.

Clinton looks like being impeached. The way things are going, Saddam may well outlast him.

Sunday, 20 December

Paul Nicholson rang. He says Martin Grant has been unable to come up with any credible offer to match the bid from the management team. However, instead of taking the obvious course and accepting the management offer, he has persuaded the board to put the supply contract for the pubs out to tender. There is a danger that one of the big breweries will put in an unrealistically low bid (funded by the profits from supplying their own pubs) and undercut Vaux.

Wednesday, 23 December

Peter Mandelson and Geoffrey Robinson have resigned,* triggering off a huge feeding frenzy in the media. Poor Peter, he flew too close to the sun.

Thursday, 24 December

The media is full of Mandelson, but this is no time for gloating. We are all damaged by this. More fodder for those who say that all politicians are the same. I resent the suggestion. We are not. Still, I can't

---

*Following the failure of Mandelson (Secretary of State for Trade and Industry) to declare a personal loan from Robinson (Paymaster General) to help buy a house in Notting Hill.

help feeling just the tiniest twinge of pity for Peter. He has nothing to fall back upon. No family. No hinterland. At least none that's visible to the naked eye. Politics is all there is and, for now at least, he is out of the loop. Many of his new-found friends will melt away. BUT ... unless there are more skeletons to be disinterred (and there may be – another Paul Routledge book is due in January) ... he will rise again. As Foreign Secretary, perhaps? What better way for The Man to demonstrate to those who flinch and sneer that they shall not prevail?

Steve Byers and Alan Milburn have been promoted to fill the gaps. The situation is not yet so desperate that anyone has suggested sending for Mullin.

Thursday, 31 December

I walked from Westminster to Greenwich, along the north bank of the river, with Caroline Adams and her friend Val Harding, pausing en route to visit St Magnus the Martyr. The scale of the transformation in Docklands is astonishing. I remember Wapping High Street when it was just a corridor of corrugated iron. Now it is full of expensive yuppie apartments. We passed David Owen's house at Limehouse and crossed to Greenwich through the foot tunnel at Island Gardens. I asked Caroline what message she wanted me to convey to our masters after the recess. She waxed strong about the 'obscenity' of the Iraq bombing, 'particularly announcing it while standing in front of that bloody Christmas tree in Downing Street'. She added that New Labour seems to live too well. 'It doesn't look good disappearing to the Seychelles, leaving the rest of us in the winter gloom.'

CHAPTER SIX

1999

Friday, 1 January 1999

And so begins another year in the life of the 'dank Tudor court', as *Tribune*'s Hugh MacPherson calls the New Labour elite. I foresee a tough year ahead. The magic has gone, thanks to misbehaviour by Messrs Ecclestone, Mandelson et al. The Man still soars above us but even he is tarnished. He, after all, chooses to surround himself with such people. If only he wasn't so impressed by the rich and the clever. All is not gloom, however. We are gradually making inroads into the benefit culture. Wealth, and even a little bit of power, is gradually redistributed. A minimum wage, some basic trade union rights, the removal of most hereditary peers from the House of Lords, devolution in Scotland, Wales and London. All achievements that will endure …

With the small people and one of their little friends to the Natural History Museum to see dinosaurs and blue whales. Best question: 'Do snakes go to the toilet?'

Thursday, 7 January

Another visit from Paul Nicholson. Again he insisted on coming to St Bede's Terrace to avoid being seen. He says Martin Grant is determined to close the brewery and has now obtained a valuation of between £6 and £12 million for the site once the plant is razed. Paul reckons the crunch will come at next week's board meeting.

Monday, 11 January

Peter Mandelson and Robin Cook are the talk of the Tea Room. Robin because his wife's memoirs are currently being serialised. Sympathy is the order of the day so far as he is concerned. The same cannot be said for Peter. Today's *FT* leads with an unsourced report that he may become 'a roving ambassador' in Europe, whatever that means. The feeling among the troops is that he is doing us serious damage and that The Man's apparent refusal to part with him is only prolonging the agony. Only Dennis Skinner is upbeat: '1998 was a good year for Old Labour,' he remarked with a twinkle in his eye.

Tuesday, 12 January

'Who is Michael Wills?'* The question is on many lips, but no one seems to know much about him. Still less, how he comes to be qualified for office after so short a time in this place. I dimly recollect a row when he was selected at Swindon in preference to the local frontrunner, but that is the only ripple he has made on my consciousness. I went to the Library and looked him up, but even his picture rings no bells. He is obviously bright, a double first from Cambridge, but as Peter has just demonstrated, brilliance is not everything. The consensus seems to be that he is a friend of Gordon's, to whom he owes his miraculous rise.

I came across Peter Mandelson in Upper Corridor South, where he had just been inspecting the office lately vacated by Geoff Hoon. It seems we may soon be neighbours. Upper Corridor South seems to be a repository for the dismissed and the disgraced. It was the same in the last parliament (Mellor, Yeo etc.). So far in this parliament we have accumulated David Clark, Ron Davies (briefly) and now Peter.† All we lack to complete the set is Geoffrey Robinson.

Clive Soley, the chairman of the parliamentary party, sought my

---

*MP for Swindon North, appointed a junior minister at the Department of Trade and Industry.
† In the event, he went elsewhere.

advice as to what we should be saying to The Man about recent events. As ever, Clive looks anxious. He takes his role very seriously, but usually ends up trying to walk down the middle of the road with the result that he gets run over by traffic from both directions. I suggested we open by asking The Man what lessons he has learned from the events of the past fortnight and let him do the talking. If it becomes clear that he is in denial, we should go in hard. The bottom line should be that speculation about Peter's future should be ended until after the election.

Wednesday, 13 January

To a packed meeting of the parliamentary party. Margaret Beckett addressed us very competently about plans for Lords reform and when she had finished Clive asked for questions. No one moved. He asked again. Still no hands went up. Such was the anxiety to reach Any Other Business that the self-restraint was unprecedented.

Gwyneth Dunwoody made an impassioned speech. Recent events, she said, had been far more distressing for Labour Party members than was generally realised. She began by attacking talk of coalition with the Liberal Democrats. Then she launched into what she called 'the swill of sewage' that spilled out of the pubs in Westminster every Friday as rival spin doctors briefed the Sunday press. 'It is extremely regrettable that, after only eighteen months, this Labour government has got itself into a situation where most discussion is about individual differences between colleagues.' She went on, 'Many of our supporters are dismayed that we have lost our way so rapidly.' For good measure, she added, 'This parliamentary party is by far the most quiescent I have seen.' Applause was warm, but by no means universal. Many of the new intake did not join in. Unsurprisingly, they don't like being told they are toadies.

Then Clive Soley spoke, with John Prescott looking grim beside him. The current crisis, said Clive, was by far the most serious since the election. 'My key message – and one I will be delivering to the government – is that we backbench Members of Parliament exercise self-restraint and we expect the same from members of the government.'

He disagreed with Gwyneth's opinion of the parliamentary party ('We are self-disciplined, not quiescent') and concluded on an upbeat note. This was a radical, reforming government. We must not allow ourselves to be distracted by infighting.

Throughout all this Peter Mandelson was sitting quietly in the front row, making the occasional note, but mostly making a show of listening intently, chin on hand, icily calm and detached. As though all this has nothing to do with him. Indeed, his name was not once mentioned.

I asked Alan Clark what he thought of Woodrow Wyatt's diaries. 'Not much. He was a courtier, not a vizier. There were bits and pieces of interest, but Woodrow wasn't in the inner circle, unlike Chips Channon.' I asked Alan why his diaries, which have so far sold half a million copies, had been so severely edited. He said that his publishers were not initially convinced they would sell. There might be an expanded edition in due course. Plus, of course, he is still writing, which is no doubt why he went to such trouble to get back into Parliament. He made one curious remark which I should have followed up, but didn't. 'My greatest fans are those who understood what I was trying to say.' I nodded vaguely, but I haven't a clue what he meant.

Ben Bradshaw, whose sister is a neighbour of Peter Mandelson, says that several journalists are camped out in the street opposite his house. 'The man can't fart without something appearing in a diary column.' I was sitting in the Library, reflecting on what to say at the parliamentary committee, when up came Jim Marshall and, making no effort to lower his voice, said, 'I am absolutely opposed to Peter Mandelson having any involvement in the affairs of government for the foreseeable future – or ever, in fact.' I was taken aback, because Jim is normally such a mild-mannered guy who usually keeps to himself. Further evidence, if any is needed, of the strength of feeling.

Clive Soley kicked off the parliamentary committee in exactly the manner I suggested. 'What lessons have been learned?' he asked. The Man replied with an inadequate little homily about the need to put the past behind us. Andrew Mackinlay was the first into the breach.

'The Prime Minister,' he said, looking The Man squarely in the eye, 'was mistaken to let Peter Mandelson represent the government in discussions with the Germans only days after his resignation'. The Man, looking mildly irritated, as he often does when Mackinlay speaks, lamely attempted to defend the decision on the grounds that the talks with the Germans had been at a delicate stage and Peter had been involved from the outset. He then became animated. 'I can't remember a Cabinet or Shadow Cabinet more united than this one. Most of what appears in the media is rubbish. Contrary to rumour, I have a good working relationship with Gordon. Gordon and I looked at Sunday's newspapers together and we didn't know whether to laugh or cry. There is a struggle going on for control of the agenda. The media want to set the agenda and we have to get it back.'

For a moment it looked as though Mackinlay might be isolated so I repeated that Peter's meeting with the Germans had been a mistake. It was in everyone's interests, including Peter's, to end speculation about his future. He should concentrate on representing his constituents and making his presence felt on the back benches, where he should remain for the foreseeable future. I added, 'And by the foreseeable future, I mean until after the next election.' Ann Clwyd said The Man should understand that the continual speculation about Peter was damaging him personally. Jean Corston endorsed everything Ann and I had said. Sylvia Heal said that Gwyneth Dunwoody had spoken for the whole parliamentary party this morning. By now The Man was looking chastened. 'I hear what you are saying,' he said meekly. 'I've got the message.'

Thursday, 14 January

To Thames House to commune with the head of MI5, Stephen Lander. My first visit to the new building. When the select committee visited Stella Rimington in Gower Street six years ago we were pursued across London by photographers on motorbikes. This time we strolled down Millbank in glorious sunshine, loitered for five minutes at the entrance to await stragglers – and no one took the blindest bit of notice.

First impression: the apparent emptiness of the building; although the best part of 1,800 people are housed within, they are mainly invisible. The public spaces are huge, furnishing minimal. At the centre a huge atrium, around which people can be glimpsed through plate glass, sitting at computer terminals, conferring with neighbours, so distant that one might be watching them on a TV screen. The atrium is devoid of people.

We were taken to a white-panelled boardroom on an upper floor with fine views across the Thames to Lambeth Palace. Lander, I notice, was born in the same year as me. A meritocrat with no pretensions to grandeur. Marks & Spencer rather than Jermyn Street. No cufflinks, no handkerchief protruding from breast pocket, a weakish chin, classless accent, spectacles. If ever there was a man born to look anonymous, it is he. But he was impressive, exuding quiet competence and honesty. On occasion, surprisingly frank. A diminishing amount of MI5 resources were taken up with Ireland. Islamist terror was the big growth area. F2, the department that used to keep an eye on trade unions, CND and the like, had been wound up in 1992 leaving a large database of redundant information. The service no longer takes an interest in the BBC, except the World Service. The historic interest in so-called domestic subversives had been triggered by a directive from the Attlee government. The 1950s, when the security services had devoted a lot of time to searching out communist sympathisers and preventing their employment in the public sector, he described as 'a sad period'. He agreed with David Bickford's interesting assertion that Whitehall was more wary of parliamentary scrutiny of the security service than the service itself. Asked about scrutiny by a select committee he was non-committal, saying only that it was a matter for ministers. Pressed, he said, 'I have no baggage either way.'

Afterwards I ran into John Hutton, who said that just before the election he and Ian Cawsey, officers of the backbench Home Affairs Committee, had been invited over by Lander, who told them he was anxious to establish contact with the Labour Party.

'Just one caveat,' he said.

'What's that?'

'This meeting never took place.'

Old habits die hard.

Monday, 18 January

Ann Clwyd drew my attention to a report in today's *Independent* headed, 'Mandelson to Become EU Aide for Cook'. She had just heard on the radio that the Foreign Office had confirmed the story and Clive Soley had been on the airwaves saying he didn't think MPs would object. We immediately cornered Robin, who confirmed that he had recently dined with the Great Ingratiator and asked him to report back on his travels in Europe, which, apparently he is undertaking on behalf of the party. 'You do realise he is after your job,' I said.

'I know, but I thought it better to keep tabs on him.'

We then spoke to Clive, who conceded he had been unwise. Clive added that he had asked to attend next week's Cabinet meeting to convey backbench angst about feuding in high places. He says The Man isn't keen on the grounds that, if the story got out – as it is bound to do – there would be another feeding frenzy.

Over the weekend, I accidentally left the answerphone on at the flat. As a result it was full of fatuous messages from journalists wanting sound bites on every subject under the sun. Sample:

1. Gloria from *On the Record*. They are making a programme about 'feuding' in the government. Would I like to contribute? Would I, hell.

2. A man from the *Express* with an inquiry about police discipline in the wake of news that all the policemen allegedly responsible for bungling the Stephen Lawrence inquiry have retired.*

3. Martin Bright of the *Observer*, wanting to talk about British-based Islamists who get involved in murky business.

4. A posh young woman called Victoria from the *Today* programme who wanted to talk about Pinochet.

5. A horrible, seedy-sounding man from the *News of the World* wanting to talk about drugs. He sounded as though he was selling drugs rather than writing about them.

---

* Stephen Lawrence was a black teenager stabbed to death in south London in April 1993; the handling of the case by the Metropolitan Police was much criticised.

I could spend my entire life concocting instant opinions on every subject under the sun to satisfy the insatiable demand for rent-a-quotes – and have precisely no impact on anything.

Tuesday, 19 January

A talk with Ken Livingstone, who says there is no chance of a deal over the London mayoral ticket. He talked to The Man in November. 'I made all the offers, but he was like ice.'

Wednesday, 20 January

To great cheers, Margaret Beckett announced the government's Bill for reforming the Lords. The plan is to get rid of the hereditaries before there is any discussion of the numerous alternatives. She was brilliant. The Tories huffed and puffed and looked very unhappy. They know they've been completely shafted.

The only churlish note on our side came from Tony Benn. The scale of his dissent is so vast that he is more isolated than at any time in his career. There are all sorts of good things going on and he can't bring himself to acknowledge any of them. When I was called I made clear that I disagreed with Tony. 'You'll get a life peerage,' he said to me later, only half in jest.

The Mandelson problem cropped up again at the parliamentary committee. Clive Soley kicked off, referring to the article in Monday's *Independent*. As he was speaking I slid the cutting across the table towards The Man, who was sitting directly opposite. He looked irritated and peered at it from a distance, as though he didn't want to soil his hands by touching it. Then he flicked it back across the table without looking me in the eye, his displeasure tangible. He denied knowing anything about the allegation that Peter was advising Robin. 'We must be careful,' he said. 'Peter has left the government, but he has not been cast into outer darkness. We must stop apologising.' At this point the tide began to turn. Several people spoke up for Peter. Prescott said it wasn't just the media who were obsessed with him: 'Let's face it, we are, too.' Margaret McDonagh said she wouldn't hesitate to ring Peter and ask for advice. No one else said anything from our side. I detect a feeling that the subject is exhausted. John is right. We are obsessed with Peter to a degree that is unhealthy, but then of course he has done us enormous damage.

The Man then surprised us all by revealing that Paddy Ashdown would be announcing his retirement as Leader of the Liberal Democrats this evening and he hoped we wouldn't mind if he said something nice about him. He did not expect Ashdown's departure to have any effect on engagement with the Lib Dems. There was a brief flurry followed by mild amusement when it was realised that Paddy hadn't yet made the announcement and that it wouldn't look good if the outside world were to hear the news via a Labour leak. We were all sworn to secrecy but, by the time we emerged, the news was out.

Thursday, 21 January

To the Home Office to see Gareth Williams, one of the unsung successes of this government. An unusual combination of cleverness and modesty, combined with a dry sense of humour. A couple of civil servants from the Prison Department gave a little presentation on the work they were doing to encourage prisoners to face up to their offending behaviour. I pressed them on what could be done for those who decline to cooperate on the grounds that they are innocent and who, as a result, end up serving longer than the guilty. The officials acknowledged there was a problem, but said – reasonably enough – that it wasn't their job to second-guess the courts. We reached no very satisfactory conclusion, but then of course there is no obvious answer.

I asked why prisoners were allowed to paper their cells with degrading pictures of women when we were supposed to be encouraging them to treat women with respect. The men from Prisons hummed and hawed about censorship and where lines should be drawn, but Gareth took my side. There was a bright, attractive young blonde woman present whom I at first assumed to be the minute-taker, but she turned out to be a governor-grade prison officer who had recently joined Gareth's office from Feltham Young Offenders Institution. Gareth asked her opinion and she said she had just drawn up a censorship policy at Feltham. Gareth asked her to consider a policy for the entire prison estate. He will come back to me in a month or so.

Monday, 25 January

As I changed tube trains at Victoria, a vagrant picked up my case and started to make off with it. 'Can I have that back, please?' I called after him. Without a word he turned and handed it to me and disappeared.

At ten o'clock there was a free vote on equalising the age of consent for heterosexuals and homosexuals. I voted in favour, which will go down badly with most of my constituents.

Tuesday, 26 January

Tam Dalyell had a little ten-minute-rule Bill which would have required the Prime Minister to seek the permission of Parliament before going along with any new attacks on Iraq. A very reasonable proposition which he moved skilfully. A lot of people stayed to hear him and listened respectfully. On all sides people are, I suspect, secretly dismayed at our isolation over Iraq. I sat uneasily, knowing that I really ought to vote for Tam's Bill but not wanting to find myself in the same lobby as the Soft on Saddam brigade. In the event no vote was called. The whips decided to let it through unopposed, knowing it will disappear into the ether, and so we were spared the embarrassment of having to take a stand.

Wednesday, 27 January

Robin Cook addressed the party meeting. It was the Robin of old. Confident, robust, impressive. He was well received, but the truth is he has few, if any, real friends and has made little effort to cultivate any. Instead he relies on his undoubted brilliance to see him through, although as Denis Healey discovered, that's not quite enough.

Robin talked of 'hair-raising' stories from Russia, which he described as being in a post-industrial state. The Russians aren't capable of either storing or reprocessing their nuclear waste. We want to help them, but it isn't clear that they wanted to be helped.

On Kosovo he said, 'We aren't going to get peace in the Balkans until we get rid of Milosevic and his poisonous machine of ethnic hatred.' That's the first time I have heard anyone in authority talk about getting rid of Milosevic. He did not elaborate.

Robin made two other memorable points: (1) 'I accept that foreign policy should be about our national interest, but promotion of our values is in our national interest'. (2) 'There is no future for us creating a fortress to protect our comfortable society. It will in any case be undermined by drugs and migration.'

The Man was in an ebullient mood at the parliamentary committee. I asked about Kosovo, saying that I hoped we weren't going to sit on the sidelines until we had to go in anyway, as the Tories did with Bosnia. The Man said he didn't rule out being part of a peacekeeping force, but there were problems with our allies. The Americans weren't interested in contributing to a ground force and the Kosovo Liberation Front was a problem. The Americans had recently sent them a strong signal which he hoped would restrain them. We were, however, working well with the French.

At this point Charles Williams came in, getting off to a bad start by referring to 'defence experts in the Lords'. Jean smiled and I whispered, 'There are 1,250 defence experts in the Lords.' The Man beamed indulgently at Charles and then glanced at me, almost winking.

Maybe it's my imagination, but there seems to be some sort of charm offensive on. The Man, Gordon and JP were all spotted in the Tea Room this afternoon. Jean, Ann, Clive and I had tea with JP, who was in good spirits. He said that he was trying to avoid sitting next to Tony at questions because on television he always looked as if he disapproved of what was being said. Sometimes he had difficulty keeping awake. 'Why aren't you supporting me?' The Man had demanded during the debacle over the Lone Parent Premium. To which JP had replied, 'I am.' But when he looked at the video of himself, slumped grim and semi-conscious on the bench beside his leader, he could see the problem. 'I can't help my face. It's just how it is.' We joked that he needed surgery. The first time I've ever heard Prescott laugh at himself.

Thursday, 28 January

David Clark reckons there will be a Liberal Democrat in the Cabinet within three years. 'Sooner if Paddy hadn't stood down.' I don't agree, unless our majority after the election is so low that we are forced into some sort of coalition. David says, 'Tony's much more at home with Liberals than he is with Labour MPs. You can see it in his body language.'

I asked the Chief Whip Ann Taylor for the names of those who have applied for the vacancy on the select committee. She replied, 'It's already been announced, didn't you know?' (Silly me, I'm only the chairman.) Later, Ann rang to apologise for failing to consult me.

A call from Paul Nicholson, in advance of tomorrow's Vaux AGM. 'Things are rather desperate. The bastards are trying to impose unacceptable conditions and our people are too wet to resist.' Paul says he has drafted three possible versions of his Chairman's Statement for tomorrow and hasn't yet decided which to use. One version he describes as 'explosive – it might well cost me the chairmanship, but I might as well go out with all guns blazing'.

Friday, 29 January

To the Vaux AGM, attended by several hundred mostly well-heeled people. Not a very typical Sunderland audience and not very relevant to what was going on since there were more than eighty million proxy votes controlled by a handful of City slickers who didn't even bother to show up. Paul Nicholson had left a message saying that I should ask Martin Grant why he was still living in the West Midlands when he was chief executive of a company based in the North East. I duly obliged, triggering a small round of applause. Grant, not a man easily embarrassed, replied affably that he had made clear from the outset that he would not be moving north. Paul made an excellent speech, his swansong as chairman, saying he believed in straight dealing and treating people decently. No prizes for guessing who that was aimed at. At the last moment a deal was signed giving the management team four weeks to conclude the sale. We must now keep our fingers crossed.

Saturday, 30 January

Ian rang to say that Jacky* has cancer. It began in her kidneys and has spread to her brain. Poor, dear, kind, frail Jacky, such a good friend since the day we met fourteen years ago. She has been allowed out of hospital for the weekend. I bought a card with a cat on the front and took it round to her. Inside I wrote, 'Thank you for all your help and kindness which I look forward to repaying in the years ahead.' I just stopped myself from writing 'months' rather than 'years'. Months is what it will be, of course.

Tuesday, 2 February

The public sector pay awards were announced today. A whopping 12 per cent for new nurses and more than 4 per cent for everyone else. Also, substantial increases for teachers, some dependent on performance. These are the biggest increases for ten years yet still the papers are full of whingeing trade unionists. The local Unison branch secretary is quoted in the *Echo* describing the nurses' award as 'a slap in the face'. All of which only goes to prove that wage militants can never be satisfied. They will ruin us if we let them. We must never surrender.

Ben Chapman was on the bus going home. I asked if he was on a select committee and he replied that he was a Parliamentary Private Secretary.

'Who for?'

'Richard Caborn.'

---

*Jackie Breach, my secretary. Ian was her husband.

'Does he need a PPS?'

'No.'

Doesn't that say it all? It's just a mechanism for extending the payroll vote and satisfying ministerial egos. The effect is to render impotent a number of talented people who might otherwise do something useful.

Wednesday, 3 February

I came across Caroline Benn, emerging from the Members' Lobby on the arm of her son Stephen. Frailer than when I last saw her, but still in good spirits. 'Permanently terminal,' she replied when I asked how she was. So many of my friends are dying from cancer. Joan (Maynard), Caroline, Jacky … who next?

On my way to Millbank for an interview, I encountered Virginia Bottomley, Golden Virginia as I like to think of her. She always calls me 'Mullin', but in a friendly way. I like her. She has a sunny disposition and, for someone who was in government for ten years, has worn extraordinarily well. Virginia was banging on about the alleged arrogance of our masters and how beastly we were being to her constituents in 'poor old Surrey'.

'Pull the other one,' I said.

Undaunted, she protested that the public spending settlement for Surrey is very mean and that resources are being shifted elsewhere. Her constituency was full of articulate elderly people who made great demands on the health service – and on their MP. On reflection, she may have a point. The cost of living – especially property prices – must make it very difficult to recruit nurses and teachers and I bet the local authorities have sold off their council houses which will have made matters worse.

At the parliamentary committee Charlotte Atkins raised Steve Byers' speech at the Mansion House last night, which was very pro-business.

The Man, in shirtsleeves signing photographs of himself, with a plate of half-eaten egg-and-tomato sandwiches on the table in front of him, replied lamely, 'You have to create wealth before you can distribute it.'

'That's not what he said,' Charlotte responded.

Suddenly The Man became strangely tongue-tied. A couple of times he started to say something and then changed his mind. In the end he said meekly, 'I take the point.' What he was going to say, indeed what he started to say, was that we are going out of our way to suck up to business because, contrary to the general view, we are actually inflicting some large new burdens – the minimum wage, shorter working hours, trade union rights, tougher penalties for unfair dismissal. He is obviously afraid that, were he to say that, word would leak – we have been a bit leaky lately – and the City might realise, if they don't already, that they are having their tummies tickled. Something similar is going on with the Lib Dems.

Ann Clwyd raised The Man's recent appearance on *Richard and Judy* which resulted in some unwise remarks about England manager Glenn Hoddle. Several people, she said, had suggested he shouldn't have accepted the invitation. The Man disagreed. The programme had reached a large audience. Calls to the nurses' hotline (set up to encourage former nurses to rejoin the NHS) had nearly doubled after his appearance. He conceded, however, that shows like *Richard and Judy* could be dangerous because they lulled you into a false sense of security. 'You know where you are with *Today*. They are trying to trick you into saying something indiscreet and you're trying to avoid doing so. On *Richard and Judy* you relax, and that's when, as I discovered, you can get into trouble.'

Frank Dobson added, to general agreement, that the *Jimmy Young Show* was the most dangerous. 'He asks such simple questions that you feel a pillock if you give a long answer.'

After The Man had departed I triggered what turned out to be a long discussion about what I perceive is the growing contempt with which select committees are treated by the government. They are laden with lightweights and regularly raided to provide parliamentary private secretaries for ministers who don't need them. I cited my conversation with Ben Chapman last night and mentioned Melanie Johnson, who stayed on Home Affairs for only five weeks before being wafted away to the Treasury. Why didn't we make more use of the growing number of ex-ministers? Gareth Williams remarked that anyone who hadn't been made a PPS by the age of fourteen thought they were a failure. Clive said select committee chairmen should be paid in order to raise their status, but I saw Ann Taylor mouthing that that debate was dead. She said there were no more PPSs now than there had been under the last Labour government.

Thursday, 4 February

To the Chamber to hear Paul Boateng and Norman Fowler debating the police revenue settlement. Paul spoke fluently for forty-five minutes, far too long. He is one of those people who can speak at any length on any subject without any notice. After a while one switches off because you know that, like all clever lawyers, he could make the opposite case with equal facility.

A fascinating old gent on the train going home this evening. A retired British Rail executive who now tours the Third World offering advice on transport systems. Aged about seventy, healthy, happy and, above all, full of optimism. Secure in the knowledge that his life has been worthwhile. He described an occasion when he had been in Bangladesh, advising the state railway. 'How many of your passengers have valid tickets?' he inquired of the management.

They didn't know so he persuaded them to conduct a straw poll. They arranged for a train to be stopped in the middle of the countryside and for the area to be cordoned off by troops while the tickets were checked.

Result: just three people out of 1,500 were carrying valid tickets. The rest were either travelling free or had bought tickets at inflated prices on the black market.

'What shall we do?' they asked.

'Close your ticket offices,' he replied. 'They are a waste of time.'

Needless to say, his advice was not accepted.

Saturday, 6 February

Paul Nicholson rang. Further drama at Vaux. He alleges that the chief executive and the finance director have been bad-mouthing the management buy-out in the City. 'I'm hoping it will come to a head this week, if the board have the balls to get rid of them.'

I remarked that I'd enjoyed his speech at the annual meeting the other day. Paul said, 'I'm told that sort of morality is out of date these days.'

He added, 'The investors behind the proposed management buy-out are holding firm so far – but they will be lean and mean. There will be redundancies.'

Tuesday, 9 February

The Vaux board have sacked Martin Grant. The finance director has also gone. A long overdue triumph for the one-nation Tories over the asset-strippers. With any luck the management buy-out will now proceed unhindered.

To Ipswich to address the Suffolk Book League on 'My brief career as a writer'. Among the audience, Peter Hardiman Scott, the former BBC political correspondent, who told an interesting little story: When *A Very British Coup* was published in 1982 he was three-quarters of the way through a novel based on precisely the same thesis – the election of a left-wing government and its overthrow by the Establishment. The similarities between his manuscript and my book were so striking that, after a discussion with his publishers, he decided he had no alternative but to shelve the project. A close shave. Had he got there first, *A Very British Coup* might never have seen the light of day.

Wednesday, 10 February

Jack Straw addressed this morning's meeting of the parliamentary party. Jack is by no means a great orator, but he does have an endearing, common-sense way of talking, with just a touch of self-deprecation. As a result he went down well. In passing he remarked that he was aiming for a 30 per cent reduction in car crime. Why? 'Because the Prime Minister has said so and it would be a bad career move not to.'

Neil Gerrard raised the plan to withdraw cash benefits from asylum seekers. It would, he said, be bad for race relations if our streets were full of black beggars. Jack rejected this. First, he said, only about 3 per cent of asylum seekers were black. Most came from the former Yugoslavia, Turkey, northern Iraq and China. Second, those who applied for asylum from within the country didn't qualify for benefit anyway and they had not resorted to begging because most of them had networks of family and friends to support them.

Fiona Mactaggart said she was not confident that the Home Office was capable of speeding up the asylum system. On the contrary, it was getting slower. This elicited a surprisingly frank response. 'I've managed in the last three months to make the system run so badly and so slowly that, from this base, it can only get better. The Tories left us with an IT system that doesn't work. Everything that can go wrong has gone wrong.'

As we were leaving Gareth Williams told me that he had 'had some fun' at a recent meeting with the senior judges to discuss the government's proposed reforms to the judicial system. Lord Bingham had remarked that there was 'outrage and disbelief' among the entire judiciary that the government could be contemplating whatever it is they are contemplating. To which Gareth had replied drily that he vividly recalled the outrage and disbelief throughout the judiciary at the proposition that six innocent men had been convicted of the Birmingham pub bombings. No one pursued the point.

To the Channel Four Political Awards. I had been nominated in the Questioner of the Year category and, having a premonition of victory (which I was careful to conceal from the other contestants), I wore my Number One suit. Sure enough I duly won and was rewarded with a useless slab of Dartington Crystal with my name engraved on the side. Unfair, really. Andrew Mackinlay, who was sitting beside me, undoubtedly asked *the* question of the year and I could see that he was disappointed. William Hague, who was also nominated, is often brilliant at Question Time (he was again today), but the choice was made by a ballot of MPs and there is no way Hague was going to win that in the present climate. It was really a popularity contest for back-benchers and, for the moment, my star is high.

The Man, who has just returned from King Hussein's funeral, was in relaxed mode at the parliamentary committee. The longest discussion was about hunting with hounds. Amazing what passions this issue arouses. I can see that The Man is bemused by it when he has so many more important matters to worry about. I expressed the hope that it could be sorted out, once we had reformed the Lords, pointing out that this played big with Middle England. This provoked Prescott, who came crashing in with a little speech about how we mustn't shoot ourselves in the foot. We had never said we would abolish fox-hunting in our first year. To general merriment he then launched into a little tirade about 'Guy' Prentice (he meant Gordon) and his Right to Roam Bill. Andrew Mackinlay, who is fearless, replied that all he was seeking was reassurance that the matter would eventually be addressed. The present uncertainty was doing us a lot of damage. The Man assured us, none too convincingly, that he was working on it. To concentrate his mind, I pointed out that the International Fund for Animal Welfare, the main pressure group (with whom I had a meeting this morning), has a million subscribers.

When we had finished going round the table The Man said, a propos of nothing, 'Shall I say a word about genetically modified food?' He was, he said, keen to ensure that we didn't overreact by launching into what he called 'populist mode'. There were all sorts of genetic modifications that we wouldn't wish to discourage. We wanted strict regulation and clear labelling, but we mustn't be stampeded into rejecting genetic modification out of hand. He added that it was a big industry and there were a lot of jobs at stake.

I didn't think anything of it at the time, but soon after we emerged from the meeting I ran into Alan Simpson, who said there were rumours that Bill Clinton had been leaning on The Man at the behest of Monsanto, which has already bought its way into the American political system and is no doubt burrowing away at ours. Jean Corston later asked Ian Gibson, who knows a lot about genetic modification, how many jobs were involved in this country. 'Very few,' he replied. Curiouser and curiouser.

Thursday, 11 February

Lunch with Bruce Grocott in the Millbank Room. I remarked that, barring another upset, Peter would return as Foreign Secretary after the election and Ron Davies would disappear without trace. Bruce replied that, on the contrary, Ron Davies appeared to be on the point of resurfacing in the murky world of Welsh politics, whereas Peter could easily disappear into obscurity. 'Three years is a long time. The parade moves on.' Knowing that it would get back to The Man, I took the opportunity to bend Bruce's ear on the forthcoming, and in my view avoidable, Livingstone crisis. Bruce, however, was not convinced. He believes that, outside London, Ken is unpopular and that, were he to be vetoed, the fuss would soon blow over.

Home on the 20.00. Elliot Morley showed me a paper on genetically modified foods drafted by Jack Cunningham for MISC 6, the cabinet committee dealing with the subject. Clearly this was the document that prompted The Man's remarks to the parliamentary committee yesterday. It was dated 9 February and addressed four key issues. (1) A moratorium. EU law prevents a moratorium on commercial production and a ban on trials was not desirable. (2) Food Labelling. The government is 'vulnerable'. (3) Animal feed labelling. Government vulnerable here, too. (4) The suggestion that ministers and officials are too close to the biotech industry. This, said Dr Jack, must be vigorously rebutted. The memo went on, 'Some aspects of our position are stronger than others.' GM foods were 'an exciting area of scientific advance encompassing human health as well as food ... a real opportunity for improving our quality of life'. There was a health science base and an emerging industrial sector which could be jeopardised. 'Our strategy,' Jack concluded, 'should include placing articles in selected newspapers and scientific journals, accepting appropriate media interviews and circulating key messages to ministerial colleagues.'

According to Elliot, the government (mindful of what happened to the Tories over BSE) is being careful not to endorse GM foods. Contrary to what Jack asserts, he says that some MAFF officials are too close to the industry. Ministers were having to go outside the department for expert advice because they weren't confident about the officials. He had seen an incredible letter from Monsanto demanding that the government take steps to reassure the public about genetically modified food. They obviously hadn't realised that there had been a change of management at MAFF.

Saturday, 13 February

Bill Clinton, faced with impeachment, has been acquitted on all counts. Proof, if any were needed, that you can get away with anything provided you get the economy right. A message which, I am sure, won't be lost on Our Great Leader.

Monday, 15 February

A chat in the Tea Room with Tony Banks, who complained that he spent all his time opening sports centres. 'Look on the bright side,' I responded, 'you might have been put in charge of social security or prisons.' Grudgingly he conceded that his lot was not a bad one, although ending up as Minister of Sport is a far cry from those heady days when we plotted to rule the world.

Tuesday, 16 February

The newspapers report Ken Livingstone's rally at Central Hall last night. More than 1,000 people turned up, but it appears to have been by and large a gathering of the irrevocably alienated plus a sprinkling of luvvies. Notes were passed to the platform calling for support for this strike and that strike. Ken vowed to oppose what he called the privatisation of the London Underground. All very 1980s. Not hard to see why the regime is so nervous of him. For the first time I begin to wonder whether or not they might be right.

There is a tremendous row going on about genetic modification, 'Frankenstein food', as the tabloid press has labelled it. The Man has said he has no problem eating it, thereby conjuring up visions of John

Gummer force-feeding his child beefburgers at the height of the BSE scare. The Tories are homing in on David Sainsbury, who, it appears, has a large stake in the industry. The Chief Scientific Adviser to the government, Sir Robert May, was on the radio this morning saying that Sainsbury leaves the room whenever the subject comes up at cabinet committee – a rather unfortunate position for the Science minister to be in, although I'm sure he's honourable to his fingertips.

Michael Meacher gave a fascinating talk about GM foods to the What's Left group this evening. He said there was no great difference between ministers on policy, although the government should be encouraging an open debate whereas Downing Street and Jack Cunningham appeared to want to dampen it down. The key, he said, was transparency. The Americans were opposed to labelling, but EU regulations would be enforced from April. He was pressing for a three-year moratorium on production and confident that he would win that argument. Three years, however, might not be long enough. The truth is that no one knows the long-term consequences for wildlife, the environment and the human immune system. Michael also wants a commission on the ethics of GM crops. He added, 'The question which haunts me is, "What's it all for?" The real problem is that the public thinks we are doing nothing, whereas quite a lot is going on, only we are not allowed to talk about it.' He said the biotech industry was over-represented on the advisory committees and he was taking steps to rectify that. The industry was putting pressure on Number 10. There were also problems with officials. He had been surprised to read that there had been eighty-one meetings between representatives of the industry with ministers and officials. He, the Environment minister, had only taken part in one. Who were the others with?

After the ten o'clock vote I put my head round Jack Straw's door. He was sitting at the table working his way through his red box. I want sight of his statement on Stephen Lawrence next week (which he agreed to arrange). Also, I wanted to sound him out about my proposal for a select committee inquiry on the handling of immigration and asylum. The system is in chaos and threatens to undermine support for the Asylum and Immigration Bill. The Bill contains some harsh measures which can only be justified if the whole process is speeded up. Jack confirmed the chaos and said the problem was that the Tories had never got a grip on it. Howard had never been interested in detail. 'The secret truth about the Tories is, they weren't good managers.'

Saturday, 20 February

To see Jacky. Uncomplaining and cheerful as ever, but visibly shrinking. She hasn't eaten properly for weeks and the treatment has knocked the stuffing out of her, although it has made talking easier. Her daughter Emma had a baby girl at 7 a.m. this morning, but, sadly, the child will never know her grandma.

Wednesday, 24 February

To the party meeting, where I introduced the report of the parliamentary committee. I'd gone to some trouble to think about what I was going to say, inserting a few little jokes, but for some reason hardly anyone laughed. Was it them or me? Am I losing my touch? Tam Dalyell asked about Iraq. I was rather short with him. I could see he was upset. I must apologise. Afterwards Mo Mowlam said I had been 'brilliant', but that's nothing to go by because Mo is a serial flatterer.

Jack Straw rang at lunchtime to tip me off about his statement on the Stephen Lawrence inquiry. He was scathing about the Met: 'Incompetence on a grand scale. Makes your hair stand on end. You wonder what we pay these guys for.' Paul Condon will be staying, but it is clear that he has survived only by the skin of his teeth and on condition he eats a big helping of humble pie. He has only ten months of his contract to run. It would be different, said Jack, if it was ten years. Mrs Lawrence had asked who was likely to succeed Condon and Jack had replied, 'I can tell you one thing – all the candidates will be white, male and over forty-five.'

The statement itself was a subdued affair. The Tories were on their best behaviour. Mr and Mrs Lawrence were in the special gallery. There were lots of tributes to their dignity. I heard later that she was not happy, but it is hard to see how the report could have gone much further. Condon was on the television this evening exuding humility.

The Man was on good form at Questions. Hague led on the euro, mention of which always has the Tories jumping up and down like a lot of Pavlov dogs. Hague has got himself into an impossible position, saying he might be in favour of our signing up – but not for ten years. The Man was merciless. Over the top, even. Twice he even went so far as to question Hague's future as Tory leader.

'You were a bit hard on young William,' I remarked when we assembled for the parliamentary committee an hour later. 'Is it in our interests to see him overthrown?'

He smiled. 'Probably not. Alastair has already told me off about that.'

A fifteen-minute discussion on GM food followed. At the mention of the subject, The Man, who had been yawning, suddenly sprang to life. He leaned back with one foot on the table and beamed at us. 'You're talking to a world expert now. How long have you got? I can talk about this all evening.'

Clearly he has boned up on the subject since we last met. He cited a paper by Robert May which, he suggested, we all ought to read. He didn't seem to think there was any problem with food. Biodiversity, he conceded, was 'the real worry', but he didn't dwell on that. Instead he talked glibly about not sending the wrong message to the industry. This was a twenty-first-century industry. We were at the cutting edge. We mustn't scare them off. Our main problem, he seemed to think (on this as with so much else), is the media. 'We must look for more imaginative ways of getting our message across.'

I said the debate about GM reminded me of the argument over nuclear reactors in the seventies when half the scientists involved turned out to be in the pay of vested interests. Monsanto, I said, had already bought into the American political system and we mustn't let it buy into ours.

Jean told a story about a friend who had bought soya, not knowing it contained genetically modified Brazil nuts to which she was allergic. As a result she had been seriously ill.

Charlotte expressed concern about the environmental aspects and someone else referred to the effect on Third World farmers of the so-called 'terminator gene'.

But our masters were having none of it. Margaret Beckett chipped in to say that we must be clear about the hypocrisy of the Tories over labelling – which they had opposed. Then The Man came back in, saying, 'We must be the calm voice of reason. We are proceeding with great care and caution.' He claimed to have gone over all the objections minutely with the officials.

Personally, I am not reassured. Nor were Jean and Charlotte. The Man, on the other hand, appears to have bought the whole package.

Later, at the division, I recounted the exchanges with The Man to Elliot Morley, who said, 'I sent word to Number 10, asking Tony to be careful because the advice from MAFF can't be relied on.'

I also told Michael Meacher, who said The Man's attitude was worrying. Four fields – which is all we have under GM crops – was not enough to enable conclusions to be drawn. 'Tony has been persuaded by his business friends.' He added, 'In the old days ministers would have got together and thrashed out our differences. Now Tony takes a decision and it is imposed. It was the same with nuclear waste.' Michael said he was reasonably confident of being able to persuade the industry to agree a significant extension – the word 'moratorium' will be avoided – of the embargo on production. 'I can get it past the industry, but I'm not sure I can get it past Tony.'

Thursday, 25 February

To the Liaison Committee, where, after we had approved the usual long list of overseas visits, an interesting discussion broke out about the status of select committees. It was triggered by Donald Anderson, who was very peeved about the way The Man and Robin Cook had rubbished his Foreign Affairs Committee report on the Sierra Leone arms affair. Bruce George said that the relationship between select committees and the government appeared to be modelled on the Supreme Soviet pre-1990. The powers of Parliament, he alleged, had peaked in the reign of Edward III and it had been downhill all the way since. 'The time is coming,' he concluded ominously, 'when we are going to have to play dirty pool.' Peter Brooke complained about the length of time it took to get replies from the Northern Ireland Office to his committee's reports. Archie Kirkwood said committee chairmen were treated with 'an attitude bordering on contempt'. I chipped in, saying we should insist that the security services were made properly accountable and that the power to appoint members of select committees should be taken out of the hands of the whips. Martin O'Neill said commercial secrecy was being misused by the DTI as an excuse for not cooperating with his select committee. Nick Winterton said, 'I have longed for years to have this discussion.'

I proposed an inquiry, but Bob Sheldon insisted we start by asking members of the committee for written submissions. An encouraging discussion.

Friday, 26 February

The fallout from the Lawrence report is damaging everyone connected with it. I'm beginning to wonder whether it was a good idea after all. Jack is under fire today because, incredibly, the published appendices contained the names and addresses of people who had offered information to the police. No one is happy. Mrs Lawrence, because she wants to see the killers brought to justice, and there was never any possibility that the inquiry would achieve that. The police, because, unfairly, they have been branded racists (arrogance and incompetence are more likely explanations). Meanwhile, the race relations industry is having a field day. I fear we may be in for a big bout of political correctness without any tangible results. There are signs that, far from healing wounds, the report will reopen them. Someone wrote in the *Telegraph* that it may give rise to a culture of permanent grievance such as is said to exist among some black people in America. There may be something in that.

Monday, 1 March

'Can anyone not entirely on message hope to be appointed to government?' asked Bob Sheldon during a division. He was referring to one of my little jokes at the party meeting last week that none of us on the parliamentary committee ought to harbour ministerial ambitions. Bob said that he had been a critic of the Wilson government over devaluation and withdrawal from East of Suez, but that Wilson had still brought him into government in 1974. 'Could that happen under New Labour?'

'Tony Banks?' I suggested.

'He's a jester, jesters are allowed licence.'

'Dawn Primarolo?'

'She's been on message for years ... I'm talking about a critic, a constructive critic of government policy.'

'I'm not holding my breath,' I replied.

Tuesday, 2 March

David Bickford, the former legal adviser to MI5, gave evidence to the select committee. All part of my little plot to keep the dispute about accountability bubbling.

He was an impressive witness. I first came across him six years ago when the committee lunched with Stella Rimington. He favours giving Parliament power to trawl through everything – even operations. His erstwhile masters won't be happy at the prospect. A man in the public seats, who bore a passing resemblance to Hitler and a permanent look of disapproval, noted his every word. The only time that the note-taker smiled was when Bickford was asked if MI5 and MI6 got on together. Over and over again he made the point – also made by Stephen Lander when we saw him in January – that the main resistance to proper scrutiny comes from Whitehall, not the security services.

During Bickford's evidence Betty Boothroyd made a brief appearance with a party of boys from Eton, among them Prince William. We were tipped off at the start of the meeting that they would be coming. A shy, well-scrubbed, rosy-cheeked youth, he stared at the floor for most of his brief visit, although I did once see him whisper to his neighbour. Later, I had a call from someone at the *Sun* asking for confirmation that William had been present. I told him to get lost.

Someone pointed out that the seven shortlisted candidates for the Conservative nomination at Leominster are all white males, four of whom were educated at Eton. I ribbed Archie Norman, who is in charge of creating a new, clean, modern Tory Party, about this. 'We're now down to four white males,' he replied cheerfully, 'two educated at Eton and one a colonel.' He added, 'I feel like a production director turning out a product that no one wants to buy.'

Wednesday, 3 March

The Man, in shirtsleeves, gave one of his little pep talks to the parliamentary party. Beautifully clear, as always. Eye firmly on the big picture. No one was scared of the Tories any longer, he said, so we couldn't play that card. Many of the good things we were doing – minimum wage, increased public spending – had yet to work their way through into the public consciousness.

There was an amusing little exchange at the beginning of The Man's address. David Pitt-Watson, the party treasurer, who had just given a presentation on party finance and organisation, referred to ELPAC, an election computer programme which many New Labourites are using. Half of the assembly looked bemused and the other half nodded vigorously. The Man remarked on this, saying that he was on the side of the bemused – 'In that sense I'm Old Labour.'

Whereupon Dennis Skinner called out, 'You've made my day.'

Saturday, 6 March

Lord Denning has died, aged 100. The media are full of eulogies, but I shall always remember the old rogue for that disgraceful judgment he gave in the Birmingham Six case.

I shared a car with him once, on the night in January 1988 that the Appeal Court threw out the Birmingham Six appeal. We were commuting between television studios in Oxford Circus and White

City. At either end he was expressing his absolute confidence in the appeal judgment. During the journey, however, it was a different story. 'I don't know why they've invited me,' he said. 'I don't know anything about this case.' After he had repeated this two or three times, I remarked that I'd met the people who carried out the bombings and that they were alive and well and living in Ireland.

'Oh,' he said, 'that's very anxious.'

I said I thought it was a bit anxious, too.

'I suppose you know more about this case than anybody else?'

'Possibly.'

'More than those Appeal Court judges?'

'Possibly.'

'If I were you, I'd write a book about it.'

The book, of course, was on its third edition and had been one of the main causes of the case being referred to the Appeal Court in the first place.

He was still saying how 'anxious' it all was as I helped him up the steps to the *Newsnight* studio, but as soon as the red light came on his certainty returned. When we had finished, he said, 'Well, Mr Mullin, I suppose you'll be going back to Ireland now.'

Tuesday, 9 March

I didn't go in for the Budget. It's impossible to get a seat on our side without turning up an hour in advance. Instead I sat in a comfortable armchair in the deserted Tea Room and watched. Gordon was on good form. Having collected a lot of revenue in his first two years, he is now starting to give it back – and on a scale that no one dreamed of. There was something for everyone. Business, pensioners, families, the poor. He even froze duty on alcohol. Only smokers and motorists were clobbered and even then he slashed road tax on small cars. Everyone on our side was very cheerful. Hague, who must have been astonished by the scale of the largesse, had to make the most difficult speech of his life, which he did brilliantly, accusing Gordon of raising taxes by stealth and making some excellent jokes. A wonderfully self-assured performance, but I doubt it will make any impact. The tide of history, not to mention the awful state of his party, is against him. In five years it might be different, if he can hang on that long.

Wednesday, 10 March

Awoke to hear Gordon on the *Today* programme skilfully resisting the suggestion that he was redistributing wealth. Over and over again John Humphrys pressed the point. Over and over Gordon declined to own up. Such is our terror of the tabloids that we daren't admit to something fundamentally honourable.

The Metropolitan Police Commissioner Paul Condon came to the select committee, a grey man, in both appearance and demeanour, but capable. And skilled, I suspect, in the art of survival. His tone was deferential. He called everyone 'sir'. Re Stephen Lawrence he ate exactly the right quantity of humble pie for everyone to be satisfied, but without conceding too much. What are his real feelings, who can say? To be fair, I think his heart is in the right place. Several people have said that he is the best ever Commissioner. Afterwards, I asked what he was going to do when his contract expires at the end of the year. Again, he gave just the sort of answer a Labour MP wants to hear: 'I'm not going to look for non-executive directorships or anything of that sort.' I said I was sure he would end up at the other end of this building and he didn't demur.

To Central Hall for a concert to mark the fortieth anniversary of the Tibetan uprising, where I was asked to do a short reading alongside Paul McCartney and others. The first time I've seen a Beatle in the flesh. He seemed a decent, down-to-earth sort of guy who – like Michael Meacher – has retained the secret of eternal youth. I chatted to him backstage for about five minutes. I don't think he knows much about Tibet, except that it is a good cause. He said he had written to ask the Dalai Lama why he still ate meat, given that he was one of the world's leading Buddhists. (The same thought occurred to me when I sat opposite HH at lunch in the Lords a while back.) He had received a courteous reply saying that he had been advised to do so by his doctors.

Paul said he had stopped eating meat about twenty years ago, mainly due to the influence of his wife, Linda. They'd been rearing lambs on their farm and they couldn't bear the thought of killing them.

Spoke to Ian. Jacky is slipping into a coma. She will soon be gone.

Thursday, 11 March

'You are causing ructions,' Dale Campbell-Savours remarked as I passed him on the Library Corridor. A reference to my request for Tom King to give evidence on the accountability of the security services. It was discussed at the Intelligence and Security Committee on Wednesday. Dale wouldn't say what had been decided, but it sounded as though Tom is very reluctant to come. 'This is the ugliest issue I've dealt with in twenty years on committees. It's causing all kinds of tensions. They think I'm your spy. They keep talking about "The Mullin Agenda". They think you want to take it over. I've told them you don't, but they won't believe me.' Dale added, 'I've told them, the issue will never go away.'

Rang to find out how Jacky was, just before I left to catch the train. A neighbour answered and said in a strained voice, 'Jacky died an hour and a half ago.'

Wednesday, 17 March

Michael Meacher addressed the party this morning. Michael, despite all the briefing against him, is one of the big successes of this government and he had a good story to tell. He has forced the water companies to invest more, cut prices, stop dumping untreated sewage and reduce leaks. Against all predictions, a legally enforceable right to roam is on the way. A moratorium on GM foods exists in all but name. 'I emphasise, we will not allow commercial planting of GM crops until we are satisfied that it is safe.' He added, 'The real issue is unresolved. If you take the view that there should be no cross-pollination,

I do not see how it is possible, even in the long term, to grow GM food on this small island.'

I asked Doug Hoyle whether he stands by his erstwhile dire predictions about Gordon's stewardship of the economy. To my surprise he cheerfully owned up to having been wrong. Gordon, he said, was a much better Chancellor than he could ever have imagined. Jack, he added, was also a much better Home Secretary.

A long session with a Home Office minister about the chaos at the Immigration and Nationality Department. The papers have been full of horror stories about lost documents and queues which start forming before dawn. He says the problem started under the Tories, who signed up to a contract for a new computer system which hasn't yet been delivered. The deadline has been extended, but even now it is still far from clear that the company concerned will deliver. The crisis threatens the credibility of the Asylum Bill and much else besides. He says the trade unions are a more reliable source of information than management about what is going on. The Tories couldn't bring themselves to talk to the unions so they were largely in the dark. Morale is low, management incompetent and it isn't even clear whether the project was ever feasible. He added that about 80 per cent of public service computer contracts have gone wrong. This one has all the makings of a disaster, but it might still, just, work out. He wants me to hold off from launching an inquiry until after the summer recess, by which time the outcome should be clear.

Thursday, 18 March

Home on the 20.00. Derek Foster was on the train. He said, 'I gather Tony is learning to live without Peter Mandelson. Tony has it in him to be a very good Prime Minister, but if he brings back Peter, the poison will start to flow again.'

Saturday, 20 March

To Brancepeth to see Paul Nicholson. Paul reported that negotiations between Vaux and the management team have all but broken down. The difference between the two sides is small, but the financial advisers are calling for scorched earth. The only hope is to put the wind up them by getting the Trade Secretary, Steve Byers, to call them in for a chat. I promised to get on to Steve on Monday. I warm to Paul. A real one-nation Tory with a genuine loathing for City slickers with their greed and short-termism.

Monday, 22 March

I rang Steve Byers and explained about Vaux, emphasising the need for speed.

Tuesday, 23 March

The Man made a statement on Kosovo. War is imminent. He was heard in silence. Hague said the Tories would support bombing, but not the use of ground troops. The Man did his best to avoid mentioning troops, but didn't rule them out. The big unanswered question is, 'What happens if, as most people seem to think, the Serbs are unmoved by bombing?'

The Vaux bid has collapsed. It was announced this afternoon that talks have broken down. Paul Nicholson says the only hope is to generate a big political row, but I am not optimistic. Steve Byers, as a result of our conversation last night, has asked Bob Dobbie, a senior official, to meet the Vaux financial advisers and see what, if anything, can be salvaged. I spoke to Dobbie, who said he would do what he could 'to rattle their cages'. He said that one of the advisers had the temerity to question the government's locus in the matter. As if the offer of £1 million of regional assistance and the prospect of having to clear up the mess after they have laid waste to one of Sunderland's best employers isn't locus enough. Bob said, 'I do doubt the judgement of some of these City types.' The meeting takes place tomorrow.

Wednesday, 24 March

'On what authority does NATO attack another sovereign state?' inquired the new Vietnamese Ambassador with whom Ann Clwyd and I had lunch. Needless to say, the sight of B-52s taking off to bomb Serbia brings back bad memories for the Vietnamese.

While awaiting the Ambassador at St Stephen's entrance we noticed an elderly, erect and immaculately pinstriped gent making his way up the steps on crutches. 'Where have I seen that face before?' asked Ann. It was Jack Profumo. He was having lunch with Oona King. Oona said to me afterwards, 'He's still a ladies' man.'

The bombing of Serbia started at around 7.00 p.m. At nine o'clock Prescott made a statement to the House. He made a hash of it, stumbling repeatedly, especially over 'Milosevic'. No one was in a mood to quibble, but at times people were just staring at the floor with embarrassment. Was he nervous, tired or what? He seemed out his depth. At one point he compared what is happening to the build-up to World War II. The mood was sombre and subdued rather than gung-ho. No one is happy at the sight of B-52s taking off from British bases to bomb another sovereign state, but there again no one has a better idea. Also, a feeling that no one can see how this is going to end. It could be much bigger than Iraq. The usual dissidents – Benn, Dalyell and Galloway – were on parade. Tony was jeered when he spoke of 'utter shame and disgust' among people of his generation. There were cries of 'No, no.'

'Why does he always go over the top?' murmured Jim Cousins who was sitting next to me.

There was dissent on the Tory side, too. Edward Leigh asked for a guarantee that ground troops would not be used. Douglas Hogg said we did not have sufficient national interest at stake to justify military action.

For a moment the doubters seemed to have the upper hand until the whips began to move among us, encouraging positive contributions. I just sat quietly. I can't think of anything useful to say. The Tories were notably more subdued than we were. 'We are the War Party now,' remarked Jim Cousins. Nick Soames said something similar earlier today.

Thursday, 25 March

Denis Healey was on the radio this morning saying that the attack on Serbia could lead to the overthrow of Yeltsin and his replacement by an extreme nationalist regime, which could complicate matters still further. He was wrong about Iraq. I hope he's wrong about this.

Paul Nicholson rang. Very down. He thinks the game's up. Today's papers are full of hostile comments. Most commentators seem to have bought the City line. Paul was particularly upset by a piece by Alex Brummer (financial editor) in the *Guardian* which, incredibly, tells the government to keep its nose out of City business. 'I'm on the point of throwing in the towel. It's not worth going on. I wish I could see a way forward, but minds are set.' He added, 'My view of the City is coming close to yours.'

So that's it, then.

A good debate on the crisis in the Balkans. Powerful speeches from Ken Livingstone and Patrick Cormack, who favour intervention, and an electrifying one from George Galloway, who is opposed. I find myself being pulled one way and then the other. I don't believe bombing alone will work. On the other hand, I don't have any better suggestions and we can't just sit back and do nothing. At the same time I have a terrible feeling that we are getting into something that could spin completely out of control. Oh, for the old black-and-white certainties of the Cold War. Now everything is grey and murky and confusing. I feel so useless.

Saturday, 27 March

The killing in Kosovo has intensified, arguably as a direct result of the bombing. John Humphrys gave Doug Henderson a going over on the subject on *Today* this morning. It is hard to see how bombing alone is going to drive the Serbs out of Kosovo. Sooner or later ground troops are going to have to be committed. It's becoming clear that we should either have done nothing or gone the whole hog.

Monday, 29 March

To London, loaded down with correspondence from Friday's surgery. The scale and the dreariness of it casts a dark cloud. It blights any useful contribution I might make to the debates on Kosovo or the Stephen Lawrence debate which takes place today. Fortunately, I have someone taking over Jacky's job next week. Otherwise I don't know how much longer I could cope. I remember dear old Arthur Bottomley's advice soon after I was elected. 'Don't hold surgeries.' At the time it seemed preposterous, but now I realise what he was getting at. You can't hope to scrutinise the executive effectively if you spend all your time being a social worker.

I made a brief intervention in The Man's statement on Kosovo, avoiding any hint of dissent. Oh what a boring, statesmanlike figure I have become. 'Questioner of the Year' indeed.

In the evening the Attorney General of Trinidad and Tobago, a smooth, affable Asian called Ramesh Maharaj, came in to discuss the select committee system which he is in the process of setting up back home. Trinidad has about 100 people waiting to be hanged so I took the opportunity to bend Mr Maharaj's ear on the death penalty, which, in his previous incarnation as a human rights lawyer, he used to oppose. He wasn't in the least rattled, pointing out smoothly that Trinidad has horrendous levels of violent crime and the public were baying for blood. He even claimed that evidence from the United States showed that the death penalty worked. As we were walking to the lift he told me that, privately, he was still opposed, but there would have to be a few hangings before the public could be persuaded to look again at the issue. One of the committee clerks who sat in on the meeting said afterwards that he'd found the exchange fascinating. 'So far capital punishment for me has been an issue for school debating societies. I've never met a practitioner.'

A chat with Steve Byers about Vaux. The government has upped its offer of assistance to £6 million, which is really very generous – and absolutely contrary to our stated policy of non-intervention. Steve added that it would be helpful if the city council was to make clear that it will never grant permission for housing on the Vaux site. Apparently, the scorched-earth brigade are basing their calculations on the assumption that they can sell this site for housing, and they need to be disabused. I immediately rang the chief executive Colin Sinclair and he promised to see what he could do.

I asked Steve about Nissan, in which Renault have just taken a large stake. Are we about to see work disappearing in the direction of France? That would be a disaster of unimaginable proportions for Sunderland. Steve thinks Nissan is safe. The Washington plant is the most productive part of the Nissan empire. He added, however, that there were bound to be big closures in the car industry. There was enormous overcapacity and in the long run two or three giant corporations would produce all the cars in the world. The Americans and the French, whose car plants are the least efficient, were most vulnerable. He seemed hopeful that Longbridge would survive, for the time being at least.

Tuesday, 30 March

It is becoming clear that the NATO air strikes have triggered a huge catastrophe, or at least made the situation much worse. Refugees are pouring out of Kosovo. The entire province is emptying. A huge tide of human misery is flowing into Albania and Macedonia, which are ill-equipped to cope. It doesn't seem to have occurred to anyone to make provision for refugees before the bombing started. Although the killing had already started, the bombing has exacerbated the situation. I ran into George Robertson in the corridor behind the Speaker's chair. 'Sooner or later, you are going to have to confront the issue of ground troops,' I said.

'I agree, but you'd need 150,000 to go in safely and that's impossible without the Americans. We're having enough trouble raising 30,000 for the peacekeeping force.' The Germans, he said, have 300,000 men in uniform, but only about 10,000 are any use for combat. He added that the other problem was the terrain. There were only two ways in, both through narrow mountain passes. George looked remarkably cheerful, considering the burden he bears. Or perhaps he doesn't. Perhaps he's just a spectator like the rest of us.

Wednesday, 31 March

To the meeting of the parliamentary party, which was addressed by a grim-faced Robin Cook. He spoke of increased bombing, aid for refugees, and war-crimes trials. Most of the questions were about ground troops, which he again ruled out until there was a ceasefire. 'If we have been wrong, it may be that we haven't been ruthless enough.' He was heard in silence. No table thumping, no hear, hears. There are deep misgivings about where all this is leading.

Also at the party meeting I asked why the Export Credit Guarantee Department was still being used to underwrite arms sales to tyrants. I received a bland reply, the drift of which was that the matter was under review. Twenty minutes later, when I ran into Steve Byers in the Members' Lobby, he said, 'What I couldn't tell you is that there is a huge row going on. Robin vetoed an arms deal with Turkey on anti-personnel grounds. I received advice that I must object. I asked "Why?" and they backed off.'

He went on to describe how ECGD had objected to providing £15 million of cover to help the cashmere industry over a temporary crisis until he asked how come they could afford a £3.4 billion guarantee for arms sales to Nigeria. 'They don't like it, but they're changing. Until now they've lacked clear political direction. Margaret [Beckett] was beginning to get on top of it. Peter wasn't interested. It takes years to turn round a department like the DTI.' Steve is obviously a breath of fresh air, but he had better leave clear advice for his successor, otherwise the officials will be up to all their old tricks as soon as he is out of the door.

The news from Kosovo grows steadily worse. It's absolutely clear that we were unprepared for the huge new exodus of refugees, although Clare Short indignantly denied this when she made a statement this afternoon. More and more voices are being raised about the futility of the bombing without ground troops. There are even signs that the Americans are beginning to have doubts. Crispin Blunt, a Tory who used to work in the Foreign Office, told Ann Clwyd that it was 'the worst foreign policy decision since Suez'.

The Man didn't show at the parliamentary committee this

evening. The third week running that he has been absent. Bruce told me he arrived back from Ireland at two o'clock, spent twenty-five minutes preparing for PM's Questions, went to Downing Street for a briefing on Kosovo and flew back to Ireland. The trouble with the Irish is that they won't even start talking unless the Prime Minister is present.

Thursday, 1 April

The Serbs have captured three American soldiers so attention has immediately moved away from the hundreds of thousands of exhausted, destitute Kosovars. I suppose this is good news, if it helps to interest the Americans in what is going on. We have to face the fact that the American army is for all practical purposes useless outside Hollywood. They are not willing to sustain a single casualty. Odd that America has wasted lives in so many bad causes, but has difficulty recognising a good one until it hits them in the face. Reading Harold Nicolson's diaries, I can see we had a similar problem in World War II until the Japanese obligingly detonated the American Pacific Fleet.

Saturday, 3 April

The evening news shows Macedonian police beating back refugees. A huge convoy of misery stretches back ten miles into Kosovo. Exhausted, desperate people pleading for help. The very old and the very young are beginning to die. What somehow makes it worse is that they look so like us. They have trainers and baby carriers and even cars. The Man was on TV this evening guaranteeing that they will return home one day. An empty promise. There is talk of evacuation.

In Nicolson's diaries, it is striking how often he seems to run into Churchill in the Smoking Room, even at the height of the war when the great man must have been heavily preoccupied. How seriously Churchill took the House of Commons. He was always making statements and opening debates. How times have changed.

Sunday, 4 April

To Chelmsford to see Mum and Dad. Mum asked if my political views had changed over the years. 'You used to be very left-wing.' She was going to say 'extreme', but the word didn't quite come out. To some extent, I suppose I have mellowed. Any illusions I once had about the Vietnamese and Chinese communists have long ago disappeared. I am more willing to recognise two sides of an argument and to accept compromise, but have I changed so much? I am still a paid-up member of CND and the Campaign for Labour Party Democracy. I pointed out that my route to respectability was via what appeared at the time to be an extreme cause, the proposition that the people convicted of all the big IRA bombings of the mid-seventies were innocent. On that issue, all the responsible, sensible people, capable of forming balanced judgements, turned out to be wrong.

Tuesday, 13 April

The Man made a statement on Kosovo. The mood was subdued. A modest 'hear, hear' when he sat down, but no cheers. There is a growing realisation that the war is not going well. Anywhere up to half a million refugees are still trapped inside Kosovo, most living rough without food or shelter. What will become of them? Once again The Man ruled out ground troops and insisted that the bombing was gradually incapacitating the Serbs in Kosovo. If it is, I wanted to ask (but didn't), surely there will come a point where ground troops are viable.

Later, a session with Robin Cook at the Foreign Affairs Committee. About thirty people attended, remarkably few considering the gravity of the situation (fox-hunting attracted more than 100). Robin was upbeat, but once again conceded nothing on ground troops. Morale among Serb troops, he claimed, was crumbling. The bombing had knocked out half the Serb air force, damaged their communications and greatly reduced their fuel supplies. There were even reports of deserters. I asked about ground troops, but Robin repeated that there was no prospect of fighting our way in. An invasion force would take months to assemble (so why haven't we started?), the Serbs had three hundred tanks in the region to our fourteen. He added that we had had details of Serb plans since November to ethnically cleanse Kosovo (which makes our lack of preparation all the more surprising). His only concession was to say that it might be possible to go in without a formal agreement, if it was clear that we would meet little or no resistance. The more I hear of this, the more I begin to wonder whether we haven't made a dreadful mistake after all.

I also asked about reports that cluster bomb units, of the sort I have seen scattered all over Laos, were being used. Robin replied that he understood that these were designed to take out tanks and were, therefore, different from what had been used in Vietnam and Laos. I tackled George Robertson about this later. He confirmed that these were a new 'improved' version, but they sounded remarkably similar to the ones that caused such carnage to civilians in South East Asia. 'Ask what percentage fail to explode on impact,' I suggested, and George promised he would.

Wednesday, 14 April

Sunderland AFC have won promotion to the Premier League. A huge boost for morale in our battered city.

Prescott turned in a truly awful performance at PM's Questions today (The Man was abroad on war business). He was thrown off balance early in the proceedings when a Tory asked about the Withholding Tax, of which he (and indeed most of us) had never heard. Instead of saying he would write to the Honourable Member JP went off completely at a tangent, much to the amusement of the Tories and to the embarrassment of our side. After that it was downhill all the way. For much of the time he was incoherent. Words just tumbled out one after the other in no particular order and with no particular meaning. The Tories were cheering for more. Our side squirmed. For reasons that I don't entirely understand, the House (like the Labour Party) has a soft spot for JP. A certain amount of incoherence is tolerated, but today's performance was too much. It was obvious to everyone that he was out of his depth. Had he been a junior minister, his card would have been marked. If The Man fell under a bus tomorrow, there is no way he could take over.

It was a chastened JP who appeared at the parliamentary committee an hour later. He opened with a self-deprecating little joke. There was none of the usual bluster or hectoring. We had a brief discussion on Kosovo. I said it was essential to do something for the several hundred thousand refugees trapped inside Kosovo, hiding in forests and mountains. They couldn't afford to wait for the bombing to yield results. JP said that the powers that be were well aware of the problems and agonising over what to do. 'The difficulty is, do we try to negotiate a ceasefire with Milosevic, while we try to help these people?' We could have done with the presence of The Man. This is the fourth meeting in succession he has not attended and it is rumoured that he will not be around next week either. Everyone is sympathetic to the pressure he's under, but the general view is that this is not good enough.

Thursday, 15 April

A convoy of refugees has been attacked by planes in Kosovo. The Serbs are claiming at least sixty dead. NATO hasn't yet owned up, but the evidence looks fairly clear. This follows an attack on a bridge with a train on it, which left many dead. In the case of the train, the pilot – who is said not to be British – fired a second missile after he knew he had accidentally hit the train. NATO spokesmen are being very blasé. Weasel words like 'collateral damage' and 'uncanny accidents' are being used.

Saturday, 17 April
Sunderland

An hour in the Market Square collecting signatures on a petition to save Vaux, but we were really just going through the motions. To make matters worse several people confused us with a group of Social-ist Workers petitioning against the war in Kosovo. One, a Unison shop steward called Sean, came over and berated me. 'What would you do?' I asked. 'Call on the Serb people to organise a general strike and bring down Milosevic,' he replied without hesitating. How comforting to have all the answers. I suppose I did once.

Monday, 19 April

NATO has at last, after a good deal of obfuscation, owned up to both of last week's attacks on refugees. In both cases, needless to say, the pilots were American.

George Robertson, the Defence Secretary, was in the Tea Room. I pressed him on what could be done for the thousands trapped inside Kosovo, many of whom are living out in the open. He said that a great deal of thought had been given to the problem, but the conclusion was that nothing could be done. Air drops would require slow-moving Hercules planes which would make easy targets and give away the location of those hiding in the forests and mountains. The terrain rendered any kind of land corridor impossible. God knows what we are going to find when we eventually get in there.

Tuesday, 20 April

The Commons is full of armchair generals. Nick Soames drew my attention to an article in the *Wall Street Journal* saying that NATO had totally misread Milosevic and that he wouldn't give way on Kosovo under any circumstances. 'Spot on,' says Soames, who, like his distinguished ancestors, comes into his own in times of war. An awful mess, he says, but having started we can't afford to lose. 'If we're going to do it, do it. We should pour more lead on them.'

Keith Simpson, who used to work in the MoD, comes to my room. 'The PM is "riding point" for Clinton,' he says. 'Call me a cynic, but I think Clinton will fudge it and the PM will be left exposed.' Kosovo is different from the Gulf, he says. Then, the Americans were fully signed up. This time they're not. He adds, 'Lots of my officer friends are ringing up saying, "We're in a mess."'

Meanwhile, Clare Short has given a foolish interview, comparing those who are sceptical about the official line on Kosovo with those who appeased Hitler.

The *Independent* is running extracts from Donald Macintyre's forth-coming biography of Mandelson, containing an amazingly detailed account of the bitter feud at the heart of New Labour, much of it petty in the extreme. Peter must have supplied Donald with the relevant documents, including letters from The Man.

Jean Corston says she recently remarked to Sally Morgan, the political officer at Number 10, that, 'The roof hasn't fallen in as a result of Peter's departure.'

To which Sally replied, 'It has been noted.'

Wednesday, 21 April

To Number 10 for the parliamentary committee meeting which had been brought forward because The Man is off to Washington this afternoon. There was a pile of luggage in the hallway when we went in and when we came out it had gone. The Man's schedule is horren-dous. Up at six yesterday for trips to Belgium and Germany. Back at 8 p.m. An hour with the children and then a meeting on Kosovo.

He was in shirtsleeves. Buoyant and good-humoured, but with pale shadows under his eyes. His fingers drummed the Cabinet table as we started, but he soon relaxed.

'How many people are still trapped?' I asked.

'Six or seven hundred thousand.'

'How can we help them? Air drops? A land corridor?'

'There is nothing anyone has suggested that we haven't considered.'

'Might we go in once Milosevic's army has been degraded?'

It was at this point that the word 'possibly' cropped up. To which he added, 'Don't expect too much,' but he definitely gave the impression that something is moving.

'What's the timescale?'

'Several weeks.'

'Then it will be too late to save those living in the open.'

He didn't challenge that.

Jean said later that Sally Morgan had confirmed that The Man had not approved the publication of his correspondence with Peter. Sally had added that, had he time to worry about it, The Man would be seriously pissed off.

Tuesday, 27 April

Robin Cook approached me during a division and said that he had checked up on the points I had raised at the Foreign Affairs Committee the other day. We are not using uranium-tipped missiles and only 3 per cent of cluster bombs don't explode on impact (a likely story). I asked if we had any documentary evidence about Operation Horseshoe (the Serb plan to ethnically cleanse Kosovo) and he said we don't. A pity because we urgently need to demonstrate that Kosovo would have been cleansed if we hadn't gone to war.

Wednesday, 28 April

The Man again absented himself from the parliamentary committee. This is becoming a habit. He was on the premises until a few minutes before. I know because I saw him in the corridor behind the Speaker's chair, chatting to Mo Mowlam.

Thursday, 29 April

An interesting little discussion at the Liaison Committee. Everyone has been asked to submit a note detailing problems in relations between select committees and the government together with suggestions for change. There was general dissatisfaction with the role of the whips in selecting members. Strong language was used. Nick Winterton, never one to understate his case, described the present system as 'fraudulent, corrupt and wrong'. Malcolm Wicks said it was wrong in principle that the executive should decide who scrutinises it. David Davis (a former whip) said we would be hard put to devise a system which the whips couldn't manipulate.

We agreed to hold a formal inquiry into the relationship between Parliament and the executive. A sub-committee, of whom I am one, is to draft the terms of reference.

In the afternoon the Home Affairs Committee had our long-awaited informal session with Tom King about the accountability of the security services. He was surprisingly affable, given that, I am reliably informed, he thinks we are poking our noses into matters that are none of our business. I began by assuring him that we weren't engaged in a turf war, simply an argument about the right mechanism. He didn't rule out the possibility that the Intelligence and Security Committee might in due course become a committee of Parliament. His line was that the process was still evolving and that the existing arrangement should be given more time to work. The more we go into this, the more I get the feeling that everyone realises that change is inevitable in the end. We must keep up the pressure. Another scandal would help.

I had the adjournment debate on Vaux. Steve Byers replied and half a dozen local members stayed to listen. Journalists keep asking, 'What do you want the government to do?' To which I can give no very adequate reply. The sad truth is that it's all over bar the shouting.

Tuesday, 4 May

Alan Howarth drew my attention to a leader in the *Sun*, responding to the nail bombs in Soho, Brick Lane and Brixton. It says, 'You can bomb us – but you will never defeat us. Hitler found that out. And everyone else who attempts to use terror for evil purposes will find that out. Brits unite when we are attacked.' Indeed, and what makes us think that the Serbs will react differently?

Wednesday, 5 May

To the House to hear George Robertson address the parliamentary party. George was down to earth, but robust. He conceded nothing. He did, however, spend a lot of time justifying the bombing, dwelling on the horrors and the lengths we had gone to avoid war. 'This is,' he said, 'a defining moment for our generation.' The only outright dissent came from Alice Mahon and Harold Best, who described himself as 'a near pacifist' and called lamely for more talks. Julia Drown said she could justify everything so far except the targeting of Serb television. Harry Barnes, who supports intervention, complained that the bombing was too indiscriminate. He read a list (faxed to him by trade unionists in Belgrade) of civilian targets, including schools and hospitals, which he said had been damaged, which George dismissed as Serb propaganda. Dale Campbell-Savours called for the bombing to be intensified.

'What,' I asked, 'are we were going to do if the Serbs do not back down and the Americans continue to veto ground troops?'

'I'm not going to tell you,' replied George, adding that there were plans. 'Yes, it looks bleak, but cracks are starting to appear.'

The Man, in contrast to George, was much more forthcoming at the parliamentary committee. He is clearly fired up by his visit to the camps in Macedonia. 'I've never felt so unequivocal about anything.' He said he had talked to Bill Clinton (who is in Germany) this morning and urged him to visit the camps. He made no secret of his frustration with our allies. Several times he used the phrase, 'I keep telling people …' After a while I realised he was referring to other heads of government. He agreed with Ann Clwyd's suggestion that UNHCR had bungled its response to the refugee crisis and said we were still trying to unblock EC aid. 'There has to be an upgrading of seriousness at every level,' he said.

I asked the question that I put to George this morning. 'What if the Serbs don't back down and the Americans refuse ground troops?'

A long pause. A sigh. Then he said hopelessly, 'Carry on bombing.'

We asked about ground troops. He didn't challenge Ann when she said, 'You've been left swinging.' Planning, he said, was going on and a slow build-up was taking place. Kosovo was only the size of Yorkshire. The military were saying it could be taken. 'We won't let this drag on through the winter … I keep saying to the other leaders … When we get inside we are going to find things so horrible that people will say "Why weren't you there?"'

'The public,' he added, 'have a clear view and the one thing they won't forgive us for is not doing what we said we would do.'

Thursday, 6 May

To Sunderland in time to do some knocking up in the local elections. An hour loudspeakering with Lennie Lamb, our candidate in St Michael's ward. The apathy is truly shocking. In the evening I knocked up for Bryn Sidaway, the council leader, who has pulled out all the stops in Hendon. About twenty members turned out and we called on every known Labour voter, but the apathy was militant. Several people said they had voted at the library (which proved they were lying since the polling station was in a school), some declared baldly that they weren't voting and others said they would come out later, but didn't. I pointed out to several people that the seat was marginal and they seemed surprised. In the event Bryn lost his seat by just two votes after two recounts.

Friday, 7 May

A crisis at breakfast. Today is Red and White Day. Every child in the city is expected to go to school wearing the Sunderland strip or something resembling it. The only household in the city to be unaware of this is that of the MP. We searched high and low and could come up with nothing remotely suitable. I rang several neighbours, but they had nothing to spare. Sarah faced the prospect of being the only child in her class not wearing the colours. Humiliation beckoned. Tears. Happily, the head teacher Mrs Crawford saved the day. Quick as a flash someone was dispatched to rummage through the lost property and came up with a red and white shirt. Relief all round. Disaster narrowly averted. Hurray for Mrs Crawford.

Saturday, 8 May

NATO has bombed the Chinese embassy in Belgrade, killing at least three people. The Chinese have gone ballistic. It is hard to imagine a worse disaster. With every day that passes the pit is getting deeper.

Monday, 10 May

At Bob Sheldon's request I drafted a letter setting out the terms of reference for the Liaison Committee's inquiry into the select committee system. I included scrutiny of the security services and 'ways in which select committees might be made more attractive to those who might otherwise seek a career in government', which is code for paying committee chairmen, to which Bob is strongly opposed. I shall watch with interest to see whether that sentence survives.

Paddy Ashdown was on the bus going home. I asked what would happen in Kosovo. 'I think we are going to let them down,' he said quietly. The bombing will stop. Milosevic will still be in power. The refugees still on the border. 'It's going to reflect badly on all of us. Especially on Tony, which is very unfair because he has taken a principled stand from the outset.' He added, 'I bet the Americans are just bombing what they want and telling us afterwards.'

Paddy also thinks we are in trouble in Scotland over tuition fees. 'Either Donald will have to back down or the Parliament will vote him down.' He said he had been privately cautioning the Lib Dems in Scotland not to go for broke over fees. 'Important though student fees are, they not worth abandoning the prospect of stable government for.'

Tuesday, 11 May

A brief chat with Dale Campbell-Savours about Kosovo. He remains optimistic and thinks the crisis over the bombing of the Chinese embassy in Belgrade will blow over and might even cause the Chinese to join up with the Russians in persuading Milosevic to settle in the long run. On the other hand he accepts that morale on our side is low. 'It reminds me of the day, during the Falklands War, when HMS *Sheffield* was hit – and we recovered from that. He added, 'On the other hand, Tony's luck may have run out.'

Wednesday, 12 May

The Man arrived a few minutes late for the meeting of the parliamentary committee, looking tired and depressed. Andrew Mackinlay, never one to mince words, remarked loudly, 'The Prime Minister looks absolutely knackered.'

The Man's face lit up. 'Until now I was feeling great. Actually, I'm off to make a speech in Germany in a few minutes ...' He said it as though he were going to address a ward branch meeting in Battersea. No wonder he looks tired.

Kosovo and the Welfare Reform Bill were the main topics of discussion. The Man said the Chinese were slowly coming round after the bombing of their embassy. Apologies were now being broadcast in China (he apologised again at this afternoon's Question Time). It was important that we now regain our poise. The Tories seemed to be back on board (Hague was noticeably more constructive than Howard was yesterday). 'The bottom line is that the refugees must go back. They won't go back accompanied only by a few Russians and Ukrainians or while the Serbs are still there ... The issue is ground forces – everyone knows where I stand on that.' He added that there was a danger of underestimating the success of the bombing. 'We had a very good day yesterday.' There was evidence of a lot of unhappiness in Serbia. The Kosovo Liberation Army were making a comeback. Ethnic cleansing was reducing. He added that the parliamentary party had been magnificent.

I asked if the Americans consulted us about targets, pointing out that this was not the first time they had bombed an embassy – they killed the French Consul General in Hanoi in 1972 and had also hit the Swedish embassy. (Everyone seemed surprised at that. How easily people forget.) 'Do they just bomb first and tell us about it afterwards?'

'It's better than that ...' he said cautiously.

'... But not as good as it might be?'

He was on the brink of conceding this and then thought better of it. 'The targets are agreed with NATO. In the case of the Chinese embassy, what happened was what the CIA say happened.'

During the meeting I noticed a small panel with three buttons on the floor under a table by the Prime Minister's chair. Upon examination afterwards the buttons proved to be labelled, 'secretary', 'messenger' and the third I forget. Bruce Grocott went and stood in the outer office by the secretary's desk and, sure enough, when the right button is pressed there is a loud buzz. A useful device for summoning help when delegations of whingeing backbenchers have outstayed their welcome.

Thursday, 13 May

To Claridge's to see the Dalai Lama. What, I wondered, is a simple Buddhist monk doing staying at Claridge's? Apparently it was the work of over-enthusiastic acolytes. According to Mr Dorjee, the Tibetan representative in London, to whom I chatted before being ushered into the presence, His Holiness took one look at the hotel and declared that it was far too grand. Find something smaller, Mr Dorjee was instructed. Panic ensued. Especially when it was discovered that Claridge's would require payment of a large cancellation fee.

HH was as warm and down to earth as when I first met him twenty-five years ago. Nowadays he is a superstar. This week he has been received by the Prime Minister, the Foreign Secretary, the Speaker and the Archbishop of Canterbury. Tickets for his lectures at Wembley were booked up four months in advance. Hard-faced Tibetan bodyguards in sharp suits and American secret service-style earpieces paced up and down in the corridor outside.

As ever he exuded optimism, although the basis for optimism is as slender now as it ever was. There has, he said, been no contact with the Chinese government since last summer. The quality of Indian politics and politicians is going down and down, 'and this is bad for us … We need India to be strong.'

We discussed the weakness of the Tibetan system, namely the fact that there is a long interregnum between Dalai Lamas. He picked up my arm and felt my pulse. 'My doctors say I will live to be 103.'

'Then you are the equivalent of two Dalai Lamas, the fourteenth and the fifteenth.'

Monday, 17 May

Out of the blue a call from Lord Longford, with whom I have never previously had any dealings. He wants to discuss penal reform. Do I have time for a drink? He adds, 'I've been poking my nose into the subject for nearly half a century and I want to know what's going on.'

We chatted for an hour in the Peers' Guest Room, during which time he consumed two enormous glasses of sherry to my glass of lemonade and lime. Although in many ways exactly as caricatured, he is in remarkably good shape, considering that he is ninety-three years old. Hair unkempt (hark who's talking), eyesight failing, but both his hearing and his mind are in good shape. He has been in the Lords for fifty-four years and has both a life peerage and a hereditary one so he will survive reform whatever happens. He reminisced briefly about Beveridge and Keynes, both of whom he knew (he worked for Beveridge), and asked if I knew any historically significant people. After a moment's hesitation I came up with the Dalai Lama. Longford still does the prison visits which have gained him such notoriety. It was scandalous, he said, that Myra Hindley was still inside after so long. She was a perfectly normal woman who, when young and impressionable, had fallen under the spell of a madman.

He said he was glad that Tony Blair was a Christian because that gave him a moral base. He wanted to know what my select committee had been up to and whether Jack Straw was really as reactionary as some of his earlier pronouncements had suggested. He conceded that being in the Lords and not being exposed to constituents made it easier to be a liberal on issues like prison reform. He kept saying, 'I regard you as the leader of the prison reformers.' I'm not sure that's a mantle I am anxious to assume, least of all if it is bestowed by Frank Longford. In some ways I do admire the old boy, however. He has stuck to his guns over a very long period and he retains a lively interest in everything going on around him. I doubt whether I shall be worth talking to about anything when I am ninety-three.

We were kept here until dawn by the report stage of the Welfare Reform Bill. I am one of sixty-seven people on our side who have signed amendments and an even bigger rebellion is brewing in the

Lords. There are a lot of good things in the Bill and I am completely signed up to the notion that we have to confront the benefit culture. Unlike many colleagues, I can live with means testing. I just don't want to make poor people poorer. To bed at 5.30 a.m.

Tuesday, 18 May

A meeting with Jack about the Freedom of Information Bill, which is to be published on Monday. It is a watered-down version of David Clark's draft, but doesn't seem too bad, despite rumours to the contrary. Jack claims his Bill is more liberal than in most other countries. He said no work on freedom of information had been done in opposition. 'Our only research material came from enthusiasts.'

Wednesday, 19 May

The parliamentary committee met around the circular table in Gordon's office because The Man was having another of his interminable meetings with the Ulster Unionists. He joined us later, looking, in the circumstances, remarkably laid-back. The circumstances being the looming rebellion over incapacity benefit (which threatens to be the biggest of his reign) and the fact that he was in Bulgaria on Monday, Albania on Tuesday – not to mention Germany at the end of last week.

He lay back in an armchair, feet on the table, occasionally leaning around Alan Haworth to address Margaret Beckett and myself, who were otherwise eclipsed. On Kosovo he tried to be upbeat, but no longer troubles to hide his frustration with our allies. 'I'm convinced that in the end the alliance will do what is necessary. I don't quite understand why some of my colleagues (a reference to the German Chancellor's remarks in today's papers) are saying they will under no circumstances contemplate ground troops. The Russians are moving closer to our position. There is a lot going on behind the scenes.' He added, 'I go round the front-line states to see what's going on. I wish more of them (other NATO leaders) would go and see for themselves.'

We talked about the Welfare Reform Bill. The mood was sombre. The government is facing its biggest test so far.

The Man made soothing noises. 'We must listen. It's important not to give the impression that we can do what we want and still get elected.' But he added with a hint of menace that there were people who were difficult to please on anything. 'The method of dissent is important. People who attack the Labour Party on the media will suffer in the end, along with the rest of us. All people will say is, "You're divided."'

Thursday, 20 May

A day of anguish. I came in to find an urgent message from Ann Coffey (Alistair Darling's PPS) who wanted to know if I would be willing to intervene on Alistair with a view to eliciting a promise that he would review the rate at which incapacity benefit was deducted from those with second pensions. I agreed. Her next question was, 'Will you vote with the government?' I said I hadn't yet made up my mind. My inclination was to abstain. There was a long silence, but I didn't budge. At 12.30 I had a message to go and see the Chief Whip, Ann Taylor. She was friendly, but tense. 'I am trying to introduce a new style into the Whips Office. I'm trying to get ministers to listen, but I can't do that if they don't get a response.' She understood, she said, that my objection was not to means testing, but to the threshold and the rate at which benefit was clawed back from those with second pensions. I confirmed that this was so. Well, she said, since the figures were not in the Bill and would have to come before Parliament a year or so hence, wasn't that the time to consider voting against the government? She wasn't trying to bully me, she said, but she did need my help. After all, she added, 'You are vice-chairman of the parliamentary party.' I fell for it. I told her that, if Alistair's reply to my intervention was satisfactory, I would rise for a second time and say that I would vote for the government.

The debate began just before two o'clock. I went in feeling like Judas with my two interventions written out. Roger Berry moved his amendment brilliantly. He was calm, persuasive, generous and went out of his way to praise the government and bash the Tories. I spoke to Jean Corston and realised I couldn't vote with the government and retain my self-respect. I went back to Ann Taylor and told her I was going to abstain after all. I would make the first intervention, but not the second. She was decent and didn't try to dissuade me. I went back into the Chamber to listen to an impassioned speech from Audrey Wise and felt for the first time this afternoon that I could look her in the eye.

Despite the differences, it was a good-natured debate. Alistair's response was mildly conciliatory. I intervened on him as planned. Although he made no promises, there are clearly going to have to be concessions. When the vote came, sixty-five Labour members voted against the government and another thirty (of whom I was one) abstained, a majority of forty – the biggest rebellion of this Parliament. As Jim Cousins said afterwards, 'A good night for the party. No one can complain about control freakery now.'

Monday, 24 May

Jack made his long-awaited announcement about the proposed Freedom of Information Act. As long foretold, he has considerably watered down David Clark's version. He has also seen off Derry Irvine, a considerable feat. More evidence, if any were needed, that Jack is a serious player, although of course he will have had just about the entire Civil Service on his side. Some of his changes are sensible enough, but there is a fear that the effect of the new test of disclosure of information, ('likely to prejudice' in place of 'substantial harm') means that little or nothing will change. The two examples he gave of information that would be in the public domain as a result of the Act were both already available, which did nothing to bolster his claim that this is a radical step forward. Richard Shepherd was scathing, but everyone else was polite, including David Clark, who I know holds a quite different view in private.

A letter from a Tory neighbour full of the usual bombast. He wants a war on car crime with mandatory prison sentences, boot camps in the wilderness and all the rest of it. 'You can rest assured,' he goes on, 'that if Tony Blair or Jack Straw had their car stolen or vandalised, there would be legislation in the blink of an eye.' I don't know about Jack, but I know Tony has had his car vandalised – when he was Shadow Home Secretary – the tyres were slashed at Darlington station. I remember him telling me.

Tuesday, 25 May

I spotted one of my constituents, an electrician, in the gallery and took him for a drink on the terrace. He's working on the Jubilee Line and is full of stories about the venality of the London contingent, who he says are greedy, obstructive and stupid. They are working only an hour or two a day. Cables have been sabotaged and some are drinking. When he insisted on doing the job he was paid for he was threatened with violence. Exactly the kind of boneheaded trade unionists Murdoch took on at Wapping. I thought Thatcher had put an end to all this, but not so. They are alive and well and working – if that's not too strong a word – on the Jubilee Line.

Asked Jack if he had ever had his car vandalised. Yes, his stereo has been stolen twice and the car once. My Tory neighbour can put that in his pipe and smoke it.

Wednesday, 26 May

The select committee's report on Freemasons is published today. I did a little spot on the *Today* programme. Alan Keen remarked afterwards that I sounded diffident. In truth I am. I am bored with the subject and anxious to be rid of the endless letters from paranoids and lunatics. The committee has recommended legislation as the only hope of obliging Masonic judges and policemen to disclose, but I doubt whether anything will come of it.

The Man addressed the party meeting. The papers were full of stories that he had come to give us a bollocking over last week's little uprising, but in fact he was in good humour and no one took offence. There was a brief nod in the direction of the dissenters with talk of dialogue and sensitivity, but by and large he stuck to his guns. 'We have to recognise,' he said, 'that part of the appeal of New Labour is that we are willing to reform the Welfare State. If we opt out of that, the Tories will move in, not to reform the Welfare State but to do away with it.'

On Kosovo he remained firm. Milosevic must be defeated. There were lots of 'hear, hears' at this and more when Malcolm Wicks remarked, 'It's wonderful to see a government determined to take on tyranny.' The only note of dissent came from Tam who was (unfairly) jeered. The parliamentary party is holding together very well. It may be my imagination, but I detect that something is about to give in Kosovo.

Friday, 4 June

At last, good news from Kosovo. The Serbs have acceded to NATO's demand for a complete withdrawal. The war will be over by Sunday.

Sunday, 6 June

The Serbs are refusing to sign up to the Kosovo deal that everyone thought they had accepted. Reports of victory, it seems, were premature.

Monday, 7 June

Emma went to nursery in uniform for the first time this morning. Only the shirt was new. The skirt and socks came from her friend Naomi, but the little nugget was excited. She said, 'My socks make me very happy.'

Tuesday, 8 June

To London on the 10.43. A crowd of Masons on the platform at Durham, on their way to some knees-up in London. All grey and ageing and instantly identifiable by the thin black cases in which they carry their regalia.

To a meeting of the backbench Home Affairs Committee to hear Jack Straw outline his concessions on the Asylum Bill. About forty people attended and a gaggle of journalists loitered outside. He opened disarmingly by thanking his critics and saying that the Bill was better as a result of their efforts. The concessions he announced are fairly substantial – an increase in cash benefits, a presumption in favour of bail and fast tracking for asylum seekers with families. As a result criticism was muted. A couple of unlikely people – Diane Abbott and Bob Marshall-Andrews – thanked him for listening to their complaints. Two or three others asked why, if he was confident of being able to process applications swiftly, the complicated voucher system that he has devised was still necessary. Jack replied that it was needed to prevent fraud and no one seemed to challenge that. Such was the lack of tension that a dozen people had drifted away before the meeting ended. My guess is the rebellion will fizzle out.

Jonathan Aitken has been jailed for eighteen months for perjury. One or two hacks were ringing round trying to find someone who would say he had got off lightly, but why kick a man when he is down?

Wednesday, 9 June

Jack addressed a well-attended meeting of the parliamentary party on the Immigration and Asylum Bill. There was scepticism about the ambitious targets he has set for the processing of asylum seekers and about the need for vouchers, but everyone was full of praise for the way in which he had handled the uprising. One or two people also remarked that Jack's approach provided a model which other ministers – no names mentioned – might care to emulate.

Lunch on the terrace with Mo Mowlam, at her suggestion. She

wanted, as she put it, to tap my brain about the proposed inquiries into security force collusion in the deaths of Rosemary Nelson and Patrick Finucane.* Every possible objection is being raised by the usual suspects – MI5, the RUC and the MoD – and they are obviously hoping she will be reshuffled because all sorts of things are suddenly being pushed back to the end of July. She is looking for someone with sufficient credibility to conduct an inquiry – 'And who, if he meets obstruction, would have the balls to say so.'

I never quite know what to make of Mo. During the course of our short lunch she burped loudly several times, made liberal use of the F-word, including telling a passing pigeon to f— off, and waved at bemused tourists in a passing cruise boat (they did not respond). Is it all an act? She has certainly been a success with the punters in Ireland, although I imagine that the Establishment can't wait to be rid of her. In her way, she's a class act. It is a paradox. The Northern Ireland job is one that requires consummate diplomatic skills which, at first glance, she appears entirely to lack (she is reputed once to have told Ian Paisley to f— off) and yet she appears to have had more success than all the upper-class gents that the Tories sent over there put together.

On Kosovo, The Man said there was intelligence that the Serbs were preparing to leave. The Yugoslav generals were angry, but their troops (who are mainly conscripts) want out. He had spoken to Yeltsin this morning and he was saying all the right things, but the Russians were urgently in need of consistent leadership from a new generation of politicians. I enquired about what impact the cost of reconstructing the Balkans would have on our spending plans. He replied that the cost would be big, but spread over a number of years. 'If we get the growth we forecast, it is within our means.'

In the evening I chaired a meeting on Agent Orange for the Britain–Vietnam Association. About twenty-five people attended, including a man from Monsanto, one of the companies which used to make the stuff. We were addressed by Hugh Warwick, an ecologist, and then

*Irish civil rights lawyers murdered by loyalist paramilitaries.

watched a video showing the horrendous birth defects that are alleged to have resulted. What made it so moving was the fact that the victims were mainly poor peasants living in utter poverty. They have received no help from anywhere. One poor woman had four or five deformed, blind children. Every moment of her life must be a nightmare. And who will look after them when their parents are gone? Sadly, the Vietnamese government has chosen not to make an issue of it. I remember saying to the Vietnamese Foreign Minister eighteen years ago that it wouldn't be hard to find American lawyers willing to run a test case against the manufacturers, but at that time he was more interested in normalising relations. These people have been abandoned.

The war in Kosovo appears to be over. The Serbs finally put their thumbprints on a timetable for withdrawal at around nine o'clock this evening. George Robertson made a statement at ten. The first contingent of troops under General Mike Jackson is expected to go in tomorrow. There is a hell of a lot of clearing up to do. George's statement was well received, but there was no triumphalism. The main feeling is one of relief that we have dug ourselves out of a very deep pit.

Friday, 11 June
Sunderland

The surgery lasted three hours. Full of people locked into the benefit culture. Three were threatened with loss of disability benefit on the grounds that they were no longer deemed to be disabled. Two were men in their mid-fifties and one a woman of only thirty who had never worked in her life. They all huffed and puffed about the wickedness of it all, but increasingly I find it hard to sympathise. They all seemed to have given up on life and could not envisage living without benefit. The woman claimed a combination of gynaecological problems and stress. So far as the stress was concerned, I couldn't resist suggesting that work was the best antidote. The men, one of whom was middle class and seemed to be recovering from a nervous breakdown, both used the phrase 'I have worked all my life'. When probed, that turned out to mean in one case until the age of forty-two and, in the other, until the age of about fifty-three. As if that somehow entitled them to take a holiday, funded by the taxpayer, for the remaining one or two decades of their working life. The forty-two-year-old, who was the most indignant and laid claim to a vast range of symptoms, also used the phrase 'I am a socialist', which I find often features in conversations of this kind. This definition of socialism never seems to place any burden on the person laying claim to it. On the contrary, it usually implies entitlement to live for the rest of his life at the expense of his fellow citizens. Am I getting too cynical? Have I been too long in this job? The more I reflect, the more I am certain that we are right to challenge the benefit culture, however painful this may be to some of our natural supporters.

Monday, 14 June

Ann Clwyd says she is having doubts about continuing with sanctions against Iraq. Her select committee is conducting an inquiry and, she says, all the evidence suggests that only the poor are being hit. The elite can obtain everything they want. It's all being smuggled in from Turkey and the various Kurdish factions are creaming off huge kickbacks. I wrote to Robin four months ago saying that I was having increasing doubts about both the morality and effectiveness of sanctions and, despite a reminder, he hasn't replied. It's very significant if Ann has changed her mind because she takes a hard line on Iraq. Tam Dalyell may have been right all along.

Tuesday, 15 June

To Winson Green, Birmingham, as part of our inquiry into drugs in prison. I travelled with Paul Stinchcombe, a bright young barrister who once worked in Derry Irvine's chambers where he got to know Cherie Blair. Paul recounted a couple of amusing exchanges with Cherie. The first, two or three years ago, was when Clare Short got into trouble for saying that cannabis should be decriminalised. Cherie said she agreed and had had an argument with Tony about it. She added, 'But, of course, I am a dangerous left-winger and there is no place for me in the present Labour Party.'

The other exchange occurred after Tony became Prime Minister. Cherie was complaining about money problems (barristers being paid months in arrears) and Paul said not to worry, after Tony retired there would be fat fees from lectures. To which Cherie replied, 'Paul, you don't understand. I'm married to an idealist. When Tony retires, he wants to go and teach in Africa.'

Wednesday, 16 June

In Clive's absence I took the chair at the weekly meeting of the parliamentary party. Hilary Benn, elected in a recent by-election, made a nice little speech saying that while we were rightly anxious to keep in with Middle England we shouldn't forget the people of 'Middle Leeds'. Hilary will take to this place like a fish to water. I wouldn't be surprised if he is a minister before long.

The main business was a discussion of priorities for the Queen's Speech. Many people made the point that we had to find a way of cheering up our core supporters. Bills on hunting with hounds, the right to roam and free TV licences for pensioners were among the suggested remedies.

Later, at the parliamentary committee, Charlotte raised the London mayoral elections and warned that interfering in the selection of our candidate for mayor would only create more disillusion. I backed her up, saying this was an avoidable disaster and we should avoid it. 'If you've got a better candidate than Ken, run him or her against him, but you must allow a free election.'

The Man looked sceptical. 'I remember canvassing in London in the eighties ...'

'So do I. Ken is a rare example of a Labour politician who was more popular at the end of eight years in office than he was at the beginning.'

There was a brief discussion about Ireland. The Man no longer bothers to hide his exasperation. Yesterday he had a meeting with representatives of the Orange Order which had got nowhere. 'Unbelievable people,' he called them, shaking his head. 'There is nothing more irritating than sitting in a room with someone who claims to be British, but who treats you as though you are nothing to do with Britain, even though you are the Prime Minister.' On Sinn Féin, who are refusing to budge over decommissioning, he said they would have to distance themselves from the IRA if they wanted a place in the assembly. 'If they are willing to let the agreement go down, one has to ask "Why?"' He confirmed that there will be no moving from the 30 June deadline. 'They have got to be brought to the precipice and asked to look over it.'

The meeting lasted for a little over an hour, one of the longest we have had.

Thursday, 17 June

A call from the Home Affairs correspondent of the *Daily Mail* about the select committee's report on accountability of the security services which is published next week. One of the Tories on the committee – I have a shrewd idea which one – has leaked the gist of it either directly to the *Mail* or to his own front bench. The reporter read out a quote from 'a senior Tory' who he said was not Tom King, alleging it was all a plot by Dale Campbell-Savours and myself. I declined to comment, but secretly I am pleased. A denunciation in the *Daily Mail* will do wonders for my street cred.

Tuesday, 22 June

The select committee's report on the accountability of the security services was published today. I did about half a dozen interviews, starting with the *Today* programme, but there is hardly anything in the newspapers. Tom King, who keeps a careful eye on the way the wind is blowing, said he didn't think the government would take much notice because we hadn't succeeded in taking Tory members of the committee with us. I fear he may be right about that. David Davis said it had always been the (Tory) government's intention that proper parliamentary accountability would eventually evolve. It would be useful if he would say that on the record.

A chat with Clive Soley, during the course of which I indicated that I would be interested in a job in the government – adding, however, that I lived in dread of being offered an under-secretaryship at the Department for Folding Deckchairs and feeling obliged, for reasons of self-respect, to turn it down. He thought an offer was possible, but perhaps not this time round. I said I'd like Overseas Development when Clare eventually moved on. It may come to nothing, but I thought I would just float the idea and see what comes of it. He did say that The Man likes me, whatever that means.

Wednesday, 23 June

The meeting of the parliamentary party was jam-packed for a guest appearance by The Man, billed as his response to the Euro-election results. About half the Cabinet were on parade. He was on top form. Relaxed, good-humoured, unapologetic but with just the right air of humility. The gist was that our alliance with the middle classes will be maintained. Without the middle classes we couldn't hope to deliver any of the good things that we were promising the poor and oppressed. This went down surprisingly well. Scarcely an Old Labour voice was raised. The only dissent came from Tam Dalyell, who told Tony that his style of government was 'Napoleonic' and called for a resumption of cabinet government.

Friday, 25 June

An invitation from the Palace. The Queen is holding a reception for MPs in ten days' time. Lounge suits only. RSVP the Master of the Household, Major General Sir Simon Someone. My instinct was to accept on the grounds that the Palace is the one part of the Establishment I haven't yet penetrated, but as luck would have it Bill Etherington and I are due that evening to have our much-postponed meeting with Health minister John Denham to discuss the shortage of GPs in Sunderland and I daren't cancel.

Sunday, 27 June

A picnic at Wallington, on our favourite seat by the China Pond. Then on to Capheaton, which opens one day a year for the Red Cross, by which time it was raining.

'Lived here long?' I asked the owner.

'On the wife's side, since 1168,' he replied.

When we got home there was a message on the answerphone saying that Tony Benn is standing down. The reason he has given is that he wants to devote more time to politics.

Tuesday, 29 June

Lunch with John Gilbert, who, for the last three months, has been helping to run the intervention – or at least our bit of it – in Kosovo. Our big mistake, he says, was not to go for Serbia's electricity supplies from the outset. 'If we'd bombed in the first week of the war the sort of targets we were hitting in the last week, it would have been over much quicker.'

'Were we right to go in?'

'As a matter of principle? Yes.'

'How long will we be there?'

'Fifty years.'

He was joking – I think.

This is John's second time at the Ministry of Defence. He was there under the last Labour government. 'It's a tremendous advantage having been here before. You can see through all the lies – and I mean lies – they tell you.'

He said he had run into a former Tory Defence Secretary who complained of being lied to. John had replied that the same thought had occurred to him, but until now he had never felt able to use the word.

As a parting shot, I asked if the continued bombing of Iraq was doing any good.

'Not much.'

Which confirms what I have long suspected.

Jack Straw is becoming accident prone. He's forever having to come to the Dispatch Box apologising for things that have gone wrong. Today it was passports. It's the usual story. New computers combined with new regulations (in this case a requirement that children should have their own passports) equals chaos. Huge queues at the Passport Office winding their way around Petty France in the rain. Just like those outside the Immigration and Nationality Department in Croydon. The difference here is that this is Middle England. And if Middle England can't go on holiday because of a bureaucratic cock-up, they are going to be mightily pissed off. And guess who they will blame?

Last week's cock-up was the Prevention of Terrorism Act. Someone had noticed that Clause 16A, B, and C had somehow been omitted when it came before Parliament for renewal last year. As a result we had to spend several hours last Thursday evening rushing through the missing clause.

Before that it was the accidental publication of the names and addresses of witnesses in the Stephen Lawrence case. Another statement to the House. More apologies. Jack is always engagingly frank and so far he has got away with it, but all this apologising is beginning to take the shine off an otherwise excellent record.

The recent spate of hangings in the Caribbean reminded me of a story I was told by a privy councillor who had been attending upon the Queen. In the mid-seventies, together with several colleagues, he stood waiting while Her Majesty, seated at her desk, signed documents. The last was a rejection of an appeal for mercy by the man who was due to be hanged in Bermuda for murdering the Governor General. She signed with a flourish. 'He's got a cheek, asking me for clemency,' she said indignantly. 'Do you know, he even shot the dog.'

Wednesday, 30 June

In the absence of The Man (who was away bringing peace to Ireland), JP stood in at PM's Questions. The first time he has been allowed out on his own since the Great Withholding Tax Disaster. We held our breath each time an elephant trap appeared. He came through okay, but there was general relief when it was over.

Thursday, 1 July

I ran into Donald Brind, the parliamentary party press officer, and bent his ear about the need to avoid a crisis over Ken Livingstone. He takes the view that in the long term the fallout from a rigged selection will be as nothing to the damage that will be caused if Ken is allowed to set up in opposition to the government on the South Bank. 'Ken is an oppositionist. Look at it from the other end of the telescope. The problem is not the next election, which we will win anyway, but the one after. The Mayor of London is going to be one of the five or six biggest figures in the Labour Party. Can we afford, in five years' time when times are hard, to have Ken sounding off on everything? He could do a lot of damage.' He added that, if the call comes, Frank Dobson will agree to serve, whatever he is saying now.

Friday, 2 July

To the Queen Street Freemasons' Hall (one of only two Grade I listed buildings in Sunderland) to launch a restoration project. The photo when it appears in the *Echo* and the Freemasons' newsletter should raise a few eyebrows, but it will help to make the point that I have nothing against Masons per se, only their obsession with secrecy.

Monday, 5 July

A talk with Nick Soames, re the proposed ban on hunting with hounds. 'You can expect real trouble,' he says. He repeated the phrase several times.

'Like what?'

'Like a million people on the streets. The last countryside demonstration will be nothing compared to this.' All bluster, of course. Providing we keep our nerve, we have nothing to fear from a few hundred thousand Tories on the march. Indeed, it will do wonders for our spirits, as Soames seemed to realise. 'The Lords and hunting are,' he said, 'the two issues that the government can use to distract its troops while they have a go at single mothers and the disabled ...'

'Can't you make do with drag hunting?'

'Not the same thing at all,' he snorted. 'Drag-hunting is like kissing your sister.'

Tuesday, 6 July

David Omand, the Permanent Secretary at the Home Office, came to the select committee this morning and we grilled him for two hours about the Great Passport Crisis and the Immigration Computer Fiasco. Not at all a great mandarin of popular imagination. About my age, the product of a Glasgow grammar school. Competent, middle class, lacking arrogance. As with Stephen Lander at MI5, Marks & Spencer rather than Fortnum & Mason. He performed well, studiously avoiding landing anyone in it. All the same, it came across clearly that all is not well. When I put it to him that his use of the word 'flawed' to describe what had gone on at the Immigration and Nationality Department was, to say the least, generous, there was a long pause. It also emerged that all those responsible for the screw-up at IND have, in the best traditions of the civil service, gone on to better things. When I saw Jack in the Tea Room afterwards, he confirmed that this was so. 'They all got out in time. I am very angry about it.'

After much agonising, I have penned the following note to the Prime Minister:

'Personal'

Dear Tony,

You may recall that some years ago you asked if I would be interested in a place in government. At the time I indicated that my first preference was to be chairman of the Home Affairs Select Committee. I have now been on the committee for seven years, two as chairman, and feel the time has come for a change. I would, therefore, be grateful if you would bear me in mind should an appropriate vacancy arise.

I handed it to Bruce Grocott, who undertook to place it before The Man. I also mentioned my interest to Jack, who undertook to see what can be done. Events must take their course.

An hour on the terrace with Mike O'Brien, who is worried about being scapegoated for the passport disaster. Mike said he has been involved in meetings with the Prime Minister on only a couple of occasions in the entire two years he has been a minister. Ministers outside the Cabinet have almost no access. John Gilbert said something similar the other day. I begin to realise what an advantage my membership of the parliamentary committee confers – and how much I would miss it were I to be favoured with office.

Wednesday, 7 July

Charles Falconer (rotund, amiable, plausible) addressed the party meeting re the Millennium Dome. So persuasive was he that I – almost – began to warm to the Monstrous Carbuncle.

To the *Guardian*'s summer party, held in the garden of Home House, a stunning Wyatt/Adam mansion in Portman Square. Who should I meet but one of my Sinn Féin contacts from when I was investigating the Birmingham bombings fourteen years ago. Our paths last crossed on a bleak housing estate in Belfast in the spring of 1986, since when he has served several years inside. And yet here he was, large as life and as cheerful as ever. He signalled to me to keep my lip zipped and we moved to a table out of earshot. I asked about the prospects for peace and he became animated. The IRA won't disarm, he said, because their constituents wouldn't allow it. 'Adams and McGuinness have gone way beyond their constituency. Way ... way beyond.'

The Unionists, he said, were fools. They've got just about everything they wanted – amendment of the Irish constitution, no unity without consent. They were even going to get Stormont back. Yet still they wouldn't sign.

So what is his solution? 'Get the IRA to take the guns down to the Republic. Ask General de Chastelain to verify. The IRA would go along with that.' He added, 'Whatever happens, the Good Friday Agreement will be the template for any future settlement.'

Later, back at the House, I travelled up in the lift with a couple of Unionists and asked if they would agree to the setting up of an assembly. 'No,' they said. 'We've got to take notice of our constituents.' Exactly what my Sinn Féin friend said.

Friday, 9 July
Sunderland

To the Health Authority for a discussion on the great GP shortage. The chairman, Joe Mills, was fuming. For years the doctors have been telling us that Sunderland is thirty GPs below establishment and now it turns out that most of them are anxious to keep it that way. Joe has had some research done which demonstrates that only three practices in the city have made any effort to recruit partners in the last twelve months. Others are sitting tight on huge lists. It's basically all about money. GPs are paid according to the number of patients on their list so they have a vested interest in keeping as many patients as possible. For that reason they are resisting Health Authority plans to recruit salaried doctors. Joe was livid. Me, too.

Monday, 12 July

To London, where a handwritten note from The Man awaited on the message board, acknowledging the letter I entrusted to Bruce last week.

At six I went with Bill Etherington and Fraser Kemp to the Department of Health for our long-awaited meeting with minister John Denham about Sunderland's GPs. John had been doing his homework. A civil servant present described GPs in Sunderland as resistant to change, male, elderly, foreign-trained (for which read Asian). The feeling is that they will flatly refuse to reduce their lists and so any attempt to introduce salaried GPs could be strangled at birth. We agreed that the standard of service provided by GPs with the biggest lists would be monitored in the hope of persuading some of them to downsize, but the plain truth is that if they won't cooperate, there is precious little the Health Authority or the government can do.

Tuesday, 13 July

Lunch on the terrace with Jean Corston. She said she had heard it suggested that, come the reshuffle, I might be made an offer. I asked if she thought it would be a good idea to refuse a job I didn't want. She thought not. It is unlikely that there will be other chances. The parade is passing ...

Jean reported on last night's reception at Buckingham Palace. About 150 members and spouses were invited. Many of the New Labour types were fawning. One was even seen to curtsey. They were kept hanging around for ages until HM and Philip arrived. Then they were marshalled into a queue. HM shook hands with everyone, peering at their name tags and saying things like, 'Bristol, oh how nice.' Jean says she has a way of shaking hands and simultaneously easing them in Philip's direction with a single wrist movement. As a public relations exercise, Jean didn't think it was a great success.

We were kept up for hours voting on the Northern Ireland Bill. It was 2 a.m. before I got back to Brixton Road.

Wednesday, 14 July

Gordon Brown addressed the party meeting. Never has a Labour Chancellor had such a good story to tell and Gordon made the most of it. Unemployment at a twenty-year low; inflation down to 1960s levels, oodles of money being pumped into the public sector. And, coming shortly, the Working Families Tax Credit which will make the lowest paid families up to £60 a week better off. As he couldn't resist pointing out, at this stage in the second Wilson government we were having to defend devaluation and two years into the last Labour government we were going cap in hand to the IMF. Even the great 1945 government was in trouble by '47. These days Gordon exudes an aura of competence and self-confidence which, in opposition, he lacked. At last, a Labour Chancellor who is not at the mercy of events.

A few complaints, but not many. Mike Connarty complained about the benefit changes, but received short shrift. 'We have to raise revenue from somewhere. It can't be painless.' Gordon added that too many people were reaching the age of fifty and then retiring with a pension and a lump sum and then, on top of that, claiming disability benefit. We couldn't go on like this. Our priority was to make work pay. By and large, however, the natives were friendly.

To Number 10 for what will probably be my last meeting of the parliamentary committee. As we hovered outside the Cabinet Room Ann Taylor whispered that the Tories were threatening to wreck the government's programme in defence of fox-hunting. She hoped that members of the parliamentary committee would do their best to maintain morale among the troops in the long nights ahead. 'For as long as you remain on it,' she added. I took that to be a hint that the Department of Folding Deckchairs beckons.

The meeting was good-humoured. The Man relaxed. Outside on the terrace a television crew was setting up for a live insert into the Ulster TV news. At one point Alastair Campbell wandered in and tried unsuccessfully to open the French windows. 'Why are you prowling around?' asked The Man.

'It's my job to prowl.'

There was much merriment when pagers kept buzzing and vibrating. Gordon's attendance at this evening's meeting of the backbench Treasury Committee was messaged a record four times. It became apparent, as I have long suspected, that The Man and I are the only members of the committee without pagers.

On Ireland he said that it was not the end of the world if Trimble failed to talk his people round by tomorrow. I groaned inwardly. Deadlines that, a week ago, we were assured were final are suddenly not final after all. Clearly this nonsense could go on all summer.

To the Northern Ireland Office for drinks with Mo Mowlam. While we were there word came through that the Unionists have declined to sign up to the new Assembly. Poor Mo, she's absolutely exhausted and desperate to be out of Ireland but there is no way she can be moved now. She told me, 'I won't move unless Tony insists.'

Thursday, 15 July

To Manchester to address the police chiefs at their summer conference. As the title implies there is also an autumn and winter one. My goodness, the police top brass live well. The event lasts three days and includes a great deal of feasting and freeloading. They all seem to have staff officers and chauffeurs. This week's festivities culminate in a black-tie event at Chatsworth to which I was invited but made my excuses. I prepared carefully, since I was in uncharted waters. The reception was polite but unenthusiastic. By four o'clock I was on the way home, having spent less than three hours on the soil of Manchester.

Monday, 19 July

People have been pulling my leg all day about a report in yesterday's *Observer* that I will be given Glenda Jackson's job at Transport. Tony Banks advised me not to accept. 'You're a senior figure in this place. You shouldn't accept anything less than a Minister of State.' My instincts precisely, although my feeling is that if I dig my heels in too hard, I am likely to end up with nothing. Later I had a quiet chat with Ann Taylor. I told her that I didn't feel I could trade in the chairmanship of one of the main select committees for one of the most junior jobs in government. There would only be two reasons for doing it: the money (which I don't need) and the prospect that it might in due course lead to something better. Ann advised caution. Government, she said, was very different from select committee work. There was a steep learning curve, she said, and there might be some advantage to starting at the bottom since high-flyers sometimes came unstuck. She agreed that The Man, who has never had the slightest interest in select committees (to my knowledge he has never appeared before one, let alone served on one) would be bewildered by the notion that anyone should attach importance to a select committee chairmanship. I said

I didn't want to upset him by rejecting whatever was on offer and that, if it meant waiting another year or so until the right job came up, I would not be unduly upset.

In passing, Ann remarked that I was an 'agoniser'. Naturally I denied the charge. But, of course, she is right.

Tuesday, 20 July

To Millbank to record a reading for Iain Dale of Politico's bookshop, who is producing a CD of contemporary politicians reading famous speeches. I opted for an outspoken piece by John Bright opposing the Crimean War. It included the following:

> I do not trouble myself whether my conduct is popular or not. I care only that it shall be wise and just as regards the permanent interest of my country, and I despise from the bottom of my heart the man who speaks a word in favour of the war, or any war which he believes might have been avoided, merely because the press and a portion of the people urge the government to enter into it.

Friday, 23 July

An historic day. After twelve years in Parliament I piloted through my first piece of legislation, the Criminal Cases Review Commission (Insanity) Bill, which allows the Commission to deal with cases involving a verdict of 'guilty but insane', thereby closing a loophole in the 1995 Criminal Appeal Act. It would have gone through in half an hour but for the fact that Eric Forth and his playmates dragged out proceedings in order to squeeze out Maria Eagle's Bill on mink farming. In the event it was over by midday and I arrived back in Sunderland just in time for the surgery, customers at which included a twenty-two-year-old woman, accompanied by her mother who did most of the talking. The young woman had been on the sick ('trouble with her nerves') since November and the Jobcentre were beginning to ask questions. 'How can she be expected to support herself on £40 a week?' the mother kept saying indignantly. 'She's worked since she left school,' the mother went on, as though five years' insurance contributions entitled the girl to a lifetime on benefit. 'All my friends got pregnant and were given a flat,' whined the young woman, as if she were doing the nation a favour by not getting pregnant.

Why wasn't she living at home? (She was only a street away from her mother.) Answer: she didn't get on with her sister.

I advised her to seek work. She looked as though she was about to burst into tears. The more I see of this nonsense, the more I believe we are right to challenge the benefit culture.

Monday, 26 July

To Derry Irvine's summer party at his grand apartment in the Lords. There I fell into conversation with a pleasant man who rejoiced in the title of Lord Chancellor's Purse-bearer. He has been in the job for fourteen years and described himself as Old Labour. 'It's much more democratic up this end,' he said. 'Of course, by the time they get here, they've made it. Or if they haven't made it at least they've got here.' He made some friendly remarks about my role in freeing the Birmingham Six. 'You really stuck your neck out. When I get home tonight I shall tell my wife I've met you.' A nice compliment in a room stuffed with the Great and the Good. As we parted he said cheerfully, 'You never know, you might end up in here one day.' Oh, please God, no.

Tuesday, 27 July

Helen Liddell announced the part privatisation of Air Traffic Control. A complete reversal of what we were saying before the election. Not since Harriet Harman tried to reduce single-parent benefit has a minister received such a pounding. No one on our side spoke up for her. Gavin Strang, her immediate predecessor, fired the first shot and from there on the mood turned uglier. She kept her head down and ploughed on regardless. She was followed by Jack Straw announcing his Bill on the funding of political parties, which cheered up everyone on our side. The Tories had no choice but to go along with it but they did not look happy bunnies. A lot of their shadier donors are simply going to disappear rather than risk exposure to daylight. Jack announced an overall cap on election spending of £20 million. Exactly as the Neill committee recommended, but still far too much.

My advance copy of the White Paper was accompanied by a letter from Jack which said, 'While the immediate impetus for the draft Bill is the Neill committee report, its provisions are also a tribute to your own advocacy of the need for openness and transparency in the funding of political parties in your minority report following the select committee inquiry into these matters in the 1993/4 session.' How good of him to remember.

Still no sign of this blessed reshuffle. The word now is that it will be tomorrow.

***

On 28 July 1999 I was appointed a Parliamentary Under-Secretary at the Department of Environment, Transport and the Regions. For a graphic account of life at the bottom of the ministerial pile, see A View from the Foothills.

Illustration Credits

The author and publisher would like to extend their thanks for permission to reproduce the photographs in this book: Getty Images/Pool 17; Parliamentary Recording Unit 13, 14; Press Association 12; Reuters/Simon Kreitem 9; Reuters/Paul McErlane 10; Steve Bell 18; *The Sun*/NI Syndication 11. All other photos are author's own.

While every effort has been made to contact copyright-holders of illustrations, the author and publishers would be grateful for information about any illustrations where they have been unable to trace them, and would be glad to make amendments in further editions.

Index